IN AND AROUND RECORD REPOSITORIES IN GREAT BRITAIN AND IRELAND

JEAN COLE
AND
ROSEMARY CHURCH

Armstrong
Boon
Marriott
Publishing

Fourth edition 1998
ABM Publishing, 61 Great Whyte, Ramsey, Huntingdon, Cambs PE17 1HL Tel: 01487 814050
First published as *In and Around Record Offices in Great Britain & Ireland* by Wiltshire Family History Society 1987.

By Jean Cole
Tracing Your Family History (3rd ed. 1988 Family Tree Magazine).
Tracing Your Family Tree (1st ed. With Michael Armstrong, published Thorson Equation 1988. 2nd ed. With John Titford, published Countryside Books 1997).
A series of transcribed and edited Wiltshire records published by Wiltshire FHS.

By Rosemary Church
Various Wiltshire records transcribed and edited for publication by Wiltshire FHS + parish register transcriptions for the historic county of Berkshire (The Vale of the White Horse), for the Oxfordshire FHS.

ISBN 0 9533492 0 9

Cover design - Darren Marriott.

Acknowledgements

We wish to thank all archivists, local studies librarians and museum curators who replied to our detailed questionnaire, and the *Family Tree Magazine* readers who wrote to us with various suggestions and amendments to the information in this edition.
To Mary and Michael Armstrong and Helen and Darren Marriott of the *Family Tree Magazine* for their help in producing this edition, particularly to Darren Marriott for all his assistance at the beginning and end of this project and for designing a bright and new eye-catching cover.
Last, but not least, to our long-suffering husbands, Reg and David, for their tolerance during the many hours we have worked on this book.

Introduction

The 3rd edition of *In and Around Record Repositories in Great Britain and Ireland*, published in 1992, contained 538 entries. This edition, now revised and enlarged, contains in excess of 740 entries. Whilst every effort has been made to ensure that the information supplied is accurate and as up-to-date as possible, it is inevitable that some changes will have occurred during the compilation of this guide. We would be pleased to hear of any major changes so that these may be shown in the *Family Tree Magazine* from time to time.

It will be noticed that the format of this edition has changed, this is in order to make it easier for readers to use. Repositories are now under their place names, with cross references where necessary, thus eliminating the need for an index. We also decided that we would like to include more repositories, libraries and museums including service museums, where possible. In an endeavour to incorporate this we removed 'places of interest' as in the last edition, and have now included what we have termed 'brief entries' and 'useful addresses'. This extra information, we hope, will be of help to researchers. Although some of the entries are not strictly within the realm of archive repositories they are, nevertheless, of utmost relevance for family, local and social historians.

Many changes have occurred since the last edition, not the least are the various government alterations to some counties and the growth of unitary authorities during the last two or three years. A number of record offices have been, and will be in the future, subject to great change including changes of venues up to and beyond the millennium e.g. County Record Offices in Berkshire, Kent and Surrey. So far as is possible, we have included these changes in 'Remarks'.

Addresses

When making enquiries from the following addresses please enclose a SAE or IRCs.

Association of Genealogists and Record Agents, Joint Secretaries, AGRA, Badgers Close, Horsham, W. Sussex RH12 5 RU. Members of AGRA agree to conform to their high standard of efficiency and integrity. They also operate a Code of Conduct and a complaints procedure if required. For a list of members with their areas of expertise send £2.50 or 6 IRCs.

Church of Jesus Christ of Latter-day Saints. For addresses of Family History Centres reference may be made to the *The Family Historian's Enquire Within* by Pauline Saul (5th ed. FFHS) or write to The Area Manager, The Genealogical Society of Utah, 185 Penns Lane, Sutton Coldfield B76 1JU.

Family Tree Magazine, 61 Great Whyte, Ramsey, Huntingdon, Cambs PE17 1HL. A long established monthly magazine published by ABM Publishing. Britain's foremost family history magazine with informative articles, news about archives, record offices and family history activities, readers' interests, letters, questions & answers, book reviews, genealogical miscellany, computer section etc.

Practical Family History Magazine (address as for Family Tree Magazine). Formerly a bi-monthly magazine but, owing to popular demand, now a monthly magazine which is specially formulated for the beginner in family history with practical features, reviews, advice for beginners, hints & tips, dating old photographs, your questions answered, readers' interests etc.

Federation of Family History Societies, The Administrator, c/o The Benson Room, Birmingham and Midland Institute, Margaret Street, Birmingham B3 3BS. For information about the Federation, its activities and publications.

Guild of One-Name Studies, Box G. 14 Charterhouse Buildings, Goswell Road, London EC1M 7BA.

Irish Genealogical Research Society, c/o Irish Club, 82 Eaton Square, London SW1 9AJ.

Scots Ancestry Society, 29b Albany Street, Edinburgh EH1 3QN.

Scottish Association of Family History Societies, c/o Aberdeen & N.E. Scotland FHS, 164 King Street, Aberdeen AB2 3BD.

The British Association for Local History (BALH), Phillimore & Co., Shopwyke Hall, Chichester, W. Sussex PO20 6BQ. Publishes a quarterly magazine with a periodic newsletter.

Local History Magazine, 3 Devonshire Promenade, Lenton, Nottingham NG7 2DS.

Reading: Amongst the numerous books which will be of help to researchers we are only able to supply a few titles here, most of which will be shown on the *Family Tree Magazine* and *Practical Family History* booklists: ABM Publishing, 61 Great Whyte, Ramsey, Huntingdon, Cambs PE17 1HL.

Bevan A. *Tracing Your Ancestors in the Public Record Office* (5th ed. November 1998 HMSO).

Blunsom C. *Civil Registration of Births, Deaths and Marriages in Ireland* (Ulster Historical Foundation).

District Register Offices in England & Wales (E. Yorkshire FHS).

Federation of FHS publications for family historians: *Basic Facts...* and *Introduction to...* series. FFHS also publishes bi-annually *The Federation News & Digest* – a 'must' for family historians.

Fitzhugh T. *The Dictionary of Genealogy* (5th ed. S. Lumas).

Genealogical & Historical Map of Ireland (Heraldic Artists Ltd.)

Johnson K. & Sainty M. *Genealogical Research Directory* (GRD). A national & international directory of surnames being researched + informative articles and information – published annually.

Gibson Guides *Record Offices: How to find them* (7th ed.) + many more informative guides which indicate the whereabouts of records held by county and other record offices.

Humphery Smith C. *Phillimore Atlas & Index of Parish Registers* (1995) – includes Scotland.

Irvine S. & Hickey N. *Going to Ireland: A Genealogical Researcher's Guide* – includes thirteen pages of useful addresses for Ireland, U.K. & N. America. (available SoG bookshop).

Istance J. & Cann E.E. *Researching Family History in Wales.*

Lumas S. *An Introduction to Census Returns in England & Wales (FFHS).*

Lumas S. *Basic Facts about Archives* (FFHS).

Price V.J. *Register Offices in Great Britain & Northern Ireland.*

Rose J. & Sheppard J. *British Archives* (3rd ed. 1995).

Saul P. *The Family Historian's Enquire Within* (5th ed. 1995 FFHS).

Short Guides to Records (2 vols.) published by the Historical Association – series of informative guides for local, family and social historians e.g. *Churchwardens Accounts; Settlement Papers; Overseers of the Poor Records; Coroners' Records* etc. Obtainable from: The Historical Association, 59A Kennington Park Road, London SE11 4JH or from BALH (see address above).

Sinclair C. *Tracing Your Ancestors in the Scottish Record Office* (HMSO).

The Society of Genealogists maintains a bookshop with a large selection of genealogical, local and social history publications which includes their own publications, microfiche and maps.

Tate W.F. *The Parish Chest* (3rd ed. Phillimore).

Tracing Your Ancestors in Northern Ireland (HMSO).

Wood T. *Basic Facts about Using Record Offices for Family Historians* (FFHS).

The World of Learning (in most major reference libraries) – guide to UK and overseas repositories.

Explanatory Notes

Opening Hours and other facilities are liable to change and it is always advisable to telephone before contemplating a visit. All record offices and libraries close on public holidays but these dates vary from area to area. Museums generally open on public holidays but their genealogical collections are not always available. Owing to prevailing financial restrictions, record repositories may be liable to unforeseen closures.

Telephone numbers: International code dialing for Eire 010 353. When we began compiling this edition we decided to include Fax, E-mail and Internet where possible. We asked for details about these addresses but not all repositories supplied them. It should be realised that E-mail and Internet addresses are always subject to change. The Royal Commission on Historical Manuscripts has, at present, ARCHON – updated regularly, which includes E-mail and Internet addresses of repositories which have these facilities. However, it is likely that ARCHON will be subject to a possible change in the near future. (see entry for RCHM under London Other Repositories). The main British Genealogical web site is "Genuki" at http://www.midas.ac.uk/genuki/

Parking: Unless otherwise stated public car parks are pay parks. Spaces – these are usually free. Limited – usually only a few spaces and these are liable to be filled quickly.

Disabled: 'Disabled friendly' indicates that all facilities such as ramps, lift, toilets and access to search rooms have been provided. In some cases it will be seen that extra facilities have been noted, such as priority parking and so on.

Children: Most libraries and many record repositories allow children in their searchrooms, but, of course, children are subject to the same rules as adults.

Appointments: Where no reference is supplied about readers' tickets it is still wise when visiting a repository, especially for the first time, to take some ID such as driving licence, pension book, passport or a recent bill showing your name and address. Some repositories ask for passport photographs for their readers' tickets and when booking an appointment this should be ascertained in advance. Where CARN (County Archive Research Network) ticket is not specified, the repository's own reader's ticket system may be in operation. Typing (electronic typewriters only), taping, laptops and cameras, where permitted, obviously should not be of disturbance to other researchers. Although many repositories state 'power supply' is provided for laptops, it is still advisable to take batteries.

Ordering System: Prior ordering by letter/tel means that documents may be ordered in advance of a visit. Four ordered, two produced indicates that four items may be ordered at a time and two produced to the researcher and that repeat orders will be allowed during the day. We have been asked to point out that 'hand held photocopiers' and 'scanners' are not permitted in archive offices. Photocopying of archives may be restricted because of their fragile nature, this includes pages from bound volumes which have also become increasingly fragile throughout the years. We would suggest that enquiries should always be made about indexes and transcripts of parish registers and various county records made by members of Family History Societies, Local History Societies and County Record Societies. Copying of records is subject to copyright restrictions.

Records: Where possible the geographic area covered by the repository has been indicated and the Diocesan Record Offices noted. Most county and other such record offices mainly contain the same type of records but some also have records of national importance.

Research Service: Charges made for research are subject to VAT (Value Added Tax). Overseas exemptions to this tax are Australia, Canada, New Zealand, South Africa and the USA. The fee charged does not usually include photocopies, microform printouts and photographed copies.

Facilities: As many researchers travel some distance to a repository or library we thought it essential to include various facilities such as whether toilets, public telephone, restaurant etc are available for those much needed breaks. Where these are not provided it has been indicated whether a café, public house or shops are nearby.

Publications: In these days of 'cut-backs' we decided to make enquiries from our own county record office and were told that stamped addressed envelopes (SAE/IRCs) for specific enquiries, free information leaflets and publications lists are most appreciated.

O. R: Other repositories in the vicinity have been noted here, but usually only very brief details have been included.

Tourist Offices: These have been included mainly for visitors from some distance away and for overseas visitors who may need accommodation, coach, rail or local 'bus information and local places of interest.

Remarks: If not stated as such, bags and briefcases are allowed in searchrooms. Where lockers are provided it may be that a refundable £1 coin or 20p piece will be required. Donations, in these days of under funding, are usually welcomed to assist with conservation work, acquiring local records, microfilming and other such purposes. Station: the name of the station, metro or underground has been given where it differs from the actual place name of the repository.

Finally, record offices are always pleased to hear of any archives for their areas which need to be placed in their care for safe keeping. Libraries and museums welcome deposits for their particular collections. To prevent damage to irreplaceable archives researchers are only allowed to use pencils. Eating, drinking and smoking are strictly forbidden.

Terms and Abbreviations.

Appt – Appointment.
BMD – Births, marriages, deaths.
BTs – Bishops Transcripts.
CARN – County Archive Research Network reader's ticket.
C: Cs – century, centuries.
CRO – County Record Office.
DIY – Do It Yourself.
Docs – documents.
FFHS – Federation of Family History Societies.
FHS – Family History Society.
FRC - Family Records Centre.
GRO – General Register office.
ID – identification.
IGI – International Genealogical Index.
Info – information.
IRC – international reply coupon.
M/f – microform.
MIs – Monumental Inscriptions.
MSS – manuscripts.
ONS – Office for National Statistics.
OPRs – Old Parish Registers.
O.S.: O/S – Ordnance Survey maps.
P/copying – photocopying.
PLU – Poor Law Union.
PRO – Public Record Office.
PRs – Parish Registers.
Pub – public house selling food & drink.
RO – Record Office.
SAE – stamped self addressed envelope.
SoG – Society of Genealogists.
Ts – transcripts.

ABERDARE

Cynon Valley Libraries, Central Library, Green Street, ABERDARE CF44 7AG Tel: 01685 885318. Usually open. Local History collection. Council mins. Newspapers. Maps. Photographs. M/f-census.

Aberdeen City Archives, Town House, Broad St., ABERDEEN, Aberdeenshire AB10 1 AQ. Tel: 01224 522513 **Fax:** 01224 522491
Opening Hours: W.-F. 9.30-4.30 Closure: Mon/Tues+Public hols.
Parking: None.
Disabled: No facilities.
Children: Accompanied: Not allowed. Unaccompanied: Educational purposes only.
Appointments: Prior booking for seats/viewers essential. Entry-register. 7 seats+1 film+1 fiche-1 reader/printer.
Ordering System: Prior ordering by letter/tel. Number ordered & produced at archivist's discretion. P/copying restricted, by staff-same day. Laptops permitted. Cameras by prior arrangement.
Records: for Aberdeen. Former Burgh & Town Councils of Aberdeen from 1398, registers of Sasine from 1484. Burghs of Old Aberdeen 17th-19thC's & Woodside 19thC. Accounts & letter books from 16thC. Burial registers for cemeteries within the City District 19/20thC's. Congregational records of churches of Aberdeen. Kirk Session of St. Nicholas & St. Clements. The Burgh Sasine register 1680-1809. Shipping Register for port of Aberdeen. Collection of Hall/Russell, shipbuilders.
Research Service: Charge made.
Facilities: Toilets. No refreshment facilities. Café/pub/shops nearby.
Publications: Free: Info leaflet: *Lists of holdings.* (SAE).
O. R: Registrar of Cemeteries & Crematoria- same address as repository Tel: 01224 522513 Ext 2485; **University of Aberdeen**, Dept of Archives & Special Collections, King's College, OLD ABERDEEN AB9 2UB; **Registrar of BMD**, St. Nicholas House, ABERDEEN AB9 1EY; **Northern Health Services Archives**, Aberdeen Royal Infirmary, Woolmanhill, ABERDEEN AB1 1LD
Tourist Office: Tel: 01224 632727

Aberdeen City Archives (Old Aberdeen Branch), Old Aberdeen House, Dunbar St, ABERDEEN, Aberdeenshire AB24 1UE Tel: 01224 481775
Opening Hours: M.-W. 9.30-1; 2-4.30 Closure: Thurs/Fri+Public hols.
Parking: Limited-free.
Disabled: Access. Toilet.
Children: Accompanied: At archivist's discretion. Unaccompanied: 10 yrs+
Appointments: Prior booking for seats essential. Entry-register. 12 seats.
Ordering System: Prior ordering by letter/tel. Number ordered at archivist's discretion, three produced. P/copying by staff-same day/post. Typing/taping not permitted. Cameras/laptops (battery) allowed.
Records: for Aberdeenshire/Banffshire/ Kincardineshire/Moray. PRs-originals. Minutes & registers of
Parochial boards. Education incl admission registers & log books. Valuation rolls. Electoral registration 20thC. County Councils 1890-1975. Town Councils.
Research Service: Charge made.
Facilities: Toilets. No public tel/refreshment facilities. Cafe/pub nearby.
Publications: Free: Info leaflet: *List of Holdings* (SAE).
Remarks: Bags not allowed-hangers. Transport: 15 mins bus ride to City Centre.

Reference & Local Studies Dept., Central Library, Rosemount Viaduct, ABERDEEN, Aberdeenshire AB25 1GW Tel: 01224 652512 Usually open. Public carpark behind Library. Disabled: Lift. M/f 4 film-2 reader/printers+3 fiche-1 reader/printer. PRs-film/fiche. Collections of local books/maps/plans/photographs/newspapers. MSS material requires 48 hrs prior notice. Booklets pub. by Libraries & Cultural Service+maps/photographs.

Gordon Highlanders Museum, St. Luke's, Viewfield Road, ABERDEEN AB15 7XH Tel: 01224 311200/31874. Appt. Archives of the 75th & 92nd Regiments incl. Local auxilliary regiments.

ABERDEENSHIRE, see Aberdeen; Oldmeldrum; Peterhead.

Archifdy Ceredigion Archives, Swyddfa'r Sir, Glan Y Mor, ABERYSTWYTH, Ceredigion SY23 2DE (County Offices, Marine Terrace, ABERYSTWYTH, Ceredigion SY23 2DE) Tel: 01970 633697
Opening Hours: M.-F. 10-1; 2-4 Closure: Public hols+Tues following May/Aug hols+2 days following Christmas.
Parking: None.
Disabled: Access. Toilet.
Children: At archivist's discretion.
Appointments: Prior booking unnecessary. Entry-register+CARN. 15 seats+4 film+1 fiche-1 film reader/printer.
Ordering System: Prior ordering by letter/tel. Catalogue nos sometimes required. Four ordered & produced. Delivery approx 3 mins. P/copying restricted, by staff-same day/post dependent on quantity.

Typing/taping/cameras/laptops (power supply) permitted.
Records: for the old County of Cardigan. PRs-film/Ts/photocopies. County/District/Borough/Town Councils. Chapel. School. PLUs of Cardigan/Newcastle Emlyn/Lampeter/Aberaeron/Tregaron/Aberystwyth. Shipping registers c1790-1900. Petty Sessions 19th/20thC's. Business. Hospital. Valuation lists. Newspapers. M/f-census.
Research Service: Limited specific enquiry.
Facilities: Toilets/public tel. No refreshment facilities. Café/pub/shops nearby.
Publications: Free: Info leaflets: *General information. Tracing your Family Tree.* (SAE).
Tourist Office: Tel: 01970 612125 Fax: 01970 612125
Remarks: Donations appreciated.

National Library of Wales (Department of Manuscripts & Records) ABERYSTWYTH, Ceredigion SY23 3BU Tel: 01970 623816 **Fax:** 01970 625713 **E-mail:** holi@llgc.org.uk
Internet: http://www.llgc.org.uk
Opening Hours: M.-F. 9.30-6; Sat 9.30-5 Closure: Public hols+1st full wk in Oct.
Parking: Yes-free.
Disabled: Lifts. Access by prior arrangement.
Children: 18 yrs+
Appointments: Prior booking unnecessary. Entry-register+ID. 30 seats+20 film+10 fiche.
Ordering System: Prior ordering by letter/telephone. Catalogue nos required. Number ordered & produced at archivist's discretion. Delivery 45 mins. Last order: 4.30. P/copying by staff-same day/post. Typing/taping/cameras not permitted. Laptops (power supply) allowed.
Records: for Wales & border counties. Diocesan RO for all dioceses within the Church of Wales. PRs-film/photocopies/Ts. BTs available. Taxation records. Estate. Nonconformist. Quarter Sessions. Court of Great Sessions. Probate. Manorial. Marriage bonds. Poor Law. Education. Electoral registers. Politics. Photographs. Maps. Newspapers. M/f-GRO indexes/census/IGI.
Research Service: Charge made.
Facilities: Toilets/public tel/restaurant/room for own food/drink vending machine. Café/pub/shops nearby.
Publications: Free: Info leaflets: *Sources for the History of Houses. Records of the Court of Great Sessions. Probate Records in the NLW. Family History at the NLW.* (SAE) Publications catalogue. For sale: *Guide to the Department of Manuscripts & Records.*
O. R: Ceredigion Museum, The Coliseum, Terrace Road, ABERYSTWYTH; **Ceredigion County Library,** Corporation Street, ABERYSTWYTH Local Studies; **University of Wales,** Penglais, ABERYSTWYTH; **National Monuments Record,** Queens Road, ABERYSTWYTH.
Remarks: Bags not allowed-guarded storage area at front entrance. Donations appreciated.

ABERYSTWYTH-USEFUL ADDRESS:

National Monuments Wales, Crown Building, Pas Crug, ABERYSTWYTH, Ceredigion SY23 1NJ

Aberystwyth Public Library, Stryd y Gorfforaeth, Corporation Street, ABERYSTWYTH, Ceredigion SY23 2BU Tel: 01970 617464/617581. Usually open. Local History collection. Welsh Local History collection.

ABINGDON, see Oxfordshire Useful Addresses.

Accrington Central Library, St. James Street, ACCRINGTON, Lancs BB5 1NQ Tel: 01254 872385. Local history of Hyndburn. 11th Service Battn. of East Lancs Regiment (WW1).

ADMIRAL BLAKE MUSEUM, see Bridgwater.

AIRBORNE FORCES MUSEUM, see Aldershot.

Airdrie Library, Wellwynd, AIRDRIE, Lanarkshire ML6 0AG Tel: 01236 763221/760937 Usually open. Disabled: 1st floor-no lift. 2film+2 fiche-1reader/printer. Laptops permitted. PRs-film. Toilet/public tel. Records for Old & New Monkland. Local History collection. Estate. Aidrie & Coatbridge Burgh minutes. Newspapers. OPRs. Census. Photographs.

Society Museum, The Old School, High Street, ALDERNEY, Channel Islands GY9 3TG Tel: 01481 823222-am; 01481 822746-pm. Appt. Alderney collection. Genealogy. Maps. Military occupation 1940-45. Publication available on Alderney militia. **Note:** This museum is only open part of the year.

Airborne Forces Museum, Browning Barracks, ALDERSHOT, Hants GU11 2BU Tel: 01252 349619 Appt. Archives. Documents. Photographs.

Aldershot Military Museum, Queen's Avenue, ALDERSHOT, Hants GU11 2LG Tel: 01252 314598. Appt. Aldershot. Military Historical Trust. Photographs.

Army Physical Training Corps Museum, Queen's Avenue, ALDERSHOT, Hants GU11 2LB Tel: 01252 347131. Appt. Various docs & photographs 1860 on.

ALDERSHOT

Queen Alexandra's Royal Army Nursing Corps Museum, Army Medical Services, Keogh Barracks, Ash Vale, ALDERSHOT, Hants GU12 5RQ Tel: 01252 340294 Appt. MSS collections & some private papers. Photographs.

Roman Catholic Record Office, The Bishopric of the Forces, AGPDO, Middle Hill, ALDERSHOT, Hants GU11 1PP Tel: 01252 349007 Appt. The office houses all records of marriages, baptisms, confirmations, dispensations & deaths which have taken place in an R.C. Service Church anywhere in the world where Service personnel in any of the Armed Services have served. Registers from St. Michael's Military Church & St. Patrick's Church at North Camp, Aldershot go back to 1856. Netley & Shorncliffe registers from 1864. Most of the others begin c1900.

Royal Army Medical Corps Historical Museum, Keogh Barracks, Ash Vale, ALDERSHOT, Hants GU12 5RQ Tel: 01252 340212. Appt. **Note:** Part of this collection has been deposited with the Wellcome Institute, London.

Alnwick Library, Green Batt, ALNWICK, Northumberland NE66 1TU Tel: 01665 602689 Usually open. M/f-census copies 1841-1891.

The Fusiliers of Northumberland Museum, The Abbot's Tower, Alnwick Castle, ALNWICK, Northumberland NE66 1NQ Tel: 01665 602152 Appt. Archives of the Regiment 1688 on.

ANDOVER, Hants see Netheravon

ANGLESEY, ISLE OF, see Llangefni.

ANGUS DISTRICT LIBRARIES & MUSEUM, see Forfar.

ANGUS, see Montrose.

Scottish Fisheries Museum, Harbourhead, ANSTRUTHER, Fife KY10 3AB Tel: 01333 310628 Appt. Fishing vessel/Scottish fishing industry. Plans. Photographs.

ANTRIM, COUNTY, see Ballymena; Belfast.

North Devon Maritime Museum, Odun House, Odun Road, APPLEDORE, Devon Tel: 01237 474852 Appt. M/f-PRs/tithe maps & apportionments for area. **Note:** This is a Devon RO Service point-a member of the Devon RO attends once a month in the afternoon-Tel: 01271 388607 for info.

Royal Electrical & Mechanical Engineers, Isaac Newton Road, Arborfield Garrison, ARBORFIELD, Reading, Berks RG2 9LN Tel: 0118 9763567 Appt. Military history only-records held by Ministry of Defence. Photographs. Catalogue of archive collection.

ARCHIFIDY CEREDIGION ARCHIVES, see Aberystwyth.

North Ayrshire Libraries, Local History Library, 39-41 Princes Street, ARDROSSAN, N. Ayrshire KA22 8BT Tel: 01294 469137 **Fax:** 01294 604236 **E-mail:** mccoll@naclibhq.prestel.co.uk
Opening Hours: M.T.Th.F. 9-5; Sat 10-1; 2-5. Closure: Wed+Public hols.
Parking: 12 places-free but always busy.
Disabled: Access. Toilet.
Children: At librarian's discretion.
Appointments: Prior booking for seats/viewers-1 day. 10 seats+4 film+1 fiche-2 reader/printers.
Ordering System: Prior ordering by letter/tel. Catalogue nos sometimes required. Number ordered & produced at librarian's discretion. P/copying by staff-same day. Typing not permitted. Taping/cameras by prior arrangement. Laptops (battery) allowed.
Records: for North Ayrshire. Local History collection. Scottish history. Major Stevenston family papers from early 1600s. Royal Borough of Irvine archive from late 1500s. Newspapers. Photographs. M/f-OPRs/census/newspapers.
Research Service: 1st 15 mins free, charge made for further research.
Facilities: Toilets. No public tel/refreshment facilities. Café/pub nearby.
Publications: For sale: *Cunninghame Maps. Burgh of Saltcoats. History of Irvine. Auchenharvie Colliery: an early history. Old Irvine. Witchcraft in Ayrshire.*
O. R: Ayrshire Museum, Kirkgate, SALTCOATS, N. Ayr.

Armagh County Museum,The Mall East, ARMAGH, co. Armagh, N. Ireland BT61 9BE Tel: 01861 523070 Social/military history.

The Cardinal Tomás Ó Fiaich Memorial Library & Archive Trust, Ara Coeli, Cathedral Road, ARMAGH, N.Ireland BT61 7QY Tel: 01861 522045 It is intended that this library & archive will be officially opened by May 1998. It will contain the Roman Catholic Diocesan records for Armagh, Cardinal Tomás Ó Fiaich collection of documents relating to Irish history, Irish language, culture & music & various other Cardinals' collections.

Southern Education & Library Board, Library Headquarters, 1 Markethill Road, ARMAGH, co. Armagh, N. Ireland BT60 1NR Tel: 01861 525353 Appt. Local history. Irish Studies. Local Newry families.

ARMY PHYSICAL TRAINING CORPS MUSEUM, see Aldershot.

Buckinghamshire Record Office, County Hall, Walton St, AYLESBURY, Bucks HP20 1UU Tel: 01296 382587 **Fax:** 01296 382405
Opening Hours: M.-Th. 9-5.15; F. 9-4.45; 1st Thurs of mth 9-7.45 Closure: Public hols+2nd full wk in Feb.
Parking: None.
Disabled: Stairlift for w/chair. New entrance planned.
Children: Accompanied: 10 yrs+. Unaccompanied: 12 yrs+.
Appointments: Prior booking for seats/viewers for late night essential, other times advisable-a few days. Entry-register+ CARN+ID. 16 seats+6 film+1 fiche, I film & 1 fiche reader/printer.
Ordering System: No prior ordering. Up to four ordered & produced. Delivery 10-15 mins. Last order: 30 mins before closure, lunch times restricted if short staffed. P/copying restricted, by staff-same day/post. Typing/taping/ cameras not permitted. Laptops (battery) allowed.
Records: for County of Buckingham pre 1965 boundaries. Diocesan RO for Archdeaconry of Buckingham (diocese of Oxford, formerly Lincoln). PRs-film/some Ts/originals if not copied. BTs-film. Estate. Family collections. Police.
Research Service: Charge made.
Facilities: Toilets/public tel. No refreshment facilities. Café/pub/shops nearby.
Publications: Free: Info leaflets: List of Publications. *Genealogical Sources. Original PRs deposited. Public House History Sources* (SAE). For sale: *House History: Short Guide to Sources. The Buckinghamshire Sheriffs 992-1992*. Maps. Fiche index of names from Settlement papers.
O. R: County Reference Library, Walton Street, AYLESBURY, Bucks HP20 1UU Tel: 01296 382250. Usually open. Directories. Local history. M/f-GRO indexes/census incl. 1881 census index/newspapers. Info leaflets available (SAE).
Remarks: Bags not allowed-lockers. Donations appreciated.
Buckinghamshire RO provides an archive service for the new unitary authority of Milton Keynes, renewable in 2000.

Aylsham Town Council Archives, Town Hall, Market Place, AYLSHAM, Norwich, Norfolk NR11 6EL. Tel: 01263 733354 Appt. to Town Clerk-address as above. Free long & short term parking. Town Hall archives only-parish council mins. Poor Law-not PLU. Aylsham Navigation Co. Turnpike Trustees. Posters. Oral history. Photographs & slides. **Note:** PRs, PLU & other Aylsham records are at the Norfolk RO, Norwich (see entry)

Ayrshire Archives, County Buildings, Wellington Square, AYR, Ayrshire KA7 1DR Tel: 01292 612138 **Fax:** 01292 612143
E-mail: wilbraha@south-ayrshire.gov.uk
Opening Hours: W. only 9.30-1; 2-4.30 Closure: Mon/Tues/Thurs/Fri+Public hols.
Parking: None.
Disabled: Ramp. Lift-by appt.
Children: Accompanied: At archivist's discretion. Unaccompanied: Not allowed.
Appointments: Prior booking for seats necessary-1 wk. Entry-register. 6 seats+1 fiche.
Ordering System: Prior ordering by letter/tel. Catalogue nos required. Three ordered & produced. Delivery 10 mins. Last order: 4.15. P/copying by staff-same day. Typing not permitted. Taping/cameras/laptops (power supply) allowed.
Records: for Ayrshire. Local authority 17th-20thC's. Estate. Solicitors. Kirk sessions. Local History collections.
Research Service: Charge made.
Facilities: Toilets/public tel/drink vending machine. Café/pub/shops nearby.
Publications: Free: Info leaflets: *Guide to Records. Commissioners of Supply.* (SAE).
Tourist Office: Tel: 01292 288688
Remarks: Note: Possible move of premises in the near future.

South Ayrshire Council, Carnegie Library, 12 Main St, AYR, Ayrshire KA8 8ED Tel: 01292 286385 **Fax:** 01292 611593 **E-mail:** carnegie@south-ayrshire.gov.uk
Internet: http://www.south-ayrshire.gov.uk
Opening Hours: M.T.Th.F. 9-7.30; W.Sat 9-5 Closure: Christmas+New Year's Days.
Parking: Public nearby.
Disabled: Disabled friendly. (Entrance in Garden St).
Children: At librarian's discretion.
Appointments: Prior booking for viewers-2 wks. 25 seats+4 film+3 fiche-4 reader/printers.
Ordering System: Prior ordering by letter/tel at librarian's discretion. Number ordered at librarian's discretion, one produced. Delivery a few mins. P/copying restricted, by staff-same day. Typing permitted. Taping/cameras not allowed. 2 PCs available for hire in Library.
Records: for Ayrshire. Ayr Burgh records. Burns collection. Galt collection. Newspapers from 1803. Societies. Maps. Photographs. M/f-OPRs/census/IGI.
Research Service: Charge made.

AYRSHIRE

Facilities: Toilets/public tel/coffee shop. Café/pub/shops nearby.
Publications: For sale: Local/Scottish history-send for leaflet (SAE).
Remarks: Bags not allowed.

AYRSHIRE, see Ardrossan; Ayr; Cumnock; Kilmarnock.

BAIRD INSTITUTE HISTORY CENTRE & MUSEUM, see Cumnock.

North Eastern Education & Library Board, Library Services, Local Studies Dept., Area Reference Library, Demesne Avenue, BALLYMENA, co. Antrim, N. Ireland BT43 7BG Tel: 01266 664100. North Eastern Local History collection.

South Eastern Education Library and Information Service, Library Headquarters, Irish & Local Studies, Windmill Hill, BALLYNAHINCH, co. Down, N. Ireland BT24 8DH Tel: 01238 566400. Irish & Local Studies collection especially for South Antrim & co. Down. Index to local newspapers.

BANBURY, see Oxfordshire Useful Addresses.

BARKING, see London Borough of.

BARNET, see London Borough of.

Barnoldswick Library, Fern Lea Avenue, BARNOLDSWICK, Colne, Lancs BB8 5DW Tel: 01282 812147. Appt. Barnoldswick Local History collection. Maps & plans. Photographs. Indexes to census/newspapers/ maps.

Barnsley Archives & Local Studies Dept, Barnsley Central Library, Shambles St, BARNSLEY, West Yorks S70 2JF Tel: 01226 773950 **Fax:** 01226 773955 **E-mail:** archives@barnsley.ac.uk.
Internet: http://www.barnsley.ac.uk
Opening Hours: Archive Service: M.W. 9.30-1; 2-6; T.F. 9.30-1; 2-5.30; Th. 9.30-1; Local Studies: (as Archive Service)+Sat 9.30-1 Closure: Public hols.
Parking: None.
Disabled: Ramp. Lift.
Children: At archivist's discretion.
Appointments: Prior booking for viewers-2 wks. Entry-register. 6 seats+1 film+1 fiche-1 reader/printer.
Ordering System: Prior ordering by letter/tel. Number ordered at archivist's discretion, three produced. Delivery 10-15 mins. P/copying by staff-same day/post. Typing/taping/laptops not permitted. Cameras allowed.
Records: for Barnsley Metropolitan Borough. PRs-film/fiche/photocopies/Ts. Local authority. Register of miners killed in local pits. Poor relief. Deeds. Nonconformist. Rate books. School. Business. Societies. Photographs. Newspapers.
Research Service: None.
Facilities: Toilets. No public tel. Coffee bar. Cafe/pub/shops nearby.
Publications: Free: Info leaflet. (SAE) For sale: *Family History Handbook. Archive Photograph Series.*
Tourist Office: Tel: 01226 206757
Remarks: Donations appreciated. **Note:** West Yorks Archive Service (Wakefield) hold Barnsley related material.

North Devon Record Office, Library & Record Office, Tuly St, BARNSTAPLE, Devon EX31 1EL Tel: 01271 388608
Opening Hours: M.T.Th.F. 9.30-5; W. 9.30-4, Sat (twice a mth) 9.30-4 Closure: Public hols+Christmas wk.
Parking: Public-paying.
Disabled: Lift. Toilet.
Children: Accompanied: At archivist's discretion. Unaccompanied: Not allowed.
Appointments: Prior booking for viewers-2/3 days. Entry-register+CARN+fee+ID. 10 seats+5 film+5 fiche-3 reader/printers.
Ordering System: Prior ordering by letter/tel. Catalogue nos required. Three ordered, number produced at archivist's discretion. Delivery 5 mins. No production 12-2. Last order: 20 mins before closure. P/copying restricted, by staff-same day/post/collection. Typing not permitted. Taping/cameras/laptops (power supply) allowed.
Records: for North Devon. Diocesan RO for Exeter-Archdeaconry of Barnstaple. PRs-film/ fiche/photocopies/Ts/original if not copied. BTs available. Barnstaple Borough. Nonconformists. Poor Law. Solicitors. Estate. Chichester family archives. Beaford Photographic archive. M/f-GRO index/census /IGI in Local Studies Centre.
Research Service: Charge made.
Facilities: Toilets/public tel. No refreshment facilities. Café/pub/shops nearby.
Publications: Free: Info leaflets: Lists of PRs, accessions etc (SAE).
O. R: Museum of N. Devon, The Square, BARNSTAPLE; **Bideford & District Council Archive**, Council Offices, NORTHAM.
Tourist Office: Tel: 01271 388583 Fax: 01271 388599
Remarks: Bags not allowed-storage area.

Cumbria Record Office, Barrow, 140 Duke Street, BARROW-IN-FURNESS, Cumbria LA14 1XW Tel: 01229 894363 **Fax:** 01229 894371
Opening Hours: M.-F. 9-5 Closure: Public hols+Tues following Easter & Spring+Christmas to New Year.
Parking: None.
Disabled: Access. Assistance on request.

Children: Accompanied: At archivist's discretion. Unaccompanied: Educational purposes only (by school certification).
Appointments: Prior booking unnecessary. Entry-register+CARN or other reader's ticket. 13 seats+2 film+3 fiche.
Ordering System: Prior ordering by letter/tel. Catalogue nos helpful. Number ordered at archivist's discretion, two produced. Delivery 5 mins. P/copying restricted, by staff-same day. Typing/taping/cameras/laptops (power supply if indemnity form signed+circuit breaker used), at archivist's discretion.
Records: for South-West Cumbria-Barrow/ Ulverston/Millom/neighbouring parishes & chapelries. Diocesan RO for Carlisle. PRs-mainly Ts. Poor Law. Manorial-Court Books & rentals. Borough Council. Nonconformists. Business. Education. Shipping registers & crew lists. Professional directories. MIs. Maps. Photographs. M/f-Protestation Returns/Hearth Tax/Quaker registers/Furness Railway staff registers/ census.
Research Service: Charge made.
Facilities: Toilets. No public tel/refreshment facilities. Café/pub/shops nearby.
Publications: Free: Info leaflets: *PRs. Poor Relief. Manorial Records. Directories. Maps. Ships & ship building in Furness. Development of Modern Barrow. Local Industries. Introduction to House/Family History.* (SAE). For sale: *Cumbrian Ancestors.*
O. R: Central Library, Ramsden Square, BARROW-IN-FURNESS, Cumbria LA14 1LL Tel: 01229 894377 Usually open. Directories. Local History collection. Burgess Rolls. Registers of electors. Maps. Photographs. M/f-census; **Workington Library**, Vulcans Lane, WORKINGTON CA14 2ND Tel: 01900 325170; **Superintendent Registrar**, 74 Abbey Road, BARROW-IN-FURNESS LA14 5UB Tel: 01229 894511; **Superintendent Registrar**, St. George's Road, MILLOM LA18 4DD Tel: 01229 772357; **Superintendent Registrar**, Town Hall, Queen Street, ULVERSTON LA12 7AR Tel: 01229 894170; **Barrow-in-Furness Public Library,** Ramsden Square, BARROW-IN-FURNESS, Cumbria LA14 1LL Tel: 01229 820650. Local History. M/f-census/newspapers.
Tourist Office: Tel: 01229 870156 Fax: 01229 432289
Remarks: Note: Central Library's Local History collection may be combined with RO in the future.

Bath & North East Somerset Record Office, Guildhall, High Street, BATH, Som BA1 5AW Tel: 01225 477421
Opening Hours: M. 9-1; 2-8; T.-Th. 9-1; 2-5; F. 9-1; 2-4.30 Closure: Public hols.
Parking: None.
Disabled: W/chair access. Lift. Toilets.
Children: Accompanied: 6 yrs+ Unaccompanied: 11 yrs+
Appointments: Prior booking unnecessary. Entry-register. 6 seats+1 film+4 fiche-1 reader/printer.
Ordering System: Prior ordering by letter/tel. Six ordered & produced. Delivery a few mins. P/copying by staff-same day. Typing/taping/ cameras/laptops (power supply) permitted.
Records: principally for Bath but also North East Somerset. PRs-fiche/Ts. Local authority. Deeds. Hospitals. Schools. Coroners. Quarter/Petty Sessions. Board of Guardians. Business. Family. Societies. Photographs. Maps.
Research Service: None.
Facilities: Toilets/public tel/drink vending machine. Café/pub/shops nearby.
Publications: Free: Info leaflet: *Bath RO.* (SAE).
O. R: Bath Police Museum, Manvers Street, BATH, Som BA1 1JN Tel: 01225 444343. Appt. Police custody records.
Tourist Office: Tel: 01225 462831 Fax: 01225 477221

Bath Central Library, 19 The Podium, Northgate Street, BATH, Som BA1 5AN Tel: 01225 428144. Usually open. Disabled: Access. Lift. 4 film+10 fiche-3 reader/printers. Laptops (battery). PRs-film/Ts. Napoleonic collection (newspapers). Walcot estate. Local societies. Directories. Scrapbooks. Local History collection. Maps/plans. Photographs/ slides/illustrations. M/f-GRO indexes/census/ newspapers/IGI.

BATH-USEFUL ADDRESS:

Fashion Research Centre, Bath Museum & Historical Buildings, 4 Circus, BATH, Som BA1 2EW

West Lothian District Library, Wellpark, Marjoribanks Street, BATHGATE EH48 1AN Tel: 01506 652866/630300. Usually open. Local History collection. Local district council mins. Maps. Newspapers. Photographs. M/f-census/parish records.

Battersea, see London Borough of Wandsworth.

The North of England Open Air Museum, BEAMISH, co. Durham DH9 ORG Tel: 01207 231811 Appt. North East of England social history collection. Archives ref. Trade catalogues/advertising. Photographs.

Brookwood Library, 166 Drymen Road, BEARSDEN, East Dumbartonshire Tel: 0141 9426811

BEDFORD

Opening Hours: M.-Th. 10-8; F.Sat 10-5 Closure: Public hols.
Parking: Yes-free.
Disabled: Disabled friendly.
Children: At archivist's discretion.
Appointments: Prior booking unnecessary. Entry-ID for consulting archive material.
Ordering System: No prior ordering. Number ordered & produced at librarian's discretion. P/copying by staff-same day/post/collection & DIY. Typing/taping not permitted. Cameras/laptops (power supply) allowed.
Records: for Bearsden/Milngavie. Local authority. Newspapers. Valuation rolls 20thC. Directories. MIs. Photographs. Maps. M/f-OPRs/census/IGI.
Research Service: None.
Facilities: Toilets. No public tel/refreshment facilities. Café/pub/shops nearby.
Publications: Free: Info leaflets: *Look It Up-Family History/Archives/Local History/Local Publications.* (SAE A5). For sale: *Remains to be Seen: a brief history of Bearsden & Milngavie. Bearsden in old picture postcards. Milngavie in old picture postcards.*

Bedfordshire & Luton Archives & Record Service, Record Office, County Hall, BEDFORD, Beds MK42 9AP Tel: 01234 228833 or 228777 **Fax:** 01234 228854
Opening Hours: M.-F. 9-1; 2-5. 1st Th. in each month 10-1; 2-5 Closure: Public hols.
Parking: Limited.
Disabled: W/chair access limited. Appt. essential. Car spaces in County Hall car park. Toilet in County Hall main building.
Children: At archivist's discretion.
Appointments: Prior booking unnecessary. Entry-register, ID may be required. 22 seats+4 film+10 fiche-1 reader/printer.
Ordering System: No prior ordering. Up to four ordered & produced. Delivery 5 mins. P/copying by staff-same day. Typing/taping/cameras/laptops (power supply) permitted.
Records: for Bedfordshire including Luton. Diocesan RO for St.Albans, Archdeaconry of Bedford. PR's-film/fiche/Ts/originals only if film/Ts unsatisfactory. BTs available. Assizes. Quarter/Petty Sessions. Poor Law. Probate. Education. Hospital. Charity. Nonconformists. Prison. Title deeds. Land Tax. Manorial-especially good for Biggleswade/Leighton Buzzard/Potton. Business. Apprenticeship. Turnpike Trust. Local authority. Council archives (formerly in Bedford Muniments Room). Public utilities. Militia. Poll books. Electoral registers from 1834. Inclosure. Tithe. Estate. County/town maps. Architectural plans from local authorities & local firms. Photographs-indexed. Newspapers. Directories. M/f-census/cemetery/IGI.
Research Service: Charge made.
Facilities: Toilets/restaurant/room for own food available. Café/pub/shops nearby.
Publications: Free: Info leaflets: *An access guide for disabled visitors. User guide. List of PR Ts to 1812. List of holdings.* (SAE). For Sale: *Tracing Ancestors in Bedfordshire* C. R. Chapman (1995)
O. R: Bedford Museum, Castle Lane, BEDFORD.
Tourist Office: Tel: 01234 215226 Fax: 01234 215226
Remarks: Bags/handbags not allowed-lockers. Donations appreciated. **Note:** Collection of books on Bedford & photographs previously at Bedford Muniments Room now at Bedford Museum.

Local Studies Library, Bedford Central Library, Harpur Street, BEDFORD, Beds MK40 1PG Tel: 01234 350931 **Fax:** 01234 342163
Opening Hours: M.W. 9.30-7; T.Th.F. 9.30-5.30; Sat 9.30-4 Closure: Public hols.
Parking: None.
Disabled: Lift. Toilet.
Appointments: Prior booking unnecessary. 3 film+6 fiche-3 reader/printers.
Records: for Bedfordshire. Bedfordshire collection-PRs/local histories/biographies/crafts & industries/directories. Frank Mott Harrison John Bunyan collection-rare editions of Bunyan's works. Fowler Library-Camden & Seldon Society publications, the Pipe Roll Series, Patent Rolls & State Paper series. M/f-census/IGI.
Remarks: Station: Bedford 10 mins walk.

BEDFORDSHIRE, see Bedford; Luton

General Register Office, Oxford House, 49-55 Chichester Street, BELFAST, N.Ireland BT1 4HL Tel: 01 232 252021/2/3/4 **Fax:** 01 232 252044
Internet: www.nics.gov.uk/nisra/gro
Opening Hours: M.-F. 9.30-4 Closure: Public hols
Parking: Public nearby.
Disabled: Access.
Children: 18 yrs+
Appointments: Prior booking for seats essential-1 day, or 6 mths if need assistance. Entry-register+fee. 2 seats+1 fiche-1 reader/printer.
Ordering System: No prior ordering. Four ordered & produced (more at extra fee). P/copying restricted, by staff-same day. Typing/cameras not permitted. Taping/laptops (battery) allowed.
Records: for Northern Ireland BMD. Births & deaths from 1864. Marriages for N.Ireland 1845-1863. Non Roman Catholic marriages in all Ireland 1864-1921. All marriages, including

Roman Catholic, 1922 to present. Marine register of births & deaths from 1922. Consular returns of births from 1927 & deaths from 1922 & marriages from 1923. Foreign marriages from 1947. War deaths 1939-48. Service department registers from 1927. Adopted children register from 1931.
Research Service: None.
Facilities: Toilets. No public tel/refreshment facilities. Café/pub/shops nearby.
Publications: Free: Info leaflets: *Records & Search Services.* (SAE).
O. R: Belfast Public Libraries, Royal Avenue, BELFAST BT1 1EA Tel: 01 232 243233 Usually open. Local History collection. Newspapers 1761 on. Theatre posters.
Remarks: Station: Central.

Linenhall Library, 17 Donegall Square North, BELFAST BT1 5GD, Co. Antrim, N.Ireland Tel: 01 232 321707
Opening Hours: M.-F. 9.30-5.30; Sat 9.30-4 Closure: Public hols+1 wk after 12th Jul hols.
Parking: None.
Disabled: Lift.
Children: At librarian's discretion.
Appointments: Prior booking unnecessary. Entry-register+ID. 35-40 seats+2 film+2 fiche.
Ordering System: Prior ordering by letter/tel. Catalogue nos sometimes required. Number ordered & produced at librarian's discretion. Delivery 5-10 mins. P/copying DIY. Typing/taping not permitted. Cameras/laptops (power supply-donations welcome) allowed.
Records: for Ireland. Printed books of Church Registers & Transcripts/family histories & pedigrees/English Marriage Licences & Musgrave Obituaries/Irish wills/Irish Marriage Licences/emigrant lists/peerage & gentry reference books/poll books & electoral registers for Belfast/school records/Army List/ directories/MIs. Griffiths Valuations. Index of Belfast newsletter BMDs.
Research Service: None.
Facilities: Toilets/public tel/restaurant. Café/pub/shops nearby.
Publications: Free & for sale: Leaflets: General cultural events & local history. (SAE).
Remarks: Donations appreciated. Station: Great Victoria Street.

Presbyterian Historical Society of Ireland, Church House, Fisherwick Place, BELFAST, N.Ireland BT1 6DW Tel: 01 232 322284
Opening Hours: M.T.Th.F. 10-12.30; W. 10-12.30; 2-4 Closure: Public hols+2 wks in Summer.
Parking: None.
Disabled: Lift.
Children: Accompanied: At librarian's discretion. Unaccompanied: Not allowed.
Appointments: Prior booking unnecessary. Entry-register+ID. 8 seats+1 film.
Ordering System: Prior ordering by letter/tel. Two ordered & produced. Delivery 10 mins. P/copying restricted, by staff-same day. Typing/taping/laptops (power supply) permitted. Cameras at librarian's discretion.
Records: mainly for Province of Ulster. PRs-film/photocopies. Presbyterian Church in Ireland including baptismal & marriage registers-indexes available. Bound volumes of *The Witness* newspaper. Pamphlets. M/f-records of local congregations.
Research Service: Limited specific enquiry.
Facilities: Toilets. No public tel/refreshment facilities. Cafe/pub/shops nearby.
Publications: For sale: *A History of Congregations: The General Assembly of the Presbyterian Church in Ireland 1840-1990*+others.
Remarks: Donations appreciated.

Public Record Office of Northern Ireland, 66 Balmoral Avenue, BELFAST, N.Ireland BT9 6NY Tel: 01 232 251318 **Fax:** 01 232 255999 **E-mail:** proni@nics.gov.uk
Internet: http://www.proni.nics.gov.uk/index .htm
Opening Hours: M.-W.F. 9.15-4.45; Th. 9.15-8.45 Closure: Public hols+2 wks in late Nov/early Dec.
Parking: 10 places-free.
Disabled: W/chair access except to Church M/f room, but these films can be viewed in main Reading Room if required.
Children: Accompanied: 7 yrs+ Unaccompanied: 12 yrs+
Appointments: Prior booking unnecessary. Entry-register+ID+reader's ticket. 42 seats+22 film+3 fiche.
Ordering System: No prior ordering except for a few documents stored off site-letter advisable for these. Five ordered & one produced. Delivery within 40 mins. Last order: 4.15; Thurs 8.15. P/copying restricted, by staff-same day/post/collection. Typing/taping/cameras not permitted. Laptops (power supply) allowed.
Records: for Northern Ireland, some parish records relating to Counties of Donegal/ Monaghan/Cavan/Louth. PRs-film/some p/copies. Poor Law. Landed estate. Some emigrant letters & passenger lists. Family. Manor rolls. Militia & army lists. Courts. School. Wills & testamentary papers. Local authorities. Public bodies. Business. Nonconformists. Catholic. Solicitors. Griffiths Valuation & Tithe Applotments (Householders' Index lists surnames). Maps & plans. Photographs.
Research Service: None. List of researchers available.
Facilities: Toilets/public tel. Restaurant.
Publications: Free: Info leaflets: *A Guide to PRONI.* Publications list. (SAE).

BELFAST

Tourist Office: Tel: 01 232 246609 Fax: 01 232 312424
Remarks: Bags not allowed-lockers. Station: Balmoral.

Royal Ulster Constabulary Museum, Brooklyn, Knock Road, BELFAST, N. Ireland BT5 6LE Tel: 01232 650222 Appt. Documents. Photographs. Reference library being established.

The Royal Ulster Rifles Regimental Museum, 5 Waring Street, BELFAST, N. Ireland BT1 2EW Appt. Royal Ulster Rifles. Royal Irish Rifles. 83rd & 86th Regimental units & associated units. Personal papers. War diaries. Casualty lists. Medal rolls. Regimental journals/histories. Photographs. Records In process of being computerised.

BERKSHIRE RO, see Shinfield Park.

BERKSHIRE, see Arborfield; Maidenhead; Reading; Shinfield Park; Sulhamstead.

Berwick Library, Church Street, BERWICK-UPON-TWEED, Northumberland TD15 1EE. Tel: 01289 307320 Usually open. M/f 1841-1881 census for North Northumberland **Note:** On Wed/Thurs the census M/f are in the Berwick-upon-Tweed RO & **not** in the library.

Berwick-upon-Tweed Record Office, Council Offices, Wallace Green, BERWICK-UPON-TWEED, Northumberland TD15 1ED Tel: 01289 330044 Ext. 230 **Fax:** 01289 330540 **E-mail:** Archives@berwickc.demon.co.uk
Internet: http://www.swinhope.demon.co.uk/genuki/NBL/NorthumberlandRO/Berwick.html
Opening Hours: W.Th. 9.30-1; 2-5. Closure: Mon/Tues/Fri+Christmas-New Year.
Parking: Public nearby+on street-paying.
Disabled: Special entrance. Toilet.
Children: Accompanied: At archivist's discretion. Unaccompanied: School age.
Appointments: Prior booking for viewers & GRO Indexes-2/3 wks. Entry-register. 12 seats+3 film+2 fiche.
Ordering System: Prior ordering by letter/tel. Catalogue nos required. Three ordered & produced. Delivery 5 mins. P/copying restricted, by staff-post/collection. Typing/taping/cameras not permitted. Laptops (power supply+donation) allowed.
Records: for the history of North Northumberland area+Berwick-upon-Tweed Borough Council. PRs-film/Ts. Berwick Borough archives 16-20thC's. MIs incl some for Scotland. Nonconformists incl Roman Catholic. Workhouse-relief/pauper service book. Cold Stream Bridge/Lamberton Toll Marriages. Miscellaneous Ts. Charity School admissions. Crew lists. Freemasons. Freemens rolls. Militia/Muster rolls. Land Tax. Electoral registers. Enclosures. Ship registers. Civil cemeteries-Berwick/Tweedmouth/N. Sunderland. Computer database for burials at Berwick 1856-1875. M/f-GRO Indexes/census/Durham Diocese wills/OPR Indexes-bapt & marr for Berwickshire & Roxburghshire/IGI (Border Archives, Selkirk-see entry).
Research Service: Charge made.
Facilities: Toilets. No public tel/refreshment facilities. Café/pub/shops nearby.
Publications: Free leaflets: *Family History Resources for N. Northumberland. Family History Resources in Berwick-upon-Tweed RO. Transcripts in the Berwick-upon-Tweed RO.* Genealogical Publications list. (A5 SAE). For sale: *RO Ts on fiche, census+1851 census indexes+Ts. Marriages at Lamberton Toll 1833-49. Guide to Anglican Churches in Newcastle Diocese. Berwick on Tweed Illustrated 1894-1994. A History of the Tweed Bridges Trust.*
O.R: King's Own Scottish Borderers, The Barracks, BERWICK-UPON-TWEED TD15 1DG Tel: 01289 307426 Appt. Archives.
Tourist Office: Tel: 01289 330733 Fax: 01289 330448
Remarks: Bags not allowed. Donations appreciated. See entries for Morpeth Records Centre & Northumberland RO, North Gosforth.

Beverley Reference/Local Studies Library, Champney Road, BEVERLEY, East Riding of Yorks HU17 9BQ Tel: 01482 885358 Usually open. Prior booking for viewers-several days. 20 seats+1 film+ 1 fiche+1 reader/printer. Beverley & the East Riding of Yorkshire. Local History collection.

East Riding of Yorkshire Archive Office, County Hall, BEVERLEY, East Riding of Yorks HU17 9BA Tel: 01482 885007 **Fax:** 01482 885463
Opening Hours: M.W.Th. 9-1; 2-4.45; T. 9-1; 2-8; F. 9-1; 2-4 Closure: Public hols+last complete wk in Jan.
Parking: Public nearby-paying.
Disabled: Access. Toilet. Prior arrangement for space in search room.
Children: Accompanied: 10 yrs+ Unaccompanied: 14 yrs+ (or 12 yrs by arrangement with school).
Appointments: Prior booking for seats/viewers 5-10 days. Entry-register. 14 seats+1 film+5 fiche+2 dual.
Ordering System: Prior ordering by letter/telephone-essential for Tues evening before 4pm of that day. Six ordered, three produced. Delivery 5 mins. Last order: 15 mins

before lunchtime & 30 mins before end of day. P/copying by staff-post/collection. Typing/cameras not permitted. Taping/laptops (power supply) allowed.
Records: for Historic East Riding to 1974/North Humberside 1974-1996/present East Riding/parts of North Yorkshire for parish records only. Diocesan RO for the Archdeaconry of the East Riding. PRs-fiche/Ts/original if not copied. East Riding Register of Deeds 1708-1976. Quarter Sessions. Education. Manorial. Nonconformists. Local authority. Business. Maps.
Research Service: Charge made.
Facilities: Toilets/public tel/drink vending machine. Café/pub/shops nearby.
Publications: Free: Info leaflets: *General Information.* List of Publications. (SAE) For sale: *Guide to the East Riding Register of Deeds. PRs. Non-Anglican Church Records. Manorial Records. Quarter Sessions Records. Education Records.*
Tourist Office: Tel: 01482 867430 Fax: 01482 883913
Remarks: Bags not allowed-lockers. Donations appreciated. Station: Beverley-10 mins walk.

BEXLEY, KENT, see London Borough of.

Wirral Archives Service, Reference & Information Sevices, Central Library, Borough Road, BIRKENHEAD, Wirral L41 2XB Tel: 0151 6526106/7/8 Usually open. Parking: Yes-free. Disabled: Access. Lift. Prior booking for viewers-1 day. PRs-film/Ts. Metropolitan Borough of Wirral/local authority. Schools. Workhouse. Hospitals. Courts. Business. Cammell Laird Shipbuilders Ltd. Societies. Private.

Birmingham City Archives, Central Library, Chamberlain Square, BIRMINGHAM, B3 3HQ Tel: 0121 2354217 **Fax:** 0121 2129397 or 0121 2334458
Internet: http://birmingham.gov.uk/libraries/archives
Opening Hours: M.T.Th.-Sat 9-5 Closure: Wed+Public hols+Tues following Spring/Aug hols+Good Friday-Easter Tues.
Parking: None.
Disabled: No w/chair access. Lift to Local Studies where material can be seen by prior arrangement.
Children: At archivist's discretion.
Appointments: Prior booking unnecessary. Entry-register+CARN. 24 seats+1 film+1 fiche+1 reader/printer in Local Studies.
Ordering System: Prior ordering by letter/tel. Catalogue nos necessary. Number ordered at archivist's discretion, approx three produced. Delivery 5-15 mins. No production 12-2. Last production 4.45. P/copying restricted, by staff-same day/post. Typing/taping permitted in study booths. Laptops (battery) allowed. Cameras allowed but no flash.
Records: for Birmingham but some collections relate to Staffordshire/Warwickshire/Worcestershire. Diocesan RO for Birmingham, few BTs. PRs-film/photocopies/originals if not copied. City Council. West Midlands County Council. Sutton Coldfield Borough Council. Nonconformists. Courts. Probate. Hospitals. Business. Societies. Family & estate. Tithe. Inclosure. Manorial. Wills. Rate books. Solicitors. Charities. Matthew Boulton/James Watt papers. Brewery History Society. Imperial Metal industries. Major collections for the study of music including composers, teachers & performers. Charles Parker archives (recordings & discussions of folk song & the oral tradition).
Research Service: Charge made.
Facilities: Toilets/public tel/cafe. Café/pub/shops nearby.
Publications: For sale: *List of PRs. Catalogue of James Watt Papers.* other source lists in preparation.
O. R: Local Studies & History Dept, same building. Tel: 0121 2354549/2354220. Newspapers. Maps. Photographs. M/f-census/GRO indexes/IGI.
Tourist Office: Ground floor of building. Tel: 0121 235 4511/2
Remarks: Bags not allowed-lockers. **Note:** Computerised cataloguing system being installed. Station: Birmingham New St or Snow Hill - 5 mins walk.

Birmingham Roman Catholic Archdiocesan Archives, Cathedral House, St.Chad's Queensway, BIRMINGHAM, B4 6EX Tel: 0121 2362251
Opening Hours: By appt only.
Parking: 12 places-free.
Disabled: No facilities.
Children: Accompanied: At archivist's discretion. Unaccompanied: 16 yrs+
Appointments: Prior booking for seats essential-1/2 wks. Entry-register. 4 seats.
Ordering System: Prior ordering by letter/tel. Catalogue nos sometimes required. Number ordered & produced at archivist's discretion. P/copying restricted, by staff-same day. Typing/taping/laptops permitted (power supply). Cameras by arrangement.
Records: for Warwickshire/Worcestershire/Staffordshire/Oxfordshire/West Midlands from 1850. Before 1850 most of Central England (except for registers). Diocesan RO for Roman Catholic Archdiocese of Birmingham. PRs-original/film.
Research Service: None.
Facilities: Toilets. No public tel/refreshment facilities. Cafe/pub/shops nearby.
Publications: For sale: List of all registers of BMD & confirmations.

Remarks: Donations appreciated. Station: Birmingham New St or Snow Hill.

BIRMINGHAM RAILTRACK, see London Other Repositories-Railtrack.

BISHOPDALE, see Leyburn.

BLACK WATCH, THE REGIMENTAL ARCHIVES OF, see Perth.

West Lothian Council Libraries Local History Library, Library HQ, Hopefield Rd, BLACKBURN, EH47 7HZ Tel: 01506 776331 **Fax:** 01506 776345 **E-mail:** libhq@libhq .demon.co.uk
Opening Hours: M.-Th. 8.30-5; F. 8.30-4; 1st Sat in mth 9-1. Closure: Public hols.
Parking: Yes-free.
Disabled: Access.Toilet.
Children: Accompanied: At archivist's discretion. Unaccompanied: 8 yrs+
Appointments: Prior booking unnecessary. Entry-register. 10 seats+3 film+1 fiche-1 reader/printer.
Ordering System: No prior ordering. Number ordered & produced at archivist's discretion. P/copying by staff-same day/post/collection. DIY restricted. Typing/cameras not permitted. Taping/laptops (power supply) allowed.
Records: for West Lothian (present boundaries)+some material on old County now in other Local Authority areas. OPRs-film. Burgh/County/District Council mins. Valuation rolls. Electoral rolls. MIs. Maps. Photographs. Videos. Films. M/f-census/newspapers/IGI.
Research Service: None.
Facilities: Toilets. No public tel/refreshment facilities.
Publications: Free: Info leaflets: *Digging up your Family Tree. Guide to West Lothian Local History Collection.* (SAE)
Tourist Office: Tel: 01254 53277 Fax: 01254 683536
Remarks: Station: Bathgate.

BLACKHEATH, see London Borough of Greenwich.

Blackpool Central Reference Library, Queen Street, BLACKPOOl, Lancs FY1 1PX. Tel: 01253 23977 Appt. for m/f readers & bound vols. of newspapers. Local History collection for Blackpool & area. Photographs. Postcards. **Note:** Blackpool will become a Unitary Authority in 1998.

The Royal Corps of Signals Museum, Blandford Camp, BLANDFORD FORUM, Dorset DT11 8RH Tel: 01258 482248 Appt. The Museum's library & archives cover the history of military communications since the Crimean War. Photographs. Info leaflet available-with map (SAE).

Blyth Library, Bridge Street, BLYTH, Northumberland NE24 2DJ Tel: 01670 3511269 Usually open. M/f-census copies 1841-1891

Duke of Cornwall's Light Infantry Museum, The Keep, BODMIN, Cornwall PL31 1EG Tel: 01208 72810 Appt. Library & archives (originally 32nd & 46th Regiments of Foot).

BODMIN, see Cornwall

Bolton Archives & Local Studies, Central Library, Civic Centre, Le Mans Crescent, BOLTON, Lancs BL1 1SE Tel: 01204 522311 Ext 2179 **Fax:** 01204 363224
Opening Hours: T.Th. 9.30-7.30; W. 9.30-1; F.Sat 9.30-5 Closure: Mon+Public hols.
Parking: None.
Disabled: Access. Ramp. Kurzweil reading machine.
Children: At archivist's discretion.
Appointments: Prior booking for viewers-essential for Tues eve/Thurs eve/Sat-up to 4 wks ahead. 22 seats+5 film+5 fiche.
Ordering System: Prior ordering by letter/tel. Number ordered at archivist's discretion, four produced. Delivery 5 mins. P/copying by staff-same day. Typing not permitted. Taping/cameras/laptops (battery) allowed.
Records: for Bolton. PRs-film/Ts. Local authority (those relating to Engineering Dept require 2 wks prior notice). Family. Estate. Business. Nonconformist. Poor Law. Quarter Sessions. Workhouse. Charities. Societies. Enclosure. Maps. Photographs. Oral history. Directories. M/f-nonconformist registers/Bolton burgess rolls 1837-1922/GRO indexes/ census/newspapers/IGI.
Research Service: None. Leaflet available for list of record & research agents.
Facilities: Toilet/public tel. No refreshment facilities. Café/pub/shops nearby.
Publications: Free: Info leaflets: *Archives & Local Studies Service. Catalogues & Indexes. Starting Your Family Tree. M/f readers-new advance booking system.* (SAE). For sale: *Handlist of Registers.*
O. R: Chorley Family History Centre, (LDS Church), Water Street, CHORLEY, Lancs Tel: 01257 233687; **Superintendent Registrar, Bolton** Tel: 01204 525165
Tourist Office: Tel: 01204 364333 Fax: 01204 3981-1

BORDER REGT & KINGS OWN ROYAL BORDER REGT, see Carlisle.

BORDERS, see Motherwell.

BORTHWICK INSTITUTE OF HISTORICAL RESEARCH, see York.

Royal Bovington Camp Armoured Corps & Royal Tank Museum, BOVINGTON CAMP, Nr. Wool, Dorset BH20 6JG Tel: 01929 405096 Appt. Regimental war diaries/histories/handbooks/documents of the Royal Armoured corps & Royal Tank Regiment. Library.

Bradford Cathedral Archives, The Cathedral, Stott Hill, BRADFORD, West Yorks BD1 4EH Tel: 01274 777721 (Cathedral Administrator) Not open to the public. There is a part-time archivist who will look up information on request-charge made. Holds registers for Bradford Parish Church (now Cathedral), which are available on film from the County Archives, & miscellaneous papers concerning the Church.

West Yorkshire Archive Service (Bradford), 15 Canal Rd, BRADFORD, West Yorks BD1 4AT Tel: 01274 731931 **Fax:** 01274 734013
Opening Hours: M.-Th. 9.30-1; 2-5; alternate Thurs eve 5-8 Closure: Fri+Public hols+1st wk in Feb.
Parking: None.
Disabled: No facilities.
Children: At archivist's discretion.
Appointments: Prior booking for viewers-a few days. Entry-register. 12 seats+6 fiche-1 reader/printer.
Ordering System: No prior ordering. Four ordered & produced. Delivery 5 mins. P/copying by staff-same day. Typing not permitted. Taping/laptops (power supply) allowed. Cameras allowed-fee required.
Records: for Bradford Metropolitan Borough. Diocesan RO for Bradford. PRs-fiche/film. Nonconformists. Borough/District Council records. Business-especially textiles. Family & estate. Trade unions. Political.
Research Service: Charge made.
Facilities: Toilets. No public tel/refreshment facilities. Café/pub/shops nearby.
Publications: Free: Info leaflets: *West Yorkshire Archive Service Bradford.* For sale: *Bradford Archives 1974-1995.* (SAE).
O. R: Bradford Central Library, Princes Way, BRADFORD, W. Yorks BD1 1NN Tel: 01274 753600 Local History collection. Photographs.
Tourist Office: Tel: 01274 753678 Fax: 01274 739067
Remarks: Bags not allowed-lockers. Donations appreciated. Station: Bradford Interchange & Forster Square.

Brecknock Museum, Captain's Walk, BRECON, Powys LD3 7DW Tel: 01874 624121 Appt. Enclosure. Railways. Canals etc. Photographs.

South Wales Borderers & Monmouthshire Regimental Museum of the Royal Regiment of Wales, The Barracks, BRECON, Powys LD3 7EB Tel: 01874 623111 Appt. South Wales Borderers/Monmouthshire Regiment/24th & 41st Regiments of Foot/Royal Regiment of Wales. Letters/diaries/journals. Citations. Paybooks. Officers' records. Battle reports. Photographs.

BRECON, see Brecknock.

BRENT, see London Borough of.

Admiral Blake Museum, Blake Street, BRIDGWATER, Som TA6 3NB Tel: 01278 456127 Local History collection. Monmouth Rebellion. Admiral Blake (Civil War) collection.

Local History Centre, Bridport Museum, South Street, BRIDPORT, Dorset DT6 3NR Tel: 01308 422116 Appt. PRs-Ts. Tudor Muster Rolls. Protestation Returns. Hearth Tax. Yeomanry etc. Tithe maps. Directories. Photographs. Local History. Card index of family history/local history research interests. M/f-PRs/census for area/IGI.

BRIERLEY HILL, see Coseley.

Brighton Reference Library, Church Street, BRIGHTON, Sussex BN1 1UE Tel: 01273 296969/296968 **Fax:** 01273 296965 **E-mail:** brightonlibrary@pavilion.co.uk
Opening Hours: M.T.Th.F. 10-7; Sat 10-4; Closure: Wed+Public hols.
Parking: Public nearby-paying.
Disabled: No facilities.
Children: At librarian's discretion.
Appointments: Prior booking for viewers-up to 1 wk. Entry+ID for some items. 55 seats+3 film+3 fiche-3 film/1 fiche reader/printer.
Ordering System: Prior ordering by letter/tel. Four ordered, number produced at librarian's discretion. P/copying restricted, by staff-same day/post/collection, or DIY. Typing not permitted. Camera/laptops (battery) allowed.
Records: for East & West Sussex with special emphasis on Brighton. PRs/BTs-Ts. Brighton church rates. Poor rates. Valuation registers. Trade union material. Burgess roll for Brighton 1854-1915. Electoral registers. Maps. Prints. Sussex Survey photographs 1880-1900. Poll books. General photographs. Newspaper & railway photographs. Ephemera. Directories. Local government publications. Periodicals. School & local church magazines. Newspapers from 1826 (not all complete). M/f-court rolls/census.
Research Service: Charge made.
Facilities: In Museum area-Toilets/public tel/restaurant. Café/pub/shops nearby.

BRISTOL

Publications: Free: Info leaflet: *The local studies collection-a brief guide.* (SAE).
O. R: Brighton Museum, same address; **Preston Manor**, Preston Park, BRIGHTON, Sussex BN1 6SD Appt. Manorial records. Deeds. Photographs.
Tourist Office: Tel: 01273 323755
Remarks: Note: Currently shares a building with Brighton Museum. A regeneration project requires the library to be housed elsewhere by Jun 1999. Eventually the complex plans to include a local studies centre & would house some of the Library's Local History collection.

Bristol Record Office, "B" Bond Warehouse, Smeaton Rd, BRISTOL, BS1 6XN Tel: 0117 9225692 **Fax:** 0117 9224236
Opening Hours: M.-Th. 9.30-4.45; 1st Th. of month 9.30-8 Closure: Fri+Public hols+last 2 wks in Jan.
Parking: Yes-free.
Disabled: Disabled friendly.
Children: At archivist's discretion.
Appointments: Prior booking for seats helpful-essential for Thurs eve. Entry-register. 24 seats+1 film+17 fiche-1 reader/printer. Charge made for use of micro fiche readers.
Ordering System: Prior ordering by letter/tel. Catalogue nos preferred. Number ordered at archivist's discretion, three produced. Delivery 10-15 mins. No production 11.45-1.30 & after 3.45. P/copying restricted, by staff-same day/post. Typing/taping/laptops by arrangement. Cameras permitted.
Records:for City & County of Bristol. Diocesan RO of Bristol. PRs-fiche/some Ts/originals if not on fiche. BTs available. Nonconformists. Poor Law. Shipping. Probate. Directories. Marriage licences. Apprentices. Business. J.S Fry & Sons W.D & HO Wills, Slavery. Cemeteries. Solicitors. Land Tax. Hospitals.
Research Service: Charge made.
Facilities: Toilets/public tel/café in another part of building. Room for own food/drink vending machine.
Publications: Free: Info leaflets: *Bristol RO Introductory Leaflet. Planning a visit to Bristol RO? Read this first. Bristol RO Publications.* (SAE). For sale: *List of registers. School admission records. Index to Bristol Wills 1793-1858. The Poor Law in Bristol. Sources for Ships, Seamen and Emigrants. Records relating to Slavery. Records of Cemeteries & Burial Grounds. Bristol Apprentice Books 1566 –1593.* Maps. Views.
O. R: Bristol Industrial Museum, Princes Wharf, City Docks, BRISTOL BS1 4RN Tel: 0117 9251470 Appt. Company. Maritime. Social & industrial histories. Photographs.
Tourist Office: Tel: 0117 9260767 Fax: 0117 9297703
Remarks: Bags not allowed-staffed cloaks cupboard. Donations appreciated. Station: Temple Meads.

Bristol Reference Library, College Green, BRISTOL, BS1 5TL Tel: 0117 9299147
Opening Hours: M.-Th. 10-7.30; F. 9.30-7.30; Sat 9.30-5 Closure: Public hols.
Parking: Public nearby-paying.
Disabled: W/chair access. Lift.
Children: Accompanied: At librarian's discretion. Unaccompanied: 14 yrs+
Appointments: Prior booking for viewers-2/3 days. 116 seats+6 film+10 fiche-2 reader/printers. Charge made for m/f readers.
Ordering System: Prior ordering by letter/tel especially for newspapers/Southwell Papers/the Ellacombe Collection which relates to Hanham/Oldland/Bitton/Kingswood. Number ordered & produced at librarian's discretion. Delivery 10 mins. Last order: 15 mins before closure. P/copying by staff/DIY. Typing/taping not permitted. Cameras/laptops (battery) allowed.
Records: for Bristol-mainly published books. PRs-fiche/Ts. BTs available. Electoral rolls. Directories. Photographs. Tithe maps. OS maps. Plans. Oral history. M/f-Jefferies Slavery Volume/GRO index/newspapers/census/IGI.
Research Service: None.
Facilities: Toilets/public tel. No refreshment facilities. Café/pub/shops nearby.
Publications: For sale: *Guide to Family History Sources; Guide to Local Studies.*
O. R: John Wesley's Chapel, The New Room in the Horsefair, 36 The Horsefair, BRISTOL BS1 3JE Tel: 01454 773158/0117 9264740. Appt. Methodist subjects+info on individual chapels. Methodist periodicals. Small library.
Remarks: Note: Possibility of opening hours being reduced.

BRITISH WATERWAYS ARCHIVE, see Gloucester; Watford.

Broadstairs Library, The Broadway, BROADSTAIRS, Kent CT10 2BS. Tel: 01843 862994. Local Studies collection. Directories. M/f-census. For Local Studies information & appt. contact Heritage Officer, Margate Library. Tel: 01843 223626

BROMLEY, Kent, see London Borough of.

BROOKWOOD LIBRARY, see Bearsden.

BUCKINGHAMSHIRE, see Aylesbury.

BUDE, see Cornwall

BUFFS, see Canterbury.

Burton upon Trent Archives, Burton Library, Riverside, High Street, BURTON-ON-TRENT, Staffs DE14 1AH Tel: 01283 239556 **Fax:** 01283 239571
Opening Hours: M.-F. 9.15-12; 2-6 Closure: Public hols.
Parking: Public nearby-paying.
Disabled: Ramp. Toilets.
Children: At archivist's discretion.
Appointments: Prior booking for seats/viewers-1/3 days. Entry-register+ID. 8 seats+2 film+2 fiche.
Ordering System: Prior ordering by letter/tel. Catalogue nos sometimes required. Number ordered at archivist's discretion, two produced. Delivery a few mins. P/copying restricted, by staff-same day. Typing/taping/laptops (battery) permitted.
Records: for old county borough of Burton-on-Trent. PRs-fiche. Local authority from 16thC. Magistrates court. Hospital. Poor Law. Business. Schools. Societies. Estate. Family. M/f-census/newspapers/IGI.
Research Service: None.
Facilities: Toilets/public tel. No refreshment facilities. Café/pub/shops nearby.
Publications: Free: Info leaflet: *Burton upon Trent Archives.* (SAE).
O. R: Bass Museum, Horninglow Street, BURTON ON TRENT, Staffs; **Burton Library,** Riverside, High Street, BURTON ON TRENT, Staffs DE14 1AH Tel: 01283 543271 Appt. Borough. PLU records. Methodist. Education.
Tourist Office: Tel: 01283 516609 Fax: 01283 517268

Bury Archive Service (1st Floor Derby Hall Annexe), Edwin St (off Crompton St), BURY, BL9 0AS Tel: 0161 7976697
Opening Hours: T. 10-1; 2-5; Appt only-M.W.Th.F. 10-1; 2-5; 1st Sat in mth 10-1 Closure: Public hols.
Parking: Public nearby-paying.
Disabled: Parking in street directly outside. Access to ground floor room for consulting documents-prior appt essential.
Children: At archivist's discretion. No younger than 8 yrs.
Appointments: Prior booking essential. Entry-register+CARN+ID required (access to certain items restricted, if no ID). 7-12 seats+1 fiche.
Ordering System: Prior ordering by letter/tel. Three ordered & produced. Delivery 1-2 mins. P/copying restricted, by staff-same day/post. Typing/taping permitted if not causing disturbance. Laptops (power supply at archivist's discretion) allowed. Cameras allowed by arrangement.
Records: for Ramsbottom/Tottington/ Radcliffe/Bury/Whitefield/Prestwick. Nonconformists registers. Education. Business. Trade Unions. Deeds. Maps & plans.
Research Service: None.
Facilities: No toilet/tel/refreshment facilities. Café/pub/shops nearby.
Publications: Free: Info leaflets: *Quarterly newsletter. General Leaflet.* (SAE) For sale: *Interim Guide*-brief listing of records; various others-send for publications list.
O. R: Reference & Information Services Dept, Bury Central Library, Manchester Rd., BURY BL9 0DR Tel: 0161 2535871 Local publications. M/f-census/newspapers/IGI; **Textile Hall**, Manchester Road, BURY, Lancs BL9 0DG Tel: 0161 7055872/3 Local History. Genealogy.
Tourist Office: Tel: 0161 7055111 Fax: 0161 7055919
Remarks: Bags not allowed-no storage facilities. Donations appreciated. Station: Bolton or Manchester Victoria-latter linked by Metrolink tram to Bury Interchange which is 5 mins away from office.

Suffolk Record Office, Bury St. Edmunds Record Office, 77 Raingate St., BURY ST.EDMUNDS, Suffolk 1P33 2AR Tel: 01284 352352 **Fax:** 01284 352355 **E-mail:** gwyn.thomas@libber.suffolkcc.gov.uk
Internet: http://www.suffolkcc.gov.uk/ libraries_and_heritage/
Opening Hours: M.-Sat 9-5 Closure: Public hols.
Parking: 12 places-free..
Disabled: Parking space. Access.
Children: At archivist's discretion.
Appointments: Prior booking unnecessary. Entry-register+CARN. 28 seats+13 film+11 fiche-1film/1 fiche reader/printer.
Ordering System: Prior ordering by letter/tel. Catalogue nos preferred. Number ordered at archivist's discretion, four produced. Delivery within 15 mins. Occasional limitations 12-2. Last order: M.-F. 4.45. Documents required for Sat should be ordered by 1pm on Fri. P/copying restricted, by staff-same day/post/collection. Typing not permitted. Taping by prior arrangement. Laptops (power supply) allowed. Cameras by arrangement+fee.
Records: for historic County of West Suffolk. Diocesan RO for St. Edmondsbury & Ipswich, Sudbury Archdeaconry & Hadleigh Deanery. PRs-film/fiche/Ts/original if not copied. BTs-film. Suffolk Regiment Archives 17th-20thC-printed histories/Suffolk Regimental Gazette/militia/yeomanry/Army List/honours & awards/lists of names for different categories of serving men/diaries/photographs/maps & plans. Marriage licences. MIs. Nonconformists. Cemetery records. Probate. Poor Law. Parish records. Directories. Electoral registers. Poll books. Manorial. School. Rates & taxes. Newspapers. Periodicals. Maps. M/f-census/Boyd's Marriage Index/IGI. Galaxy 2000 & Viewpoint-computerised catalogue

currently used by public libraries in Suffolk. **Note:** Suffolk Regimental Museum now closed, records deposited here-Archives of Duke of Norfolk's Regiment/12th Regiment of Foot/East Suffolk Regiment.
Research Service: Charge made.
Facilities: Toilets. No public tel/refreshment facilities. Café/pub nearby.
Publications: Free: Info leaflets: *Sources for Family History. The Local Studies Collection. The Suffolk Regiment Archives.* (SAE).
Tourist Office: Tel: 01284 764667 Fax: 01284 757124
Remarks: Bags not allowed-lockers. Donations appreciated.

BUTE, Isle of, see Rothesay.

Gwynedd Archives & Museums Service, County Offices, CAERNARFON, Gwynedd LL54 7EF Tel: 01286 679095/679088 Fax 01286 679637.
Opening Hours: M.T.Th.F. 9.30-12.30; 1.30-5; W. 9.30-12.30; 1.30-7 Closure: Public hols+Christmas period+2nd full wk in Oct.
Parking: Public nearby-paying.
Disabled: Disabled friendly.
Children: At archivist's discretion.
Appointments: Prior booking for viewers-1 day. Entry-register+CARN. 24 seats+5 film+2 fiche.
Ordering System: Prior ordering unnecessary except for some classes of local government records-3 days. Number ordered at archivist's discretion, three produced . Delivery 5 mins. P/copying by staff-same day. Typing/taping/ cameras not permitted. Laptops allowed.
Records: for old counties of Anglesey/Merioneth. Diocesan RO for Bangor & St.Asaph (parish records). PRs-film/fiche/ originals. Local authority. Business. Shipping. Photographs. Prints. Newspapers. Oral history.
Research Service: Charge made.
Facilities: Toilets/public tel. No refreshment facilities. Cafe/pub/shops nearby.
Publications: Free: Info leaflets: Short guides to genealogical sources. (SAE). For sale: wide range of publications & photographic reproductions.
Tourist Office: Tel: 01286 672232
Remarks: Bags not allowed-storage available.

CAITHNESS, see Wick.

CALDERDALE, see Halifax.

CAMBORNE, REDRUTH, see Cornwall

County Record Office Cambridge, Shire Hall, Castle Hill, CAMBRIDGE, Cambs CB3 0AP Tel: 01223 717281 **Fax:** 01223 717201
E-mail: county.records.cambridge@camcnty .gov.uk
Opening Hours: T.-Th. 9-12.45; 1.45-5.15; F. 9-12.45; 1.45-4.15; Late night Tues 5.15-9 appt. only. Closure: Mon+Public hols.
Parking: Yes-free but often full.
Disabled: W/chair access from rear of building-consult car park attendant. Toilets. With prior notice space can be allocated in search room.
Children: At archivist's discretion.
Appointments: Prior booking for seats/viewers advisable-essential for Tues eve-3 days. Entry-register+CARN. 16 seats+2 film+1 fiche+5 dual-1 reader/printer.
Ordering System: Prior ordering by letter/tel. Number ordered & produced at archivist's discretion. Orders for Tues eve required by 3pm of that day. Delivery 2-15 mins. P/copying by staff-same day/post. Taping not permitted. Typing/laptops (power supply) by prior arrangement. Cameras by prior arrangement+fee.
Records: for Cambridgeshire. Diocesan RO for Ely Archdeaconry/Ely & March Deaneries. PRs-film/fiche/Ts/originals. BTs-Ts. Nonconformists. Local authority. Overseers. Poll books. Electoral registers. Taxation. Quarter Sessions. Business. Manorial. Family/ Estate. Bedford Level Corporation. Mls. Probate. Directories. M/f-GRO indexes/wills 1853-1943/census/IGI.
Research Service: Charge made.
Facilities: Toilets/public tel/drink vending machine. Café/pub nearby.
Publications: Free: Info leaflets: *General Information. Historical Research Service. Principal Services for Genealogists. Publications List.* (SAE) For sale: *Genealogical Sources in Cambridgeshire. Education Records in CRO Cambridge.*
O. R: Cambridge University Library, West Road, CAMBRIDGE CB3 9DR; **Cambridge Central Library,** 7 Lion Yard, CAMBRIDGE, Cambs CB2 3QD Tel: 01223 65252 Ext. 209 Cambridgeshire Collection-Cambridge/Cambridgeshire/Isle of Ely. Newspapers. Maps. Photographs; **Cambridgeshire Libraries & Heritage,** Ground Floor, Babbage House, CAMBRIDGE, Cambs CB3 OAP Tel: 01223 317064. Local History collection for Cambridge. **Note:** Other Local History collections are at Huntingdon, Peterborough & Wisbech libraries.
Tourist Office: Tel: 01223 322640 Fax: 01223 463385
Remarks: Bags not allowed-left in office. Donations appreciated.

CAMBRIDGE, Westminster College, see United Reformed Church History Society, London.

CAMBRIDGESHIRE, see Cambridge; Huntingdon; Peterborough; St. Ives; Wisbech.

CAMDEN, see London Borough of.

Buffs (Royal East Kent Regiment-3rd Regiment of Foot) Museum, Royal Museum & Art Gallery, High Street, CANTERBURY, Kent CT1 2JE Tel: 01227 452747 Appt. Archive of documents. Photographs.

Canterbury Cathedral Archives, The Precincts, CANTERBURY, Kent CT1 2EH
Tel: 01227 463510 **Fax:** 01227 762897
Internet: http://crane.uhc.ac.uk/english/cmed.htm
Opening Hours: M.-Th. 9-5 & 1st/3rd Sat 9 -1. Groups & classes on Fri. Closure: Fri+Public hols+last 2 wks in Jan+3rd Tues in Nov.
Parking: None.
Disabled: Lift. Parking.
Children: 10 yrs+
Appointments: Prior booking for seats. Entry-CARN. 12 seats+12 film+1 fiche.
Ordering System: Prior ordering by letter/tel. Catalogue nos required. Number ordered at archivist's discretion, three produced. Delivery 5-10 mins. P/copying restricted, by staff-same day. Taping/cameras not permitted. Typing/laptops (power supply) allowed.
Records: for Canterbury. Diocesan RO for Canterbury. BTs/PRs-fiche/film/Ts/originals if not copied. Dean & Chapter. City Council. Archdeaconry parish records.
Research Service: Charge made, minimum ½ hr.
Facilities: Toilets. No tel/refreshment facilities. Café/pub/shops nearby.
Tourist Office: Tel: 01227 766567 Fax: 01227 459840
Remarks: Bags not allowed-shelves. Donations appreciated.Station: Canterbury East or West.

The Institute of Heraldic & Genealogical Studies, Northgate, CANTERBURY, Kent CT1 1BA Tel: 01227 768664 **Fax:** 01227 765617 **E-mail:** ihgs@dial.pipex.com
Opening Hours: M.W.F. 10-1; 2-4.30; Bookshop open M.-F. 9-5 Closure: Public hols+Christmas period.
Parking: Public nearby-paying.
Disabled: No facilities, assistance can be given with prior notice.
Children: Not allowed.
Appointments: Prior booking for seats/viewers-1 wk. Entry-register+fee if not a member. 5 seats+1 film+2 fiche.
Ordering System: Prior ordering by letter/tel. P/copying by staff-same day. Typing/taping/cameras/laptops permitted.
Records: An establishment for the study of history & structure of the family, constituted to train those who wish to acquire skill in family history research. PRs-fiche/Ts. Large reference/genealogical source collection. Many indexes/finding aids-Pallot Marriage Index/Crisp's London Marriage Licences/Catholic Marriage Index/The Tyler Collection (East Kent)/the Sussex Collection/the Hackman Collection (Hampshire BTs)/Lang family/Gretha marriages/General Persons Name Index of the Institute's archives/the Andrews Index (notices from newspapers)/ Freemasons index. Large collection of directories for the whole country. Directories for clergymen/doctors & surgeons/journalists/ vets/teachers/dentists/lawlists/army/navy/airforce. Heraldic collection. M/f-GRO indexes/indexes to censuses/index to OPRS of Scotland/Boyd's Marriage Index/Australian Civil Registration indexes/Apprentices' Indentures & Masters 1710-1774/wills index 1837-1983/IGI.
Research Service: Charge made.
Facilities: Toilets. No public tel. Room for own food/drink vending machine. Café/pub/shops nearby. Overnight accommodation available for visitors to the Library-write for details.
Publications: Free: Info leaflets: *Guide to the Library*. Publications list. (SAE A4). For sale: Institute series of maps. Teaching packs & many other publications.
Remarks: Bags not allowed-locked cupboard.

Cardiff Central Library, St. David's Link, Frederick Street, CARDIFF CF1 4DT Tel: 01222 382116 Usually open. Glamorgan Local History collection. Trade directories. M/f-census.

Glamorgan Record Office, Glamorgan Building, King Edward VII Avenue, Cathays Park, CARDIFF, Glamorgan CF1 3NE Tel: 01222 780282 **Fax:** 01222 780284
Internet: http://www.llgc.org.uk/cac for info on Welsh County Record Offices
Opening Hours: T.Th. 9.30-1; 2-5; W. 9.30.1; 2-7; F. 9.30-1; 2-4.30 Closure: Mon+Public hols+Tues following.
Parking: None.
Disabled: Access. Toilet.
Children: At archivist's discretion but not encouraged.
Appointments: Prior booking for viewers, essential for Wed eve-2/3 days. Entry- register. 20 seats+2 film+8 fiche.
Ordering System: Prior ordering by letter/tel. Catalogue nos required. Number ordered at archivist's discretion, three produced. Delivery 5-10 mins. Last order: 30 mins before closure. Documents for Wed eve must be ordered before 4pm on that day. P/copying by staff-same day. Typing permitted. Taping/laptops (power supply) allowed if no disruption to others. Cameras not allowed.
Records: for historic county of Glamorgan/former Mid & South Glamorgan-Cardiff/Bridgend/Caerphilly/Merthyr Tydfil/Rhondda Cynon Taff/Vale of Glamorgan. Diocesan RO for Llandaff (parish

records). PRs-film/Ts/p/copies. BTs-film. Quarter Sessions. County Council. Electoral registers. Nonconformists. Quaker records for Wales. National Coal Board. Business. Dowlais Iron Company collection. Shipping. Seamen. Police. School. PLU. Maps. M/f-census.
Research Service: Charge made.
Facilities: Toilets. Facilities limited & prone to change due to various uses of the building. Café/pub nearby.
Publications: Free: Info leaflets: *Tracing your Family Tree in the Glamorgan RO. Records of Poor Relief. School & Education Records. Police Records. The Dowlais Iron Company Collection.* (SAE). For sale: *A Glossary Of Medieval & Post-Medieval Terms for South Wales. Poor Relief in Merthyr Tydfil Union in Victorian Times.*
Tourist Office: Tel: 01222 227281 Fax: 01222 239162
Remarks: Bags not allowed-cupboard at reception. Donations appreciated. Station: Cardiff Central (main line). Cardiff Queen Street (branch line).

The Welch Regiment Museum, The Castle, CARDIFF, Glamorgan CF1 2RB Tel: 01222 229367
Opening Hours: Museum: M.W.-F. 10-6 (Mar 1st-Oct 31st); 10-4.30 (Nov 1st-Feb 28th), last entry 10 mins before closure. **Archives:** Tues & Sat 10-2 Appt only. Closure: Christmas/Boxing Day/New Year's Days.
Parking: Public nearby-paying.
Disabled: No facilities.
Children: Educational purposes only.
Appointments: Prior booking for seats essential. 1 seat.
Ordering System: Prior ordering by letter/tel. No p/copying. Typing/taping/laptops at curator's discretion. Cameras by special arrangement.
Records: for 41st & 69th Regiments of Foot (later 1st & 2nd Battalions Welch Regt), associated Militia & Volunteer Corps of South Wales.
Research Service: Limited specific enquiry-charge made for more extensive research..
Facilities: Toilets/refreshment facilities in Castle grounds.
Publications: Various. (SAE).
Remarks: Bags not allowed.

Welsh Industrial & Maritime Museum, Bute Street, CARDIFF CF1 6AN. Tel: 01222 481919 Library & Archive Photographic research rooms open M.-F.10-4.30. Appt. No parking. P/copying. Industrial/Maritime/ Transport histories of Wales-early modern times to present day. Substantial photographic collection (over 180,000). Notable collection of documents-share certificates/personal papers/plans/maps/technical drawings/posters etc. (c30,000). HM Inspector of Mines Reports. Lloyds Registers. Significant Ref. Library of large number of extant & dead journals. Publications: Several catalogues for photographic collection-contact Museum for list & availability. Lists of holdings for photographic & document collection available for perusal only. **Note:** There may be a move to new premises dependent on application to the Heritage Lottery Fund. Station: Cardiff Bay.

CARDIFF, see St. Fagan's.

CARDINAL TOMÁS Ó FIAICH MEMORIAL LIBRARY, see Armagh.

Cumbria Record Office Carlisle, The Castle, CARLISLE, Cumbria CA3 8UR Tel: 01228 607285 **Fax:** 01228 607299
Opening Hours: M.F. 9-5 Closure: Public hols+Tues following Easter & Spring+Christmas wk.
Parking: Yes-free.
Disabled: Parking. Toilet. Ring at front door for assistance.
Children: Accompanied: At archivist's discretion. Unaccompanied: School children to produce special form certified & stamped by their school.
Appointments: Prior booking unnecessary. Entry-register+CARN. 24 seats+6 film+2 fiche-1 reader/printer.
Ordering System: Prior ordering by letter/tel for documents held in outstore. Catalogue nos sometimes required. Two ordered & produced. Delivery up to 20 mins. P/copying restricted, by staff-same day. Typing/taping/cameras/ laptops (power supply-after signing declaration) permitted.
Records: for historic county of Cumberland (South & West of River Derwent) including city of Carlisle. Diocesan RO for Carlisle. PRs-film/photocopies/original. BTs available. Ecclesiastical. Electoral registers. Wills. Deeds. Quarter Sessions. Poor Law. Directories. Family. Estate. Local authorities. Schools. Solicitors. Shipping. Societies. Photographs. Maps. M/f-census.
Research Service: Charge made.
Facilities: Toilets. No public tel. Room for own food/drink vending machine. Café/pub/shops nearby.
Publications: Free: Info leaflets: *Archives.* Publications list. *Cumbria RO Carlisle searchroom information.* (SAE) For sale: *Cumbrian Ancestors. On the Right Track* (Cumberland railways). Maps. Posters.
O. R: Carlisle Library, 11 Globe Lane, CARLISLE CA3 8NX Tel: 01228 607310; **Records Management Unit**, Ashley Street, CARLISLE CA2 7BD; **Border Regiment & King's Own Royal Border Regiment**

Museum, Queen Mary's Tower, The Castle, CARLISLE, Cumbria CA3 8UR Tel: 01228 32774 Appt. Records from 1702.
Tourist Office: Tel: 01228 512444 Fax: 01228 511758
Remarks: Bags not allowed-lockers. Outdoor clothing at reception. Donations appreciated.
Note: See also entry for RO at Whitehaven.

Tullie House Museum & Art Gallery, Castle Street, CARLISLE, Cumbria CA3 8TP Tel: 01228 34781 Tells the story of the Reivers families from the 14thC to the late 17thC. Offers a team of professional genealogists called Reivers Research. They will produce a fully researched document of one known & named ancestor-apply to Tullie House for details. For sale: CD-Rom *In Search of the Border Reiver*

Carmarthenshire Archives Service, County Hall, CARMARTHEN, Carmarthenshire SA31 1JD Tel: 01267 224180 **E-mail:** archives@carmarthenshire.gov.uk
Internet: http://www.carmarthenshire.gov.uk/
Opening Hours: M. 9-7; T.-Th. 9-4.45; F. 9-4.15 Closure: Public hols.
Parking: None.
Disabled: Access.
Children: Accompanied: At archivist's discretion. Unaccompanied: 12 yrs+
Appointments: Prior booking for seats/viewers-2/3 days. Entry-register. 10 seats+4 film+4 fiche.
Ordering System: Prior ordering not allowed except for documents at outstore which require 1 wk notice. Four ordered & produced. No production 12.30-1.30. Last order: 15 mins before closure. P/copying restricted, by staff-same day/post/collection. Typing not permitted. Taping/laptops (power supply) allowed. Cameras-fee.
Records: for Carmarthenshire. PRs-original. Cawdor Archive. Dynevor Archive. Poor Law. Hospitals. Police. Military. Local authority. Rate books. Pedigrees. Family. Business. Maps.
Research Service: None.
Facilities: Toilets/public tel/restaurant/drink vending machine. Café/pub/shops nearby.
Publications: Free & for sale. (SAE).
O. R: Carmarthen Reference Library, St. Peter's Street, CARMARTHEN.
Tourist Office: Tel: 01267 231557 Fax: 01267 221901
Remarks: Bags not allowed-lockers. Donations appreciated. **Note:** Possibility of a move to a new site in 1999/2000.

CARMARTHENSHIRE, see Carmarthen.

CEREDIGION, see Aberystwth.

CHANNEL ISLANDS, see Alderney; St. Helier, Jersey; St. Peter Port, Guernsey.

CHAPLAINS, ROYAL ARMY CHAPLAIN'S DEPT, see Netheravon.

The Royal Engineers Library, Brompton Barracks, CHATHAM, Kent ME4 4UG Tel: 01634 822416 Appt. Letters/documents/ diaries (WW1). Photographs 1885 on.

Chelmsford & Essex Museum, Oaklands Park, Moulsham Street, CHELMSFORD, Essex CM2 9AQ Tel: 01245 353066 Appt. Local History collection. Essex Regiment records. Card Index of Essex county servicemen for family history research.

ESSEX POLICE MUSEUM, see Springfield.

Essex Record Office, County Hall, CHELMSFORD, Essex CM1 1LX Tel: 01245 430067 **Fax:** 01245 430085 **E-mail:** ero.enquiry@essexcc.gov.uk
Internet: www.essexcc.gov.uk
Opening Hours: M. 10-8.45; T.-Th. 9.15-5.15; F.Sat 9.15-4.15 Closure: Public hols+additional day at Christmas.
Parking: Public nearby-paying.
Disabled: Parking by prior arrangement. Disabled friendly.
Children: At archivist's discretion.
Appointments: Prior booking for seats/viewers-a few days. Entry-register+ CARN+ID. 24 seats+12 film+14 fiche-1 fiche/1 film reader/printers.
Ordering System: Prior ordering by letter/tel. Catalogue nos preferred. Some records e.g. local authority & some nonconformist require 24 hrs notice. Five ordered & produced. Delivery 15-20 mins. Last order: 45 mins before closure. P/copying restricted, by staff-same day/post/collection. Printing from M/f DIY. Typing/cameras not permitted. Sound booth available for taping. Laptops (power supply) allowed.
Records: for historic county of Essex including London Boroughs of Barking & Dagenham/Havering/ Newham/Redbridge/ Waltham Forest (parish records for the latter held at Vestry House Museum). Diocesan RO of Chelmsford. PRs-fiche/film/Ts/original if not copied. BTs available. Quarter Sessions from 1530s. Courts. Coroners. Local authority. Probate. Family. Estate. Business. Nonconformists. Charities. District Councils. Schools. Boards of Guardians. Petty Sessions. Electoral registers. Militia. Deeds. Rate books. Tithe maps. Photographs. Sound archive. M/f-Boyd's Marriage Index/marriage licences/Poor Law/hearth tax/tithe awards/census/IGI.
Research Service: Charge made.
Facilities: Toilets/public tel/restaurant/room for own food/drink vending machine. Café/pub/shops nearby.

CHELMSFORD

Publications: Free: Info leaflets: *Notes for Users.* Publications list. *The history of your house/family.* (SAE). For sale: *Rural Essex 1700-1815. Meagre Harvest: the Essex farm workers' struggle against poverty 1750-1914. The Smugglers' Century 1730-1830. Seedtime & Harvest: a diary of an Essex farmer 1807-23. Return of Owners of Land in Essex 1873. Parish Census Listings 1797-1831. Name Index to Poor Law Settlement Papers.* Essex Wills Series.
Tourist Office: Tel: 01245 283400 Fax: 01245 354026
Remarks: Bags not allowed-lockers. Donations appreciated. **Note:** M/f access proposed for Thurrock, points already at Saffron Walden & Harlow. Station: Chelmsford-5 mins walk.

CHELMSFORD, Essex, also see Springfield

CHELSEA, see London Borough of Kensington & Chelsea.

Chertsey Museum, 33 Windsor St., CHERTSEY, Surrey KT16 8AT Tel: 01932 565764 Open in pm T.-Fri; Sat 11-4.30. Disabled: access. 4 seats. Local History collection for Runneymede Borough-photographs/prints/rate books/maps/cuttings /paintings/costumes.

CHESHIRE, see Chester; Northwich; Sale; Stalybridge; Warrington.

Cheshire Military Museum, The Castle, CHESTER, Cheshire CH1 2DN Tel: 01244 327617 Appt. Charge made. Archives of 22nd (Cheshire) Regiment & Cheshire (Earl of Chester's) Yeomanry. Photographs. Index to collections.

Cheshire Record Office, Duke Street, CHESTER, Cheshire CH1 1RL Tel: 01244 602574 **Fax:** 01244 603812 **E-mail:** recordoffice@cheshire-cc.btx400.co.uk
Opening Hours: M.-F. 9.15-4.45 Closure: Public hols+Tues following late Spring & late Summer.
Parking: None.
Disabled: Access. Toilet.
Children: At archivist's discretion.
Appointments: Prior booking for seats/viewers-3/5 days. Entry-CARN or own reader's ticket. 15 seats+12 film+2 fiche.
Ordering System: Prior ordering by letter/telephone. Catalogue nos required. Three ordered & produced. Delivery 10 mins. P/copying by staff-same day/post. Typing/taping/laptops at archivist's discretion. Cameras permitted.
Records: for Cheshire. Diocesan RO for Chester. PRs-film/Ts/original if not copied. County Council. Local authority. Quarter Sessions. Education. Police. Railways. Nonconformists.
Research Service: Charge made.
Facilities: Toilets. No public tel/refreshment facilities. Cafe/pub/shops nearby.
Publications: Leaflets on records. (SAE).
Tourist Office: Railway Station Tel: 01244 322220 Fax: 01244 322221
Remarks: Bags not allowed-storage. Donations appreciated. See *Cheshire RO guide* ed. C.M. Williams (1991): *Guide to the civil registration districts of Cheshire 1837-1974* (1996).

Chester Archives, Town Hall, CHESTER, Cheshire CH1 2HJ Tel: 01244 402110 **Fax:** 01244 324338 **E-mail:** m.lewis@chestercc .gov.uk
Internet: http://www.chestercc.gov.uk/ chestercc/htmls/heritage.htm
Opening Hours: M.-F. 10-4 Admission at other times by appt only. Closure: Public hols.
Parking: None.
Disabled: Disabled friendly.
Children: At archivist's discretion.
Appointments: Prior booking unnecessary. Entry-register+CARN. 10 seats+2 film+3 fiche-1 reader/printer.
Ordering System: Prior ordering by letter/tel. Catalogue nos sometimes required. Number ordered at archivist's discretion, one produced. Delivery 5-10 mins. P/copying by staff-post. Typing not permitted. Taping/laptops (power supply) allowed. Cameras by arrangement+fee.
Records: for Chester City. Education. Nonconformists. Assembly books. Quarter Sessions. Hospitals. Guild records. Records of Grosvenor family of Eaton Hall, if permission granted by Duke of Westminster.
Research Service: Charge made.
Facilities: Toilets. No public tel/refreshment facilities. Room for own food. Cafe/pub/shops nearby.
Publications: Free: Info leaflets: *Tips for using a RO. Tips for starting Family History.* (SAE). For sale: *Family History Source Guide. Archives & Records of the City of Chester.*
O. R: Chester Heritage Centre, St. Michael's Church, CHESTER; **Chester Cathedral Library**, CHESTER Appt only;
Tourist Office: Tel: 01244 317962 Fax: 01244 400420
Remarks: Bags not allowed-lockers. Donations appreciated. Also see Warrington Library.

Chesterfield Local Studies Library, New Beetwell Street, CHESTERFIELD, Derbyshire S40 1QN Tel: 01246 209292 **Fax:** 01246 209304
Opening Hours: M.-F. 9.30-7; Sat 9.30-1 Closure: Public hols.
Parking: Public nearby-paying.
Disabled: Lift.
Children: At librarian's discretion.

Appointments: Prior booking for viewers. 17 seats+3 film+3 fiche-1 reader/printer.
Ordering System: Prior ordering by letter/tel. Catalogue nos required. Three ordered & produced. Delivery up to 15 mins. P/copying by staff-same day. Typing/cameras not permitted. Taping/laptops (battery) allowed.
Records: for Chesterfield & North Derbyshire. PRs-film/Ts. BTs-Ts. Local studies collection. Estate. Business. Family. Nonconformists. Education. Deeds. Photographs. Newspapers. Directories. M/f-census.
Research Service: Charge made.
Facilities: Toilets/public tel/restaurant/drink vending machine. Café/pub/shops nearby.
Publications: For sale: *Family History in Derbyshire. Microfilms in Derbyshire Libraries. Local newspapers in Derbyshire Libraries. How to start tracing your Family Tree in Derbyshire.*
Tourist Office: Tel: 01246 207777/8 Fax: 01246 556726
Remarks: Station: Chesterfield- ¾ mile away.

CHETHAM'S LIBRARY, see Manchester.

West Sussex Record Office, Sherburne House, Orchard Street, CHICHESTER, Sussex; for postal enquiries-County Hall, Chichester, Sussex PO19 1RN **Tel:** 01243 533911 **Fax:** 01243 533959 **E-mail:** recordsoffice@westsussex.gov.uk
Internet: http://www.westsussex.gov.uk/ro/rohome.htm
Opening Hours: M.-F. 9.15-4.45; Sat 9.15-12.30; 1.30-4.30 Closure: Public hols+1 wk in Dec.
Parking: 6 spaces-free. Public nearby-paying.
Disabled: Disabled friendly-parking requires notice. Carrels.
Children: Accompanied: At archivist's discretion. Unaccompanied: 9 yrs+
Appointments: Prior booking unnecessary. Entry-register+CARN. 24 seats+14 film+11 fiche-2 reader/printers.
Ordering System: Prior ordering by letter/tel. Catalogue nos required. Numbers ordered at archivist's discretion, three produced. Delivery 5 mins. No production 12.15-1.30. Last order: 4.15. P/copying by staff-post/collection after 2 days. Typing/taping/cameras by prior arrangement. Laptops (power supply if valid certificate produced) permitted in carrel which needs prior booking.
Records: for all Sussex for PRs/BTs, probate & Diocesan; West Sussex for other collections. Diocesan RO for Chichester. PRs-film/Ts (fiche during 1998). BTs-film. Royal Sussex Regiment-MSS Military 18th-20thC's. West Sussex Constabulary. County/City/District Councils. Education. Quarter/Petty Sessions. Nonconformists. Coroners. Manorial. Tithe. Solicitors. Estate. Shipping. Maps. Photographs. M/f-Land Tax/Probate/Poor Law/wills/electoral registers/Marriage Licence registers/directories/National Probate Calendars/census/ IGI.
Research Service: Charge made.
Facilities: Toilets/public tel. No restaurant. Room for own food. Café/pub/shops nearby.
Publications: Free: Info leaflets: Publications list. (SAE). For sale: *Roots of America: An Anthology of documents relating to American History in the West Sussex RO. West Sussex Probate Inventories. Genealogists Guide to the West Sussex RO.*
Tourist Office: Tel: 01243 775888 Fax: 01243 539449
Remarks: Bags not allowed-lockers. Donations appreciated.

CHISWICK see London Borough of Hounslow.

CHORLEY FAMILY HISTORY CENTRE, see Bolton.

North West Sound Archive, Clitheroe Castle, CLITHEROE, Lancs BB7 1AZ Tel: 01200 427897. Appt. 100,000 recordings largely relating to the N. West incl. regional oral history material.

CLOGHER DIOCESAN ARCHIVES, see Monaghan, co. Tyrone.

Tipperary S.R.Co.Museum, Parnell Street, CLONMEL, Co.Tipperary, Eire Tel: 052 25399 Appt. Local History collection for South Tipperary. Moving to new premises on Suir Island, Clonmel in 1999

Essex Record Office, Colchester & N.E. Essex Branch, Stanwell House, Stanwell Street, COLCHESTER, Essex CO2 7DL Tel: 01206 572099 **Fax:** 01206 574541
Opening Hours: M. 10-5.15; T.-Th. 9.15-5.15; F. 9.15-4.15; 2nd Mon in mth 10-8.45 Closure: Public hols.
Parking: None.
Disabled: Ramp. Lift. Toilet.
Children: At archivist's discretion.
Appointments: Prior booking for seats/viewers-1/2 days. Entry-register+CARN. 10 seats+2 film+4 fiche-1 reader/printer.
Ordering System: Prior ordering by letter/tel. Catalogue nos sometimes required. Number ordered at archivist's discretion, five produced. No production 1-2, sometimes 12-2. Last order: 45 mins before closure. P/copying restricted, by staff-same day/post. Taping/cameras not permitted. Typing allowed on silent keyboard. Laptops (power supply) allowed.
Records: for Colchester Borough & Tendring District. Diocesan RO for Chelmsford parishes within the Colchester & Tendring areas. PRs-fiche. Colchester Borough records from

COLNE

14thC. District Councils. Quarter Sessions. Nonconformist. Poor Law. Schools. Business. Societies. Deeds. Family. Estate. Index to Essex wills 1400-1858. Maps & plans. M/f-census/IGI.
Research Service: None.
Facilities: Toilets/public tel. No refreshment facilities. Café/pub/shops nearby.
Publications: As Essex RO, Chelmsford.
O. R: Local Studies Dept, Colchester Library, COLCHESTER; **University of Essex Library**, Wivenhoe Park, COLCHESTER, Essex CO4 3SQ Tel: 01206 873333 Appt. by written application. Society of Friends meetings for Colchester & Coggeshall.
Tourist Office: Tel: 01206 282920 Fax: 01206 282924
Remarks: Bags not allowed-rack & hooks. Donations appreciated.

Colne Library, Market Street, COLNE, Lancs BB8 0AP Tel: 01282 871155 **Fax:** 01282 865227
Opening Hours: M. 9.30-7; T. 9.30-12; W.Th.F. 9.30-5; Sat 9.30-4 Closure: Public hols+Easter Sat.
Parking: Yes-free.
Disabled: Access. Lift.
Children: Accompanied: At librarian's discretion. Unaccompanied: Educational purposes only.
Appointments: Prior booking for viewers-2/3 days. 12 seats+2 film+4fiche-1 reader/printer.
Ordering System: Prior ordering by letter/tel. Number ordered & produced at librarian's discretion. P/copying by staff-collection. Typing not permitted. Taping/cameras/laptops (power supply) allowed.
Records: for Colne/Foulridge/Trawden/Wycoller.
PRs-fiche/film also for Lancashire & Yorkshire. Parish records. Nonconformists. Local authority. Business. Associations. Societies. Directories. Newspapers. Photographs.
Research Service: None.
Facilities: Toilets. No public tel/refreshment facilities. Café/pub/shops nearby.
Publications: In house indexes to photographs, wills of Colne, newspapers, maps of Colne, surname index to Census returns 1841-91.
Remarks: Donations appreciated.

Colyton Local History Centre, COLYTON, Devon. Service point-moved to the upper floor of Colyton St. Andrew's Sunday School in the church precincts. Collection of documents, maps & photographs held by the Colyton Parish History Society administered by the Society (Enqs. Tel: 01297 552828) together with the facilities of the service point for the Devon RO, Exeter (PRs/tithe maps & apportionments/ Registers of Methodist & URC churches of E. Devon & Society of Friends/Colyton 1891 census/IGI). Tel. 01392 38452 for info.

COMMONWEALTH WAR GRAVES COMMISSION, see Maidenhead.

CORNISH STUDIES LIBRARY, see Redruth.

CORNWALL RO, see Truro.

CORNWALL-USEFUL ADDRESSES:

Penzance Library, Morrab Gardens, PENZANCE-membership/day fee. Useful library for family historians incl some Scilly Isles material.

District Probate Registry, Market Street, BODMIN PL31 2JW Tel: 01208 72279-all Cornish wills from 1858

Superintendent Registrar's Offices:-

12 Carlyon Road, ST. AUSTELL PL25 4AJ Tel: 01726 68974

Lyndhurst, St. Nicholas Street, BODMIN PL31 1AG Tel: 01208 73677

Roskear, CAMBORNE TR14 8DN Tel: 01209 612924 (Camborne-Redruth)

12/14 Berkeley Vale, FALMOUTH TR11 3PH Tel: 01326 312606

Plougastel Drive, SALTASH PL12 6DL Tel: 01752 842624 (St. Germans)

The Willows, Church Street, HELSTON TR13 8NJ Tel: 01326 562848 (Kerrier)

Hendra, Dunheved Road, LAUNCESTON PL15 9JG Tel: 01566 772464
Graylands, Dean Street, LISKEARD PL14 4AH Tel: 01579 343442

St. John's Hall, PENZANCE TR18 2QR Tel: 01736 363848

The Parkhouse Centre, BUDE EX23 8LD Tel: 01288 353209 (Stratton)

Register Office, The Leats, TRURO TR1 3AG Tel: 01872 272842

CORNWALL, DUKE OF CORNWALL'S LIGHT INFANTRY MUSEUM, see Bodmin.

CORNWALL, see Bodmin; Redruth; St. Mary's, Isles of Scilly; Torpoint; Truro.

Dudley Archives & Local History Service, (Dudley M.R.C.), Mount Pleasant Street,

COSELEY, West Midlands WV14 9JR Tel: 01384 812770 **Fax:** 01384 812770 **E-mail:** archives.pls@mbc.dudley.gov.uk
Internet: http://dudley.gov.uk
Opening Hours: T.W.F. 9-5; Th. 9.30-7; 1st & 3rd Sat 9.30-12.30 Closure: Mon+Public hols+2 wks in Nov or Dec.
Parking: Yes-free.
Disabled: Disabled friendly.
Children: Accompanied: At archivist's discretion. Unaccompanied: 10 yrs+
Appointments: Prior booking for viewers-1/2 days. Entry-register+reader's ticket+ID. 12 seats+8 film+5 fiche-1 reader/printer.
Ordering System: Prior ordering by letter/tel. Catalogue nos preferred. Three ordered & produced. Items produced on the hour & half hour. No production 1-2. P/copying restricted, by staff-usually same day. Typing/taping/ cameras/laptops (power supply by arrangement) permitted.
Records: for present Metropolitan Borough. Diocesan RO for Worcester-Deaneries of Dudley/Stourbridge/Himley. PRs-fiche/film/p/copies/Ts/originals if not copied. BTs not held. Earls of Dudley estate 12-20thC's. Local authority. Schools. Poor Law. Business. Nonconformists. Newspapers. Electoral rolls. Rate books. Directories. Maps. Photographs. M/f-GRO indexes/census/ newspapers/maps/IGI.
Research Service: Charge made.
Facilities: Toilets. No public tel. Room for own food/drink vending machine. Café/pub/shops nearby.
Publications: Free: Info leaflets: *Black Country Archives & Local History Services.* Publications list. (SAE). For sale: *Handlist of PRs. Handlist of nonconformist records. Local newspapers: list of holdings. Directories: list of holdings. Census, electoral rolls & rate books: lists of holdings.*
O. R: Brierley Hill Library, High St., BRIERLEY HILL DY5 3ET Tel: 01384 812865; **Halesowen Library**, Queensway Mall, The Combow, HALESOWEN B63 4AJ Tel: 01384 812 980; **Black Country Museum**, Tipton Rd, DUDLEY DY1 4SQ
Remarks: Bags not allowed-lockers. Donations appreciated.

COURTNEY LIBRARY, see Truro.

LORD COUTANCHE LIBRARY, see St. Helier, Jersey.

Coventry City Archives, Mandela House, Bayley Lane, COVENTRY, West Midlands CV1 5RG Tel: 01203 832418 **Fax:** 01203 832421
Opening Hours: M. 9.30-8; T.-F. 9.30-4.45 Closure: Public hols
Parking: Public nearby-paying.
Disabled: W/chair access.
Children: At archivist's discretion.
Appointments: Prior booking for seats essential for Mon after 4.45. Prior booking for viewers. Entry-register+CARN. 16 seats+3 film+2 fiche.
Ordering System: Prior ordering by letter/tel-essential for late night Mon. Numbers ordered at archivist's discretion, three produced. Delivery 10 mins. P/copying restricted, by staff-same day/post. Typing/taping/laptops (power supply-after being checked) permitted. Cameras by arrangement.
Records: for Coventry within its present boundaries/C. of E. records-Coventry & surrounding area of Warwickshire. PRs-film/some Ts. Freemens & apprentice 1781 to present. City Council 12thC to present. WWII & post war reconstruction. 19/20thC industrial records. Nonconformists. Quarter Sessions. Electors & Burgess Rolls. Coroners. Hospital. Education. Business. Plans. M/f-registers of the London Road Cemetery/indexes of wills proved in the Bishop's Consistory Court of Lichfield & Coventry c1520-1860/census/IGI.
Research Service: Charge made.
Facilities: Toilets/public tel nearby. No refreshment facilities. Café/pub/shops nearby.
Publications: Free: Info leaflets: *Family History Sources. Coventry Archive.* Publications list. (SAE) For sale: Various guides to records. *Coventry's Civil War. Coventry through the Ages. Men & Mining in Warwickshire.* Coventry Apprenticeship Enrolment Registers 1822-1831 (on microfiche). *Foleshill Union Workhouse Punishment Book.* Maps.
O. R: Coventry City Library, Smithford Way, COVENTRY CV1 1FY Local History collection for Coventry & Warwickshire includes maps/papers/photographs.
Tourist Office: Tel: 01203 832303/4 Fax: 01203 832370
Remarks: Bags not allowed-lockers. Donations appreciated.

Modern Records Centre, University of Warwick Library, COVENTRY, West Midlands CV4 7AL Tel: 01203 524219 **Fax:** 01203 524211 **E-mail:** archives@warwick.ac .uk
Internet: http://www.warwick.ac.uk/www/ services/library/mrc/mrc.html
Opening Hours: M.-Th. 9-1; 1.30-5; F. 9-1; 1.30-4 Closure: Public hols+10 days at Christmas+6 days at Easter.
Parking: Yes-restricted in term time.
Disabled: Toilet. Lift. Access. By appt.
Children: Accompanied: 16 yrs+ Unaccompanied: Not allowed.

Appointments: Prior booking for seats/viewers-2/3 days. Entry-register+research form. 14 seats+1 film+1 fiche
Ordering System: No prior ordering. Approx three ordered & delivered. Delivery approx 5 mins. P/copying restricted, by staff-same day/post. Typing not permitted. Taping/laptops (power supply) allowed. Cameras at archivist's discretion.
Records: National repository for Industrial Relations. Trade Unions. TUC registry files pre 1960. Employers & trade associations including the CBI & its predecessors. Business particularly the motor industry & road haulage. Photographs. **Note:** The BP Archive is located next to the Modern Records Centre & may be consulted in the joint searchroom.
Research Service: None.
Facilities: Toilets. No tel/refreshment facilities-available in main library building. Café/pub/shops nearby.
Publications: Free: Info leaflets: *Notes for Researchers.* (SAE) For sale: *Summary Guide* & supplements. *Holdings Guide.*
Remarks: Bags not allowed-lockers. Donations appreciated. **Note:** Accommodation facilities on campus-contact the Centre.

Cowes Library & Maritime Museum, Beckford Road, COWES, Isle of Wight PO31 7SG. Tel: 01983 293341 Usually open. Isle of Wight Maritime history books. Photographs.

Cricklade Museum, Calcutt Street, CRICKLADE, Wilts Tel: 01793 750756. Appt. Charge made. Local History collection incl some original material for Cricklade. Photographic collection.

CROYDON, see London Borough of.

CUMBRIA, see Ambleside, Barrow-in-Furness; Carlisle; Grasmere; Kendal; Whitehaven.

Baird Institute History Centre & Museum, 3 Lugar Street, CUMNOCK, Ayrshire KA18 1AD Tel: 01290 421701 **Fax:** 01290 421701
Opening Hours: M.T.Th.F. 10-1; 1.30-4.30 Closure: Wed+Public hols.
Parking: None.
Disabled: No facilities-several steps to entrance.
Children: At staff's discretion.
Appointments: Prior booking unnecessary. 15 seats+2 film+2 fiche.
Ordering System: Prior ordering not allowed. P/copying by staff-post. Typing/cameras not permitted. Taping/laptops (power supply) allowed.
Records: for Ayrshire. Newspapers. MIs. Valuation & voters rolls. Poor Relief registers for New Cumnock/Muirkirk/Mauchline incl Catrine & Sorn. M/f-OPRs/census(selected parishes)/local newspapers/IGI for Scotland & Ireland,.
Research Service: Limited specific enquiry-charge made. Leaflet listing record researchers.
Facilities: Toilets. No public tel/refreshment facilities. Café/pub/shops nearby.
Publications: Free: Info leaflets: *Tracing Your Family Tree: sources in East Ayrshire.* Publications list. (SAE). For sale: *Pictorial Histories of Kilmarnoch/Dundonald/Darvel/Galston etc. The History of Auchinleck.* Various other Local History books.
Station: Auchinleck.

Cupar Library, 33-35 Crossgate, CUPAR, Fife KY15 5AS Tel: 01334 412285 Usually open. Old Parish records. Census. Local History collection for North East Fife. Publications: For sale: *Burgess Rolls of Fife 1700-1800. Burgess Rolls of St.Andrews 1700-50 & 1751-1775. Beginners Guide to Scottish Genealogy. Crail Deaths 1794-1854.*
Cupar Registrar, County Buildings, St Catherine St, Cupar.

Gwent Record Office, County Hall, CWMBRAN, Gwent, NP44 2XH Tel: 01633 644888/644886 **Fax:** 01633 648382 **E-mail:** 113057.2173@compuserve.com
Opening Hours: M.-Th. 9.30-5; F. 9.30-4 Closure: Public hols+Christmas wk+New Year's Day.
Parking: Yes-free.
Disabled: Access. Toilet.
Children: At archivist's discretion.
Appointments: Prior booking for seats-1 day. Entry-register+CARN. 12 seats+4 film+5 fiche-1 reader/printer.
Ordering System: Prior ordering by letter/tel. Catalogue nos necessary. Number ordered at archivist's discretion, three produced. Delivery 10 mins. P/copying restricted, by staff-same day/post/collection. Typing/taping not permitted. Laptops (power supply) allowed. Cameras at archivist's discretion.
Records: for Counties of Gwent & Monmouthshire. Diocesan RO of Monmouth (2 parishes in Swansea & Brecon). PRs-film/Ts/original. Parish records. Local authority. Shipping, docks & harbours. Crime & punishment. Maps.
Research Service: Max 1 hr-charge made.
Facilities: Toilets/public tel/restaurant/drink vending machine. Shops nearby.
Publications: Free: Info leaflets: on Gwent RO & ROs of Wales. (SAE). For sale: various guides to research.
O. R: Gwent County Library, County Hall, CWMBRAN, Newport NP44 2XL. Tel: 01633

832139 Usually open. Local Studies & Chepstow collections.
Remarks: Bags not allowed-lockers.

CYNON VALLEY, see Aberdare.

DAGENHAM, ESSEX, see London Borough of Barking & Dagenham.

Centre for Local Studies, Darlington Branch Library, Crown Street, DARLINGTON, Durham DL1 1ND Tel: 01325 349630 **Fax:** 01325 381556
Opening Hours: M.T.Th.F. 9.30-1; 2.15-7; W.Sat 9.30-1; 2.15-5 Closure: Public hols.
Parking: Public nearby-paying.
Disabled: No facilities. Access restricted-stairs.
Children: At librarian's discretion.
Appointments: Prior booking for viewers advised-1/2 days. 18 seats+3 film+4 fiche-1 reader/printer.
Ordering System: Prior ordering by letter/tel. Number ordered & produced at librarian's discretion. P/copying by staff-same day. Typing/taping/cameras/laptops (power supply) permitted.
Records: for the southern part of Durham/northern part of the North Riding/Darlington. PRs-film/Ts. Extensive railway collection-books/ photographs/maps/ephemera/photocopies from archive collection.
Research Service: None.
Facilities: Toilets. No public tel/refreshment facilities. Café/pub/shops nearby.
Publications: Free: Info leaflet: Brief details on collection (SAE). For sale: Leaflets on newspapers/directories/ Parish Registers.
O. R: Darlington Museum, Tubwell Row, DARLINGTON, Durham DL1 1PD Tel: 01325 463795 Appt. Local Government Museum. Local/Family History. Social/Agricultural history of Darlington. List of Stockton & Darlington Railway & N.E.
Tourist Office: Tel: 01325 388666 Fax: 01325 388667

DARTMOOR LIFE, MUSEUM OF, see Okehampton.

DAVID OWEN ARCHIVE, see Ellesmere Port.

Deal Maritime & Local History Museum, 22 St. George's Road, DEAL, Kent CT14 7AJ Tel: 01304 375816 Local history of Deal. Local maritime history. PRs-Ts.

The Royal Logistics Corps Museum, RLC Training Centre, Princess Royal Barracks, Blackdown, DEEPCUT, Camberley, Surrey GU16 6RW Tel: 01252 340871 Appt. Documents. Journals. Photographs of the Royal Corps of Transport/Royal Army Ordnance Corps/Royal Pioneers Corps/Army Catering Corps. Royal Engineers Postal & Courier Service. Library.

DEESIDE, see Hawarden.

DENBIGHSHIRE, see Hawarden, Ruthin.

Derby Local Studies Library, 25B Irongate, DERBY, Derbyshire DE1 3GL Tel: 01332 255393
Opening Hours: M.T. 9-7; W.-F. 9-5; Sat 9.30-1 Closure: Public hols.
Parking: None.
Disabled: Parking. Access.
Children: At librarian's discretion.
Appointments: Prior booking for viewers-1/2 days. Entry-register+ID. 4 film+3 fiche+1 fiche/1 film reader/printer.
Ordering System: Prior ordering by letter/tel. Catalogue nos sometimes required. Number ordered & produced at librarian's discretion. P/copying restricted, by staff-same day/post/collection. Typing/taping/cameras not permitted. Laptops (battery) allowed.
Records: for Derby & Derbyshire. PRs-film/Ts. Poll books. Fairs. Apprenticeship. MSS. Poor Law. Courts. Electoral registers. Land Tax. Hearth Tax. Business-Derby Canal Co/Evans Cotton Mill/Derby China Factory etc. Family. Deeds. Maps. Photographs. Surname index. M/f-newspapers/directories/census/IGI.
Research Service: Charge made.
Facilities: No toilet/public tel/refreshment facilities. Cafe/pub/shops nearby.
Publications: Free: Info leaflet: *Guide to using the Derby Local Studies Library.* (SAE).
O. R: The Superintendent & Registrar, Nottingham Road Cemetery, DERBY; **The Registrar**, 9 Traffic Street, DERBY; **Derby Museum & Art Gallery,** The Strand, DERBY, Derbyshire DE1 1BS Tel: 01332 716657/716659 Usually open. Computer database of 9th & 12th Lancers records-available from early 1998.
Tourist Office: Tel: 01332 255802 Fax: 01332 256137
Remarks: Derby became an Unitary Authority on 1 April 1997. Station: Derby Midland.

DERBYSHIRE, see Chesterfield; Derby; Matlock.

The Library of the Wiltshire Archaeological & Natural History Society, 41 Long St., DEVIZES, Wilts SN10 1NS. Tel: 01380 727369 Usually open. Disabled: No facilities. Wiltshire Tracts. Newspaper cuttings-indexed from 1850. Early newspapers-Devizes & Wiltshire Gazette/Salisbury Journal+others. Edward Kite's collection of pedigrees. Baker's Ts of MIs-23 vols. Drawings. Photographs-incl aerial/prints/drawings.

Maps-canal/railway/local/O.S. Books-large collection for Wiltshire.
O.R: Wiltshire FHS Workroom, 10 Castle Street, Devizes SN10 1HU - Limited opening. Appt.

DEVON WEST RO, see Plymouth.

DEVON, N. DEVON MARITIME MUSEUM, see Appledore.

DEVON, see Appledore; Barnstaple; Colyton; Exeter; Newton Abbot; Okehampton; Plymouth; Tavistock; Tiverton; Torquay; Totnes.

DICK INSTITUTE, see Kilmarnock.

DOCUMENTARY PHOTOGRAPHIC ARCHIVE, see Manchester.

Archifdy Meirion Archives, Cae Penarlag, DOLGELLAU, Gwynedd LL40 2 YB Tel: 01341 424444/424442 **Fax:** 01341 423984
Opening Hours: M.-F. 9-1; 2-5 Closure: Public hols+1st full wk in Nov.
Parking: Yes-free.
Disabled: Ramp. Toilet.
Appointments: Prior booking for viewers-2 days. Entry-register+CARN. 12 seats+2 film+2 fiche.
Ordering System: Prior ordering by letter/tel. Catalogue nos required. Three ordered & produced. Delivery 2-4 mins. P/copying at archivist's discretion, by staff-same day/post. Typing/taping/cameras not permitted. Laptops (power supply) allowed.
Records: for old County of Merioneth. PRs-film/Ts/p/copies. Nonconformists. Quarter Sessions. Family. Estate. Business. Local authority.
Research Service: Charge made.
Facilities: Toilets. No public tel/refreshment facilities. Café/pub/shops nearby.
Tourist Office: Tel: 01341 422888 Fax: 01341 422888

Doncaster Archives, King Edward Road, Balby, DONCASTER, South Yorks DN4 40NA Tel: 01302 859811
Opening Hours: M.-F. 9-12.45; 2-4.45 Closure: Public hols+Tues following except for May Day.
Parking: Limited-free.
Disabled: Access.
Children: 15 yrs+
Appointments: Prior booking for viewers-1 wk. Entry-reader's ticket+ID. 12 seats+1 film+1 fiche.
Ordering System: No prior ordering. Four ordered, one produced. Delivery a few mins. P/copying
by staff-same day. Typing/taping not permitted. Laptops (battery) allowed.
Records: for Doncaster Metropolitan District. Diocesan RO for Archdeaconry of Doncaster in the Diocese of Sheffield. PRs-Ts/photocopies. BTs-film. Nonconformists. Quarter Sessions. Public records. Parish.
Research Service: Limited specific enquiry-charge made.
Facilities: Toilets/public tel nearby. No refreshment facilities. Café/pub nearby.
Publications: Free: Info leaflets: *The RO.* (SAE). For sale: Family History Starter Pack.
O. R: Doncaster Central Library, Waterdale, DONCASTER, South Yorks DN1 3JE Tel: 01302 734320 Local History collection. Railways.
Tourist Office: Tel: 01302 734309 Fax: 01302 735385
Remarks: Bags not allowed.

Dorset Record Office, 9 Bridport Road, DORCHESTER, Dorset DT1 1RP Tel: 01305 250550 **Fax:** 01305 257184 **E-mail:** dcc_archives@dorset-cc.gov.uk
Internet: http://www.dorset-cc.gov.uk/records.htm
Opening Hours: M, T, Th, F. 9-5; Wed 10-5; Sat 9.30-12.30 Closure: Public hols+Tues following Spring & Summer.
Parking: Yes-free.
Disabled: Disabled friendly.
Children: At archivist's discretion.
Appointments: Prior booking for viewers. Entry-reader's ticket+ID. 42 seats+20 film/fiche+6 fiche-2 reader/printers.
Ordering System: Prior ordering by letter/tel. Catalogue nos required. Four ordered, two produced. Delivery 5-10 mins. Last order: 30 mins before closure. P/copying restricted, by staff-same day/post. Typing/taping/cameras/laptops (power supply) permitted.
Records: for Dorset. Diocesan RO for Dorset & Sherborne Archdeaconry. PRs-film/fiche/Ts/p/copies. Quarter Sessions. Manorial. Estate. Family. Coroners. Business. Inclosure. Tithe. Borough. Parish. Electoral registers. Maps.
Note: The whole of the Poole Borough Archive collection has been transferred to this R.O-some of the collection is uncatalogued at present.
Research Service: Charge made.
Facilities: Toilets/public tel/room for own food/drink vending machine. Cafe/pub/shops nearby.
Publications: Free: Info leaflet: Publications list (SAE). For sale: Short Guides to-*Settlement Papers/ Apprenticeship & Bastardy Records/Parish Registers/Probate Accounts/School Log Books/Transcripts/ Nonconformists & Catholic Registers of Dorset.*
O. R: Dorset County Reference Library, Colliton Park, DORCHESTER, Dorset DT1 1XJ Tel: 01305 224456 Local Studies collection. Census. Newspapers

Tourist Office: Tel: 01305 267992 Fax: 01305 257039
Remarks: Bags not allowed-at reception. Donations appreciated. This service is provided on behalf of Dorset County Council, Bournemouth Borough Council & the Borough of Poole. **Note:** Many Dorset Diocesan records in Wiltshire & Swindon RO, Trowbridge, Wilts. Station: Dorchester South or West.

The Keep Military Museum of Devon & Dorset, Bridport Road, DORCHESTER, Dorset DT1 1RN Tel: 01305 264066 **Fax:** 01305 250373
Opening Hours: M.-Sat 9.30-5 Closure: 23rd Dec-2nd Jan
Parking: Limited-free.
Disabled: Disabled friendly.
Children: 14 yrs+
Appointments: Prior booking for seats-14 days. Entry-ID. 14 seats.
Ordering System: Prior ordering by letter/tel. Four ordered & produced. P/copying by staff-same day. Typing/taping/cameras/ laptops (power supply) permitted.
Records: for the Military Units of Devon & Dorset. Dorset Regiment-39th & 54th of Foot/Devonshire Regiment/11th of Foot/Dorset Militia/Devon Militia/Queens Own Dorset Yeomanry/1st Dorset Rifle Volunteer Battalion.
Research Service: Fees on request.
Facilities: Toilets. No public tel/refreshment facilities. Drink vending machine.. Cafe/pub shops nearby.
Publications: Free: Info leaflet: *The Keep Military Museum* (SAE A5).
Remarks: Donations appreciated.

DORSET, see Blandford Forum; Bovington Camp; Bridport; Dorchester; Poole.

General Registry, Registries Building, Deemsters' Walk, Bucks Road, DOUGLAS, Isle of Man IM1 3AR Tel: 01624 687038/9 **Fax:** 01624 687004
Opening Hours: M.-F. 9-1; 2-5 Closure: Public hols+Jul 5th+Fri of T.T.Race wk
Parking: None.
Disabled: Disabled friendly.
Children: Accompanied: At archivist's discretion. Unaccompanied: Not allowed.
Appointments: Prior booking unnecessary. 5 seats+2 fiche.
Ordering System: No prior ordering. Number ordered at archivist's discretion, three/four produced. Delivery 30 mins. P/copying not allowed. Typing/cameras not permitted. Taping/laptops (battery) allowed.
Records: for Isle of Man. PRs index-fiche/Ts. In the Deeds Registry-wills from 1911 to date/deeds from 1911 to date.
Research Service: None.
Facilities: Toilets. No public tel/refreshment facilities. Café/pub/shops nearby.
Remarks: Donations appreciated.

Manx National Heritage Library, Manx Museum & National Trust, Kingswood Grove, DOUGLAS, Isle of Man IM1 3LY Tel: 01624 648000 **Fax:** 01624 648001
Opening Hours: M.-Sat 10-5 Closure: Public hols+last wk in Jan.
Parking: Yes-free.
Disabled: Chair lift-help available.
Children: 10 yrs+
Appointments: Prior booking unnecessary. Entry-register. 20 seats+9 film+2 fiche-1 reader/printer.
Ordering System: Prior ordering by letter/tel. Catalogue nos sometimes required. Three ordered & produced. P/copying by staff-same day. Typing/cameras not permitted. Taping/laptops (power supply) allowed.
Records: for the Isle of Man. Diocesan RO for Sodar & Man. PRs-film/Ts. Nonconformist. Deeds. Newspapers. MIs. Tithe. Presentments. Maps. Estate. Photographs. M/f-land & property books/indexes of BMD 1878 to present/census/wills/IGI.
Research Service: Charge made.
Facilities: Toilets/public tel/restaurant. Cafe/pub/shops nearby.
Publications: Free: Info leaflets: *Sources for Family History. Sources for information on the Isle of Man.* (SAE) For sale: *The Manx Family Tree* by Janet Narasimham (2nd ed. 1996)
Tourist Office: Tel: 01624 686766 Fax: 01624 627443
Remarks: Bags not allowed-at reception. Donations appreciated.

The Princess of Wales & the Queen's Regiment Museum, Inner Bailey, Dover Castle, DOVER, Kent CT16 1HU Tel: 01304 240121 Appt. Limited records of The Queen's Regiment.

DOVER, see Whitfield, E. Kent Archive Centre.

DOWN, COUNTY, see Ballynahinch; Holywood.

Dublin City Archives, City Assembly House, 58 South William Street, DUBLIN 2, Eire Tel: 01 6775877 **Fax:** 01 6775954
Opening Hours: M.-F. 10-1; 2-5
Parking: None.
Disabled: No facilities.
Children: Accompanied: 12 yrs+ Unaccompanied: Not allowed.
Appointments: Prior booking for seats-1 wk. Entry-register+ID. 4 seats+1 film+1 fiche.
Ordering System: Prior ordering by letter/tel. Catalogue nos sometimes required. Number

ordered at archivist's discretion, three produced. Delivery up to 24 hrs depending on bulk. Last order: 4pm for following day. P/copying by staff-same day. Typing/taping not permitted. Cameras/laptops (power supply) allowed.
Records: for Dublin/Rathmines/Rathgar/ Pembroke. City Council. Freedom of Dublin (Free citizens 13thC, 1468-1512, 1575-1918). The Wide Streets Commission. Mansion House Fund (relief during 1870s & 1880 famines). Court. Howth Urban District Council 1918-1940. City Council. Assembly Rolls. Charity. Title deeds. Maps. Photographs.
Research Service: Limited specific enquiry.
Facilities: Toilets. No public tel/refreshment facilities. Café/pub/shops nearby.
Publications: Free: Info leaflets: *Freedom of the City of Dublin. Dublin City Archives.* For sale: *Directory of Historic Dublin Guilds. The Dublin Guild Merchant Roll, c1190-1265.*
Remarks: Bags not allowed-lockers. Transport: DART to Pearse Street Station.

Genealogical Office, Office of the Chief Herald, 2 Kildare St., DUBLIN 2, Eire Tel: 01 6030302/6030311 **Fax:** 01 6621062
Opening Hours: M-F. 10-12.30; 2-4.30; Closure: Public hols+Good Friday-Easter Wednesday+Christmas Eve-Jan 2nd+St. Patrick's Day+Whitsun wkend.
Parking: None.
Disabled: Access through back of building. Lift.
Children: At archivist's discretion.
Appointments: Prior booking unnecessary. Entry-register+reader's ticket. 26 seats.
Ordering System: Prior ordering by letter/tel. Catalogue nos required. One/three ordered & produced. Delivery 15 mins. P/copying restricted, by staff-same day. Typing/laptops by prior arrangement. Taping/cameras permitted.
Records: For Ireland Genealogical sources. Registers of Grants of Arms & Pedigrees. Unregistered Arms & Pedigrees. Abstracts of wills. Funeral entries. Maps. 70,000 files of research carried out by the office. Miscellaneous material.
Research Service: Charge made.
Facilities: Toilets. No public tel/refreshment facilities. Cafe/pub/shops nearby.
Publications: For sale: Genealogical Research pack.
O. R: Dublin Civic Museum, City Assembly House, 58 South William Street, DUBLIN 2
Remarks: Bags not allowed-storage facilities. Station: Pearse.

Irish Theatre Archive, City Assembly House, 58 South William Street, DUBLIN 2, Eire Tel: 01 6775877 Usually open. Ephemera from 1850 relating to theatres mainly in Dublin. Modern theatre archives. Memorabilia. Unpublished plays.

Kilmainham Gaol, Inchicore Road, DUBLIN 8, Eire Tel: 01 453 5984 Documents relating to the history of Irish Nationalism 18-20thC's.

National Archives, Bishop Street, DUBLIN 8, Eire Tel: 01 4092300 **Fax:** 01 4092333
Internet: http://www.kst.dit.ie/nat_arch/
Opening Hours: M.-F. 10-5.30 Closure: Public hols.
Parking: None.
Disabled: Lifts. Toilet.
Children: Accompanied: 12 yrs+ Unaccompanied: 15 yrs+
Appointments: Prior booking unnecessary. Entry-register+reader's ticket. 48 seats+15 film+5 fiche-5 reader/printers.
Ordering System: Prior ordering by letter-1/2 days (especially for records stored at Four Courts). Catalogue nos required. Three ordered & produced. Last order: 4.30. P/copying by staff-post/collection. Typing not permitted. Taping/laptops (power supply) allowed. Cameras by prior arrangement.
Records: for Ireland. Church of Ireland PRs-film. Government Departments-agriculture/education/ health/justice/the Marine/transport. Customs & Excise. Famine Relief Commission. National School applications/registers/files pre 1922. Valuation. Chancery pleadings. Genealogical abstracts. Landed estates Court rentals. Private. Trade Union. Rebellion papers. Wills & administrations. BMD. M/f-census for 1901 & 1911/some returns for 1821, 1831, 1841, 1851 for parts of Antrim/Cavan/ Fermanagh/ Galway/King's (Offaly)/Londonderry (Derry) /Meath/heads of household in 1851 for Dublin City/Tithe Applotment books/the Primary Valuation (also known as the Griffith's Valuation). Stored at **Four Courts:** Court records. Wills 1900-76. O.S. Prison registers. Shipping agreements & crew lists. Business. Hospital. Boards of Guardians.
Research Service: None. List of researchers available.
Facilities: Toilets/public tel/room for own food. Café/pub nearby.
Publications: Free: Info leaflets: *Tracing your Ancestry in Ireland. Sources for Family History & Genealogy.*
Remarks: Bags not allowed-lockers.

National Library of Ireland, Kildare Street, DUBLIN 2, Eire Tel: 01 6030200 **Fax:** 01 6766690
Opening Hours: M.-W. 10-9; Th.F. 10-5; Sat 10-1. Closure: Public hols.
Parking: None.
Disabled: Ramps. Toilets.
Children: Accompanied: At librarian's discretion. Unaccompanied: Not allowed.

Appointments: Prior booking unnecessary. Entry-ID. 100 seats+28 film+5 fiche-1 reader/printer.
Ordering System: Prior ordering unnecessary. Approx four ordered & produced. Delivery about 10 mins. P/copying by staff-post/collection. Typing/taping/laptops (power supply) permitted. Cameras not allowed.
Records: for Ireland. PRs-film. Wills & administrations. 19thC convict register. Dublin voters list. Printed pedigrees. Maps. Assize. Books. Newspapers. Prints. Drawings. Photographic negatives. Periodicals. MSS sources for Irish History.
Research Service: None.
Facilities: Toilets/public tel. No restaurant facilities. Café/pub/shops nearby.
Publications: Free: Info leaflets.
O. R: Military Archives, Cathal Brugha Barracks, Rathmines, DUBLIN 6, Eire Tel: 01 4975499 Department of Defence & the Defence Forces records.
Remarks: Bags not allowed-cloakroom with lockers. Station: Pearse Station, Westland Row.

Religious Society of Friends in Ireland, Swanbrook House, Bloomfield Avenue, DUBLIN 4, Eire Tel: 01 6687157 Open Thurs am only-appt. Quaker records-Minute books. Family lists. Sufferings. Testimonies of denial & disownments 17th-20thC's. Registers of BMD 17th-20thC's. Letters. Diaries. School. Photographs. Pedigrees. Wills. Deeds. Marriage certificates 17th-20thC's. Pamphlets & correspondence relating to Quaker mission & service.

Representative Church Body Library, Braemor Park, Churchtown, DUBLIN 14, Eire Tel: 01 4923979 **Fax:** 01 4924770
Opening Hours: M.-F. 9.30-1; 1.45-5
Parking: 9 spaces-free.
Disabled: No facilities.
Children: Not allowed.
Appointments: Prior booking for seats/viewers advisable. Entry-register. 12 seats+3 film+1 fiche.
Ordering System: Prior ordering by letter/tel. Number ordered & produced at librarian's discretion. Delivery 5 mins. No production 12.30-1; 4.30-5. P/copying restricted, by staff. Typing/taping at librarian's discretion. Cameras/laptops (power supply) permitted.
Records: Principal theological & reference library of the Church of Ireland and the major repository for church archives & manuscripts. Diocesan RO of Republic of Ireland. PRs-film/Ts/original. BTs available. Religious census of 1766. Will abstracts. Hearth Tax. Subsidy rolls. Dissenters lists. Estate. Scottish freeholders. Plantation of Ulster. Newspapers.
Research Service: None.
Facilities: Toilets. No public tel/refreshment facilities. Cafe/pub/shops nearby.
Publications: Free: Info leaflet: Publications list. For sale: *A Handlist of Church of Ireland Parish Registers in the R.C.B.L. A Handlist of Church of Ireland Vestry Minute Books in the R.C.B.L.. Register of the Parish of St.Thomas, Dublin 1750-1791.*
Remarks: Bags not allowed-can be locked away by staff. Transport: No.14 bus to Mount Carmel from City centre.

DUDLEY ARCHIVES & LOCAL HISTORY SERVICE, see Coseley.

DUKE OF CORNWALL'S LIGHT INFANTRY MUSEUM, see Bodmin.

DUKE OF EDINBURGH'S ROYAL REGIMENT MUSEUM, see Salisbury.

Dumbarton Library, Local Studies Section, Strathleven Place, DUMBARTON, West Dunbartonshire G82 1BD Tel: 01389 733273 **Fax:** 01389 763018
Internet: http://lim.viscount.org.uk/familia/services/west_dunb artons.htm/#/GI
Opening Hours: M.W.F. 9.30-5; T.Th. 9.30-8; Sat 10-5 Closure: Public hols+Christmas wk.
Parking: Yes-free.
Disabled: Access.
Children: At librarian's discretion.
Appointments: Prior booking unnecessary. Entry-register. 6 seats+3 film+2 fiche-1 reader/printer.
Ordering System: Prior ordering by letter/tel. Catalogue nos sometimes required. Number ordered & produced at librarian's discretion. P/copying DIY. Typing/taping/cameras/laptops (power supply) permitted.
Records: for West part of West Dunbartonshire & West Stirlingshire. Burgh records 1600 on. Large photographic collection. Newspapers. Books. Maps. M/f-OPRs/census.
Research Service: Charge made.
Facilities: Toilets. No public tel/refreshment facilities. Cafe/pub/shops nearby.
Publications: Free: Info leaflets: *Local History information sheet* (SAE). For sale: Books on local subjects. Photographs. Prints.
O. R: Helensburgh Library, John Street, HELENSBURGH.
Tourist Office: Tel: 01389 742306

Dumfries & Galloway Archives, Archive Centre, 33 Burns Street, DUMFRIES, Dumfries & Galloway DG1 2PS Tel: 01387 269254 **Fax:** 01387 264126
Opening Hours: T.W.F. 11-1; 2-5; Th. 6-9 Closure: Mon+Christmas Day+Dec 26th+Jan 1st/2nd+Easter Fri & Mon.
Parking: Public nearby.
Disabled: One shallow step.

DUMFRIES

Children: Accompanied: At archivist's discretion. Unaccompanied: 12 yrs+
Appointments: Prior booking for seats-2/3 days. Entry-register+application form. 6 seats+2 film+2 fiche+1 dual.
Ordering System: No prior ordering. Number ordered at archivist's discretion, three produced. Delivery under 10 mins. P/copying restricted, by staff/DIY-same day/post. Typing/taping/laptops at archivist's discretion (power supply). Cameras by arrangement.
Records: for Dumfries & Galloway. Burgh records of Dumfries from 15thC. Estate papers of Stewarts of Shambellie from 15thC. Poor board. Business. Trade. Police. Shipping. School. Health. MIs. Valuation. Electoral. Crime. Customs & Excise. Family. Architectural plans. Motor vehicle records. Clubs & organisations. Newspapers. Maps. c8,000 plans-Walter Newall. M/f-OPRs/census.
Research Service: Specific limited enquiry-free. Charge made for more extensive search.
Facilities: Toilets. No public tel/refreshment facilities. Café/pub/shops nearby.
Publications: Free: Info leaflets: Advice sheets. Source lists (SAE). For sale: *1851 Census Returns for Applegarth/Canonbie/ Cummertrees/Durisdeer/Johnstone/ Balmaclellan. Records for Genealogists. Ancestor Hunting in Dumfries Archive Centre.*
O. R: Stewarty Museum, St. Mary Street, KIRKCUDBRIGHT; **Broughton House**, KIRKUDBRIGHT.
Tourist Office: Tel: 01387 253862
Remarks: Bags not allowed-limited storage. Donations appreciated.

Dumfries & Galloway Council Libraries, Information & Archives, Ewart Library, Catherine Street, DUMFRIES DG1 1JB Tel: 01387 253820 **Fax:** 01387 260294 **E-mail:** libs&i@dumgal.gov.uk
Opening Hours: M.-W.F. 10-7.30; Th.Sat 10-5 Closure: Public hols.
Parking: Limited-free.
Disabled: Access. Toilet.
Children: At librarian's discretion.
Appointments: Prior booking unnecessary. 26 seats+1 film+6 fiche-2 reader/printers.
Ordering System: Prior ordering by letter/tel. Catalogue nos appreciated. Number ordered at librarian's discretion, one produced. Delivery 10 mins. P/copying restricted, by staff-same day+DIY. Typing/taping not permitted. Laptops (power supply) allowed. Cameras by arrangement.
Records: for Dumfries & Galloway. Local authority. Irregular Border marriage records. Newspapers. R.C.Reid collection. Sewen trades papers. OPRs held at Archive Centre.
Research Service: Charge made.
Facilities: Toilets/public tel. No refreshment facilities. Café/pub/shops nearby.
Publications: For sale: various.
O. R: Dumfries & Galloway Family History Research Centre, 9 Glasgow Street, Dumfries DG2 9AF
Remarks: Station: Dumfries-5 mins walk.

DUMFRIES & GALLOWAY, see Dumfries; Kircudbright; Stranraer.

DUNBARTONSHIRE, see Bearsden; Dumbarton; Helensburgh; Kirkintilloch.

Dundee City Archives, 21 City Square, DUNDEE, Tayside DD1 3BY (Callers use Inshore Terrace) **Tel:** 01382 434494 **Fax:** 01382 434666
Opening Hours: M.-F. 9.15-1; 2-4.45 Closure: Public & local hols.
Parking: Public nearby-paying.
Disabled: Lift-by appt.
Children: Accompanied: At archivist's discretion. Unaccompanied: 15 yrs+
Appointments: Prior booking for seats-3 days. Entry-register. 7 seats+1 film+1 fiche.
Ordering System: Prior ordering by letter/tel. Catalogue nos sometimes required. Nine ordered, three produced. Delivery 10 mins. P/copying restricted, by staff-post. Typing/taping/laptops/cameras not permitted.
Records: for Tayside Regional Council & former County Councils of Angus/Perth/ Kinross. Burgh books. Shipping registers. Education. Police. Parish Council. Burial records. JPs records. Port authority. Registers of deed. Local authority. Cess books. School. Plans. Registers of Sasines. Customs & excise. Family. Estate. Business-extensive holdings. Solicitors. Nonconformists.
Research Service: Charge made.
Facilities: Toilets. No public tel/refreshment facilities. Cafe/pub/shops nearby
Publications: Free: Info leaflet: *Dundee City Archive & Record Centre.* (SAE) For sale: Abertay Historical Society publications.
O. R: Dundee University Archives, The University, DUNDEE DD1 4HN Tel: 01382 344095
Tourist Office: Tel: 01382 434664
Remarks: Donations appreciated. **Note:** Angus Archives are moving to Montrose Public Library. Perth Archives are moving to AK Bell Library.

Dundee City Council, Central Library, DUNDEE, Tayside DD1 1DB Tel: 01382 434377 **Fax:** 01382 434036 **E-mail:** local.studies@dundeecity.gov.uk
Internet: www.dundeecity.gov.uk
Opening Hours: M.T.F.Sat 9.30-5; W. 10-7; Th. 9.30-7 Closure: Public hols.
Parking: None.

Disabled: Lift.
Children: At librarian's discretion.
Appointments: Prior booking unnecessary. 50 seats+3 film+3 fiche.
Ordering System: Prior ordering by letter/tel. Bound volumes of newspapers require 24 hrs notice. Number ordered at librarian's discretion, one produced. P/copying restricted, by staff-same day/post/collection. Typing/taping/laptops (battery) permitted. Cameras not allowed.
Records: for City of Dundee. PRs-film/fiche. The Alexander Wilson Bequest-several thousand glass negatives of Dundee & surrounding area 1870-1905. The Lamb Collection-450 boxes of ephemera late 19thC including maps/books/photographs/prints. Newspapers & periodicals from 1803. M/f-OPRs/census/IGI.
Research Service: None.
Facilities: Toilets/public tel/restaurant. Café/pub/shops nearby.
Publications: Free: Info leaflets: *Dundee Central Library Local Studies Department. The Lamb Collection.* (SAE) For sale: Prints. Photographs. Maps. Postcards.
O. R: Family History Research Centre, 179 Princes Street, DUNDEE DD4 6DQ Tel: 01382 461845 Fee for non-members. Indexed Pedigree charts. OPRs index for Scotland. Census/OPR for Tay Valley area. IGI. Lair records. MIs. Sasine etc.

Registrar of Births, Deaths & Marriages, 89 Commercial Street, DUNDEE, Tayside DD1 2AF Tel: 01382 435222 Appt. Cost of £20 per session. A computerised link has been established to the National Indexes at New Register House, Edinburgh. Also holds BMD for Dundee 1855-1995. MD for Angus 1855-1939. Angus B 1855-1899. Tayside OPRs 1553-1854. Tayside Census.

Dunfermline Central Library, Local History Department, Abbot Street, DUNFERMLINE, Fife KY12 7NL Tel: 01383 312994 **Fax:** 01383 312608 **E-mail:** dunfermline@fife.ac.uk
Opening Hours: M.T.Th. F. 10-7; W.Sat 10-5 Closure: Usually first Mon in Apl/May/June/Oct.+middle Mon in July+1st/2nd Jan+25th/26th Dec.
Parking: None.
Disabled: Disabled friendly+2 parking spaces.
Children: Accompanied: No restriction. Unaccompanied: 8 yrs+
Appointments: Prior booking unnecessary. 12 seats+5 film+2 fiche-1 reader printer
Ordering System: Prior ordering by letter/tel. Number ordered & produced at librarian's discretion. Delivery immediate. P/copying by staff-same day. Typing not permitted. Taping/cameras/laptops (power supply) allowed.
Records: for area covered by Dunfermline District Council-roughly the triangle from Kincardine-on-Forth along the coast to Aberdoir & north to include Kelly/Ballingry/Lochgelly. Some nonconformist. Newspapers. Directories. Electoral/valuation rolls. Maps. Photographs. Some Local authority. Some Rosyth Royal Naval Dockyard. M/f-OPRs for all parishes Fife & Kinross/census.
Research Service: Limited specific enquiry.
Facilities: Toilets. No public tel/refreshment facilities. Café/pub/shops nearby.
Publications: Free leaflets: *Tracing Your Family Tree at Dunfermline Library. Andrew Carnegie. Dunfermline City Chambers. Local History in Dunfermline Library. Dunfermline Linen: An Outline History. Everyday Life in Dunfermline in the late 18th Century. Coalmining in West Fife: A bibliography of material held in Dunfermline Central Library.* (A5 SAE) For sale: *Family History Research-the ancestor hunter's ABC in Dunfermline District. The 17th century witch craze in West Fife: A guide to the printed sources.*
O.R: Dunfermline City Chambers, DUNFERMLINE; **Kircaldy Library**, War Memorial Gardens, KIRCALDY.

Durham County Record Office, County Hall, DURHAM, DH1 5UL Tel: 0191 3833253 or 3833474 **Fax:** 0191 3834500
Opening Hours: M.T.Th. 8.45-4.45; W. 8.45-8; F. 8.45-4.15 Closure: Public hols.
Parking: Yes-free.
Disabled: Access, prior notification helpful.
Children: Not allowed.
Appointments: Prior booking for seats-10/14 days, separate appointment for Wed eve. Entry-register+report to Help Desk. 13 seats+16 film+3 fiche-1 reader/printer.
Ordering System: Prior ordering by letter/tel for Wed eve only. Catalogue nos required. Three ordered, one produced. Delivery 3-10 mins. Last order: M.-Th. 4.15; F. 3.45. P/copying by staff-same day. Typing/taping/cameras/aptops (power supply) permitted.
Records: for present county of Durham & Darlington borough. Diocesan RO for Durham & part of Ripon (parish records only). PRs including those for South Tyne & Wear/North Cleveland-film/some Ts. Nonconformists. Quarter/Petty Sessions. Education. Poor Law. Colliery. Hospital. Business. Archives of the Strathmore/Londonderry/Brancepeth/Salvin estates. Solicitors. Trade Unions. Maps. M/f-census/newspapers.
Research Service: Charge made.
Facilities: Toilets/public tel/restaurant/room for own food/drink vending machine. Café/pub nearby.

DURHAM

Publications: Free: Info leaflets: *Guide for visitors. Durham Archives Research Service. User Guides.* (SAE). For sale: *The Londonderry Papers: Catalogue of documents.* Map of parish & chapelry boundaries. *Durham Family History Gazeteer. Durham Places in the mid 19thC.* Handlists of Records 1-10. Subject Guides 1-9. User Guides 1-9.
O. R: Durham Light Infantry Museum, Aykley Heads, DURHAM DH1 5TU Tel: 0191 3842214 Appt. Photographs-incls Durham Militia & Rifle Volunteers.
Tourist Office: Tel: 0191 3843720
Remarks: Donations appreciated.Station: Durham (East Coast main line).

Durham University Library (Archives & Special Collections), Palace Green, DURHAM, DH1 3RN Tel: 0191 3743202 **Fax:** 0191 3747481 **E-mail:** p6.library@durham .ac.uk
Internet: http://www.dur.ac.uk/library/asc/ index.html
Opening Hours: University term: M.F. 9-5; T.-Th. 9-6 Vacation: M.-F. 9-5 Closure: Public hols+10 days at Christmas.
Parking: Public nearby-paying.
Disabled: Access-by appt.
Children: Accompanied: 14 yrs+ Unaccompanied: At librarian's discretion.
Appointments: Prior booking advisable. Entry-register+ID. 20 seats+2 film+1 fiche.
Ordering System: Prior ordering by letter/tel. Catalogue nos required. Six ordered, three produced. Delivery 5-10 mins. No production 1-2; 5-6. P/copying at librarian's discretion, by staff-same day/post/collection depending on staff time. Typing/taping/cameras not permitted. Laptops (power supply at librarian's discretion) allowed.
Records: for historic counties of Northumberland & Durham/some of Yorkshire & Cumbria. Diocesan RO for Durham. PRs-Ts. BTs available. Probate 16th-19thC. Durham Bishopric financial & estate records. Earl Grey papers. Deeds. Guild. Family. Estate. Howard of Naworth papers (miscellaneous papers/deeds/ manorial documents). Newspapers. Photographs. Maps. Plans.
Research Service: None-list of researchers available.
Facilities: Toilets. No public tel/refreshment facilities. Café/pub/shops nearby.
Publications: Free: Info leaflets: *Introductory Guide.* Publications List. (SAE) For sale: the Library's published catalogues.
O. R: Durham Cathedral Archives, 5 The College, DURHAM DH1 3EQ Tel: 0191 3743610 Appt.
Remarks: Bags not allowed-lockers. Donations appreciated. Station: Durham-10 mins walk.

DURHAM, COUNTY, see Beamish; Darlington; Durham; Sunderland.

EALING, see London Borough of.

EAST SUSSEX, see Lewes.

EAST YORKSHIRE, see Beverley; Kingston-upon-Hull.

Edinburgh Central Library, George IV Bridge, EDINBURGH, EH1 1EG Tel: 0131 2255584 **Fax:** 0131 2258783
Opening Hours: M.-F. 9-9; Sat 9-1 Closure: Public hols+local hols.
Parking: None.
Disabled: Lift. Tight entrance for w/chairs.
Children: No restriction-creche on Tues/Thurs am.
Appointments: Prior booking unnecessary. Entry-fill in a slip for each item consulted. 85 seats+8 film+12 fiche-3 reader/printers.
Ordering System: No prior ordering. Number ordered & produced at librarian's discretion. Delivery 5 mins. Last order: 8.45. A few items held in remote stocks can only be obtained 2-4. P/copying restricted, by staff-post. Typing/taping/cameras not permitted. Laptops (power supply) allowed.
Records: for Ayrshire/Borders/Caithness/ Clackmannanshire/Dumfries & Galloway/Fife/ Kinrossshire/ Lothians/Nairn/Orkney/Ross & Cromarty/Shetland/Stirlingshire/Sutherland. Index to OPRs for whole of Scotland. **Edinburgh Room:** Education. Trade Unions. Societies. Maps & plans. **Scottish Library:** Highland Folklife collection. MIs. Professional Directories. Family histories. M/f-OPRs/ census/IGI.
Research Service: None.
Facilities: Toilets. No public tel/refreshment facilities. Café/pub nearby.
Publications: Free: Info leaflet: *Tracing your Family History in Edinburgh Central Library.* (SAE).
O. R: Royal Museum of Scotland, Chambers Street, EDINBURGH EH1 1JF Tel: 0131 2257534 Appt. Scottish/military history. Working life. Education.
Remarks: Note: The collections are separated between the Edinburgh Room & the Scottish Library. See *In Search of Scottish Ancestry* by G. Hamilton-Edwards. *Scottish Roots* by H. James.

Edinburgh City Archives, Dept of Corporate Services, City of Edinburgh Council, City Chambers, High Street, EDINBURGH, EH1 1YT Tel: 0131 5294616 **Fax:** 0131 5294957
Opening Hours: M.-Th. 9 -1; 2-4.30 Closure: Fri+Public hols.
Parking: None.

Disabled: Lift.
Children: Accompanied: 8 yrs+ Unaccompanied: 16 yrs+
Appointments: Prior booking unnecessary. Entry-register+visitor's security pass. 8 seats.
Ordering System: Prior ordering by letter/tel. Catalogue nos sometimes required. Twenty ordered, three produced. Delivery 10 mins (some documents take 2 days). P/copying restricted, by staff-same day/collection next day. Typing/taping not permitted. Laptops (battery) allowed. Cameras by prior arrangement.
Records: for the City of Edinburgh. Local authority 14thC on. Town Council. Registers of Burgesses & Guild Brothers. Police. Parochial Board. Gaol.
Research Service: None.
Facilities: Toilets/public tel/room for own food/drink vending machine. Café/pub/shops nearby.
Tourist Office: Tel: 0131 5571700
Remarks: Bags not allowed-storage facilities. Station: Edinburgh Waverley.

General Register Office for Scotland, New Register House, EDINBURGH, EH1 3YT (Access is from West Register St, opposite the Balmoral Hotel). **Tel:** 0131 3340380 **Fax:** 0131 3144400 **E-mail:** nrh.gros@govnet.gov.uk
Internet: http://www.open.gov.uk/gros/groshome.htm
Opening Hours: M.-F. 9-4.30 Closure: Public hols.
Parking: None.
Disabled: By prior arrangement.
Children: Accompanied: 16 yrs+ Unaccompanied: Not allowed.
Appointments: Prior booking for seats unnecessary but advisable if coming from distance-Tel: 0131 3144433 Entry-entrance fee. 100 places.
Ordering System: No prior ordering. Self service system-3 fiche/2 film. No p/copying. Typing/taping/cameras not permitted. Laptops (battery) allowed.
Records: for Scotland. M/f-OPRs 1553-1854/Register of neglected entries 1801-1854/BMD from 1855/ Divorces from 1984/Adopted children from 1930/Marine register of BD from 1855/Air register from 1948/Service records from 1881/War registers from 1899/Consular returns of BMD from 1914/BMD in foreign countries 1860-1965/High Commissioners returns of BD from1964/Foreign marriages from 1947/census.
Research Service: Specific enquiries-charge made.
Facilities: Toilets/public tel. No refreshment facilities. Café/pub/shops nearby.
Publications: Free: Info leaflets: *List of main records in the care of the Registrar General. Searching by our staff. Guidance for general search customers.* (SAE) For sale: Copies of OPRs on film. Index of B,CH,Banns,M on fiche. *Tracing your Scottish Ancestors. Guides for Researchers No.1. Registration districts of Scotland from 1855. Personal names in Scotland.*

Dept. of Manuscripts, National Library of Scotland, George IV Bridge, EDINBURGH, EH1 1EW Tel: 0131 2264531 **Fax:** 0131 2206662
Internet: www.nls.uk
Opening Hours: M.T.Th.F. 9.30-8.30; W. 10-8.30; Sat 9.30-1 Closure: Public hols+1st wk in Oct.
Parking: None.
Disabled: Access.
Children: At librarian's discretion.
Appointments: Prior booking unnecessary. Entry-register+ID. 18 seats. Film/fiche readers in other part of library.
Ordering System: Prior ordering by letter/tel. Catalogue nos sometimes required. Six ordered, three bound vols/one file produced. Delivery 20-30 mins. No production 1-2. Last order: 4pm. P/copying by staff-post/collection. Typing/taping/cameras not permitted. Laptops (power supply) allowed.
Records: for Scotland & the Scots home & abroad. History. Literature. Politics. Estate. etc.
Research Service: None.
Facilities: Toilets. No public tel/refreshment facilities. Café/pub/shops nearby.
Publications: Free: Info leaflets: on procedures, collections etc. (SAE). Library shop.
Remarks: Bags not allowed-manned cloakroom. Donations appreciated. **Note:** Due to building works there will be no public access to MSS collections from Sept 1997 to approx Sept 1998. On re-opening there will be an improved general enquiry service at entrance. From approx 2000 there will be a new, larger special material Reading Room with improved facilities.

National Monuments Record of Scotland, John Sinclair House, 16 Bernard Terrace, EDINBURGH, EH8 9NX Tel: 0131 6621456 Appt. Photographs & drawings of ancient monuments & historic buildings. Aerial photographs. Maps. Printed books. Pamphlets.

Royal College of Surgeons of Edinburgh, Nicolson Street, EDINBURGH, EH8 9DW Tel: 0131 5271600 Appt. Enquirers should write to Home Secretary for written permission to consult the archives before getting in touch with the archivist. List of fellows from 1581. Licentiates 1770-1873. Apprentices indentures 1709-1872. Examination records from 1581. The Surgeons Widows Fund 1820-1890. **O. R:**

EDINBURGH

Royal College of Nursing Archives, 42 South Oswald Road, EDINBURGH, EH9 2HH Tel: 0131 6621010 Appt. Papers & certificates relating to hundreds of nurses.

Scottish Record Office, H.M.General Register House, EDINBURGH, EH1 3YY Tel: 0131 5351314 **Fax:** 0131 5351328
Opening Hours: M.-F. 9-4.45 Closure: Public hols+1st fortnight of Nov.
Parking: Public nearby-paying.
Disabled: Access. Lift.
Children: At archivist's discretion.
Appointments: Prior booking unnecessary. Entry-reader's ticket+ID. 27 seats+3 film+1 fiche.
Ordering System: Prior ordering by letter/tel. Catalogue nos required. Three ordered, one produced. Delivery 20 mins. Some documents not in building require prior ordering. P/copying by staff-post. Typing/taping/cameras not permitted. Laptops (battery) allowed.
Records: for Scotland. Kirk Session PRs. Valuation rolls. Wills. Court of Sessions/Judiciary (criminal)/ Burgh/ Presbytery/Kirk Session mins. Maps. Family & estate. Business. Societies. Sheriff court, taxation & heritors records require 2 days prior notice.
Research Service: None.
Facilities: Toilets/public tel. No refreshment facilities. Café/pub/shops nearby.
Publications: Free: Info leaflets: List of publications. (SAE).
Remarks: Bags not allowed-cloakroom.

Scottish Record Office (West Search Room), West Register House, Charlotte Square, EDINBURGH, EH2 4DF Tel: 0131 5351413 **Fax:** 0131 5351430 **E-mail:** sro.gov.uk
Opening Hours: M.-F. 9-4.45 Closure: Public hols+local hols+3rd full wk in Nov.
Parking: Public nearby-paying.
Disabled: Access by lift-prior appt.
Children: Accompanied: At archivist's discretion. Unaccompanied: Senior school pupils.
Appointments: Prior booking not allowed. Entry-reader's ticket+ID+fee (fees not payable for historical & literary searches). 16 seats+2 film +2 fiche+3 soundproof glass booths.
Ordering System: Prior ordering by letter/tel. Catalogue nos required. Some records require 48 hrs notice. Three ordered & produced. Delivery 30 mins. Production not guaranteed after 4.15. P/copying by staff-same day/post/collection. Typing/taping permitted in booths. Laptops (power supply) allowed if silent. Cameras not allowed.
Records: for Scotland/Scots in UK & abroad. OPRs-film/photocopies. Register of deeds/ sasines/testamentary records-indexes of these available on fiche/Ts. Register House plans-large & varied collection including some from other countries. Court of Session. Justiciary Court post 1800. Sheriff/central civil/criminal courts. Modern Government. Nationalised industries-coal/rail/gas/electricity /steel. Maps. Plans.
Research Service: Limited specific enquiries. List of local researchers available.
Facilities: Toilets. No public tel/refreshment facilities. Café/pub/shops nearby.
Publications: Free: Info leaflets: *Using Scottish Record Office Archives & National Register of Archives (Scotland). Plans. Railways. Facilities for Historical Research. Family History. Early Family History. Short Guide to the Records. Indexes to Deeds, Sasines & Testamentary Records.* (SAE). For sale: *Scottish Record Office Family History Guide. Tracing your Scottish ancestors in the Scottish Record Office* (HMSO). *Military Source List Part One & Two. List of American Documents* (general index).
Remarks: Bags not allowed-lockers.

Scottish United Services Museum Library, National Museums of Scotland, The Castle, Museum Square, EDINBURGH EH1 2NG Tel: 0131 2257534 Ext. 404 Appt. Regimental Order books. Correspondence. MSS Scots Greys. Photograph/print collections.

The Royal Scots Regimental Museum, The Castle, EDINBURGH EH1 2YT Tel: 0131 310 5016/5017 Appt.-written application. Registers of services/diaries/paybooks/correspondence. Regimental magazines. Photographs, etc.

The Scottish Genealogical Society Library & Family History Centre, 15 Victoria Terrace, EDINBURGH, EH1 2JL Tel: 0131 2203677 **Fax:** 0131 2203677 **E-mail:** scotgensoc@sol.co.uk
Internet: http://www.scotland.net/scotgensoc
Opening Hours: T. 10.30-5.30; W. 10.30-8.30; Sat 10-5 Closure: Christmas & New Year.
Parking: None.
Disabled: No facilities.
Children: Accompanied: 5 yrs+ Unaccompanied: 12 yrs+
Appointments: Prior booking unnecessary. Entry-register+fee (if non-member). 14 seats+5 film+9 fiche-2 reader/printers.
Ordering System: Prior ordering by letter/tel. Number ordered & produced at librarian's discretion. Delivery immediate. P/copying by staff & DIY. Typing/taping/laptops (battery) permitted. Cameras not allowed.
Records: for Scotland. Library of printed works. Genealogy & family history-directories/trades & professions. Emigration lists. School & university rolls. Heraldry. Biography. Service records including Rolls of Honour/Medal

Rolls/casualty lists/pensioners. M/f-OPRs /census/MIs/IGI.
Research Service: Limited specific enquiry.
Facilities: Toilets. No public tel. Room for own food. Cafe/pub/shops nearby.
Publications: Free: Info leaflet: Publications list. (SAE) For sale: *MIs. Bathgate Mortality Records. Edinburgh 1851 Census. Edinburgh Police Register 1815-1859. Kirkcudbright Burgesses 1576-1975. Tron Parish Poll Tax 1694. Scottish Clocks & Watch Makers 1445-1900.* Leaflets: *Emigration to North America. Poll Tax.* and various others. Other publishers' books also on sale.
Remarks: Bags not allowed-behind reception counter. Donations appreciated.

EDINBURGH-USEFUL ADDRESSES:

Grand Lodge of Scotland, Freemasons' Hall, 96 George Street, EDINBURGH EH2 3DH

The National Register of Archives (Scotland), H.M. Register House, 2 Princes Street, EDINBURGH EH1 3YY. Note: The NRA(S) operates from the West Register House, Charlotte Square but postal enquiries should be addressed to the above address.

The Egham Museum, The Literary Institute, High Street, EGHAM, Surrey TW20 9EW Appt. PRs-p/copies. Local History collection for Egham. Publications for sale: *The Egham Picture Book. The Thorpe Picture Book. Runnymede: A Pictorial History. Railways from Staines to Sunningdale 1856-1996. Janes, Drapers of Egham. Four Score Years*-reminiscences by a local dairy farmer. Books. Postcards. Maps. Run entirely by volunteers so donations appreciated.

EIRE, see Clonmel; Dublin; Limerick.

Moray Libraries Headquarters, High Street, ELGIN, Moray IV30 1BX Tel: 01343 543451. Local history of Moray/Nairn/ Banffshire. Family History. M/f-BMDs/census/ newspapers.

David Owen Archive, The Boat Museum, Dockyard Road, ELLESMERE PORT, L65 4EP Tel: 0151 3555017 Appt. Canal including David Owen collection+other major collections. Weaver navigators files.

ENFIELD, see London Borough of.

Fermanagh District Museum, Enniskillen Castle, Castle Barracks, ENNISKILLEN, co. Fermanagh, N. Ireland BT74 7HL Tel: 01365 325000. Appt. School registers. Criminal books-19/20thC's. Maps. Photographs.

The Regimental Museum of the Royal Inniskillen Fusiliers, The Castle, ENNISKILLEN, co. Fermanagh, N. Ireland BT74 7BB Tel: 01365 323142. Appt. History/past members of the Regiment.

ESSEX POLICE MUSEUM, see Springfield.

ESSEX, DAGENHAM, see London Borough of Barking & Dagenham

ESSEX, ILFORD, see London Borough of Redbridge.

ESSEX, ROMFORD, see London Borough of Havering.

ESSEX, see Chelmsford; Colchester; Hastings; Saffron Walden; Southend-on-Sea; Springfield.

Devon Record Office, Castle Street, EXETER, Devon EX4 3PU Tel: 01392 384253
Internet: http://www.devon-cc.gov.uk/dcc/services/dro/homepage.html
Opening Hours: M.-Th. 9.30-5; F. 9.30-4.30 Closure: Public hols+Christmas wk.
Parking: Limited 1hr Public nearby paying.
Disabled: Ramp. Lift. Buzzer to summon staff help if required.
Children: At archivist's discretion.
Appointments: Prior booking unnecessary. Entry-CARN or other reader's ticket+ID+fee. 15 seats+5 film+17 fiche-1 reader/printer.
Ordering System: Prior ordering by letter/tel. Catalogue nos required. Some documents in outstore require 48 hrs notice. Number ordered at archivist's discretion, three produced. Delivery 5-10 mins. Last order: 15 mins before closure. P/copying restricted, by staff-same day/post/collection. Typing/taping/laptops (power supply) at archivist's discretion. Cameras permitted.
Records: for historic county of Devon. Diocesan RO for Exeter. PRs-fiche/film/some Ts. BTs available. Quarter Sessions from 16thC. Diocesan records from 13thC. City of Exeter records from 12thC. Family. Estate. Ships crew lists. Inland Revenue wills 1812-1858. Exeter prison records. Photographs. M/f-tithe maps & apportionments/nonconformists registers.
Research Service: Charge made.
Facilities: Toilets-female only. Public tel in Library. No refreshment facilities. Café/pub/shops nearby.
Publications: Free: Info leaflets: *Devon RO Service Points.* Publications list. (SAE) For sale: *Guide to Sources. Parish, Non-Parochial & Civil Registers in the Devon RO. Ships' Crew Lists. Sources for a New Maritime History of Devon. Methodism in Devon: a handlist of chapels & their records. Records of the Bishop of Exeter's Consistory Court to 1660.*

EXETER

O. R: Exeter Register Office, 1 Lower Summerlands, Heavitree Road, EXETER; **Exeter Probate Registry**, 94 Fore Street, EXETER Wills & Admins from 1942 only-those prior to this date were destroyed during WW2. Principal Probate Registry, London (see entry) has all complete for Devon from 1858
Tourist Office: Tel: 01392 265700 Fax: 01392 265260
Remarks: Bags not allowed-open shelves. **Note:** Plymouth & Torbay were unitary authorities from 1st April 1998. Plymouth will have its own separate archive service, Torbay will not. **Note:** Devonshire Regimental Archives formerly at Exeter are now deposited at the Military Museum of Devon & Dorset, Dorchester (see entry) Station: Exeter Central or St. David's.

West Country Studies Library, Castle Street, EXETER, Devon EX4 3PQ Tel: 01392 384216 **Fax:** 01392 384224. **Internet:** http://www.devon-cc.gov.uk/library/locstudy
Opening Hours: M.F. 9.30-6; T.Th. 9.30-7; W.10-5; Sat. 9.30-4
Parking: Limited-1hr. Public nearby-paying.
Disabled: Access ramp. Lift.
Children: At librarian's discretion.
Appointments: Prior booking for viewers-3 days. Entry-register, only for use of the Devon & Cornwall Record Society's collection-temporary membership can be taken out in Library. 22 seats+4 film+4 fiche-2 reader printers.
Ordering System: Prior ordering by letter/tel. Catalogue nos sometimes required. Number ordered & produced at librarian's discretion. Delivery 5 mins. No production during lunch hour. Last order: 30 mins before closure. P/copying restricted, by staff-same day/post/collection-staff unable to undertake large orders. Typing/cameras not permitted. Taping/laptops allowed.
Records: for Devon with some coverage of adjoining counties. PRs-Ts (main collection belonging to the Devon & Cornwall Record Society). MSS & Ts county/town/parish histories. MSS & Ts family histories & genealogical compilations. Will extracts. Directories. Maps/illustrations with Index. Periodicals. Electoral registers for Exeter & East Devon. Ephemera. Card Index to Exeter Flying Post newspaper 1763-1885. Burnet-Morris Index (over 1,000,000 cards with information on Devon persons/places/subjects). M/f-census/newspapers/IGI. Finding aids to collections available. **Note:** The Devon & Cornwall R.S. has a vast collection of PR Ts+Ts of other records-Handlist to this collection for sale in Library.
Research Service: None-a service is available in the Devon R.O. in same building (see entry).
Facilities: Toilets-female only. Public toilets nearby. No public tel/refreshment facilities. Café/pub/shops nearby.
Publications: Free: *Introductory Guide.* Publications List. (SAE). For sale: *Local Studies in Devon Libraries: A Guide to Resources. Handlist of Directories in Devon Libraries. The Burnet Morris Index 1940-1990* (a guide & history). *Historic Maps. Exeter Garlands*-on going series of copies of early printed material in slide binders, e.g. *Election broadsheets 1724-1806. Wars & Revolutions 1549-1803. Crime & Punishment 1782-1854. Estate Documents 1710-1800. Trade & Industry 1731-1830. Charity, Welfare & Religion 1704-1814.* etc. Resource Guides-series of leaflets detailing resources available for local studies research in Devon (3 main series).
O.R: Devon & Exeter Institution, The Close, EXETER; **Exeter Cathedral Library**, Old Bishop's Palace, Diocesan House, Palace Gate, EXETER EX1 1HX Appt. Tel: 01392 272894 (library), 495954 (archives); **University of Exeter Library**, Stocker Road, EXETER EX4 4PT Tel 01392 263870 (written application only); **Devon FHS**, Tree House, Unit 3b, 7-9 King Street, EXETER. Open T.W.Th. 10-30-4. No correspondence to this address, enqs. with SAE to the Society Librarian, Mr. C.P. Stone, 55 Marlborough Street, Exeter EX2 4LN
Tourist Office: Tel: 01392 265700 Fax: 01392 265260. Exeter Services: Tel: 01392 437581
Remarks: Donations appreciated to Kent Kingdon Trust. **Note:** Torbay & Plymouth became independent of Devon on 1st April 1998 but this will have no effect on the holdings of the West Country Studies Library. The Devon RO is in the same building along the corridor from the library. Station: Exeter Central. Exeter St. David.

Falkirk Museum, History Research Centre, Callendar House, Callendar Park, FALKIRK FK1 1YR Tel: 01324 612134 Appt. Beneficient Society records 17thC on. Maps & plans. Photographs.

History Research Centre, Falkirk Museums, Callendar House, Callendar Park, FALKIRK, FK1 1YR Tel: 01324 503770 **Fax:** 01324 503771
Opening Hours: M.-F. 10-12.30; 1.30-5 Closure: Public hols.
Parking: Yes-free.
Disabled: Lift.
Children: At staff's discretion.
Appointments: Prior booking unnecessary. Entry-report to reception. 14 seats+1 film+1 fiche-1 reader/printer.
Ordering System: Prior ordering by letter/tel. Catalogue nos required. Three ordered & produced. Delivery 5-10 mins. P/copying restricted, by staff-same day. Typing/

taping/cameras not permitted. Laptops (battery) allowed.
Records: for Falkirk District including Burghs of Denny/Grangemouth/Bo'ness/Dunipace/ Falkirk. Forbes of Callendar papers. James Love collection. Burns family papers. Local authority. Schools. Valuation rolls. Electoral rolls. Industrial. Business. Societies. Clubs. Trade unions. Family. Photographs. Plans.
Research Service: Charge made.
Facilities: Toilets. No public tel/refreshment facilities. Restaurant 200 metres.
Publications: Free: Info leaflets: *Guide to Local Social History Research in the H.R.C. Guide to Local Industrial Research. Guide to Family History Research* (SAE).
Tourist Office: Tel: 01324 620244
Remarks: Station: Falkirk High or Falkirk Grahamston.

FALMOUTH, see Cornwall

FERMANAGH, COUNTY, see Enniskillen.

FIFE, see Anstruther; Cupar; Kirkcaldy; Dunfermline; St. Andrews.

FINSBURY, see London Borough of Islington.

FLEET AIR MUSEUM, see Yeovilton.

FLINTSHIRE, see Hawarden.

South East Kent, Kent Arts & Libraries, Folkestone Library, 2 Grace Hill, FOLKESTONE, Kent CT20 1HD Tel: 01303 850123 **Fax:** 01303 242907
Opening Hours: M.T.Th.Sat 9.30-5; F. 9.30-7 Closure: Public hols.
Parking: Public nearby-paying.
Disabled: Lift. Material can be taken to ground floor Lending Library.
Children: Accompanied: At archivist's discretion. Unaccompanied: 12 yrs+
Appointments: Prior booking for seats/viewers-1/2 days. Entry-CARN. 14 seats+3 film+1 fiche-1 reader/printer.
Ordering System: Prior ordering by letter/tel. Catalogue nos preferred. Number ordered at archivist's discretion, three produced. Delivery 10 mins. No production after 5 pm on Fri+occasional lunchtimes. P/copying restricted, by staff-same day. Typing/taping/laptops (battery) permitted.
Records: for Folkestone/Hythe/Romney Marsh/Eltham Valley/Capel. **Heritage Room:** PRs-film/some Ts. BTs-film for many parishes in the Shepway area. Plans for Royal Military Canal 1805. Muster records for Folkestone 1803. Directories. Electoral registers. Poll Books. Photographs. Maps. Plans. Newspapers (some on film). M/f-census including 1801 census for Folkestone (with names)/IGI. **Archive Office:** Folkestone Town Council. Boards of Guardians for Eltham/Romney Marsh. School log books. Methodist Circuit. Photographs. Maps. Plans.
Research Service: Charge made.
Facilities: Toilets/public tel. No refreshment facilities. Cafe/pub/shops nearby.
Publications: Free: Info leaflets: *Guide to Heritage Services. List of PRs. Kent Research Service.* (SAE).
Tourist Office: Tel: 01303 258594 Fax: 01303 259754
Remarks: Note: Relocation to East Kent Archives Study Centre, Enterprise Business Park, Honeywood Road, Whitfield, Dover CT16 3EH in summer 1998 (see entry) which will house most of the above records leaving behind only a Local History collection. Contact Centre for Kentish Studies, Maidstone for info.

FOLKESTONE, see Whitfield, Dover

Angus District Libraries & Museums, Administrative Unit, County Buildings, Market Street, FORFAR, Tayside DD8 3LG Tel: 01307 461460. Scottish & Local history. M/f-parish records/census/newspapers/IGI.

Moray Council Record Office, Tolbooth, FORRES, Moray IV36 0AB Tel: 01309 673617 **Fax:** 01309 674166
Opening Hours: M.-F. 9.30-4.30 Closure: Public hols.
Parking: Public nearby-free.
Disabled: No facilities.
Children: At archivist's discretion.
Appointments: Prior booking unnecessary. Entry-register. 40 seats.
Ordering System: Prior ordering by letter/tel. Catalogue nos sometimes required. Three ordered & produced. Delivery 2 mins. P/copying by staff-same day. Typing/taping/ cameras/laptops (power supply) permitted.
Records: for Moray. Established Church Kirk Sessions. Presbytery. Family. Local government. Maps. Plans. Photographs.
Research Service: None.
Facilities: Toilets. No public tel. Restaurant. Café/pub/shops nearby.
Tourist Office: Tel: 01309 672938
Remarks: Note: Likely to be major changes in the organisation but no details available. Station: Forres.

FULHAM, see London Borough of Hammersmith & Fulham.

FUSILIERS OF NORTHUMBERLAND MUSEUM, see Alnwick.

Gateshead Libraries & Arts Service, Local Studies Dept., Central Library, Prince Consort Road, GATESHEAD, Tyne & Wear

NE8 4LN **Tel:** 0191 4773478 **Fax:** 0191 4777454 **E-mail:** local@gateslib.demon.co.uk
Internet: http://wamses.unn.ac.uk
Opening Hours: M.T.Th. 9-7; W. 9-5; Sat 9-1 Closure: Fri+Public hols+previous Sat.
Parking: Limited-free.
Disabled: Disabled friendly. Facilities for large print, audio tape or braille copies by arrangement.
Children: At librarian's discretion.
Appointments: Prior booking for viewers advisable. 31 seats+2 film+2 fiche-2 reader/printers.
Ordering System: Prior ordering by letter/tel. Catalogue nos helpful. Number ordered & produced at librarian's discretion. Delivery 5-10 mins. P/copying restricted, by staff-same day/post or DIY. Typing/taping/cameras/ laptops (power supply) permitted.
Records: for Gateshead Metropolitan Borough-Gateshead/Felling/Whickham/Blay don/Ryton/Birtley. PRs-film/Ts. Rate books. Electoral lists. Poll books. Directories. Estate. Local authority. MIs. Newspapers.
Research Service: Limited specific enquiry.
Facilities: Toilets/public tel/restaurant. Café/pub nearby.
Publications: For sale: List of holdings. Newspaper list. Postcards. Books.
Tourist Office: Tel: 0191 4773478 Fax: 0191 4777454
Remarks: Station: Newcastle upon Tyne-Central.

GENEALOGICAL OFFICE, see Dublin.

GENERAL REGISTER OFFICE FOR SCOTLAND, see Edinburgh.

Giffnock Library, Local History Dept., Station Road, GIFFNOCK, East Renfrewshire G46 6JF Tel: 0141 6386349 Appt. Local History. Collection of newspapers/letters/photographs etc. Voters rolls.

Gillingham Central Library, High Street, GILLINGHAM, Kent ME7 1BG Tel: 01634 281066 Usually open. M/f-PRs 1558-1927/census for Gillingham, Rainham & parts of N.E. Kent. See also Rochester-upon-Medway.

GLAMORGAN WEST, ARCHIVE SERVICE, see Swansea.

GLAMORGAN, see Cardiff; Newport; Treorchy.

Archdiocese of Glasgow Archive, 196 Clyde Street, GLASGOW G1 4JY Tel: 0141 226 5898 Ext. 154. Appt.-written application. Archdiocesan/Cathedral PRs 1795 on. Education papers. Catholic Union.

Glasgow City Archives, Libraries & Archives, Glasgow City Council, The Mitchell Library, North St., GLASGOW G3 7DN Tel: 0141 2872913 **Fax:** 0141 2268452
E-mail: glw_archives@cqm.co.uk
Internet: http://users.colloquium.co.uk/ⁿglw_archives/scrØØ1.htm
Opening Hours: M.-Th. 9.30-4.45; F. 9.30-4 other times by arrangement. Closure: Public hols.
Parking: None.
Disabled: Access-by appt.
Children: At archivist's discretion.
Appointments: Prior booking for viewers. Entry-register. 26 seats+2 film+2 fiche.
Ordering System: Prior ordering by letter/tel. Catalogue nos sometimes required. Number ordered at archivist's discretion, three produced. Delivery 15 mins. No production 1-2. Last order: 15 mins before closure. P/copying by staff-same day/post. Typing/taping/ cameras/laptops (power supply) permitted.
Records: for the former Strathclyde Region apart from Argyll & Ayrshire. OPRs-film/Ts. Kirk Session records of Church of Scotland within Presbytery of Glasgow. Poor Law. School. Voters rolls. Valuation rolls. Retours (printed+index). Wills (index). Sasines (index). Register of deeds from 1625. Cemetery registers. MIs. Burgess rolls for Glasgow. Estate. Port Authority. Business. Local government. Directories. Newspapers. Registers of deseased seamen 1886-1952. Photographs. Some collections require 24 hrs prior ordering. M/f-census/Ancestral File/Family History Catalogue (LDS)/IGI.
Research Service: Charge made.
Facilities: Toilets/public tel/restaurant. Café/pub/shops nearby.
Publications: Free: Info leaflets:*Tracing your Ancestors*. Research fee charges. (SAE) For sale: Various. Two collections of photographs.
O. R: Glasgow & West of Scotland FHS, Unit 15, 32 Mansfield Street, GLASGOW G11 5QP.
Tourist Office: Tel: 0141 2044400
Remarks: Bags not allowed-bag deposit system.

GLASGOW RAILTRACK, see London Other Repositories-Railtrack.

Royal Highland Fusiliers Regimental Headquarters & Museum, 518 Sauchiehall Street, GLASGOW G2 3LW Tel: 0141 332 0961. Appt. Regimental histories of the Royal Scots Fusiliers (21st Regiment of Foot). Highland Light Infantry (71st & 74th Regiments of Foot).

GLASGOW, see Giffnock Library

British Waterways Archive, Llanthony Warehouse, Gloucester Docks,

GLOUCESTER, Glos GL1 2EY Tel: 01452 318041 **Fax:** 01452 318076
Opening Hours: M.-F. 10-4 Closure: Public hols at Christmas & Easter.
Parking: Yes-paying.
Children: 16 yrs+
Appointments: Prior booking for seats/viewers-3 days. Entry-register. 3 seats+1 fiche-1 reader/printer.
Ordering System: Prior ordering by letter/telephone. Catalogue nos necessary. P/copying restricted, by staff-same day. Typing/taping/laptops not permitted. Cameras allowed.
Records: for the History of British Waterways Board. History of predecessor canal companies. British Transport Commission (docks & inland waterways executive). British Waterways Board. Photographs.
Research Service: None.
Facilities: Toilets/public tel/restaurant at Museum. Café/pub/shops nearby.
Publications: Info leaflets: at Museum. (SAE).
Remarks: Bags not allowed.

Gloucestershire Record Office, Clarence Row, Alvin Street, GLOUCESTER, Glos GL1 3DW Tel: 01452 425295 **Fax:** 01452 426378 **E-mail:** records@gloscc.gov.uk
Internet: http://www.gloscc.gov.uk/corpserv/archives/index.htm
Opening Hours: M. 10-5; T.W.F. 9-5; Th. 9-8 Closure: Public hols+2 wks in Dec.
Parking: Yes-free.
Disabled: Disabled friendly.
Children: At archivist's discretion.
Appointments: Prior booking unnecessary. Entry-register+fee+ID. 42 seats+6 film+15 fiche-1 reader/printer.
Ordering System: Prior ordering by letter/tel. Catalogue nos required. Three ordered, one produced. Delivery 20-30 mins. No production 1-2. Last order: 30 mins before closure except Thurs when 60 mins. P/copying restricted, DIY. Typing/taping/cameras not permitted. Laptops (power supply) allowed.
Records: for Gloucestershire & South Gloucestershire. Diocesan RO for Gloucester. PRs-fiche/film/Ts. BTs-original/Ts. Parish. Probate. Quarter Sessions. Borough. Nonconformist. Poor Law. Manorial. Business. Societies. Deeds. Estate. Boroughs. Courts. Solicitors. Wills. Maps. Photographs. Indexes. M/f-census.
Research Service: Charge made.
Facilities: Toilets. No public tel. Room for own food/drink vending machine. Cafe/pub/shops nearby.
Publications: Free: Info leaflets: List of publications. (SAE) For sale: *Gloucestershire Record Office Handlist.*
O. R: Gloucestershire Record Office, Shire Hall Branch, Record Centre, Shire Hall, Westgate Street, GLOUCESTER, Glos GL1 2TG Tel: 01452 425289. Appt. Entrance fee. Local Government. Education. Hospitals. 19thC Coroners for Gloucestershire.
Tourist Office: Tel: 01452 421188 Fax: 01452 504273
Remarks: Bags not allowed-lockers. **Note:** Could be a period of closure in 1998.

The Gloucestershire Collection, County Library, Brunswick Rd, GLOUCESTER, Glos GL1 1HT Tel: 01452 426979 **Fax:** 01452 521468
Opening Hours: M.T.Th. 10-7.30; W.F. 10-5; Sat 9 -1 Closure: Public hols.
Parking: Public nearby-paying.
Disabled: Access. Lift.
Children: At librarian's discretion.
Appointments: Prior booking for viewers-2 days. Entry-register. 15 seats+2 film+5 fiche-2 reader/printers.
Ordering System: No prior ordering. Five ordered & produced. Delivery 5 mins. Last order: 30 mins before closure. P/copying restricted, DIY. Typing not permitted. Taping/cameras/laptops (power supply) allowed.
Records: for Gloucestershire. Houses the largest collection of printed material about the county. Many of the sources on M/f-census/IGI. Electoral lists. Directories. Hockaday abstracts & collections. Visitation. Subsidy & muster rolls. MIs. Wills & obituaries. Small American Civil War collection. Emigrants. Newspapers. Cuttings. Periodicals. Journals. VCH. Photographs. Maps. Prints & slides. Videos. Tapes. Indexes.
Research Service: Charge made.
Facilities: No toilet/public tel/refreshment facilities. Café/pub/shops nearby.
Publications: Free: Info leaflets: *Routes to Roots. Your local history.* (SAE).
O.R: Stow on the Wold Library, STOW-ON-THE-WOLD Small English Civil War collection.

GLOUCESTERSHIRE, see Gloucester, Stow on the Wold

GORDON HIGHLANDERS MUSEUM, See Aberdeen.

Royal Navy Submarine Museum, Archive Dept., Haslar Jetty Road, GOSPORT, Hants PO12 2AS Tel: 01705 529217. Appt. Data on submariners/submarines. Photographic archive.

Great Yarmouth Central Library, Tolhouse Street, GREAT YARMOUTH, Norfolk NR30 2SH Tel: 01493 844551 Local history of Great Yarmouth & area. Local genealogical info. Local History collections. Maps. Newspaper cuttings.

GREATER MANCHESTER

GREATER MANCHESTER, see Irlam; Manchester; Oldham; Salford; Rochdale; Stockport.

GREEN HOWARDS REGIMENT MUSEUM, see Richmond.

Watt Library, 9 Union St., GREENOCK, Inverclyde PA16 8JH Tel: 01475 720186 Usually open.18 seats+2 film. M/f-Inverclyde & Renfrewshire OPRs/census.

GREENWICH, see London Borough of.

GREFFE, THE, see St. Peter Port.

Grimsby Museum & Heritage Service, Welhome Museum Store, Welhome Road, GRIMSBY, N.E. Lincolnshire DN32 9LP Tel: 01472 323575 Appt. Lincolnshire history. Social history. Fishing industry. Railway history. Photographs.

North East Lincolnshire Achives, Town Hall, GRIMSBY, Lincs DN31 1HX Tel: 01472 323585
Opening Hours: M.-F. 9.30-12; 1-4.30 Closure: Public hols.
Parking: None.
Disabled: W/chair access. Toilet.
Children: At archivist's discretion.
Appointments: Prior booking for viewers. Entry-register. 6 seats+1 film+2 fiche.
Ordering System: Prior ordering by letter/tel. One ordered & produced. Delivery 2 mins. Last order: 15 mins before closure. P/copying restricted, by staff-post. Typing/taping/laptops (power supply) permitted. Cameras by prior arrangement.
Records: for North & North East Lincolnshire unitary authorities. PRs-fiche. Great Grimsby 13thC on. Registers of ships 1825-1918. Fishing vessels. Crew lists (1863-1914 require prior ordering-3 days). Dock records. Merchant marine/fishing apprentice. Education. Poor Law. Burial Boards. Pastures Rolls (freemen & widows 1849-1925). Nonconformist. Business. Winn papers 1860-1941. Engineers' plans & records. Some crew lists indexes, approx 30,000, available without prior notice. Oral history recordings.
Research Service: Specific limited enquiry. List of local researchers supplied.
Facilities: Toilets. No public tel/refreshment facilities. Café/pub/shops nearby.
Publications: Free: Info leaflets: *Sources for tracing family history/shipping and fishing/education and school/ public health.* Archive Office information leaflet. (SAE) For sale: *Guide to the Archive Office. Grimsby's War Work 1914-19. Index to the Freeman's Roll Book of Grimsby 1780-1980.*
O. R: Local Collection, Central Library, Town Hall Square, GRIMSBY DN31 1HG Tel: 01472 323600 Directories. Newspapers. Census. Ts of PRs. Indexes to MIs; **Superintendent Registrar**, Register Office, Town Hall Square, GRIMSBY DN31 1HX Tel: 01472 324865 Registers of BMD in Grimsby Registration District.
Tourist Office: Tel: 01472 342422 Fax: 01472 268542
Remarks: Bags not allowed. **Note:** Archives collected by the Scunthorpe Borough Museum & Art Gallery are now deposited here, but can be returned to the Museum for study by arrangement with the Keeper of Local History there. Tel: 01724 843533. See *Guide to South Humberside RO* by John Wilson (C.C. 1993).

GUERNSEY, see St. Peter Port.

GUILDFORD MUNIMENT ROOM, see Woking.

GWENT, see Cwmbran.

GWYNEDD, see Caernarfon; Dolgellau.

HACKNEY, see London Borough of.

HALESOWEN, see Coseley.

West Yorkshire Archive Service, Calderdale, Calderdale District Archives, Central Library, Northgate House, Northgate, HALIFAX, West Yorks HX1 1UN Tel: 01422 347284 Ext. 2636 **Fax:** 01422 341083
E-mail:calderdale@wyashq.demon.co.uk
Internet: http://www.wyashq.demon.co.uk
Opening Hours: M.T.Th.F. 10-5.30 (M/f 5.30-8); Sat M/f 10-5 Closure: Wed+Public hols+1 wk in Feb.
Parking: None.
Disabled: Lift.
Children: At archivist's discretion.
Appointments: Prior booking unnecessary. Entry-register. 10 seats+15 film+4 fiche-2 reader/printers.
Ordering System: Prior ordering by letter/tel essential-no ordering at the office. Catalogue nos sometimes required. Number ordered at archivist's discretion, one produced. P/copying by staff-post/collection. Typing/taping/ cameras/laptops (power supply) permitted.
Records: for the ancient parish of Halifax. PRs-film/Ts. LBT's. Calderdale Metropolitan Borough Council records & its 9 predecessor authorities-County Borough of Halifax/B oroughs of Brighouse/Todmorden/Urban Districts of Ellend/Hebden Royd/Queensbury & Shelf/Ripponden/Sowerby Bridge/Rural District of Hepton. Civil townships from 1665. Boards of Guardians. Family. Estate. Manorial.

Solicitors. Nonconformist. Political & trade unions. Charities. Societies. Oral history. Newspapers. Directories. Electoral. Poll books. Business records especially those to do with the textile industry from 1736/banking from 1735/brewing from 1808/clay & brickmaking from 1800/clock making 1750-1812/coal mining from 1633/engineering from 1849/ stone quarrying from 1773/wire manufacturing from 1868. Shibden Hall muniments include-Notebooks of Jonathan Hall of Elland upholsterer 1701-56. Eye witness accounts of battle during the American War of Independence. Travel journals of Anne Lister 1806-40. M/f-census.
Research Service: Charge made.
Facilities: Toilets. No public tel/refreshment facilities. Café/pub/shops nearby.
Publications: Free: Info leaflet. (SAE) For sale: Lists of holdings. *Calderdale Guide with supplements.*
Tourist Office: Tel: 01422 368725 Fax: 01422 354264
Remarks: Donations appreciated. **Note:** Reference Library at the same address.

Hamilton Library, 98 Cadzow Street, HAMILTON, S. Lanarkshire ML3 6HQ Tel: 01698 894044 Ext. 2403 Appt. Hamilton Burgh. Hamilton Poor House minute books 1864 on. Estate papers. Newspapers. Local History collection. M/f-census for Hamilton area.

HAMMERSMITH, see London Borough of.

HAMPSHIRE, see Aldershot; Gosport; Portsmouth; Southampton; Southsea; Winchester.

HANLEY LIBRARY, see Stoke on Trent.

HARINGEY, see London Borough of.

HARROW, see London Borough of.

Hartlepool Central Library, 124 York Road, HARTLEPOOL TS26 9DE Tel: 01429 263778/272905. Local History collection. Maps. Newspaper Index. Photographs. **Note:** Hartlepool is now a Unitary Authority.

Lancashire Library, Deardengate, HASLINGDEN, Lancs BB4 5QL Tel: 01706 215690 Usually open except for Wed. Parking: Yes-free. Disabled: Access to Library only. Local Studies on 1st floor. PRs-film. Rossendale & Lancashire pre 1974. Local History collection incl Halstead collection of books/pamphlets /scrapbooks/notebooks/MSS. Publications: *Local Studies in Lancashire: A guide to Resources* (1986).

Hastings Area Library, Brassey Institute, 13 Claremont, HASTINGS, Essex TN34 1HE Tel: 01424 420501. Local/military/ shipping histories.

Hastings Museum & Art Gallery, Cambridge Road, HASTINGS, Essex TN34 1ET Tel: 01424 721202 Appt. Archives of Hastings & the Cinque Ports. Family. Photographs.

Pembrokeshire Record Office, The Castle, HAVERFORDWEST, Pembrokeshire, SA61 2 EF Tel: 01437 763707
Opening Hours: M.-Th. 9-4.45; F. 9-4.15; 1st Sat in mth 9.30-12.30 (public holiday wk/ends excepted). Closure: Public hols+Tues following Spring/late summer+days between Christmas & New Year.
Parking: Limited-free.
Disabled: Access. Taping allowed with prior permission.
Children: At archivist's discretion.
Appointments: Prior booking unnecessary. Entry-register. 15 seats+5 film+2 fiche.
Ordering System: No prior ordering. Number ordered at archivist's discretion, two produced. Delivery approx 5 mins. Last order: 15 mins before closure. P/copying restricted-by staff same day/post. Typing/taping not permitted. Cameras/laptops (power supply) allowed.
Records: for the old county of Pembrokeshire. Diocesan RO for St. Davids (registers & papers). A few PRs-film/Ts. Local authority. Family incl. Starbuck family of America. Shipping. Coal mining. Elections. Railways. Quarries. Newspapers. Maps. Haverfordwest Borough papers.
Research Service: Charge made.
Facilities: Toilets. No public tel/refreshment facilities. Café/pub nearby.
Publications: Free: Info leaflets: *Tracing Your Ancestors. History of Houses. Summary of main collections.* (SAE) For sale: *Documents in Haverfordwest. Railways in Pembrokeshire. Slate and Limestone Quarries. Skokholm Island. Haverfordwest Castle. Shipping Records. Coal Mining. Rebecca Riots. Oil Industry. Politics and Parliamentary Elections. A Guide to PRs in St David's Diocese. A Guide to Local Newspapers.* Maps.
Tourist Office: Tel: 01437 763110 Fax: 01437 767738
Remarks: Bags not allowed.

The County Library, Dew Street, HAVERFORDWEST, Pembrokeshire SA61 1SU Tel: 01437 762070 Usually open. Disabled: No facilities. 3 seats+1 film+1 fiche. County of Pembrokeshire. Francis Green collection-relating to prominent families of Pembrokeshire/Cardiganshire/Camarthenshi re which includes-Ts of wills/church records/pedigree sheets etc. Photographs. Maps. Newspapers. See: *Genealogical Sources at Haverfordwest Library*-being revised.

HAVERING, see London Borough of.

Flintshire Record Office, The Old Rectory, HAWARDEN, Deeside CH5 3NR Tel: 01244 532364 **Fax:** 01244 538344
Internet:
http://www.Ugc.org.uk/cac0011.html
Opening Hours: M.-Th. 9-4.45; F. 9-4.15 Closure: Public hols+1 wk in Jan or Feb.
Parking: Yes-free.
Disabled: Access. Toilet.
Children: At archivist's discretion.
Appointments: Prior booking for seats/viewers-1 wk. Entry-register+CARN+ID. 6 seats+5 film+2 fiche.
Ordering System: Prior ordering by letter/tel. Catalogue nos usually required. Number ordered at archivist's discretion, three produced. Delivery 5-10 mins. No production 12-1.30 Last order: 15 mins before closure. P/copying restricted, by staff-same day/post/collection. Typing not permitted. Taping/cameras by special arrangement. Laptops (battery) allowed.
Records: for historic Flintshire with coverage of areas (registers & census) previously in Denbighshire. PRs-film/Ts/p/copies/originals if not copied. Local authority. Quarter Sessions. Nonconformist. Schools. Poor Law. Magistrates. Estate. Hospitals. Police. Shipping. Business. Societies. Trade unions. Family. Glynne-Gladstone papers (held at St. Deniol's Library but produced here). Photographs. Maps. M/f-census/probate/newspapers/tithe apportionments/some trade directories.
Research Service: None.
Facilities: Toilets. No public tel. Room for own food/drink vending machine. Café/pub/shops nearby.
Publications: Free: Info leaflets: List of publications. (SAE) For sale: *Guide to Parish Records. Handlist of Denbighshire Quarter Sessions Records.*
Remarks: Donations appreciated. **Note:** There will be a new enlarged search room in Spring/Summer 1998.

HAY FLEMING LIBRARY, see St. Andrews

HENDON, See RAF Museum, London other repositories.

HENLEY-ON-THAMES, see Oxfordshire Useful Addresses.

Hereford (& Worcester) Record Office, Old Barracks, Harold Street, HEREFORD, Herefordshire HR1 2QX Tel: 01432 265441 Fax 01432 370248.
Opening Hours: M. 10-4.45; T.W.Th. 9.15-4.45; F. 9.15-4 Closure: Public hols-Mon. only+last 2 wks in Nov.
Parking: 8-10 places.
Disabled: 1st Floor Search Room. Records may be consulted on ground floor by appt. Toilet.
Children: At archivist's discretion.
Appointments: Prior ordering for viewers-1 wk. Entry-register+CARN. 18 seats+ 8 film+6 fiche-5 dual purpose-1 film/fiche+1 fiche reader printer.
Ordering System: No prior ordering. Number ordered at archivist's discretion, one produced. Last order: 30 mins before closure. Delivery 20 mins max. P/copying DIY. Typing not permitted. Taping/ laptops allowed. Cameras+fee permitted.
Records: for county of Hereford. Diocesan RO for Hereford-incl parts of Shropshire & Powys. PRs-film/Ts/originals if not copied. BTs-film. County/City. Leominster Borough, District & Parish Councils originating in Hereford. Quarter/Petty Sessions. Magistrates Courts. Hospitals. Probate. Manorial. PLU. Schools. Tithe. Business. Trade. Family. Newspapers. Directories. Maps. M/f-GRO Indexes/census /nonconformist/IGI.
Research Service: Charge made.
Facilities: Toilets. No public tel. Area for own food. Café/pubs nearby. Shops-10 mins.
Publications: For sale: *Census Returns/ PRs/Parish Officer/School Log Books & Admission Registers at Hereford RO.*
O.R: Hereford Cathedral Library, The Cathedral, HEREFORD. HR1 2NG. Tel: 01432 359880. Appt. Records of Dean's Consistory Court+Administrative papers of Dean & Chapter & prebends. Manorial; **Hereford City Library**, Broad Street, HEREFORD.
Tourist Office: Tel: 01432 268430 Fax: 01432 342662
Remarks: Bags not allowed-lockers. Donations appreciated. **Note:** This office split from Worcester on 1st April 1998. There may be some alterations but major changes unlikely.

Hertfordshire Archives & Local Studies, County Hall, Pegs Lane, HERTFORD, Herts SG13 8EJ Tel: 01992 555105 **Fax:** 01992 555113 **E-mail:** iris.white@hertscc.gov.uk
Internet: http://hertslib.hertscc.gov.uk
Opening Hours: M.W.Th. 9.30-5.30; T. 10-8; F. 9.30-4.30; Sat 9-1 Closure: Public hols+1st wk in Nov.
Parking: Yes-free.
Disabled: Access. Toilet.
Children: 7 yrs+
Appointments: Prior booking for seats/viewers-2/3 days.

Entry-register+CARN+ID. 40 seats+11 film+13 fiche-4 reader/printers.
Ordering System: Prior ordering by letter/telephone-essential for Tues eve before 4pm/for Sat am before 3pm on the previous Fri. Catalogue nos sometimes required. Three ordered, one produced. Delivery 20 mins. Last order: 60 mins before closure. P/copying restricted, by staff-same day/post. DIY in Local Studies Library. Typing/taping/cameras/ laptops (power supply) permitted.
Records: for Hertfordshire. PRs-film/Ts/original if not copied. Diocesan RO for St. Albans. BTs available. Panshanger Archive of the Earls Cowper 12th-20thC's. Local government. Nonconformist. Probate. Allen index of marriages pre 1837. Estate. Family. Wills. Plans. Business. Education. Maps. Photographs.
Research Service: Charge made.
Facilities: Toilets. No public tel. Restaurant/room for own food/drink vending machine. Café/pub/shops nearby.
Publications: For sale: Info leaflets: *Source guides to PRs & nonconformist holdings.* (SAE)
Tourist Office: Tel: 01992 584322 Fax: 01992 505876
Remarks: Bags not allowed-lockers. Donations appreciated. Station: Hertford North or East.

HERTFORDSHIRE, see Hertford; Hitchin; St. Albans; Watford.

Hexham Group Library, Queen's Hall, Beaumont Street, HEXHAM, Northumberland NE46 3LS Tel: 01434 603156 Usually open Local Studies collection. Electoral rolls. Newspapers. M/f-census.

Heywood Public Library, Church Street, HEYWOOD, Lancs OL10 1LL Tel: 01706 306947 Usually open. Disabled: No facilities. Prior booking for viewer. 4 seats+1 film+1 fiche. Heap, Heywood Borough collection. Methodist archives. Newspapers. Maps.

HIGHLAND NORTH, see Wick.

HIGHLAND, see Inverness.

HILLINGDON, see London Borough of.

Hitchin Museum, Paynes Park, HITCHIN, Herts SG5 1EQ Tel: 01462 434476 Usually open.Disabled: No facilities. Prior booking for seats-1 wk. 2 seats+1 fiche. Local History on history of Hitchin. Maps. Documents. Ephemera.

HOLBORN, see London Borough of Camden.

Ulster Folk & Transport Museum, Cultra, HOLYWOOD, co. Down, N. Ireland BT18 OEU Tel: 01232 428428 Appt. Information & material which illustrates the way of life & traditions of Northern Ireland people. Local history. Oral history. Business. Transport. Photographs. M/f-newspapers.

HOUNSLOW, MIDDX see London Borough of Hounslow

West Yorkshire Archives; Kirklees, Central Library, Princess Alexandra Walk, HUDDERSFIELD, West Yorks HD1 2SU Tel: 01484 221966
Opening Hours: Archives: M.Th. 10-5; T. 10-8; F. 10-1 Closure: Wed+Public hols+1st wk in Feb. **Local Studies Dept:** M.T.Th.F 9-8; W. 9.30-5; Sat 9-4 Closure: Public hols.
Parking: None.
Disabled: Ramp. Lift.
Children: Accompanied: At archivist's discretion. Unaccompanied: 15 yrs+
Appointments: Prior booking for seats/viewers-2 days. Entry-register. 8 seats+5 film+5 fiche-1 reader/printer.
Ordering System: Prior ordering by letter/tel. Catalogue nos required. Four ordered & produced. Delivery 5 mins. P/copying by staff-same day. Typing/taping not permitted. Cameras/laptops (power supply) allowed.
Records: Archives: for Kirklees Metropolitan Borough Council-Batley/Dewsbury/ Huddersfield/Holne Valley/Colne Valley/Spen Valley. PRs-fiche /film/Ts/originals if not copied. Nonconformist. Poor Law. Schools. Family. Estate. Local authority. Business-mainly relating to the textile industry (these require 2 wks prior notice). **Local Studies Dept:** PRs-Ts. M/f-PRs/nonconformist registers.
Research Service: Specific enquiry-charge made.
Facilities: Toilets. No public tel/refreshment facilities. Café/pub/shops nearby.
Publications: Free: Info leaflets: Relating to all the ROs in West Yorkshire. (SAE) For sale: *Guides to other ROs in West Yorkshire.* Subject/topic lists.
Tourist Office: Tel: 01484 430808 Fax: 01484 451798
Remarks: Donations appreciated.

HULL, see Kingston upon Hull.

County Record Office Huntingdon, Grammar School Walk, HUNTINGDON, Cambs PE18 6LF Tel: 01480 425842 **Fax:** 01480 459563 **E-mail:** county.records.hunts@ camcnty.gov.uk/
Opening Hours: T. 1.45-5.15; W.Th. 9-12.45; 1.45-5.15; F. 9-12.45; 1.45-4.15; 2nd Sat in mth 9-12 by appt. only. Closure: Public hols.
Parking: Public nearby-paying.

Disabled: No facilities-steep staircase. Prior appt to have documents produced elsewhere.
Children: Accompanied: At archivist's discretion. Unaccompanied: Educational purposes only.
Appointments: Prior booking for viewers. Entry-register+CARN or ID. 21 seats+3 film+2 fiche-1 reader/printer.
Ordering System: Prior ordering by letter/tel. Catalogue nos sometimes required. Three ordered & produced. Delivery 5 mins. P/copying restricted, by staff-same day. Typing/taping not permitted. Cameras/laptops (power supply) allowed.
Records: for the ancient county of Huntingdonshire & the soke of Peterborough. Diocesan RO for Archdeaconry of Huntingdon in the Diocese of Ely. PRs-Ts/originals. BTs available. Manchester collection (Duke of Manchester). Hinchingbrooke collection (Earls of Sandwich). Cromwell-Bush collection. Manorial. Rate books. Deeds. Directories. Maps. Inclosure. Tithe. Marriage index. MIs. Nonconformist. Poor Law. Probate. Quarter Sessions. Local authority. Photographs. M/f-census/IGI.
Research Service: Charge made-leaflet available.
Facilities: Toilets. No public tel/refreshment facilities. Café/pub/shops nearby.
Publications: Free: Info leaflets: *Tracing the History of your House. Tracing your Family Tree.* (SAE) For sale: *Genealogical Sources In Cambridgeshire*-includes Huntingdon & Peterborough.
Tourist Office: Tel: 01480 388588
Remarks: Bags not allowed-supervised corner of reception area. Donations appreciated. **Note:** Peterborough Unitary Authority inaugurated in Apr 1998-however no records are likely to be transferred for some years.

Knowsley Reference & Information Services, Local History & Archives Library, Huyton Library, Civic Way, HUYTON, Knowsley, Merseyside L36 9GD Tel: 0151 4433738 **Fax:** 0151 4433739
Internet: http://www.knowsley.gov.uk
Opening Hours: M.-F. 10-7; Sat 10-4 Closure: Public hols.
Parking: Yes-free.
Disabled: Access.
Children: At librarian's discretion.
Appointments: Prior booking for viewers essential. Entry-reader's ticket. 8 seats+7 film+7 fiche-2 reader/printers.
Ordering System: Prior ordering by letter/tel. Catalogue nos sometimes required. Number ordered & produced at librarian's discretion. Last order: 6.40. P/copying restricted, by staff-same day. Taping/cameras not permitted. Typing/laptops (battery) allowed.
Records: for Knowsley & part of Merseyside. PRs-film/fiche/Ts/photocopies. Local authority. Harold Wilson material. National Coal Board. Cronton Parochial Trust 1755-75. Prescot Grammar School 15th-19thC's. Huyton Cricket Club 1860-1970. Maps. Photographs-indexed in part.
Research Service: None.
Facilities: Toilets. No public tel/refreshment facilities. Café/pub/shops nearby.
Publications: For sale: *Prescot Parish Memoirs. Huyton & Roby-a History of 2 Townships. Inns of Prescot & Whiston. Prescot Records* (Court Rolls). Archive photographic series.

Hythe Town Archives, Town Council Offices, Stade Street, HYTHE, Kent CT21 6BG Tel: 01303 266152/3 Appt essential. Hythe Borough records which include items usually found in parish records e.g. settlement certificates/charity. **Note:** In 1998 a new repository, the East Kent Archive Centre, will be opened at Whitfield, Dover (see entry). The archival records from Hythe, Folkestone & Ramsgate will be housed there. The Hythe office will then only house the local studies collection.

ILFORD, ESSEX, see London Borough of Redbridge.

INSTITUTE OF HERALDIC & GENEALOGICAL STUDIES, see Canterbury.

INVERCLYDE, see Greenock.

Highland Council Archives & Genealogy Service, Inverness Library, Farraline Park, INVERNESS, Highland IV1 1NH Tel: 01463 220330 **Fax:** 01463 711128
Opening Hours: Archives: M.-Th. 10-1; 2-5 **Genealogy**: M.-F. 11-1; 2-5 Closure: Public hols+Christmas & New Year.
Parking: None.
Disabled: No facilities.
Children: At archivist's discretion.
Appointments: Prior booking by appointment only. Entry-register. 5 seats+4 film+4 fiche.
Ordering System: Prior ordering by letter/tel. Catalogue nos required. Number ordered at archivist's discretion, three/four produced. P/copying by staff-same day/post. Typing/taping/cameras/laptops (power supply) permitted.
Records: for the Highlands. Newspapers. Local authority. MIs. Lists of emigrants. Printed genealogies. Estate. Family. Maps. M/f-OPRs/census/IGI.
Research Service: Charge made.
Facilities: No toilets/public tel/refreshment facilities. Café/pub/shops nearby.
Publications: For sale: *Guide to Highland Council Archives.*

O. R: Highland Family History Library, Highland Regional Library Service, 31A Harbour Road, INVERNESS IV1 1UA Tel: 01463 235713 Local & Family History collections for Highland & Caithness; **Inverness Museum & Art Gallery**, Castle Wynd, INVERNESS IV2 3ED Tel: 01463 237114 Appt. Estate papers. Letters. Inverness Town & district council mins. Newspapers. Photographs; **Queen's Own Highlanders Regimental Museum (Archives)**, Cameron Barracks, INVERNESS IV2 3XD Application by letter. Regimental archives of the Seaforth & Cameron Highlanders. Military history.
Tourist Office: Tel: 01463 234353

Suffolk Record Office, Ipswich Record Office, Gatacre Road, IPSWICH, Suffolk IP1 2LQ Tel: 01473 584541 **Fax:** 01473 584534 **E-mail:** gwyn.thomas@libber.suffolkcc .gov.uk
Internet: http://www.suffolkcc.gov.uk/ libraries_and_heritage/
Opening Hours: M.-Sat 9 -5 Closure: Public hols.
Parking: Limited-free.
Disabled: Disabled friendly.
Children: At archivist's discretion.
Appointments: Prior booking for viewers advisable-2/3 days. Entry-register+CARN. 28 seats+10 film+11 fiche+3 computer terminals-1 fiche/1 film reader/printers.
Ordering System: Prior ordering by letter/tel. Catalogue nos sometimes required. Four ordered & produced. Delivery approx 15 mins. Occasional limitation at wkday lunchtimes. Limited service on Sat. Last order: 4.30. P/copying restricted, by staff-same day/post/collection. Typing not permitted. Taping by arrangement. Laptops (power supply) allowed. Cameras allowed by arrangement+fee.
Records: mostly for East Suffolk though coverage of whole county for PRs. Diocesan RO for St. Edmundsbury & Ipswich, Ipswich & Suffolk Archdeaconries. PRs-fiche/film/ Ts/originals if not copied. BTs available. Local authority. Local collections. M/f-census/ National Probate indexes/IGI.
Research Service: Charge made.
Facilities: Toilets/public tel/room for own food/drink vending machine.
Publications: Free & for sale. (SAE).
O. R: Ipswich Museum, Upper High Street, IPSWICH.
Tourist Office: Tel: 01473 258070 Fax: 01473 258072
Remarks: Bags not allowed-lockers. Donations appreciated.

IRELAND N., see Armagh; Ballymena; Ballynahinch; Belfast; Enniskillen; Holywood; Monaghan; Omagh.

IRISH THEATRE ARCHIVE, see Dublin.

Salford Archives Centre, 658-662 Liverpool Road, IRLAM, Manchester M44 5AD Tel: 0161 775 5643
Opening Hours: M-F 9-4.30 Closure: Public hols.
Parking: 6 spaces.
Disabled: Toilet.
Children: At archivist's discretion.
Appointments: Prior booking for seats-1 day. Entry-register. 6 seats.
Ordering System: Prior ordering by letter/tel. Card to be signed when ordering records. Number ordered & produced at archivist's discretion. Records stored elsewhere need prior ordering-1 day. Delivery 5-10 mins. P/copying by staff-by post. Typing/taping/camera/ laptops (power supply) permitted.
Records: for City of Salford. Local Authority incl Salford PLU. Quarter Sessions. Coroners for Salford City. Hospital. Religious incl nonconformist. Education. Family. Business. Trade Unions. Societies. Charities. Apprentice indentures. Ratebooks. Maps & plans. National Collection-Bridgewater Estate records 18-20thC's (U 375)-in process of being catalogued.
Research Service: Limited specific enquiry-post only.
Facilities: Toilet/public tel/room for own food. Café/pub/shops nearby.
Publications: Free leaflets: *A Handlist of Salford City Archives. Genealogical Sources for the City of Salford. The History of Houses.* (A5 SAE).
O.R: Working Class Movement Library, Jubilee House, Crescent, SALFORD M5 4WX Tel: 0161 736 360 for archives & appt; **The Superintendent Registrar**, Salford Registration District, "Kingslea" Barton Road, SWINTON, Gt. Manchester M27 5WH Tel: 0161 7930077 for City of Salford with exception of Little Hilton area before 1937-these are in the keeping of Superintendent Registrar, Bolton Register Office Tel: 01204 525165.
Remarks: Bags allowed but may be subject to inspection. **Note:** Manchester Central Library is the Diocesan RO for Manchester Diocese which incls Salford (see entry). Other Quarter Sessions & coroners records are in Lancashire RO Preston (see entry). There is a possibility of re-location if superior premises become available.

IRLAM, see Salford.

Ironbridge Gorge Museum, Library & Archives Department, IRONBRIDGE, Telford, Shropshire. TF8 7AW Tel: 01952 432141 **Fax:** 01952 432237
Opening Hours: M.-F. 9-5.30. Closure: Public hols+Christmas & New Year.

ISLE OF ANGLESEY

Parking: Yes-free.
Disabled: Ramp. Toilet.
Children: Accompanied: At staff's discretion. Unaccompanied: 14 yrs+
Appointments: Prior booking necessary-1 day. Entry-register. 20 seats+1 film+1 fiche.
Ordering System: Prior ordering by letter/tel. Three/four ordered & produced. Delivery 5 mins. P/copying restricted, by staff-same day. Typing/taping not permitted. Cameras/laptops (power supply) allowed.
Records: for the Industrial Revolution & social history of the Ironbridge Gorge & Telford. Local business archives. Property documents. Family papers-especially the Darby family of Coalbrookdale. Thomas Telford collection. Coalbrookdale Company archives. Victorian Decorative Tile designs. Lilleshall Iron & Steel archives. Maps & plans. Photographs & postcards. Film collection (local industries). Oral history recordings.
Research Service: Limited specific enquiry-free but donations suggested. Charge for p/copying. Postal enquiries or personal visits encouraged.
Facilities: Toilets/public tel/restaurant/room for own food. Café/pub nearby.
Publications: Free leaflets: Plan of Ironbridge Gorge Museum; *Telford Collection* (SAE). For sale: Museum site guides etc.
Tourist Office: Telford: Tel: 01952 291370 Fax: 01952 291723
Remarks: Bags not allowed-lockable cupboard. Donations appreciated. Station: Telford Central (5 miles) Public transport: Tel: 0345 056785.

ISLANDS ARCHIVES SERVICE, see St. Peter Port.

ISLE OF ANGLESEY, see Llangefni.

ISLE OF BUTE, see Rothesay.

ISLE OF LEWIS, see Stornaway.

ISLE OF MAN, see Douglas.

ISLE OF WIGHT, see Cowes, Newport.

ISLES OF SCILLY, see St. Mary's.

ISLINGTON, see London Borough of.

JERSEY, see St. Helier.

JEWISH MUSEUM, see Manchester.

JOHN RYLANDS UNIVERSITY LIBRARY, see Manchester.

JOHN WESLEY'S CHAPEL, see Bristol.

JUDICIAL GREFFE, see St. Helier.

Keighley Reference Library, North Street, KEIGHLEY, West Yorks BD21 3SX Tel: 01535 618215 **Fax:** 01535 618219
Opening Hours: M.W. 9-7; T. 9-1; Th. 9.30 -7; F.Sat 9-5 Closure: Public hols.
Parking: None.
Disabled: Stairlift.
Children: At librarian's discretion.
Appointments: Prior booking for viewers-1/2 days. 12 seats+3 film+3 fiche.
Ordering System: Prior ordering by letter/tel essential. Catalogue nos sometimes required. Number ordered at librarian's discretion, one produced. P/copying DIY. Typing/cameras not permitted. Taping/laptops (battery) by prior arrangement.
Records: for Keighley & Worth Valley. PRs-fiche/Ts. Some BTs. Rate books. Voters lists. Nonconformist. Directories. Indexes to names. MIs. Maps. Photographs. M/f-Keighley News 1862-1940/census/IGI.
Research Service: None.
Facilities: No toilets/public tel/refreshments facilities. Café/pub/shops nearby.
Publications: Free: Info leaflets: *Some important sources for Family History. Welcome to Keighley Reference Library.* (SAE A4 or A5).

Cumbria Record Office (Kendal), County Offices, Stricklandgate, KENDAL, Cumbria LA9 4RQ Tel: 01539 773540 **Fax:** 01539 773439
Opening Hours: M.-F. 9-5. Closure: Public hols+Tues following Easter/late Spring+Christmas-New Year.
Parking: Yes.
Disabled: Access at rear of County Hall. Toilet.
Children: At archivist's discretion.
Appointments: Prior booking unnecessary. Entry-sign in at main entrance+register at RO+CARN. 15 seats+map table+2 film+7 fiche-1 reader printer.
Ordering System: Prior ordering by letter/tel. Catalogue nos required-items not produced until signed for in person. Two ordered & produced. Delivery 5 mins/19-25 mins for items in outstore. Occasional suspension of production lunch time. P/copying by staff-same day if possible/post/collection. Typing/taping at archivist's discretion. Cameras/laptops (power supply after signing declaration+circuit breaker) permitted.
Records: for historic county of Westmorland+Sedbergh/Garsdale/Dent area formerly in W. Riding of Yorks/Cartmel area formerly in Lancs north of the Sands. Diocesan RO for Carlisle & Bradford. PRs-film/fiche/p/copies/Ts/originals if not copied. BTs. Local authority. Solicitors. Business. Manorial. Papers of Lady Anne Clifford (1590-1676) of Appleby Castle. Sir Daniel Fleming (1633-1701) of Rydal Hall. T.H.

Mawson, landscape architect (1861-1933) of Windermere-garden plans. Photographs.
Research Service: Charge made-3 hrs max.
Facilities: Toilets. No public tel/refreshment facilities. Cafe/pub/shops nearby.
Publications: Free: Info. leaflets. Publications leaflet (SAE). For sale: *Cumbrian Ancestors* 2nd ed. (1993). *Guide to holdings*-in preparation.
O.R: Kendal Library, Local Studies Library. Stricklandgate, KENDAL M/f-census/ newspapers; **Armitt Library**, Kelswick Road, AMBLESIDE. LA22 OBZ; **Dove Cottage**, The Wordsworth Library, GRASMERE LA22 9SH.
Remarks: Bags not allowed-storage. Donations appreciated. Station: Kendal (local). Oxenholme (mainline).

KENSINGTON, see London Borough of Kensington & Chelsea.

KENT, BEXLEY, see London Borough of Bexley.

KENT, BROMLEY, see London Borough of Bromley.

KENT, see Broadstairs; Canterbury; Chatham; Deal; Dover; Folkestone; Gillingham; Hythe; Lydd; Maidstone; Margate; Ramsgate; Rochester-upon-Medway; Sevenoaks; Tonbridge; Whitfield.

KENTISH STUDIES, CENTRE FOR, see Maidstone.

KERRIER, see Cornwall

KEW. SURREY, see London, Other Repositories, Public Record Office

KILMAINHAM GAOL, see Dublin.

Dick Institute, Elmbank Avenue, KILMARNOCK, Ayrshire KA1 3BU Tel: 01563 526401 **Fax:** 01563 529661 **E-mail:** 106111.645@compuserve.com
Opening Hours: M.T.Th.F. 9-8; W.Sat 9-5 Closure: Public hols.
Parking: Yes-free.
Disabled: Disabled friendly.
Children: At staff's discretion.
Appointments: Prior booking unnecessary. 14 seats+4 dual film/fiche.
Ordering System: Prior ordering not allowed. P/copying by staff-post or DIY. Typing not permitted. Taping/laptops (power supply) allowed. Cameras by prior arrangement.
Records: for Ayrshire. Valuation rolls. Electoral rolls. Newspapers. MIs. Directories. Maps. Photographs. M/f-OPRs (all Ayrshire parishes)/census (all Ayrshire parishes except Auchinleck 1841)/local newspapers/IGI for Scotland & Ireland.
Research Service: Limited specific enquiry-charge made. Leaflet listing record searchers.
Facilities: Toilets/public tel. No refreshment facilities. Cafe/pub/shops nearby.
Publications: Free: Info leaflets: *Tracing Your Family Tree: sources in East Ayrshire.* Publications list. (SAE) For sale: *Pictorial Histories of-Kilmarnoch/Dundonald/ Darvel/Galston etc. The History of Auchinleck.* Various other Local History books.
Tourist Office: Tel: 01563 539090

KINGS OWN REGIMENT, see Lancaster.

KING'S REGIMENT COLLECTION, see Liverpool.

KING'S OWN SCOTTISH BORDERERS, see Berwick-upon- Tweed.

Hull Central Library, Albion Street, KINGSTON UPON HULL E. Yorks HU1 3TF Tel: 01482 883102 **Fax:** 01482 883080 **E-mail:** adlib@kuhlib.karoo.co.uk
Opening Hours: M.-Th. 9.30-8; F. 9.30-5.30; Sat 9-4.30 Closure: Public hols.
Parking: Public nearby.
Disabled: Reference Library-w/chair access. Local Studies-no w/chair access.
Children: No restriction.
Appointments: Prior booking for viewers in Reference Library-1 day. **Reference Library**: 50 seats+6 fiche-1 reader/printer. **Local Studies**: 12 seats+4 film+4 fiche-1 reader/printer.
Ordering System: Prior ordering by letter/tel. P/copying restricted, by staff-same day & DIY. Typing/taping/laptops (power supply) permitted. Cameras by arrangement.
Records: for Hull City & East Riding of Yorkshire & some north Lincolnshire. PRs-Ts. Poll books. Directories. MIs. Newspapers. Maps. Photographs. M/f-GRO indexes/Burgess Rolls/census/IGI.
Research Service: Charge made except to residents of Hull.
Facilities: No toilets. Public tel. No refreshment facilities. Café/pub/shops nearby.
Publications: Free: Info leaflet: *Sources for Family History*. (SAE) For sale: Range of local history publications.
Remarks: Note: Proposal to put genealogical material into a Family History Resource Centre at the library.

Hull City Archives, 79 Lowgate, KINGSTON UPON HULL, E. Yorks HU1 1HN Tel: 01482 615102 **Fax:** 01482 613051
Opening Hours: M.-Th. 9-12.15; 1.30-4.45; F. 9-12.15; 1.30-4.15 Closure: Public hols.

Parking: None.
Disabled: Access via circular stairs, alternative arrangements can be arranged with prior notice.
Children: At archivist's discretion.
Appointments: Prior booking for seats/viewers essential-3 days. Entry-register. 11 seats+2 film+2 fiche.
Ordering System: Prior ordering by letter/tel. Catalogue nos helpful. Number ordered at archivist's discretion, up to three produced. Delivery approx 5 mins. Items in the outstore may only be seen on Tues pm when main Search room is closed. P/copying by staff-same day. Typing/taping/cameras/laptops (power supply) permitted.
Records: for City of Hull/Hessle/Anlaby/ Willerby/Wolfreton/Haltemprice/Kirk Ella/ West Ellea/Swanland/North Ferriby. City Council. Borough 16/17thC's. Quarter Sessions. Nonconformists. Coroners. Insolvent debtors' court. Admiralty court. Business. Magistrates courts 1836-1974. Militia. Private organisations. Charities. PLU. Schools. Engineering & architectural drawings 19/20thC's.
Research Service: Referred to Central Library.
Facilities: Toilets. No public tel/refreshment facilities. Café/pub/shops nearby.
Publications: Free: Info leaflets: *General Information on RO. Sources for Genealogy. New Publications.* (SAE) For sale: *Anti-German Sentiment in Kingston upon Hull: The German Community & the First World War. The Old Hull Borough Asylum. De la Pole Hospital 1883-1983. Early Hull Printers & Booksellers. The Medical Profession in Hull 1400-1900. Guide to the RO. The People in Hull in 1695 & 1697* (index to Poll Tax assessments).
O. R: University of Hull, Brynmor Jones Library, Cottingham Road, KINGSTON UPON HULL HU6 7RX Records of Society of Friends for Hull & Pickering monthly meeting 17th-20thC's.
Tourist Office: Tel: 01482 223344 Fax: 01482 593718
Remarks: Bags not allowed-lockers.Station: Hull Paragon.

KINGSTON UPON THAMES, SURREY RO, see Woking.

KINGSTON UPON THAMES, SURREY see London Borough of Kingston upon Thames

Hull Town Docks Maritime Museum, Queen Victoria Square, KINGSTON UPON HULL, E. Yorks HU1 3DX Tel: 01482 613902 Appt. Whaling 18th-20thC's-journals/logs/miscellaneous. Fishing 19/20thC's. Hull's Merchant Trade 19/20thC's.

Fife Council Central Area Libraries, Central Library, War Memorial Grounds, KIRKCALDY, Fife KY1 1XT Tel: 01592 412879 **Fax:** 01592 646125
Opening Hours: M.-Th. 10-7; F.Sat 10-5 Closure: Public hols.
Parking: Limited-free.
Disabled: Access. Prior appt for help.
Children: Accompanied: At librarian's discretion. Unaccompanied: 12 yrs+
Appointments: Prior booking for viewers. 29 seats+2 film+3 fiche-1 reader/printer.
Ordering System: Prior ordering by letter/telephone. Number ordered & produced at librarian's discretion. Delivery immediate. P/copying DIY. Printouts-2 days. Typing/taping not permitted. Laptops (battery) allowed. Cameras by prior permission.
Records: for County of Fife. Military. Business. Sheriff Court Book of Fife. The Scots Black Kalendar-criminal trials 1800-1910. Local authority. Family. Newspapers. Directories. Alphabetical lists of mariners. MIs. Maps. Photographs. M/f-OPRs/census/IGI.
Research Service: None.
Facilities: No toilet/public tel/refreshment facilities. Café/pub/shops nearby.
Publications: Free: Info leaflets: *OPRs. Local Studies in Kirkcaldy District.* (SAE) For sale: *Family History Sources in Kirkcaldy Central Library.*
Tourist Office: Tel: 01592 267775

East Dunbartonshire Libraries, William Patrick Library Reference Dept., 2 West High St., KIRKINTILLOCH, Glasgow, East Dunbartonshire G66 1AD Tel: 0141 7768090 **Fax:** 0141 7760408
Opening Hours: M.-Th. 10-8; F.Sat 10-5 Closure: Public hols.
Parking: Yes-free.
Disabled: Access-ramp. Lift.
Children: At librarian's discretion.
Appointments: Prior booking unnecessary. Entry-ID for consulting archive material. 26 seats+3 film+1 fiche-1 reader/printer.
Ordering System: No prior ordering. Number ordered & produced at librarian's discretion. P/copying by staff-same day/post/collection & DIY. Typing/taping not permitted. Cameras/laptops (power supply) allowed.
Records: for Kirkintilloch/Lenzie/Twechar/ Milton of Campsie/Lennoxtown/Cadder/ Bishopbriggs/Baldernock/Bearsden/ Westerton. Local authority. Valuation rolls. Burgh. Lion Foundry collection. J.F.McEwan collection of Railway history. Family. Business. MIs. Cemetery. Newspapers from 1886. Directories. Organisations. Maps. Photographs. M/f-OPRs/census/IGI.
Research Service: None.
Facilities: Toilets/public tel. No refreshment facilities. Cafe/pub/shops nearby.

Publications: Free: Info leaflets: *Look It Up-Family History/Archives/Local History/ Local Publications.* (SAE) For sale: Auld Kirk Museum Publications e.g *The Story of Bishopbriggs. The Story of Kirkintilloch. The Story of Lenzie. Kirkintilloch Shipbuilding. Milton of Campsie: People & Places. Bishopbriggs: The Golden Years. The Forth & Clyde Canal 'a Kirkintilloch View'.*
Remarks: Station: Lenzie or Bishopbriggs.

Orkney Archives, Orkney Library, Laing Street, KIRKWALL, Orkney KW15 1NW Tel: 01856 873166 **Fax:** 01856 875260
Opening Hours: M.-F. 9 -1; 2- 4.45 Closure: Public hols+3 wks from mid Feb.
Parking: None.
Disabled: Access.
Children: 14 yrs+
Appointments: Prior booking for seats/viewers-as long as possible. 5 seats+3 film+2 fiche-1 reader/printer.
Ordering System: Prior ordering by letter/tel. Catalogue nos necessary. Five ordered & produced. Delivery 5 mins. Last order: 4.30. P/copying by staff-same day. Typing not permitted. Taping/cameras/laptops (power supply) allowed.
Records: for Orkney Islands. OPRs-film/ original. Repository for Church of Scotland/Secession Kirk records. Sheriff court. Local authority. Customs & Excise. Family. Estate. Business. Photographic archive. Sound archive.
Research Service: None.
Facilities: Toilets. No public tel/refreshment facilities. Cafe/pub/shops nearby.
Tourist Office: Tel: 01856 872856
Remarks: Note: A new library & archive is to be constructed, completion not expected before 2001. Station: Thurso.

KNOWSLEY REFERENCE & INFORMATION SERVICES, see Huyton.

LAMBETH, see London Borough of.

LANARKSHIRE, see Airdrie; Hamilton.

LANCASHIRE, see Accrington; Barnoldswick; Blackpool; Clitheroe; Colne; Haslingden; Heywood; Lancaster; Leigh; Preston; Rawtenstall; Salford; Wigan.

Lancaster Library, Market Square, LANCASTER, Lancs LA1 1HY Tel: 01524 63266 Usually open. Disabled: No facilities. Prior booking for viewers. 24 seats+4 film+6 film-1 reader/printer. PRs-Ts. Large Local History collection-apprentice registers/ maritime history. King's Own Regiment archive.

LAUNCESTON, see Cornwall

Local Studies Library, Central Library, Calverley Street, LEEDS, West Yorks LS1 3AB Tel: 0113 2478290 Usually open. Disabled: Access-with help. 18 seats+8 film+4 fiche. PRs-film/fiche/Ts. Local/family/military/ naval histories. Maps. Playbills. M/f-GRO indexes 1837-1980/census/newspapers. Donations appreciated.

West Yorkshire Archive Service: Yorkshire Archaeological Society, Claremont, 23 Clarendon Road, LEEDS, West Yorks LS2 9NZ Tel: 0113 2456362 **Fax:** 0113 2441979
E-mail: yas@wyashq.demon.co.uk but cannot accept genealogical enquiries
Internet: http://www.wyashq.demon.co.uk
Opening Hours: T.W. 2-8.30; Th.F. 930-5; Sat 9.30-5 Closure: Mon+Public hols.
Parking: 6 places-free.
Disabled: W/chair access.
Children: At archivist's discretion.
Appointments: Prior booking for seats/viewers essential-2 days. Entry-register. 8 seats+1 film+7 fiche-1 reader/printer.
Ordering System: Prior ordering by letter/telephone-essential for Sat. Catalogue nos preferred. Four ordered & produced. Delivery 5 mins. P/copying restricted, by staff-same day/post. Typing/taping/cameras/ laptops (power supply) permitted.
Records: for Yorkshire. PRs-fiche/Ts. Heraldic & genealogical MSS. MIs. Maps. Deeds. Monastic. Estate incl the Manor of Wakefield 1274-1925. Family. Freemasonry. Plans. Pedigrees.
Research Service: Charge made.
Facilities: Toilets. Use of ROs tel at cost. Room for own food/kettle for drinks. Café/pub nearby.
Publications: Free: Info leaflets: *Guide to Yorkshire Archaeological Society Archives* (being reprinted). Guides to-*Family History/Quarter Sessions.* Publications list. (SAE).
Tourist Office: Tel: 0113 2425242 Fax: 0113 2468246
Remarks: Bags not allowed-lockers. Donations appreciated.

LEICESTERSHIRE, see Wigston Magna.

Wigan Archives Service, Town Hall, LEIGH, Lancs WN7 2DY Tel: 01942 404430 **Fax:** 01942 404505
Opening Hours: M.T.Th.F 10-1; 2-4 Closure: Wed+Public hols+Christmas wk.
Parking: Yes-paying.
Disabled: Lift to search room then one step.
Children: Accompanied: At archivist's discretion. Unaccompanied: 16 yrs+
Appointments: Prior booking for seats/viewers-1 wk. Entry-register. 6 seats+1 film+1 fiche.

LERWICK

Ordering System: Prior ordering by letter/telephone. Catalogue nos sometimes required. Three ordered, number produced at archivist's discretion. Delivery 10-15 mins. Documents only ordered 11.30 & 2.15. P/copying restricted, by staff-same day/post. Typing not permitted. Taping if no disturbance to others. Laptops (power supply) allowed. Cameras by prior arrangement.
Records: for Wigan Metropolitan Borough-Wigan/ Pennington/Westleigh/Leigh/ Atherton/Abram. Diocesan RO for Liverpool-Wigan & Winwick deaneries. Schools. Local authority-Wigan Borough 1600s on. Quarter/Petty Sessions. Burgess lists. Borough Sessions. Court Leet. PLU. Edward Hall collection of diaries/letter books. Deeds. Civil War papers. Estate. Family. Business. Societies. Maps. Photographs. M/f-Roman Catholic registers/nonconformist registers/census.
Research Service: None.
Facilities: No toilets. Public tel. No refreshment facilities. Café/pub/shops nearby.
Publications: Free: Info leaflet: *Archives.* (SAE) For sale: *Guide to Genealogical Sources. Guide to the Archives.*
O. R: History Shop, Library Street, WIGAN M/f-PRs/census/electoral registers/directories; **Leigh Local History**, Leigh Library, Civic Square, LEIGH WN7 1EB Tel: 01942 404559
Remarks: Donations appreciated. **Note:** PRs/census etc which used to be available at this RO are now at Wigan History Shop (see above). Station: Atherton-3 mls.

Shetland Archives, 44 King Harald Street, LERWICK, Shetland ZE1 0EQ Tel: 01595 696247 **Fax:** 01595 696533 **E-mail:** shetland.archives@zetnet.co.uk
Opening Hours: M.-Th. 9-1; 2-5; F. 9-1; 2-4 Closure: Public hols.
Parking: Yes-free.
Disabled: Ramp. Toilet.
Children: At archivist's discretion.
Appointments: Prior booking for seats/viewers preferred. Entry-register. 7 seats+2 film+1 fiche.
Ordering System: Prior ordering by letter/telephone. Three ordered & produced. Delivery a few mins. P/copying by staff-same day. Typing/taping/laptops (battery) permitted, if feasible. Cameras not allowed.
Records: for Shetland. OPRs-film/Ts. Local authority. Sheriff court. Customs & Excise. Procurator Fiscal records 15thC on. Oral history. Local History collection.
Research Service: None.
Facilities: Toilets. No public tel/refreshment facilities. Café/pub/shops nearby.
O. R: Shetland Library, Lower Hillhead, LERWICK ZE1 0EL
Remarks: See *Shetland - Pre 1853 parish sources for Family History* by H.M. Beattie (pub. Shetland FHS 1995).

East Sussex County Library Services Headquarters, Southdown House, 44 St. Anne's Crescent, LEWES, Sussex BA7 1SQ Tel: 01273 481000 Appt. Local history of Brighton/Hastings (incls. military history)/Hove.

East Sussex Record Office, The Maltings, Castle Precincts, LEWES, Sussex BN7 1YT Tel: 01273 482349 Fax: 01273 482341
Opening Hours: M.T.Th. 8.45-4.45; W. 9.30-4.45; F. 8.45-4.15; 2nd Sat in mth 9-1; 2-4.45 Closure: Public hols+last 2 wks in Jan.
Parking: None.
Disabled: Access to main entrance. Parking. Every effort will be made to accommodate downstairs. Prior notification required.
Children: At archivist's discretion.
Appointments: Prior booking for viewers/seats advisable-2/3 days. Entry-register+CARN+ID. 26 seats+4 film+5 fiche+3 film/fiche.
Ordering System: Prior ordering by letter/tel. Catalogue nos helpful. Number ordered at archivist's discretion, three produced. Delivery approx 10 mins. No production 12.30-2. P/copying by staff-post/collection. Typing/taping/cameras/laptops (power supply) by prior arrangement.
Records: for County of East Sussex & Brighton & Hove Unitary Authority. Diocesan RO for Chichester. PRs-fiche/film/Ts/originals if not copied. BTs-Ts. Quarter Sessions. Manorial. Electoral registers. Nonconformist. Schools. Family incl. America & West Indies. Directories. Newspapers. Baptismal index. Tithe. Maps. M/f-wills proved in Lewes Archdeaconry Court & the peculiar courts of Battle & South Malling/national index of wills/census/IGI.
Research Service: Charge made.
Facilities: Toilets. No public tel/refreshment facilities. Cafe/pub/shops nearby.
Publications: Free: Info leaflets: *Introductory Notes for Searchers. How to find a Will. Tracing your Family History/House. Genealogical Research Service.* (SAE) For sale: *Handlist of Registers of Births, Baptisms, Marriages, Deaths & Burials.*
Tourist Office: Tel: 01273 483448 Fax: 01273 484003
Remarks: Donations appreciated. **Note:** Current agreement with the Unitary Authority runs to March 1999, to be reviewed thereafter.

LEWIS, ISLE OF, see Stornaway.

LEWISHAM, see London Borough of.

Bishopdale Archives, West Lane House, Bishopdale, LEYBURN, N. Yorks DL8 3TG Appt. Houses. Families. Collection of census index booklets for area.

Lichfield Record Office, The Friary, LICHFIELD, Staffs WS13 6QG Tel: 01543 510720 **Fax:** 01543 510715
Opening Hours: M.-F. 9.30-5 Closure: Public hols+Tues following Spring & Summer+Christmas Eve pm & Dec 27th.
Parking: None.
Disabled: Toilet. Lift.
Children: Accompanied: At archivist's discretion. Unaccompanied: 11 yrs+
Appointments: Prior booking for seats/viewers-a few days. Entry-register+reader's ticket+ID. 12 seats+4 film+5 fiche.
Ordering System: Prior ordering by letter/tel. Catalogue nos sometimes required. Five ordered, one/five produced. Delivery 2-25 mins. No production 12.30-2.30. Last order: 12 & 3.30. P/copying restricted, by staff-post. Typing/taping not permitted. Cameras/laptops (power supply by prior appt) allowed.
Records: for Lichfield. Diocesan RO for Lichfield. PRs-fiche/Ts/originals if not copied. BTs available. Bishops registers from 1296. Probate. Marriage bonds. Lichfield Cathedral. Tamworth/Lichfield Methodist Circuit. Local authority. Charities. Manorial. Business. Solicitors. Family wills from the Lichfield Probate Registry 1858-1928. M/f-census/ newspapers/IGI.
Research Service: Charge made.
Facilities: Toilets. No public tel/refreshment facilities. Café/pub/shops nearby.
Publications: Free: Info leaflets: *Lichfield RO. Dwelling in the Past?* (SAE) For sale: Family History Pack. *List of PRs. List of Registers of Staffs Nonconformist Churches. Staffordshire & the Great Rebellion. Canal Records. Railway Records. Staffordshire Gazetteer. Business Records. Public Utilities.*
Tourist Office: Tel: 01543 252109 Fax: 01543 417308
Remarks: Bags not allowed-lockers. Donations appreciated. Station: Lichfield City.

Staffordshire Regimental Museum, Whittingdon Barracks, LICHFIELD, Staffs WS14 9PY Tel: 0121 3113240 Appt. by letter. Staffordshire Regiment (Prince of Wales's), South & North Staffordshire Regiments (38th & 64th Regiments of Foot), 98th & 80th Regiments of Foot. Militia & volunteers. Diaries. Documents. Newspaper cuttings. Photographs. Catalogue to collections available.

Limerick Regional Archives, The Granary, Michael Street, LIMERICK, Eire Tel: 061 410777 **Note:** The Director & staff who are specialists in family history, prefer to deal with research by post as space is extremely limited-no room for personal search (deposit for costed assessment which is returned if search is pointless). Some 1.1 million records are on a computerised database which contains all church records to 1900, Roman Catholic, Church of Ireland, Presbyterian & Methodist. Civil B.M.D. records to 1911. Tithe Applotment Books. 1901 census. Manual indexes & alphabetically arranged Ts. to Griffiths Valuation c1850. Newspapers c1780-1821. Wills post 1858. Limerick's main cemetery from 1855. Re-organisation in 1998 may separate the archives from the genealogy service but should not generally change.

Lincolnshire Archives, St. Rumbold Street, LINCOLN, Lincs LN2 5AB Tel: 01522 526204 (enquiries); 01522 525158 (Search Room appts & enquiries) **Fax:** 01522 530047 **E-mail:** archives@lincsdoc.demon.co.uk
Internet: http://www.lincs-archives.com
Opening Hours: M. (Mar-Oct) 1-7; M. (Nov-Feb) 11-5; T.-F. 9-5; Sat 9-4 Closure: Public hols+Tues following Easter, Spring & August.
Parking: Limited-free.
Disabled: Access. Toilet.
Children: Accompanied: At archivist's discretion. Unaccompanied: 14 yrs+
Appointments: Prior booking for viewers-1 wk. Entry-reader's ticket requiring 2 mini photos+ID. 23 seats+6 film+25 fiche-1 fiche reader/printer.
Ordering System: Prior ordering by letter/tel. Catalogue nos sometimes required. Number ordered at archivist's discretion, up to fifteen produced. Delivery 15 mins. Last order: 75 mins before closure. P/copying by staff-same day/post. Typing/taping/laptops (power supply) permitted. Cameras not allowed.
Records: for the historical County of Lincolnshire. Diocesan RO for Lincoln. PRs-fiche/Ts/originals if not copied. BTs-film. Quarter/Petty Sessions. Probate-outstanding collection of wills & inventories. Earliest Bishop's register in western Christendom. Parish. Coroners. County Courts. Manorial. Schools. Hospitals. Poor Law. Enclosure. Local authority. Nonconformist. Marriage licences. Estate. Family. Solicitors. Business. Manufacturers. Charities. Maps. MIs. Directories. Electoral registers. M/f-GRO indexes/ wills 1858-193/census/IGI.
Research Service: Charge made.
Facilities: Toilets. No public tel/refreshment facilities. Cafe/pub/shops nearby.
Publications: Free: Info leaflets: *Tracing your Family History. Discovering the History of your Village/House. Genealogical Research Service.* (SAE) For sale: *Deposited Registers.*

LINCOLN

Poor Law Union Records. Archivists' Reports.
Tourist Office: Tel: 01522 529828
Remarks: Bags not allowed-lockers. Donations appreciated. See *Genealogical Sources in Lincolnshire.* 3rd ed (1996). Station: Lincoln Central.

Lincoln Central Library, Free School Lane, LINCOLN, Lincs LN2 1EZ Tel: 01522 549160
Opening Hours: M.-F. 9.30-7; Sat 9.30-4 Closure: Public hols.
Parking: Public nearby-paying.
Disabled: W/chair access.
Children: At librarian's discretion.
Appointments: Prior booking for viewers-2/3 days. Many seats+6 film+3 fiche-2 reader/printers.
Ordering System: Prior ordering by letter/tel. Three ordered & produced. Orders in last 15 mins likely to be refused. P/copying restricted, by staff & DIY. Typing/taping/laptops (power supply) permitted on reserving a study booth. Cameras not allowed.
Records: for Lincolnshire. Poll books. Protestation returns. Exley's Inns. Directories. Photographs. Maps. M/f-Cokayne MSS/Ross MSS/List of War dead in Lincolnshire Regiment/newspapers/census/IGI.
Research Service: None.
Facilities: Toilets/public tel. No refreshment facilities. Café/pub/shops nearby.
Publications: Free: Info leaflets: *Family History/Local Studies in Lincolnshire Libraries.* (SAE).
Remarks: Bags allowed-small lockers.

Museum of Lincolnshire Life, Old Barracks, Burton Road, LINCOLN, Lincs LN1 3LY Tel: 01522 528448. Appt. History of 10th Regiment of Foot, Royal Lincolnshire Regiment. Diaries. Digests. Photographs.

LINCOLNSHIRE, see Grimsby; Lincoln.

LINENHALL LIBRARY, see Belfast.

LISKEARD, see Cornwall

King's Regiment Collection, Regional History Dept., Liverpool Museum, William Brown Street, LIVERPOOL, Merseyside L3 8EN Tel: 0151 478 4399 Appt. Archives of the King's Regiment.

Liverpool Record Office, Central Library, William Brown Street, LIVERPOOL, Merseyside L3 8EW Tel: 0151 2255417 **Fax:** 0151 2071342 (for library). **E-mail:** ro@lvpublib.demon.co.uk
Internet: http://www.liverpool.gov.uk/public/council_info/direct-info/leisure/libraries/ro.htm
Opening Hours: M.-Th. 9-7.30; F. 9-5; Sat 10-4 Closure: Public hols+Christmas wk.
Parking: None.
Disabled: Access-ramp. Lift. Toilet.
Children: Accompanied: At archivist's discretion. Unaccompanied: 16 yrs+at archivist's discretion.
Appointments: Prior booking for viewers-2 wks. Entry-register+Liverpool RO ticket. 50 seats+8 film+4 fiche. Advance booking fee required for M/f.
Ordering System: Prior ordering unnecessary. Five ordered & produced. Delivery 10-15 mins. Ordering on the hour & ½ hr. On Fri & Sat no orders at 12.30 & 1.30. Last order: 30 mins before closure. P/copying restricted, by staff-post, & DIY. Typing/taping/laptops not permitted. Cameras by prior arrangement.
Records: for Liverpool/parts of Lancashire & Cheshire. Diocesan RO for Liverpool. PRs-film/Ts/original if not copied. Cemeteries. Nonconformist. Deeds. Schools. Crew lists. Manorial. Family. Estate. Trade unions. Business. Poor Law. Probate. Electoral rolls. Town Books. Newspapers. Directories. Photographs. Maps. M/f-GRO indexes/census.
Research Service: None.
Facilities: Toilets/public tel/restaurant/drink vending machine. Cafe/pub/shops nearby.
Publications: Free: Info leaflets: *General Information. C of E & Roman Catholic parish records. Lists of classes of records.* (SAE).
Tourist Office: Merseyside Welcome Centre Tel: 0151 7093631 Fax: 0151 7080204 Atlantic Pavilion Tel: 0151 7088854 Fax: 0151 7098129
Remarks: Bags not allowed. Station: Lime Street.

Merseyside Maritime Museum-Maritime Archive & Library, Albert Dock, LIVERPOOL, Merseyside L3 4AQ Tel: 0151 4784418 **Fax:** 0151 4784590
Opening Hours: T.W.Th. 10.30-4.30 Closure: Mon/Fri+Public hols.
Parking: Public nearby.
Disabled: Disabled friendly. Only 2 w/chair users at any one time.
Children: Accompanied: At archivist's discretion. Unaccompanied: 18 yrs+
Appointments: Prior booking for viewers-1 day. Entry-register+fee or Maritime Record Centre reader's ticket.
Ordering System: Prior ordering by letter/telephone. Catalogue nos necessary. Three ordered & produced. Delivery 15-30 mins. No production 12.30-1.30. Last order: 4pm. P/copying by staff-same day/post/collection. Typing/taping/laptops not permitted. Cameras by prior arrangement.
Records: for Maritime history. Liverpool Registers of Merchant Ships. Mersey Docks & Harbour Company. Seamens charity/educational records. Shipping. Diaries of emigrants & seamen. Accounts of Slave

Traders. Photographs. Maps. Charts. Emigration. Passenger lists.
Research Service: None.
Facilities: Toilets/public tel. in museum. Restaurant. Café/pub/shops nearby.
Publications: Free: Info leaflets. (SAE) For sale: *The Leaving of Liverpool* (emigration). *Ships & Seafarers in 19th Century Liverpool. Guide to the Maritime Archives. Emigration-a Bibliography.*
Remarks: Bags not allowed-lockers.

Merseyside Police Headquarters, Canning Place, LIVERPOOL, Merseyside L69 1JD Tel: 0151 7778568 Contact Mr Tony Mossman. Not open to the public. Limited research can be undertaken on request.

Merseyside Record Office, 4th Floor, Cunard Buildings, Pier Head, LIVERPOOL, Merseyside L3 1EG Tel: 0151 2368038 **Fax:** 0151 2365827
Opening Hours: T. 9-5 Closure: Mon/Wed/Thurs/Fri+Public hols+Christmas wk.
Parking: None.
Disabled: Lift..
Children: Accompanied: At archivist's discretion. Unaccompanied: 16 yrs+at archivist's discretion.
Appointments: Prior booking for seats. Entry-reader's ticket+ID. 10 seats.
Ordering System: Prior ordering by letter/telephone. Catalogue nos sometimes required. Five ordered & produced. Delivery 10-15 mins. P/copying restricted, by staff-same day/post/collection. Typing/taping/laptops not permitted. Cameras allowed.
Records: for Merseyside. County Council. Coroners. Hospital. Nonconformist. Estate. Societies. Business. Family. Deeds. Fire Brigade. Plans.
Research Service: None.
Facilities: Toilets. No public tel. Room for own food. Café/pub nearby.
Publications: Free: Info leaflets: *General Information.* (SAE) For sale: *Public Health on Merseyside: a guide to local sources. Education on Merseyside: a guide to local sources.*
Remarks: Note: Probable move to Central Library, William Brown Street, Liverpool (see entry) towards the end of 1998. Station: B.R.-Lime Street; Merseyrail-James Street.

Special Collections & Archives, University of Liverpool Libraries, Sydney Jones Library, University of Liverpool, P.O. Box 123, LIVERPOOL, Merseyside L69 3DA Tel: 0151 7942696 **Fax:** 0151 7942681 **E-mail:** archives@liv.ac.uk
Internet: http://www.liv.ac.uk/library/livhomep.html
Opening Hours: M.-F. 9.30-4.45 Closure: Public hols+2 wks at Christmas.
Parking: Yes-need visitor's car parking permit, can be supplied in advance or on day of visit.
Disabled: Access. Lift. Toilet.
Children: At archivist's discretion.
Appointments: Prior booking for seats/viewers appreciated. Entry-register+ID. 11 seats+1 film.
Ordering System: Prior ordering by letter/telephone. Catalogue nos preferred. Three ordered, two produced. Delivery 5 mins. P/copying restricted, by staff-same day/post/collection. Typing/taping permitted provided no disturbance to others. Laptops (power supply) allowed. Cameras not allowed.
Records: for Liverpool University & City, Cheshire. Widnes Halmote Rolls 1748-1863. Private papers. Deeds. Business. Family. Archives of the University. Gypsy Lore Society 1896-1974. Cunard Steamship Co 1840-1945. Social work archives. National sporting bodies.
Research Service: None.
Facilities: Toilets/public tel. Room for own food/drink vending machine. Café/pub/shops nearby.
Publications: Free: Info leaflets: *Business Archives. Social Work Archives. Sports Archives.* (SAE).
Remarks: Storage for bags-coin operated lockers. Station: Lime Street.

Powys County Archives Office, County Hall, LLANDRINDOD WELLS, Powys LD1 5LG Tel: 01597 826088 **Fax:** 01597 827162
E-mail: archives@powys.gov.uk
Internet: http://www.powys.gov.uk
Opening Hours: T.-Th. 10-12.30; 1.30-5; F. 10-12.30; 1.30-4 Closure: Mon+Public hols+1st two wks in Feb.
Parking: Yes-free.
Disabled: Access.
Children: Accompanied: At archivist's discretion. Unaccompanied: 12 yrs+
Appointments: Prior booking for seats/viewers-3/4 days. Entry-register+CARN+ ID. 4 seats+4 film/fiche.
Ordering System: Prior ordering by letter/tel. Catalogue nos required. Number ordered at archivist's discretion, four produced. Delivery 5 mins. P/copying restricted, by staff-same day. Typing/taping/camera/laptops (power supply) at archivist's discretion.
Records: for old Counties of Breconshire/Montgomeryshire/Radnorshire. PRs-film. Quarter Sessions 1690 on. Poor Law. Highways. Education. Boroughs. Districts. Land Valuation Registers. Electoral rolls. Deeds. Estate. Probate, Tithe maps. Maps. Newspapers. Directories. MIs. M/f-index of BMD/census/IGI.
Research Service: None.

Facilities: Toilets. No public tel/refreshment facilities. Café/pub/shops nearby.
Publications: Free: Info leaflets: *House History. Family History.* (SAE) For sale: *Office Guide.*
O. R: Llandrindod Library, Cefnllys Rd, LLANDRINDOD WELLS LD1 5LD Tel: 01597 826860; **Brecon Area Library**, Ship St, BRECON LD3 9AE Tel: 01874 623346; **Newtown Area Library**, Park Lane, NEWTOWN SY16 1EJ Tel: 01686 626934; **Radnorshire Museum**, Temple St, LLANDRINDOD WELLS LD1 5DL Tel: 01597 824513; **Powysland Museum**, The Canal Wharf, WELSHPOOL SY21 7AQ Tel: 01938 554656
Tourist Office: Tel: 01597 822600
Remarks: Bags not allowed-lockable cupboard. Donations appreciated.

Anglesey County Record Office, Shirehall, Glanhwfard, LLANGEFNI, Isle of Anglesey LL77 7TW Tel: 01248 752080
Opening Hours: M.-F. 9-1; 2-5 Closure: Public hols+1st full wk in Nov.
Parking: Yes-free.
Disabled: By prior arrangement-1 wks notice. Steps to ground floor where docs can be consulted.
Children: At archivist's discretion.
Appointments: Prior booking for viewers-2 days. Entry-register+CARN. 18 seats+2 film+3 fiche.
Ordering System: Prior ordering by letter/tel but unnecessary. Catalogue nos required. Three documents/one newspaper/one bundle/six photos ordered & produced. Delivery 5 mins. P/copying by staff-same day. Typing/taping/laptops (power supply) at archivist's discretion. Cameras not permitted.
Records: for Isle of Anglesey. PRS-film/photocopies/Ts. Quarter Sessions. Poor Law. Parish. Local Government. Nonconformist. Private. Family. Business.
Research Service: Charge made.
Facilities: Toilets. No public tel/refreshment facilities. Cafe/pub/shops nearby.
Publications: Free and for sale. (SAE).
Remarks: Bags not allowed-lockers. **Note:** There are plans for a new RO but location as yet undecided, but it will be Llangefni. Station: Bangor (main), Llanfairpwll or Holyhead.

Midlothian Council Libraries, Local Studies Centre, 2 Clerk Street, LOANHEAD, Midlothian EH20 9DR Tel: 0131 4402210 Ext. 226 **Fax:** 0131 4404635
E-mail: mc_libhq_blossoming@compuserve.com
Internet: http://www.lim.viscount.org.uk/earl/members/midlothian/inde x.html
Opening Hours: M. 9-5; 6-8; T.-Th. 9-5; F. 9-3.45 Closure: Public hols.
Parking: Yes-free.
Disabled: Ramp. Toilet.
Children: At librarian's discretion.
Appointments: Prior booking unnecessary. 9 seats+1 film+3 fiche-1 reader/printer.
Ordering System: Prior ordering by letter/telephone. Number ordered & produced at librarian's discretion. P/copying by staff-same day. Typing not permitted. Taping allowed if no disturbance to others. Cameras/laptops (power supply) allowed.
Records: for Midlothian. Burghs records of Bonnyrigg/Lasswade/Dalkeith/Loanhead/Pen icuik. School log books. Local school boards 1870-1919. Family. Local organisations. Valuation Rolls 1867-1975. Prints. Photographs. Newspapers. Maps. PRs-post 1975. M/f-OPRs/some newspapers/census/IGI.
Research Service: None.
Facilities: Toilets. No public tel/refreshment facilities. Café/pub/shops nearby.
Publications: Free: Info leaflet: *Local Studies in Midlothian.* (SAE).
Remarks: Note: Separate Archive store is being set up, some less used material may be there. Transfer arrangements are not clear yet. Station: Edinburgh.

Morpeth Records Centre, The Kylins, LOANSDEAN, Morpeth, Northumberland NE61 2EQ (Postal enquiries: Northumberland Record Office, Melton Park, North Gosforth, Newcastle upon Tyne. NE3 5QX) **Tel:** 01670 504084 **Fax:** 01670 514815
Internet: http:/www.swinhope.demon.co.uk/genuki/nbl/northumberlandro/ - Information about available records.
Opening Hours: M.F. 9.30-1; 2-5; T. 9.30-1; 2-8 Closure: Wed/Thurs+Public hols+Christmas period
Parking: 3 spaces.
Disabled: Toilet.
Children: At archivist's discretion.
Appointments: Prior booking for viewers-1 wk for locals-visitors from away may book in advance. Entry-register. 8 seats+14 film+3 fiche-1 reader/printer.
Ordering System: No prior ordering allowed. Three ordered & produced. Delivery 5-10 mins. Last order: Mon/Fri 4.30. Tues-7.30. P/copying by staff-by post/collection (within a wk). Typing/taping/cameras not permitted. Laptops (power supply) allowed.
Records: for Northumberland. Diocesan RO for Newcastle. Diocese of Newcastle & Hexham (Roman Catholic). PRs-film/Ts/originals if not copied-for Northumberland-Newcastle/Alston/Garragill/Nenthhead (Cumbria)/Edmundbyers & Muggleswick (Durham). Nonconformists. Quarter/Petty Sessions. Magistrates Courts. Coroners. Lieutenancy. Urban/Rural Districts. PLU. Highways. Constabulary. Pre-nationalisation coalmines. County/

Boroughs Council. Civil Parishes. Sanitary Authorities. Schools. Hospital/Health Authorities. Coal mining. Roman Catholic & Diocesan parish records. MSS of Hexhamshire Wills 1688-1799 which are held at the Borthwick Institute. M/f-census/GRO Indexes 1837-1980/FH sources incl pedigrees & electoral registers/Civil cemeteries/copy wills 1858-1941/nonconformist records & registers/IGI.
Research Service: Charge made
Facilities: Toilet. No public tel/refreshment facilities. Café/pub nearby.
Publications: Free leaflets: *Morpeth Records Centre* incl. Map. *Historic Census Returns for Northumberland 1841-1891. Northumberland Wills. Civil Cemetery Records. Introduction to the ROs.* Publications list. (A5 SAE). For sale: various.
O.R. Morpeth Library, Gas House Lane, MORPETH, NE61 1TH
Tourist Office: Tel: 01670 511323 Fax: 01670 511326
Remarks: Donations appreciated. **Note:** See entry for Berwick-upon-Tweed RO.

LONDON BOROUGHS
Publications of assistance to tracing a family history in London, Middlesex & Surrey (also see entries for Surrey)
P. Wolfson, rev. C. Webb, *Greater London Cemeteries & Crematoria.*
Silverthorne, E. Ed, *London local archives* 3rd ed. (1994 GLAN) (4th edition in preperation)
Webb, C. *My Ancestors were Londoners* (pub. SOG). *A guide to London and Middlesex genealogy and records* (1994). *Genealogical research in Middlesex, a collection of research aids* (1990). *A guide to London and Middlesex manorial records* (1994). *A preliminary guide to Middlesex parish documents (incl. poor law records)* 2nd ed (1993). *A provisional list of City of London poor law records* (1992). *London, Middlesex and Surrey workhouse Records: a guide to their nature and location* (1992).
Gibson Guides incl: *Record Offices: How to find them* (7th ed). *Lists of Londoners* (2nd ed). *Poor Law Union Records.* (see *Family Tree Magazine* Postal Book Listings).

London Borough of Barking & Dagenham, Valence House Museum, Becontree Avenue, DAGENHAM, Essex. RM8 3HT Tel: 0181 5958404
Opening Hours: T-F. 9.30-1; 2-4.30; Sat 10-4. Closure: Mon+Public hols.
Parking: 4 spaces.
Disabled: Ground floor toilets
Children: At staff's discretion
Appointments: Prior booking for seats-1/2 wks. Entry-register. c10 seats
Ordering System: Prior ordering by letter/tel. Number ordered & produced at staff's discretion. Delivery immediate. P/copying by staff-same day/post/ collection. Typing/ taping/laptops permitted. Cameras by arrangement.
Records: for ancient parishes of Barking/Dagenham Essex. Urban Districts-Essex Boroughs & London Boroughs of same. PRs-film/fiche/photocopies/Ts. Local Government. Title deeds. Lawes Chemical Co. archives. Fanshawe family papers incl diplomatic papers of Sir Richard Fanshawe (17thC). Maps & plans. Photographs. Local History collection.
Research Service: None
Facilities: Toilets. No public tel. Room for own food. Cafe/pub/shops nearby.
Publications: Free: Info leaflet+various others.
O.R: Valence Library also at the above address, holds maps/local histories/ PRs-film/fiche.
Remarks: Donations appreciated. Station: Chadwell Heath.

London Borough of Barnet, Local Studies & Archives Centre, Chapel Walk, Egerton Gardens, LONDON NW4 4EH (Postal address: Hendon Library, The Burroughs, Hendon, London NW4 4BQ) **Tel:** 0181 3592876 **Fax:** 0181 3592885
Opening Hours: T.W.Sat 9.30-12.30;1.30-5; Th. 12.30-7.30 Closure: Public hols.
Parking: 6 spaces.
Disabled: No facilities.
Children: At archivist's discretion.
Appointments: Prior booking for viewers-1 wk. Entry-register. 8 seats+1 film+1 fiche-1 reader/printer.
Ordering System: Prior ordering by letter/tel. Catalogue nos sometimes required. Number ordered & produced at archivist's discretion. Delivery 5 mins. Last order: 15 mins before closure. P/copying by staff-post/DIY. Typing/taping/laptops (power supply) permitted. Cameras not allowed.
Records: for London Borough of Barnet-Edgware/Chipping Barnet/East Barnet/ Finchley/Friern Barnet/Hendon/ Totteridge parishes. PRs-film/fiche/Ts. Local authority. Civil parish. Urban District Council. Borough. Manorial. Nonconformist. Tithe. Maps. Photographs. M/f-census/newspapers.
Research Service: None.
Facilities: Toilets. No public tel/refreshment facilities. Café/pub/shops nearby.
Publications: For sale: Local interest books & maps incl O/S maps, pamphlets (Publications List).
O.R: Chipping Barnet Reference Library, Stapylton Road, BARNET, Herts; **Barnet Museum**, Wood Street, CHIPPING BARNET, Herts. EN5 4QS; **Church End Reference**

Library, 24 Hendon Lane, FINCHLEY; **Barnet Libraries**, Arts & Museum Education Services, Friern Barnet Lane, LONDON N11 3DL Tel: 0181 3593164. Local History collection incl Finchley.
Remarks: Bags not allowed. **Note:** Lease expires on present building in 2 yrs-suitable premises now being sought. Station: Hendon Central.

London Borough of Bexley, Bexley Local Studies Centre, Hall Place, Bourne Road, BEXLEY, Kent. DA5 1PQ Tel: 01322 526574 **Fax:** 01322 522921
Opening Hours: M-Sat 9-5. Closure: Public hols+2 days in Dec.
Parking: Yes.
Disabled: Ramp-access.
Children: Accompanied: 5 yrs+ Unaccompanied: 8 yrs+
Appointments: Prior booking for m/f printer readers (2 hrs per day). Entry-register. 13 seats+3 film+5 fiche-3 reader/printers.
Ordering System: Prior ordering by letter/tel. Number ordered & produced at librarian's discretion-usuallly three. Delivery 11-15 mins. P/copying restricted, by staff-same day/DIY. Typing not permitted. Taping/laptops/cameras allowed.
Records: for the London Borough of Bexley-Sidcup/Welling/E. Wickham/Bexley/Bexleyheath/Crayford/Erith/Blackfen/Thame smead/Barnehurst. Diocesan RO for Rochester churches in London Borough of Bexley-Rural Deaneries of Erith/Sidcup. PRs-film/fiche/Ts/originals if not copied. Local authority. Civil parishes. Local schools. Business. Societies. Family incl Estates of Danson/Hall Place/Footscray Place/Belverdere. Special collection on William Morris resident in area 1860-65. Newspapers. Directories. Maps. Photographs. M/f-census/1881 census index/IGI.
Research Service: None.
Facilities: Toilets/public tel/café in adjacent car park. No refreshment facilities. Café/pub nearby. Shops-10 mins.
Publications: Free: *Past & Present* (general info). Catalogue of Publications+order form. (A5 SAE). For sale: *Family History in Bexley*. Studies notes on aspects of Local History. Maps. Posters, etc.
O.R: Bexley Museum (same address as above); **Erith Museum**, Erith Library, Walnut Tree Road, ERITH, Kent
Tourist Office: Central Library: Tel: 0181 3039052 Fax: 0181 3037872
Remarks: Donations appreciated. See *West Kent Sources: A Guide to Genealogical Research in the Diocese of Rochester* (N.W. Kent FHS. revised ed). **Note:** There is a possibility of re-location of this centre in the medium term.

London Borough of Brent, Grange Museum of Community History Library & Archive, Cricklewood Library, 152 Olive Road, LONDON NW2 6UY Tel: 0181 937 3540 Appt. Borough of Brent & predecessors-former Boroughs of Willesden/Wembley+medical health reports. Willesdon vestry. Churchwardens & overseers accounts. Electoral registers. Rate books. Maps. Newspapers. Photograph collection. **Note:** No reply was received from this library so the information supplied here has mainly been taken from the 3rd Ed.

London Borough of Bromley, Local Studies & Archives Section, Central Library, High Street, BROMLEY, Kent. BR1 1EX Tel: 0181 4609955 Ext 261 **Fax:** 0181 3139975 **E-mail:** bromley.cenlib@cityscape.co.uk
Opening Hours: M.W.F. 9.30-6; T.Th. 9.30-8; Sat 9.30-5 Closure: Public hols.
Parking: Public nearby-paying.
Disabled: Disabled friendly. Parking by prior arrangement.
Children: At archivist's discretion.
Appointments: Prior booking for seats/viewers-1 wk. Entry-register. 4 seats+2 film+6 fiche-2 film+1fiche reader/printers.
Ordering System: Prior ordering by letter/tel. Catalogue nos sometimes required. Number ordered at staff's discretion, three produced. Delivery 10 mins max. No production 12-2. P/copying restricted, by staff-same day. Typing/taping/cameras/laptops (power supply) by prior arrangement.
Records: for London Borough of Bromley-Bromley/Beckenham/Penge/Orping ton/Chiselhurst. Diocesan RO for Rochester-Deaneries of Bromley/Beckenham/Orpington. PRs-film/fiche/Ts/originals if not copied. Local authority. Parish. Nonconformists. Harlow Bequest-Orpington & Kent. Maps. Local collection. M/f-GRO Indexes 1837-1983/census/1881 census Index/Kent Directories/Newspapers/IGI/BigR.
Research Service: None.
Facilities: Toilets-nearby. Public tel. No refreshment facilities. Café/pub/shops nearby.
Publications: Free leaflets: *Census Returns. Beginning Your Family History in Bromley L.S. Library. Family History Sources.* (A5 SAE). For sale: Various .
Remarks: See entry for Centre for Kentish Studies, Maidstone for other local archives. See *West Kent Sources: A Guide to Genealogical Research in the Diocese of Rochester* (N.W. Kent FHS rev. ed.). Station: Bromley South.

London Borough of Camden, Camden Local Studies & Archives Centre, Holborn Library, 32-38 Theobald's Road, LONDON WC1X 8PA Tel: 0171 4136342 **Fax:** 0171 4136284

Opening Hours: M.Th. 10-7; T. 10-6; F. 10-5; Sat 10-2; 2-5 Closure: Wed+Public hols.
Parking: None.
Disabled: Access. Car parking by prior arrangement.
Children: At archivist's discretion.
Appointments: Prior booking for viewers. Entry-register. 14 seats+5 film+1 fiche-1 reader/printer-some film/fiche.
Ordering System: Prior ordering by letter/tel. Catalogue nos sometimes required. Number ordered & produced at staff's discretion. Delivery 5-10 mins. Records stored elsewhere need prior ordering. P/copying restricted/DIY. Typing/taping not permitted. Laptops/cameras allowed.
Records: for London Borough of Camden-Camden/Hampstead/Holborn/St. Pancras. PRs-film/Ts (originals are at the London Metropolitan Archives, see entry, except for those of St. Andrew Holborn which are at the Guildhall Library see entry). Parish/vestry/borough records incl mins-some on m/f 1856-1980s. Ratebooks & valuation lists. Manorial. Electoral registers. Deeds. Business. Family & estate. Societies. MIs. 1801 & 1811 brief census schedules for Hampstead. Kentish Town Rolls (19thC drawings). Maps & plans. Directories. Heal collection-maps /books/docs/illustrations/posters/playbills-mainly m/f. Wallis Collection-prints/drawings of Camden/some of Islingon & St. Marylebone. Bellmoor/Dalziel collections+others. Newspapers & periodicals. Photographs. Theatre programmes & posters. M/f-census/Highgate Cemetery 1839-May 1984.
Research Service: None.
Facilities: Toilets. No public tel/refreshment facilities. Café/pub/shops nearby.
Publications: Free leaflets: *Information Guide* with map. Publications list. *PRs. Newspapers. Local Books. Rate books & Valuation lists. Lists of researchers. Directories & Electoral Registers. Maps. MIs. Record Offices & Libraries in London.* (A4 SAE). For sale: *Camden Local Studies & Archives Centre: a brief guide to the collections. Camden now & then: a student's guide to the Local Studies Library.*
Remarks: Note: The Swiss Cottage Library and Holborn collections are now at this Centre. Most Poor Law records are at the London Metropolitan Archives. Underground: Holborn/Chancery Lane.

London Borough of Croydon, Croydon Local Studies Library & Archives Service, Central Library, Croydon Clocktower, Katherine Street, CROYDON, Surrey CR9 1ET Tel: 0181 760 5400 **Fax:** 0181 253 1004
E-mail: dparr@library.croydon.gov.uk
Internet: www.croydon.gov.uk
Opening Hours: M. 9-7; T.W.F. 9-6; Th. 9.30-6; Sat 9-5 Closure: Public hols.
Parking: None.
Disabled: Access.
Children: At archivist's discretion.
Appointments: Prior booking unnecessary. Entry-register. 45 seats+3 film+6 fiche-4 reader printers.
Ordering System: Prior ordering by letter/tel. Six ordered & produced. P/copying restricted, by staff-same day. Typing/taping not permitted. Laptops/cameras allowed.
Records: for London Borough of Croydon-ancient parishes of Croydon/Addington/Sanderstead /Coulsden. PRs-film/Ts. Local authority. School. Quarter Sessions. PLU. Vestry. Family & estate. Business. Periodicals & pamphlets. Photographs. Maps.
Research Service: None.
Facilities: Toilets/public tel/restaurant. Cafe/pub/shops nearby.
Publications: Free leaflet: General Info. (SAE). For sale: Local History & Oral history publications in Clocktower shop.
Tourist Office: Tel: 0181 2531009 Fax: 0181 2531008
Remarks: Bags not allowed-lockers. Station: East Croydon.

London Borough of Ealing, Local History Library & Archives, Central Library, 103 Ealing Broadway Centre, EALING, London W5 5JY Tel: 0181 5673656 Ext. 37.
Opening Hours: T.Th. 9.30-7.45; W.F.Sat 9.30-5. Closure: Mon+occasional lunchtimes+Public hols+preceding Sat
Parking: Public nearby-paying.
Disabled: Lift. Wide aisles. Level floor.
Children: Accompanied: 8 yrs+ Unaccompanied: Archives: 16 yrs+ Library: 14 yrs+
Appointments: Prior booking for viewer. 6 seats+1 film-1 reader printer.
Ordering System: Prior ordering by letter/tel. Catalogue nos sometimes required. Number ordered & produced at archivist's discretion. Delivery 5 mins. No production (archives only) 12-2. Last order: 30 mins before closure (archives & library). P/copying restricted, by staff-same day. Typing/taping/cameras not permitted. Laptops (power supply) allowed.
Records: for Ealing/Acton/Southall/Norwood/ Brentford/Perivale/Hanwell. PRs-p/copies/Ts. Education/ Schools. Methodist. Electoral registers. Directories. Photographic survey of Borough of Ealing+other photographs. Poor Law. Vestry. Maps. Wetherall Papers (ADC to Duke of Kent, Queen Victoria's father). Greenslade Papers (Patron of Art, Potters etc.). M/f-census (1861-1891 unindexed)/1841-1851 (Surname index-covers parishes of Ealing/Acton

/Norwood/Greenford/Perivale/West Twyford/Hanwell/Southall/Norwood (school & vessels)/Northolt/1801&1811 census Ealing only/newspapers.
Research Service: Details on application with SAE.
Facilities: Toilets/public tel. in Mall where library situated. No refreshment facilities. Cafe/pub/shops in Mall.
Publications: No free leaflets at present but some may be available soon. For sale: Local History publications. Maps.
Remarks: Bags allowed but must be kept close at all times. **Note:** Computerisation in progress to facilitate production of handlists & finding aids. There may be a change in the authority organisation in the future. Station: Ealing Broadway (Rail & Underground)-5 mins walk.

London Borough of Enfield, Archives & Local History Unit, Local Borough of Enfield Libraries, Southgate Town Hall, Green Lanes, PALMERS GREEN, London N13 4XD Tel: 0181 9827453 **Fax:** 0181 982 7378
Opening Hours: M.-Sat 9-5 Closure: Public hols.
Parking: None.
Disabled: W/chair access-not Sat.
Children: At staff's discretion.
Appointments: Prior booking for viewers-2 days. Entry-register. 5 seats+2 film+2 fiche.
Ordering System: Prior ordering by letter/tel. Catalogue nos sometimes required. Number ordered & produced at staff's discretion. Delivery 5-10 mins. P/copying by staff-same day. Typing/taping/cameras/laptops (power supply) permitted.
Records: for former districts of Enfield/Edmonton/Southgate. PRs-Ts. Societies. Turnpike Trust. Rate books. Valuation lists. Enclosure awards. Directories. Newspaper cuttings. Photographs. Maps. Local History collection. M/f-census/newspapers.
Research Service: None.
Facilities: Toilets. No public tel/refreshment facilities. Café/pub/shops nearby.
Publications: Free leaflets: Series of brief histories & fact sheets covering various aspects of Enfield history (SAE).
Remarks: Station: Arnos Grove (L.T.) Palmers Green (B.R.).

London Borough of Greenwich, Greenwich Local History & Archives Library, Woodlands, 90 Mycenae Road, BLACKHEATH, London SE3 7SE Tel: 0181 8584631 **Fax:** 0181 2934721
Opening Hours: M.T. 9-5.30; Th. 9-8; Sat 9-5 Closure: Wed/Fri+ Public hols.
Parking: 5 spaces+street.
Disabled: Library on 1st Floor but documents can be consulted on ground floor by prior arrangement.
Children: Accompanied: At staff's discretion. Unaccompanied: 8 yrs+
Appointments: Prior booking for viewers-2 days. Entry-register. 12 seats+ 4 film+4 fiche-all reader/printers.
Ordering System: Prior ordering by letter/ tel. Catalogue nos sometimes required. Number ordered at staff discretion, four produced. Delivery 10 mins. P/copying by staff-same day. Typing not permitted. Taping only permitted under certain conditions. Cameras/laptops (battery) allowed.
Records: for Deptford (St. Nicholas)/ Greenwich/Charlton/Woolwich/Plumstead/ Shooters Hill/Eltham/Kidbrooke/Blackheath (part). Diocesan RO for Southwark-Greenwich parish. PRs-Ts/originals if not copied. Local authority. Roman Catholic. Board of Health. Deeds. Family. Estate. Business incl. Woolwich Ferry. Blackheath Justices mins. Rate books. Plans & surveys. Maps. Pamphlets. Photographic collection. A.R. Martin collection-c10,000 items of antiquarian & historical relevance to Greenwich/Blackheath /Charlton-also contains genealogical material re: Martin/Fuller/Newton families.
Research Service: None.
Facilities: Toilets. No public tel/refreshment facilities. Café/pub/shops nearby.
Publications: Free & for sale.
Tourist Office: Tel: 0181 8586376 Fax: 0181 8534607
Remarks: See *Family history in Greenwich* by L. Reilly (1991). **Note:**There will be a move to the Heritage Centre in Woolwich Arsenal by the year 2000, a co-location with Greenwich Borough Museum. Station: Westcombe Park.

London Borough of Hackney, Hackney Archives Dept., 43 De Beauvoir Road, LONDON N1 5SQ Tel: 0171 2412886 **Fax:** 0171 2416688 **E-mail:** archives@hackney.gov.uk
Internet: http://www.hackney.gov.uk/archives/first1.htm
Opening Hours: M.T.Th. 9.30-1; 2-5; 1st & 3rd Sat in mth 9.30-1; 2-5. Closure: Wed/Fri+Public hols+2 last wks in Feb.
Parking: On street-free.
Disabled: Disabled friendly.
Children: At archivist's discretion.
Appointments: Prior booking for seats/viewers-2 days, 1 wk for Sat. Entry-register. 10 seats+4 film+1 fiche-1 reader/printer.
Ordering System: Prior ordering by letter/tel. Catalogue nos sometimes required. Number ordered & produced at archivist's discretion. Delivery 10 mins. Last order: 15 mins before closure. P/copying by staff-same day/post.

Typing/taping/cameras not permitted. Laptops allowed.
Records: for London Borough of Hackney-Hackney/Shoreditch/Stoke Newington. PRs-film/originals if not copied. Post 1837 nonconformist registers. Land tax. Rate books. Voters lists. MIs. Abney Park Cemetery. Maps. Visual collection-photographs/prints/films. Sound recordings/oral history collection. Business incl. Bryant & May, match manufacturers/J & W Nicholson, gin distillers. John Dawson collection of early printed books. Local theatres incl. programmes/posters. Directories. M/f-newspapers.
Research Service: Charge made. Free advice on records held & specific enquiries.
Facilities: Toilets. No public tel/refreshment facilities. Café/pub nearby.
Publications: Free leaflets: *Sources for F.H./Maps/Ratebooks/Land Tax returns/street directories/voters' lists.* (A4 SAE). For sale: *Guide to Collections. Handlist of surviving parish & nonconformist registers with listings of present whereabouts.*
Tourist Office: Tel: 0181 9859055 Fax: 0171 8332193
Remarks: Bags not allowed-lockers. Donations appreciated. **Note:** A move from these premises is under consideration but nothing definite. The Friends of Hackney Archives also serves as the Local History Society and publishes an annual newsletter, *The Hackney Terrier*. Transport:: Buses from Victoria & Waterloo stations.

London Borough of Hammersmith & Fulham, Hammersmith & Fulham Archives & Local History Centre, The Lilla Huset, 191 Talgarth Road, LONDON W6 8BJ Tel: 0181 7415159/0181 7483020 Ext 3850. **Fax:** 0181 7414882
Internet: http://www.ftech.net/~haflibs
Opening Hours: M. 9.30-8; T.Th. 9.30-1; 1st Sat in mth 9.30-1 Closure: Wed/Fri+Public hols+1 wk in Jan-usually 3rd.
Parking: None.
Disabled: Disabled friendly-free parking by prior arrangement.
Children: Accompanied: At staff's discretion. Unaccompanied: Secondary school age.
Appointments: Prior booking for seats/viewers-1 day. Entry-register. 10 seats+3 film+3 fiche-1 reader/printer.
Ordering System: Prior ordering by letter/tel. Number ordered & produced at archivist's discretion. Delivery-5 mins. P/copying by staff-same day. Typing/taping/cameras/laptops (power supply) permitted.
Records: for Hammersmith & Fulham from 17thC on-incl vestries of these parishes. Fulham Board of Works. Metropolitan boroughs of Hammersmith & Fulham/St. Paul's Church/Hammersmith. Nonconformists. West London Hospital. Electoral registers. Rate books. Cemetery. Schools. Business. Charities. Manorial-Fulham. Hammersmith Convent records 17-19thC's. Special collections relating to William Morris/A.P. Herbert & the White City Exhibition. Directories. Newspapers. Illustrations. Maps. Ephemera on history of the borough & its people. M/f-census (indexed by street)/1851 & 1881 census by personal name/IGI (London & Middx).
Research Service: None.
Facilities: Toilets. No public tel. Room for own food. Cafe/pub/shops nearby.
Publications: Free: Info leaflet with map. Publications list. (SAE). For sale: Maps. Prints. Postcards. Books of photographs. Various histories-*A History of Hammersmith. Pope's corner. Roman Catholic Institutions in Hammersmith & Fulham. Shepherds Bush. The Dickens Connection. Urania Cottage Home for Fallen Women. Shepherds Bush Markets & Traders. Fulham Hospital. The Nursery Gardens of Chelsea, Fulham, Hammersmith & Kensington.* Extensive collection of oral histories & reminiscences.
O.R: Museum of Fulham Palace, Bishops Avenue, LONDON, SW6 6EA
Remarks: Bags not allowed-lockers. Donations appreciated. See article-*Archives of Hammersmith & Fulham* by J. Farrell (West Middx. FHS Journal Mch 93). Underground: Hammersmith (District & Piccadilly) Hammersmith & City Line.

London Borough of Haringey, Haringey Archive Service, Bruce Castle Museum, Lordship Lane, LONDON N17 8NU Tel: 0181 8088772 **Fax:** 0181 8084118
Opening Hours: Twice a week+alternate Sat 1-4.45 (days vary from Wed pm to Fri pm).
Parking: 20 spaces.
Disabled: No facilities.
Children: Accompanied: 10 yrs+ Unaccompanied: Not allowed.
Appointments: Prior booking for seats/viewers-1 wk. Entry-form. 8 seats+2 film-2 reader/printers.
Ordering System: Prior ordering by letter/tel. Number ordered & produced at archivist's discretion. Delivery 5-10 mins. P/copying restricted, by staff-same day/post/collection. Typing/taping not permitted. Cameras/laptops (power supply) allowed.
Records: for Haringey-Tottenham/Wood Green/Hornsey. Local authority. Tottenham manorial rolls 1308-1732. Parish records-Tottenham/Hornsey. Tithe. Alexandra Palace. Local history books/pamphlets/maps/plans. Photographs. Newspapers. M/f-census.
Research Service: None.
Facilities: Toilets. No public tel. Room for own food. Cafe/pub nearby.
Publications: None.

Remarks: Donations appreciated. **Note:** Bruce Castle Museum is a museum of local & postal history. The archives of the Middlesex Regiment formerly at this museum are now at the National Army Museum (see entry). Station: Bruce Grove from Liverpool Street. Underground to Wood Green on Piccadillly Line, then 243 bus to Lordship Lane.

London Borough of Harrow, Harrow Reference Library, Civic Centre, Station Road, HARROW HA1 2UU Tel: 0181 4241056 (Postal address: P.O. Box 4, Civic Centre, Harrow HA1 2UU) Usually open. W/chair access. Local History collection.

London Borough of Havering, Reference & Information Library, St. Edward's Way, ROMFORD, Essex RM1 3AR Tel: 01708 772393/4 **Fax:** 01708 772391
Internet: http://www.earl,org.uk
Opening Hours: M.T.W.F. 9.30-8; Sat 9.30-4 Closure: Thurs+Public hols.
Parking: Public nearby-paying.
Disabled: Minicom Tel: 01708 772237. Induction loop at Enquiry Desk. Lift available on request. Loan of magnifying lens.
Children: At librarian's discretion.
Appointments: Prior booking for viewers-1 day. 80 seats+2 film+3 fiche-2 reader/printers.
Ordering System: Prior ordering by letter/tel. Number ordered & produced at archivist's discretion. Delivery-5 mins. Last order: 15 mins before closure. P/copying restricted-DIY. Typing/taping/cameras/laptops (power supply) permitted.
Records: for South West Essex area with majority of material relating to the area of London Borough of Havering-Havering/ Romford/Hornchurch/Upminster/Rainham. PRs-film/fiche/Ts. Local authority. Parish rate books. Council min books. Romford Local Borough of Health. Maps & plans. Local History collection. M/f-census /newspapers. Some local items held at Essex RO Chemsford (see entry) on m/f for example-South Divisional Parliamentary Committee Chelmsford for Essex minute book (17thC) & Romford PLU mins.
Research Service: None.
Facilities: No toilet/public tel/refreshment facilities. Café/pub/shops nearby.
Publications: For sale: Postcards of old local views. *Romford Market 1247-1997. From country to Cockney. Romford Market within living memory. The Queen's Theatre, Hornchurch: a history. A history of the parish of Havering-atte-Bower. Essex Stubbers: a short history. Hornchurch & the New Zealand connection: the story of the N.Z. Convalescent Hospital in Hornchurch during the First World War. The Victoria History of Essex Vol. 7-Hornchurch & Romford. Childhood memories of Hornchurch 1914-1936.*

London Borough of Hillingdon, Hillingdon Heritage Service, Central Library, High Street, UXBRIDGE, Middx UB8 1HD Tel: 01895 250702 **Fax:** 01895 811164 **E-mail:** ccotton@lbhill,gov.uk
Opening Hours: M. 9.30-8; T.W.Th. 1-5.30; F. 10-5.30; Sat 9.30-12; 1-4 Closure: Public hols.
Parking: Public nearby-paying.
Disabled: Lift. Toilets.
Children: At staff's discretion.
Appointments: Prior booking necessary. Entry-register. 5 seats+2 film+3 fiche-3 reader/printers.
Ordering System: Prior ordering by letter/tel. Number ordered at staff's discretion, three produced. Delivery immediate. Records stored elsewhere need three days prior ordering. P/copying restricted, by staff-same day/DIY. Typing/ taping not permitted. Laptops allowed. Cameras by arrangement.
Records: for N.W. Middx-Ruislip/Harefield/ Ickenham/Uxbridge/Hillingdon/Hayes/Harlin gton/West Drayton/Cowley/Harmondsworth. PRs-film/Ts/originals on order. Parish records of St. John the Baptist, Hillingdon. Manorial. Council mins. Rate books. Uxbridge Board of Health. Nonconformists. Newspapers. Maps. Photographs. Prints. Films. Minet Estate collection-properties in Hayes.
Research Service: Under review.
Facilities: No toilet/public tel/refreshment facilities. Café/pub/shops nearby.
Publications: For sale: *Guide to Local History Resources.*
O.R: Feltham Library, 210 The Centre, FELTHAM, Middx TW13 6AW. Local History collection.
Tourist Office: 01895. 250706 Fax: 01895 239794
Remarks: Underground: Uxbridge (Metropolitan/Piccadilly).

London Borough of Hounslow, Chiswick Local Studies, Chiswick Library, Duke's Avenue, LONDON W4 2AB Tel: 0181 9941008 **Fax:** 0181 7427411
Opening Hours: M.Th. 9.30-8; T.F.Sat 9.30-5.30 Closure: Wed+Public hols.
Parking: None.
Disabled: No facilities.
Children: Accompanied: 7 yrs+ Unaccompanied: 10 yrs+
Appointments: Prior booking unnecessary. Entry-register+ID. 4 seats+1 film+1 fiche-1 reader/printer.
Ordering System: Prior ordering by letter/tel. Three ordered & produced. P/copying restricted, by staff-same day/post/ collection/DIY.
Typing/taping/laptops/cameras permitted.

Records: for Brentford/Chiswick. PRs-p/copies/Ts. Parish. Local authority. Rate books. Electoral registers. Newspapers. Maps. Prints. Directories. M/f-census.
Research Service: Charge made.
Facilities: No toilets/public tel/refreshment facilities. Café/pub/shops nearby.
Publications: Free & for sale.
Remarks: Station: Turnham Green.

London Borough of Hounslow, Hounslow Library, Local Studies Dept. 24 Treaty Centre, High Street, HOUNSLOW, Middx TW3 1ES Tel: 0181 5700622 **Fax**: 0181 8627602
Opening Hours: T.Th. 9.30-8; M.W.F.Sat 9.30-5.30 Closure: Public hols.
Parking: Public nearby-paying.
Disabled: Lift+automatic doors+ground floor entrance.
Children: Accompanied: 7 yrs+ Unaccompanied: 10 yrs+
Appointments: Prior booking unnecessary. Entry-register+ID. 8 seats+3 film+5 fiche-3 reader/printers.
Ordering System: Prior ordering by letter/tel. Three ordered & produced. P/copying restricted, by staff-same day/post/collection/DIY. Typing/taping/laptops permitted. Cameras at librarian's discretion.
Records: for Heston/Isleworth/Hounslow/Cranford/Hanworth/Bedfont/Feltham. PRs-Ts/originals if not copied. Local authority. Parish. Hounslow Borough. Rate books. Electoral registers. Maps. Newspapers. Photographs. M/f-census.
Research Service: Charge made.
Facilities: Toilet/public tel/restaurant. Café/pub/shops nearby.
Publications: Free & for sale.
O.R: Gunnersbury Park Museum, Pope's Lane, LONDON W3 8LQ
Tourist Office: Tel: 0181 5728279 Fax: 0181 5694330
Remarks: Station: Hounslow Central.

London Borough of Islington, Finsbury Local History Collection, Finsbury Library, 245 St. John Street, LONDON EC1V 4NB Tel: 0171 2787343 **Fax:** 0171 2788821
Internet: http://www.islington.gov.uk/council/info
Opening Hours: Library but not necessarily the collection. M.Th. 9-8; T.Sat 9-5; F. 9-1. Closure: Wed+Public hols.
Parking: Public nearby-paying.
Disabled: No w/chair access to Local History Room but special arrangements can be made. Text magnifier in Library. Some staff with deaf awareness training.
Children: At staff's discretion.
Appointments: Prior booking for seats/viewers-1 wk. 4 seats+2 film+2 fiche-1 reader/printer.
Ordering System: Prior ordering by letter/tel. Three ordered & produced. Material produced from 10-12; 2-4.45. Delivery immediate. P/copying restricted, by staff-same day. Typing/taping/cameras not permitted. Laptops (power supply) allowed.
Records: for south part of present London Borough of Islington, roughly from Angel to City of London boundary, incls. Sadler's Wells/New River Head area but not Hoxton or Shoreditch. PRs-Ts (Harleian Socy. printed Ts St. James+Clerkenwell 1551-1754). Records of the former Metropolitan Borough of Finsbury & parishes which preceded it, incl. some Poor Law & Workhouse. Claremont Chapel Register of Bapts 1836-1973 incls. some lists of chapel members. 18/19thC's settlement exams for Clerkenwell (name indexes). Mins of the Metropolitan Boroughs incl. council mins. Deeds. Papers of local individuals & organisations. Rate books. Clerkenwell & St. Luke's vestries. Sadler's Wells Theatre-playbills/prints/cuttings/books/some archival material. Penton family & estate. Electoral registers. Finsbury Dispensary. Local History collection. M/f-census 1841 (Clerkenwell /St. Luke's/St. Sepulchre's)/newspapers/ Duplicated street indexes to census returns & name indexes to 1851 census for Clerkenwell & St. Luke's.
Research Service: Charge made-limited postal research.
Facilities: Toilet. Public tel. just outside library. No refreshment facilities. Café/pub/shops nearby.
Publications: Free: Info. leaflet with map. *Islington Local History Collections* (SAE). For sale: Maps.
O.R: St. John's Gate Museum; **Wesley's House Museum**.
Remarks: Bags allowed but must be placed away from users. Donations appreciated. **Note:** see Remarks for Islington about re-location of records. Underground: Farringdon/Angel. Rail: King's Cross.

London Borough of Islington, Islington History Collection, Central Reference Library, 2 Fieldway Crescent, LONDON N5 1PF Tel: 0171 6196931 **Fax:** 0171 6196939
Internet:
http://www.islington.gov.uk/council/info
Opening Hours: M.W.Th. 9-8; T. 9-5 Closure: Fri+Public hols.
Parking: None.
Disabled: Lift accessible by w/chair. Assistance available & special arrangements can be made. OCR reader (for printed material)-converts text to speech. Help available for deaf users.

Children: At staff's discretion.
Appointments: Prior booking for viewers-1/2 wks. Entry-register. 4 seats+2 film+3 fiche-2 reader/printers.
Ordering System: Prior ordering by letter/tel. Number ordered & produced at staff's discretion. Ordering times 10-12 & 2-4. Delivery immediate. Last order: 15 mins before closure, at staff's discretion. P/copying restricted, by staff-same day/post. Typing/taping/cameras not permitted. Laptops (power supply at staff's discretion) allowed.
Records: Parish of St. Mary, Islington-Archway area in north, to Angel in south. Northern part of present London Borough of Islington. Records for southern part are at Finsbury Library (see entry). PRs (St. Mary, Islington)-fiche (originals at London Metropolitan Archives, see entry)+parish chest records. Nonconformists. Civil parish of St. Mary, Islington. St. Mary's Vestry. Metropolitan Borough of Islington. Local maps & survey. Turnpike Trusts. Electoral registers. Deeds. Rate books. Directories. Newscuttings. Local History collection. Papers of local individuals & organisations. Some papers relating to Walter Sickert (artist). M/f-census/newspapers.
Research Service: Charge made.
Facilities: Toilets/public tel. No refreshment facilities. Drink vending machine. Café/pub nearby.
Publications: Free: Info. leaflet (SAE). For sale: various. Maps.
O.R: Islington Museum, Upper Street, LONDON N1
Tourist Office: Tel: 0171 2788787
Remarks: Bags allowed but staff may require them to be separated from user-limited storage. Donations appreciated. **Note:** Re-location is planned & merger of collections will be put into effect-likely date 2000. Underground: Highbury/Islington (Victoria line & rail). Holloway Road (Piccadilly line).

Royal Borough of Kensington & Chelsea, Chelsea Public Library, Local Studies Dept., Old Town Hall, Kings Road, LONDON SW3 5EZ Tel: 0171 3614158 **Fax:** 0171 3511294
Opening Hours: M.T.Th. 10-8; W. 10-1; F.Sat 10-5 Closure: Public hols+Sat preceding Easter & August.
Parking: None.
Disabled: Stairs-bell at street level for assistance.
Children: At librarian's discretion.
Appointments: Prior booking for viewers-1 day. Entry-register. 8 seats+2 film+1 fiche-2 reader/printers.
Ordering System: Prior ordering by letter/tel. Number ordered & produced at librarian's discretion. Delivery 5-10 mins. No production 12-2. P/copying DIY. Typing/laptops permitted. Taping not allowed. Cameras by prior arrangement.
Records: for former Metropolitan Borough of Chelsea. PRs-film/originals if not copied. Parish records. Rate books. Voters lists. Deeds. Maps. Histories & other records relating to the former borough mainly after 1700. M/f-census.
Research Service: Charge made-limited to postal research.
Facilities: Toilets. No public tel./refreshment facilities. Café/pub/shops nearby.
Publications: For sale: Works of local interest.
Remarks: Underground: Sloane Square (District/Circle Lines).

Royal Borough of Kensington & Chelsea, Central Library, Phillimore Walk, LONDON W8 7RX (postal address). Public access: Hornton Street. **Tel:** 0171 3613038 **Fax:** 0171 3612976 **E-mail:** ellsces@rbkc.gov.uk
Opening Hours: T.Th. 10-8; W. 10-1; F. 10-5; Sat 10-1; 2-5 Closure: Mon+Public hols.
Parking: Public nearby-paying.
Disabled: Ramp. Lift. Parking by prior arrangement.
Children: At librarian's discretion.
Appointments: Prior booking for viewers-1 day. Entry-register. Seats+viewers-2 reader/printers.
Ordering System: Prior ordering by letter/tel. Catalogue nos sometimes required. Ten ordered & produced. Delivery 15 mins. No production 1-2. Last order: 30mins before closure. P/copying restricted-DIY. Typing not permitted. Taping/laptops/cameras allowed.
Records: for Kensington-parish St. Mary Abbots+post 1965 Royal Borough of Kensington & Chelsea. PRs-fiche+Index on hard copy/Ts. Earl's Court & Mary Abbot Manor rolls. Vestry. Tithe. Charities. Poor Law (overseers from 1683+trustees of the poor 1777-1888+paupers exams from 1791-incomplete). Schools. Business incl. Carlisle & Gregson (Jimmy's) Ltd-military tutors 1889-1940. Kensington Housing Trust. Deeds. Family & estate. Very complete admin. records incl. Ratebooks/electoral rolls/street/naming/planning applications/drainage plans etc. Kensington Turnpike Trust. Lord Leighton letters 19thC. Prints. Engravings. Photographs. Slides. Cuttings. Newspapers. Maps & plans. Directories. M/f-census 1841(gaps)-1891/1851 /Ecclesiastical census.
Research Service: Charge made.
Facilities: No toilets. Public tel. No refreshment facilities. Café/pub/shops nearby.
Publications: For sale: *A Short Guide to the Kensington & Chelsea Local Collections* (in process of revision).
Remarks: Station: Kensington High Street (District/Circle lines).

Royal Borough of Kingston upon Thames, Museum & Heritage Service, Kingston Local History Room, Room 46, North Kingston Centre, Richmond Road, KINGSTON UPON THAMES, Surrey KT2 5PE Tel: 0181 5476738 **Fax:** 0181 5476747
Opening Hours: M.W.Th.F. 10-5; T. 10-7 Closure: Sat. **Note:** Opening hours under review.
Parking: Yes-shared with other depts.
Disabled: Toilet. No access to Local History Room but documents may be viewed in an accessible room by prior arrangement.
Children: Accompanied: At archivist's discretion. Unaccompanied: 8 yrs+
Appointments: Prior booking for viewers-1 day. Entry-register. 6 seats+1 film+1 fiche-reader/printer.
Ordering System: Prior ordering by letter/tel. Catalogue nos sometimes required. Number ordered at archivist's discretion, two produced. Ordering times: 10-12; 2-3 unless previously ordered. P/copying by staff-same day. Typing/taping not permitted. Laptops (power supply) allowed. Cameras permitted under severe copyright restrictions.
Records: for the present Royal Borough of Kingston upon Thames-Kingston/Surbiton/ Coombe/New Malden/Old Malden/Tolworth/ Hook/Chessington/Malden/Rushett. Surrey RO is the Diocesan RO. PRs-film/Ts. Vestry. Churchwardens. Manorial. Nonconformist. Private deposits. Business. Education. Deeds. Local Histories. Maps. Newspapers. Taped reminiscences. Photographs. Eadweard Muybridge Archive-internationally important motion picture pioneer. M/f-census/IGI. **Note:** Borough archives may also be consulted at Surrey RO (see entry) by appt.
Research Service: Charge made.
Facilities: Toilets/public tel/room for own food/drink vending machine. Café/pub nearby.
Publications: Free: Info leaflet: *Kingston Heritage*-with map. (SAE). For sale: *Guide to the Borough Archives: Accessions to 1965* (pub. 1974).
Tourist Office: Tel: 0181 5475592 Fax: 0181 5475594
Remarks: Bags not allowed-storage. Donations appreciated.

London Borough of Lambeth, Archives Department, Minet Library, 52 Knatchbull Road, LONDON SE5 9QY Tel: 0171 9266076 **Fax:** 0171 9266080
Opening Hours: M. 10.30-7.30; T.Th. 9.30-5.30; F. 9.30-1; Alternate Sat 9.30-1; 2-4.30 Closure: Wed+Public hols.
Parking: On street.
Disabled: W/chair access. Visual aids.
Children: Accompanied: At archivist's discretion. Unaccompanied: 12 yrs+
Appointments: Prior booking for viewers-1 day. Entry-register. 12 seats+3 film+3 fiche-2 reader/printers.
Ordering System: Prior ordering by letter/tel. Catalogue nos sometimes required. Six ordered & produced. Delivery 5 mins. P/copying restricted-DIY. Typing/taping/cameras not permitted. Laptops allowed.
Records: for London Borough of Lambeth+some records for Surrey. Archives & local history material relating to parishes of Lambeth/Clapham/Streatham from 1504. PRs-film/Ts/originals if not copied. Nonconformist. Poor Law. Hospital Trust. Vauxhall Gardens books & cuttings. South London theatres playbills. Surrey-borough of Southwark & Wandsworth council records. Deeds. Family. Estate. Incomplete series of draft registers from 1695-1855. Burial fee accounts 1811-1854. Electoral registers. Maps & plans. Newspapers & periodicals. Directories. Ephemera (cuttings etc.).
Research Service: None.
Facilities: Toilets. No public tel/refreshment facilities. Café/pub/shops nearby.
Publications: Free leaflets: Publications price list. List of Information Guides-single copies free of charge. 1. *Records of Interest to Family Historians*. 2. *Records Agents List*. 3. *Sources for Business History*. 4. *Maps & Plans*. 5. *Handlist of local newspapers*. 7. *List of periodicals*. 8. *Local History, Family History & Amenity Societies*. 9. *House History*. 10. *Resources for teachers*. 11. *The Environment in Lambeth Archives Dept* (A4 SAE). For sale: *Greater London Cemeteries & Crematoria* (1994). *London Local Archives* (1994). Maps. Local History books. Posters, etc.
Remarks: Bags not allowed-pegs for coats/bags. Donations appreciated. Underground: Brixton.

London Borough of Lewisham, Lewisham Local Studies & Archives, Lewisham Library, 199-201 Lewisham High Street, LONDON SE13 6LG Tel: 0181 2970682 **Fax:** 0181 2971169 **E-mail:** local.studies@lewisham.gov.uk
Internet: http://www.lewisham.gov.uk
Opening Hours: M. 10-5; T.Th. 9-8; F.Sat 9-5 Closure: Wed+Public hols+1st two wks in Dec.
Parking: Public behind library in Slaithwaite Road (off Morley Road)-paying.
Disabled: Disabled friendly. Parking spaces for Orange Badge holders-beside library in Limes Grove. No entry from Lewisham Street. Induction loop.
Children: At archivist's discretion.
Appointments: Prior booking for viewers-2 days. Entry-register for archive use. 16 seats+1 film+1 fiche-2 reader/printers.
Ordering System: Prior ordering by letter/tel. Catalogue nos sometimes required. One trolley

full ordered, two items/one bundle produced. Delivery 5-30 mins. No production 12-2; 5-8. Documents to be handed in 15 mins before closure. P/copying by staff-same day. Typing/taping/laptops permitted. Cameras not allowed.
Records: for Borough of Lewisham-ancient parishes of Lee/Lewisham/St. Paul's Deptford. Diocesan RO for Lewisham (not Deptford). PRs-film/Ts/originals if not copied. Borough/local authority. Poor rate books. Church & Highway rate books. Register of graves. Nonconformists. Business, Charity. Poll books/electoral registers. MIs. Directories. Photographs & prints. Maps. M/f-census (indexed by street, some by name)/newspapers.
Research Service: None.
Facilities: Toilet. Public tel nearby. Coffee shop/bookshop. Café/pub/shops nearby.
Publications: Free leaflets: Info. leaflet (with map). Details of holdings of interest to family historians. Details of services to teachers & tutors etc. (SAE). For sale: Wide range of local history publications. Maps.
Tourist Office: Tel: 0181 2978317
Remarks: Bags not allowed-lockers. Donations appreciated. Station: Lewisham (BR) 10 mins walk. New Cross/New Cross Gate (E.London Line) then Bus 136.

London Borough of Merton, Merton Local Studies Centre, Merton Civic Centre, London Road, MORDEN, Surrey, SM4 5DX Tel: 0181 5453239 **Fax:** 0181 5454037
Opening Hours: M.W. 10-7; T.F.Sat 10-5; Th. 10-1 Closure: Public hols.
Parking: Public in York Road/Safeway-limited street parking nearby.
Disabled: Disabled friendly.
Children: At staff's discretion.
Appointments: Prior booking unnecessary. 38 seats+1 film+1 fiche-1 reader/printer.
Ordering System: Prior ordering by letter/tel. Catalogue nos sometimes required. Number ordered & produced at librarian's discretion. P/copying-DIY. Typing/taping not permitted. Laptops (battery)/cameras (not flash) allowed.
Records: for London Borough of Merton incl. Morden. PRs-Ts. Local authority-Merton & predecessors. Electoral registers. Directories. Maps. Photographs. Local History collection incls Mitcham and Wimbledon. M/f-census.
Research Service: None.
Facilities: Toilets/public tel/refreshment facilities. Café/pub/shops nearby.
Publications: For sale.
Remarks: See *Finding out about your family* series.

London Borough of Newham, Local Studies Library, Stratford Library, Water Lane, LONDON E15 4NJ Tel: 0181 4721430 Ext. 25662 **Fax:** 0181 5031525
Opening Hours: M.Th. 9.30-8; T. 9.30-6.30; W.F. 9.30-5.30; Alternate Sat 9.30-5.30 Closure: Public hols.
Parking: None.
Children: At staff's discretion.
Appointments: Prior booking necessary-as long as possible. Entry-ID. 6 seats+2 film+1 fiche-reader/printer.
Ordering System: Prior ordering by letter/tel. One ordered & produced. Delivery 5-20 mins. P/copying restricted-DIY. Typing/taping not permitted. Laptops/cameras allowed.
Records: for Newham-boroughs of East & West Ham. Diocesan RO is at Essex RO, Chelmsford (see entry). PRs-film. Local authority. Nonconformist. Manorial. PLU. Landowners. Family. Charities. Deeds. Maps. Theatre posters/programmes. HMS Albion disaster. Silvertown Explosion disaster-photographs/ documents. M/f-newpapers/electoral registers/ directories.
Research Service: None.
Facilities: No toilets/public tel/refreshment facilities. Café/pub/shops nearby.
Publications: Free leaflet: Local Studies notes related to the London Borough of Newham (SAE).
Remarks: Note: There may be a possible re-location of this library sometime in the next two years. Underground: Stratford (Central line).

London Borough of Redbridge, Local History Library, Clements Road, ILFORD, Essex IGI 1EA Tel: 0181 4787145 Ext. 225 Usually open-closed Mon. Former boroughs of Ilford/Wanstead/Woodford/parts of Essex. Local History collection. Infant Orphans Asylum-Royal Infants Orphanage. Local authority. Newspapers. Maps & plans. Photographs. **Note:** No reply was received from this library so the information provided here has mainly been supplied from the 3rd Ed.

London Borough of Richmond upon Thames, Richmond Local Collection, Albert Barkas Room for Local Studies, Central Reference Library, Old Town Hall, Whittaker Avenue, RICHMOND, Surrey TW9 1TP Tel: 0181 9405529 Ext. 32 **Fax:** 0181 9406899 **E-mail:** ref@richmond.gov.uk
Opening Hours: T. 1-5; W. 1-8; Th.F. 10-6; 2nd/4th/5th Sat 10-12.30; 1.30-5 Closure: Mon+Public hols+2 wks beg of Dec.
Parking: None.
Disabled: No access to Searchroom-stairs, but material may be viewed in Ref. Library by prior arrangement.
Children: At librarian's discretion.
Appointments: Prior booking unnecessary. Entry-register. 8 seats+1 film+2 fiche.

Ordering System: Prior ordering by letter/tel. Catalogue nos sometimes required. Number ordered & produced at librarian's discretion. P/copying restricted, by staff-same day/DIY. Typing/taping/cameras/laptops (power supply) permitted.
Records: for London Borough of Richmond upon Thames-Barnes/East Sheen/Ham/Kew/ Mortlake/Petersham/Richmond. PRs-fiche/Ts. Local Government. Richmond vestry mins & workhouse. Schools. Societies & clubs. Maps. Photographs. Local History collection. Collections of Burton/Vancouver (Capt. George Vancouver)/Sladen/Walpole/playbills. M/f-census/newspapers.
Research Service: Limited specific enquiry-free.
Facilities: Toilets/public tel. No refreshment facilities. Café/pub/shops nearby.
Publications: Free Info. leaflet: *The Local Studies Collection* (SAE). For sale: Various.
O.R: Museum of Richmond, Old Town Hall, Whittaker Avenue, RICHMOND UPON THAMES TW9 1TP
Tourist Office: Tel: 0181 9409125 Fax: 0181 9406899
Remarks: Note: Some local church vestries still retain the ecclesiastical records for their areas. The ROs for Greater London (London Metropolitan Archives), the Guildhall Library, Aldermanbury & Surrey have considerable archive material relating to the Richmond upon Thames area.

London Borough of Richmond upon Thames,Twickenham Local Studies Library, Garfield Road, TWICKENHAM, Surrey TW1 3JS Tel: 0181 8917271
Opening Hours: M.F 1-6; T. 1-8; W. 1-5; 1st & 3rd Sat 10-12; 1-5 Closure: Thurs+Public hols+2 wks in Dec.
Parking: None.
Disabled: Ramp to main library. No access to Search Room (stairs) but material may be viewed by prior arrangement.
Children: Accompanied: At librarian's discretion. Unaccompanied: 11 yrs+
Appointments: Prior booking for seats unnecessary. Entry-register with address & nature of enquiry. 9 seats+1 fiche.
Ordering System: Prior ordering by letter.tel. Number ordered & produced at librarian's discretion. P/copying restricted, by staff-same day/DIY. Typing/taping/laptops/cameras permitted.
Records: for London Borough of Richmond-The Hamptons/Teddington/ Twickenham/Whitton. Former borough of Twickenham. PRs-fiche/Ts. Local History collection. Aerial surveys. Maps. Photographs. Extensive collection of paintings/prints/ drawings. Collections relating to Alexander Pope & Horace Walpole. M/f-census/ newspapers.
Research Service: None.
Facilities: No toilets/public tel/refreshment facilities. Café/pub/shops nearby.
Publications: For sale: Various.
O.R: The Chief Executive's Dept., Civic Centre, TWICKENHAM. TW1 3AA. Tel: 0181 8911411. Many archives relating to the area are held here-apply to him in writing or by application to the Local Studies Staff at this library.
Tourist Office: Tel: 0181 8911411
Remarks: Note: The ROs for Greater London (London Metropolitan Archives), the Guildhall, Library, Aldermanbury & Surrey hold considerable archive material relating to the Richmond upon Thames area. **Note:** Some local church vestries still retain the ecclesiastical records for their areas.

London Borough of Southwark, Southwark Local Studies Library, 211 Borough High Street, LONDON SE1 1JA
Tel: 0171 4033507 **Fax:** 0171 4038633
Opening Hours: M.Th. 9.30-8; T.F. 9.30-5; Sat 9.30-1 Closure: Wed+Public hols.
Parking: None.
Disabled: Access. Toilet.
Children: At librarian's discretion.
Appointments: Prior booking for viewers-1 day. 5 film+5 fiche-3 reader/printers.
Ordering System: Prior ordering by letter/tel. Number ordered & produced at librarian's discretion. Records stored elsewhere need at least 1 wk prior ordering. Delivery 1 min. P/copying restricted-DIY. Typing/ taping/cameras/laptops (power supply) permitted.
Records: for London Borough of Southwark-former boroughs of Bermondsey/ Camberwell/Southwark. Diocesan RO for Southwark is at London Borough of Greenwich Local History & Archives Library (see entry). PRs-film/Ts/originals if not copied. Some records for the former civil parish of St. Saviour (the rest are at London Metropolitan Archives, see entry). Vestry mins. Rate books. Poor Law. Churchwardens accounts etc. for St. Saviour/St. Olave/St. Mary Magdalene (Bermondsey)/St. Mary (Rotherhithe)/St. Mary (Newington)/St. Giles (Camberwell)/St. John Horsleydean/St. George, Christchurch/St. Thomas. Borough. Southwark Cathedral archives-deeds/financial & insurance/visitors' books. Business. Nonconformist. Deeds. Rate books. Electoral registers. Directories. Maps. Newspapers. Photographs. Film/video/tape collection of local people & organisations in the borough 1920s on. M/f-census./ newspapers/IGI.
Research Service: Charge made for copies from specified sources i.e. census/directories/

electoral registers/PRs for a given date-send for application form.
Facilities: Toilets. No public tel/refreshment facilities. Café/pub/shops nearby.
Publications: Free & for sale.
O.R: District Register Office, 34 Peckham Road, LONDON SE5 8PX which covers the London Boroughs of Southwark/Bermondsey/ Camberwell; **Southwark Archdiocesan Roman Catholic Archives**, 150 St. George's Road, SOUTHWARK, London SE1 6HX Tel: 0171 9285592 Appt. Collection relating to Diocese of Southwark 1850 on incls. letters from chaplains in Crimea and Indian Mutiny wars.
Remarks: Donations appreciated. Station: BR-London Bridge. Underground: Elephant & Castle (Bakerloo line)/Borough (Northern line).

London Borough of Sutton Heritage Service, Archives & Local Studies Section, Central Library, St. Nicholas Way, SUTTON, Surrey SM1 1EA Tel: 0181 770 4747 **Fax:** 0181 770 4666 **E-mail:** sutton.heritage@dial.pipex.com
Internet: www.earl.org.uk/earl/members/ sutton/
Opening Hours: T.F. 9.30-12; W.Th. 2-7.30; 1st & 3rd Sat 9.30-1; 2-4.45 Closure: Mon+Public hols.
Parking: Yes-paying.
Disabled: Disabled friendly+parking.
Children: Accompanied: At archivist's discretion. Unaccompanied: 8 yrs+
Appointments: Prior booking for viewers-2 days. Entry-register+CARN (or other reader's ticket)+ ID if required. 15 seats+1 film (library)+2 fiche (1 film/1 fiche reader/printers in library).
Ordering System: Prior ordering by letter/tel. Catalogue nos sometimes required. All archives must be ordered in advance-any number. P/copying restricted, by staff-post/collection. Typing/taping not permitted. Laptops (power supply) allowed. Cameras at archivist's discretion.
Records: for geographical area of Sutton incl. parishes of Beddington/Wallington/ Carshalton/Sutton & Cheam-also hold PR copies for rest of Surrey. PRs-fiche/p/ copies/Ts/originals if not copied. Manorial. Tithe. Nonconformist. Education. Royal Female Orphanage. Charities. Business. Maps. Photographs. Local histories. Croydon Airport. Wandle River deed. Carew family of Beddington. M/f-census/newspapers.
Research Service: Charge made.
Facilities: Toilets/public tel/refreshment facilities-coffee shop/drink vending machine. Cafe/pub/shops nearby.
Publications: For sale: *Guide to Archives & Local Studies Collection. Guide to PRs held by Sutton Archives.*
Remarks: Donations appreciated. **Note:** Sutton Archives are recognised as a place of deposit for public records, manorial & tithe awards. Expect shortly to be recognised as a sub-diocesan RO within the diocese of Southwark. The searchroom is within a very large library which contains an excellent collection of genealogical books. **Note:** Surrey CRO will be moving to Woking (see entry) in 1998 & when they move a great deal of material will be transferred to Sutton incl. relevant PRs. Station: Sutton (BR)-5 mins walk.

London Borough of Tower Hamlets, Tower Hamlets Local History Library & Archives, Bancroft Library, 277 Bancroft Road, LONDON E1 4DQ Tel: 0181 9804366 **Fax:** 0181 9834510
Opening Hours: M.T.Th. 9-8; F. 9-6; Sat 9-5 Closure: Wed+Public hols.
Parking: None.
Disabled: Ramp entrance. Lift to 1st Floor.
Children: Accompanied: At staff's discretion. Unacompanied: 11yrs+
Appointments: Prior booking for viewers-2/3 days. Entry-register. 14 seats+4 film+1 fiche-4 reader/printers-all film viewers convert to fiche.
Ordering System: Prior ordering by letter/tel. Catalogue nos sometimes required. Number ordered at archivist's discretion, six produced. Delivery 5 mins. P/copying restricted, by staff-same day/DIY-library material only. Typing/taping/cameras/laptops (power supply, if available) permitted.
Records: for London Borough of Tower Hamlets-Stepney/Whitechapel/Mile End/ Wapping/Shadwell/St. George-in-the-East/ Spitalfields/Bethnal Green/Poplar/Bow/ Bromley (Old Artillery Ground). PRs-film/p/ copies. Vestry. Poor Law. Schools. Shipping & logbooks. Marriage Notice Books (1837 on). Local authority from 16thC. Nonconformists incl. Lutheran & Huguenot. Rate books. Land Tax. Deeds. Electoral Registers. Maps. Photographs/films/videos. MIs. Published volumes of Bevis Marks Records Parts 1&3. Numerous indexes to collections. M/f-census+indexes/nonconformists/newspa pers/IGI.
Research Service: None.
Facilities: Toilets. No public tel/refreshment facilities. Café/pub/shops nearby.
Publications: Free leaflets: Handlists 1. *Personal Name Indexes.* 2. *Registers of Places of Worship.* Publications List. (A4 SAE). For sale: Booklets. Posters. Maps. Postcards.
Tourist Office: Tel: 0171 3752549 Fax: 0171 3752539
Remarks: Donations appreciated. Underground: Stepney Green.

London Borough of Waltham Forest, Waltham Forest Archives & Local History

Library, Vestry House Museum, Vestry Road, WALTHAMSTOW, London E17 9NH Tel: 0181 5091917 **Fax:** 0181 5099539
Internet: http://www.lbwf.gov.uk/
Opening Hours: T.W.F. 10-1; 2-5.15; Sat 10-1; 2-4.45 **Note:** All visits by appt only. Closure: Mon/Thurs+Public hols+Boxing Day to New Year's day+2 wks usually in Feb.
Parking: None.
Disabled: Searchroom at top of stairs-special arrangement for use of ground floor classroom-3 wks notice.
Children: Accompanied: 6 yrs+ Unaccompanied: 12 yrs+ & at staff's discretion.
Appointments: Prior booking for seats/viewers-3/4 days. Entry-register. 7 seats+ 1 film+1 fiche-reader/printer.
Ordering System: Prior ordering by letter/tel-preferable that docs are ordered prior to visit. No more than 30 docs per person ordered, four produced. Records stored elsewhere need prior ordering. Sat & alternate Fri all docs must be booked in advance. Delivery 15 mins. Last order: Tues/Wed/alternate Fri 4.45. P/copying by staff-post/collection/ DIY-reader printer. Typing/taping/laptops (power supply) by prior arrangement. Cameras not allowed.
Records: for London Borough of Waltham Forest-former boroughs of Chingford/ Leyton/Walthamstow (Essex). Local authority. PRs-fiche/film/Ts/originals if not copied. BTs held for parishes in Waltham Forest Deanery with permission of Diocese of Chelmsford. Nonconformist. Rate books for Waltham Forest parishes incl. Cann Hall 1894-1900. Civil parish records-jury lists/vestry mins/tithe/land tax. Poor Law pre 1834 incl. info. on immigration (emigration 18th/early 19thC's). Workhouse admissions 1797-1836. Apprentices. Manorial. Deeds. Militia. Voters lists. Newspapers. MIs. Directories. Histories of Essex Regiment. Periodicals. Family Histories. Chingford Mount Cemetery 1884-1970. Repton's `Red Book' of Highams, 1794. MSS works of John Drinkwater, poet & dramatist c1912-1934. Indexes to various archives. M/f-census.
Research Service: None.
Facilities: Toilets. No public tel/refreshment facilities. Café/pub nearby.
Publications: Free: General leaflet on holdings -in preparation for reprint (SAE).
O.R: William Morris Gallery, Lloyd Park, Forest Road, WALTHAMSTOW, London E17 4PP Appt. Holds MSS & printed sources relating to William Morris & his circle.
Remarks: Bags not allowed-lockers. Donations appreciated. Underground: Walthamstow Central.

London Borough of Wandsworth, Local History Library, Battersea Library, 265 Lavender Hill, LONDON SW11 1JB Tel: 0181 8717753 (direct line): 0171 9784376 (Ref. Dept.).
Opening Hours: T.W. 10-1; 2-8; F. 10-1; 2-5; Sat 9-1 Closure: Mon/Thurs+Public hols.
Parking: None. Nearby Supermarket-2 hrs free.
Disabled: Access to ground floor only-Local History Room on 1st floor.
Children: At librarian's discretion.
Appointments: Prior booking for viewers. Entry-register. 12 seats+3 film+1 fiche-2 reader/printers.
Ordering System: Prior ordering by letter/tel. Number ordered at librarian's discretion, two produced. Delivery few mins. P/copying. Typing not permitted. Taping/cameras/laptops (power supply) allowed.
Records: for London Borough of Wandsworth-Battersea/Clapham/Graveney/Putney/Streatham/Tooting/Wandsworth. PRs-film/fiche/Ts. Some material on closed access. Some Poor Law-poor coverage for Clapham/Wandsworth. Education. Electoral rolls. Rate books. Photographs/illustrations.
Research Service: Charge made-3 hrs max-in house searches only.
Facilities: Toilets. No public tel/refreshment facilities. Café/pub/shops nearby.
Publications: None.
Remarks: Bags allowed under supervision. Station: Clapham Junction.

LONDON-OTHER REPOSITORIES
British Library, Department of Western Manuscripts, Great Russell Street, LONDON WC1B 3DG Tel: 0171 4127513 **Fax:** 0171 4127511 **E-mail:** mss@bl.uk
Internet: http://www.bl.uk **Note:** From January 1999 the address will be: **The Dept. of Western Manuscripts, The British Library, 96 Euston Road, London NW1 2DB**
Opening Hours: M.-Sat 10-4.45 Closure: Public hols+1-2 wks in Nov. **Note:** The Dept. will close late Aug 1998 & re-open at St. Pancras in Jan 1999.
Parking: None.
Disabled: W/chair access.
Children: Not allowed.
Appointments: Prior booking unnecessary. Entry-on production of Manuscripts pass (ref. required-letter of recommendation by responsible person) in conjunction with the British Library (see Manuscripts Students' Room Regulations leaflet). Reader's photographic pass-one day pass available for some material+ID+other reader's ticket. 60 seats+3 film+1 fiche.
Ordering System: Prior ordering by letter/tel. Three by letter/one by tel. Catalogue nos required. Some records, i.e. Lord Chamberlains Play material requires 48 hrs notice. Some restricted material requires written application. Six ordered & produced. Delivery 20 mins. Last

order: 4.30. P/copying restricted, by staff-post. Typing/taping/cameras not permitted. Laptops allowed.
Records: for Western Europe. Historical/literary MSS. Theatre collections. Papers of scientists/medical researchers/ explorers. Maps. Illustrations. Topographical drawings. Finding aids to collections: Index of MSS in the B.L. 10 vols (Chadwyck-Healey) 1950. Catalogues of additions for later accessions. Class Catalogue of subjects+supplement.
Research Service: None.
Facilities: Toilets/public tel. Restaurant facilities in British Museum. Café/pub/shops nearby.
Publications: Free: Info. leaflet: *Department of Manuscripts*-general information+map. *Picture Research*- a reader guide. For sale: *English Literary Manuscripts. English Historical Documents. Guide to the catalogues & indexes of the Dept of MSS* (3rd Ed).
Remarks: Bags may be left in British Museum front hall. Donations appreciated. **Note:** Write or phone for more details concerning the Manuscripts Students' room, the Map Library (Tel: 0171 4127700/7747). Philatelic Collections (Tel: 0171 4127635). Latest info about move to St. Pancras available on WWW see Internet or Tel: 0171 4127527. Underground: Tottenham Court Road/Holborn/Russell Square. The National Sound Archive, 29 Exhibition Road, London, SW7 2AS Tel: 0171 4127440/7430 will be moving to St. Pancras in two stages-phone or write for up to date info.

British Library Newspaper Library, Colindale Avenue, LONDON NW9 5HE Tel: 0171 4127353 **Fax:** 0171 4127379 **E-mail:** newspaper@bl.uk
Internet: http://www.bl.uk/collections/ newspaper/
Opening Hours: M.-Sat 10-4.45 Closure: Public hols+last wk in Oct.
Parking: 10 spaces.
Disabled: Disabled friendly but prior arrangement advised.
Children: 18 yrs+ (under 18 yrs need prior permission).
Appointments: Prior booking unnecessary. Entry-ID. 78 seats+52 film+2 fiche-8 reader/printers.
Ordering System: Prior ordering by letter/tel-1/2 days. Four ordered & produced. Delivery 30-60 mins. Last orders: 4.15. P/copying by staff-post/collection/DIY-M/f only. Typing/taping/laptops (power supply) permitted. Cameras by special arrangement.
Records: National Archive Collection of newspapers. British & Irish newspapers 18thC on+substantial collection of Commonwealth newspapers & selected foreign newspapers. Periodicals. Magazines. M/f-Burney Collection (700 vols of newspapers 1602-1818).
Research Service: P/copies by post only if precise details are supplied-e.g. title, date, page, column etc.
Facilities: Toilet/public tel/room for own food/drink & snack vending machines. Café/pub nearby.
Publications: Free Info. leaflet: *Newspaper Library: an introduction*+various other leaflets+twice yearly newsletter. For sale: NEWSPCAN reports & selected other British Library publications.
Remarks: Bags not allowed-staffed cloakroom. **Note:** South Asian newspapers in English are at The British Library Oriental & India Office (see entry). The Thomason Tracts (Civil War & other 17thC newsbooks & newspapers) & the Burney Collection are housed at the British Library (see entry). Newspaper Library catalogue available, listing holdings by title & place of publication. Published indexes to the Times, New York Times & a number of other newspapers are on the Reference shelves. At present there are no plans for this library to move to the St. Pancras building. Underground: Colindale (Northern line).

British Library, Oriental & India Office Collections, 96 Euston Road, St. Pancras, London, NW1 2DB Tel: 0171 4127873 **Fax:** 0171 4127641 **E-mail:** oioc-enquiries@bl.uk
Internet: http://www.bl.uk/collections/ oriental
Opening Hours: M.-F. 9.30-5.45; Sat 9.30-12.45 Closure: Public hols.
Parking: None.
Children: Not allowed.
Appointments: No prior booking. Entry-register+ID+readers ticket/B.L. Readers pass. 92 seats+10 film+6 fiche-1 reader/printer.
Ordering System: Prior ordering by letter/tel. Catalogue nos required. Six ordered, three MSS/six books produced. Delivery 1 hr. Last order: 4 pm. P/copying restricted, by staff-post/DIY. Typing/taping/laptops (power supply) permitted. Cameras not allowed.
Records: cover India/Burma/Bangladesh/ Pakistan/neighbouring countries. Gulf States. South Africa. St. Helena. Malaysia. Singapore. Indonesia. China. Japan. PRs-film indexes on shelf. Archives of the East India Company/Burma Office. Map collection. Prints & drawings. M/f-South Asian newspapers in English & Oriental scripts originally collected by the East India Company & the India Office.
Research Service: None.
Publications: Free & for sale: Collection holdings. Subject guides. Using Reading Room. Regulations. Reprographic Service etc.
Remarks: Bags not allowed-lockers. **Note:** This office & collection have recently re-located

to 96 Euston Road, St. Pancras, London, NW1 2DB the new British Library premises.

B.T. Archives, 268-270 High Holborn, LONDON WC1V 7EE Tel: 0171 4928792. Appt.+ID. Telephone directories 1879 on. Historical records of telecommunications of the Post Office & its predecessors from 19thC. Photographic library 19thC on. Local histories. Journal & periodicals. Books.

City of London Police, Personnel Office, 26 Old Jewry, LONDON EC2R 8DJ Tel: 0171 601 2297. The office is not open for personal research-apply in writing only. All records are photocopied, if available, & a copy sent by 2nd class post-free. Personnel records for City of London police officers from 1839. **Note:** Metropolitan Police archives are with the PRO, Kew.

City of Westminster Archives Centre, 10 St. Ann's Street, LONDON SW1P 2XR Tel: 0171 6415180 **Fax:** 0171 6415179 **E-mail:** vp86@dial.pipex.com
Opening Hours: M.-F. 9.30-7; Sat 9.30-5 Closure: Public hols+Christmas-New Year+annual stocktaking-usually Dec.
Parking: None.
Disabled: Disabled friendly. Magnifiers. Induction loop in meeting room.
Children: Accompanied: At archivist's discretion. Unaccompanied: 8 yrs+
Appointments: Prior booking unnecessary. Entry-register. 30 seats+11 film+4 fiche-2 reader/printers.
Ordering System: Prior ordering by letter/tel. Catalogue nos required. Number ordered & produced at archivist's discretion. Delivery 10 mins. Last order: 20 mins before closure. P/copying restricted, by staff-same day/post/collection/DIY-at archivist's discretion. Typing not permitted. Taping by prior arrangement. Laptops (power supply)/cameras (non-flash) allowed.
Records: for City of Westminster incl. pre-1965 boroughs of Paddington/St. Marylebone. Diocesan RO for Westminster excluding St. Marylebone/Paddington. PRs-film/p/copies (some R.C.registers)/Ts/ originals if not copied or at archivist's discretion for difficult paleography. Parish. Nonconformist incl. Lutheran/Huguenot /Roman Catholic (Imperial Legation of Austria/Charles Street/St. James to 1784 then Twickenham+Neapolitan Legation). Manorial. Private. Business. St. Marylebone Charity School for Girls. Greycoat Hospital. Family incl. Grosvenor Estate. Westminster Fire Office. Programmes/playbills/scrapbooks for all West End Theatres from days of John Kemble & Sarah Siddons to present. Electoral registers. Directories. Newspapers.
Research Service: None.
Facilities: Toilet/public tel/room for own food/drink vending machine. Café/pub/shops nearby.
Publications: For sale: *Guide to sources for Family History held by Westminster City Archives* by Elizabeth Cory. *List of PRs. Nonconformist & Roman Catholic Registers.* Local & Family History publications, maps, postcards & various leaflets etc.-some free, others for sale.
Remarks: Bags not allowed-lockers & secure coat hangers. Small handbags allowed. Donations appreciated. **Note:** The archives which were formerly at Marylebone Library have been transferred to this new repository. Underground: St. James' Park.

Corporation of London Records Office, PO Box 270, Guildhall Library, LONDON EC2P 2EJ (2nd Floor North Office Block, Rooms N221-223-Guildhall access via Basinghall Street). **Tel:** 0171 3321251 **Fax:** 0171 3321119
Opening Hours: M.-F. 9.30-4.45 Closure: Public hols.
Parking: None.
Disabled: Parking by arrangement. Access-w/chair available on request for use within Guildhall. Toilet on ground floor. Induction loops.
Children: Access restricted,.
Appointments: Prior booking for seats unnecessary. Entry-ID-pass issued at Guildhall entrance (airport type security)+CLRO register. 9 seats+2 film+2 fiche-2 reader/printers.
Ordering System: Prior ordering by letter/tel. Catalogue nos sometimes required. Six ordered & produced until 4.30 (all docs to be returned by 4.45). Delivery 15 mins max. P/copying restricted, by staff-post (see Info. Sheet 4 Archive Copying Services). Typing/taping/ cameras/laptops (power supply) by prior arrangement.
Records: Administration of City of London but has responsibilities beyond the City e.g. Southwark, on the Thames (Thames Conservancy), Open Spaces (Epping Forest) etc. Charters & Custumals. Civic Courts incl. Husting/Mayors/Sheriffs/Coroners/Orphan Courts. Financial. Freedom records incl. admissions to the Freedom of the City of London 1681-1940. Architectural plans & drawings. Bridge House Estates & City Lands to 1942. Finsbury Estate 16-19thC's. Irish Society (plantation of Ulster & management of estates) 17-20thC's. Lieutenancy of London (militia) 17-20thC's. Royal Contract Estates (manors) mainly 17thC. Southwark-Coroners/ manorial/session 16-20thC's.
Research Service: None (list of AGRA members for sale in Guildhall bookshop).
Facilities: Toilets/public tel-ground floor of North Office Block. Refreshment

facilities-trolley service am & pm. Café/pub/shops nearby.
Publications: Free info. leaflets: send for Info Sheet 9 Free Publications Order Form (SAE)-*City Freedom Archives. Sworn Brokers Archives. Using the CLRO. Open Spaces. City Archives. Committee Records. The Court of Common Council. How to get to the Guildhall*+with map. **Note:** Guildhall Library has its own bookshop which sells many books pub. by Guildhall Library about archives in its care. For a full list write to Guildhall Library, Publications, Aldermanbury, London EC2P 2EJ Tel: 0171 3321858. Ts. of some of the Corporation's records have been pub. by the London Record Society-details in *An Introductory Guide to the Corporation of London Records Office* (for sale).
Remarks: Note: This office may move to another part of the Guildhall in 1998. See article in Genealogists' Magazine Vol. 20 nos 10 & 11 June/Sept 1982 *Some Genealogical Sources in the CLRO* by B. Masters. Undergrounds: St. Paul's/Bank/Moorgate/Mansion House/Cannon Street.

Family Records Centre (PRO, Central London Reading Room), 1 Myddelton Street, LONDON EC1R 1UW Tel: 0181 3925300 Certificate enqs-0171 2339233 **Fax:** 0181 3925307 **E-mail:** enquiry.pro.rsd.Kew@gtnet.gov.uk
Internet: http://www.open.gov.uk/prohome.htm
Opening Hours: M.W.F. 9-5; T. 10-7; Th. 9-7; Sat 9.30-5 Closure: Public hols+preceding Sat.
Parking: Public nearby, Bowling Green Lane (off Farringdon Road) & Skinner Street (both easy walking distance)-paying.
Disabled: Disabled friendly. Parking must be booked in advance-Tel: 0171 5336400
Children: At staff's discretion.
Appointments: Prior booking unnecessary. 220 film+30 fiche-8 reader/printers.
Ordering System: No prior ordering-self help access to indexes & films. BDM certificates: for collection-four working days/post-three working days after application. P/copying restricted-indexes cannot be copied. Typing/taping/laptops (power supply) permitted. Cameras not allowed.
Records: BMDs-England/Wales from July 1837. Adoptions from 1927. Overseas & Military BMDs. Consular/Chaplains Returns. Census 1841-1891 England/Wales/I. of Man/Channel Islands. PCC wills & Admons to 1858. Estate Duty Office registers 1796-1858-indexes from 1796-1903. Non parochial registers 1567-1858. Miscellaneous foreign returns of BMDs 1627-1960. IGI. On-line computer link to New Register House for Scottish Civil Registration Indexes of BMD from 1855/Divorces from 1984/OPRs 1553-1854/Index to 1891 census for Scotland (not available Sat). Time on computer terminals must be booked+fee for this service.
Research Service: Charge made for census & wills holdings. Tel: 0181 3925300.
Facilities: Toilets/public tel/baby changing room/room for own food/drink vending machine. Café/pub/shops nearby. Advice provided for local & social historians-tel: 0181 3925300 for information.
Publications: Free: Info. leaflet (with map). PRO Information leaflets re. census. Info point selling publications on family history.
Remarks: Bags allowed-storage-£1 coin lockers. Donations appreciated towards the work of the Friends of the PRO-box on 1st Floor. Postal applications to be directed to ONS, Postal Applications Section, Smedley Hydro. Trafalgar Road, Birkdale, Southport, PR8 2HH. There is a Family history reference area including books, maps, CD Roms etc. **Note:** The same indexes as previously provided at St. Catherine's House/Census Reading Rooms at Chancery Lane have been transferred to the Family Records Centre. There are several `finding aids'-census surname indexes/directories/maps/nonconformist lists & indexes/some printed PRs for London, etc. The Family Records Centre is run jointly by the PRO & ONS. Essential reading: *Basic Facts About.Using The Family Records Centre* by Audrey Collins (FFHS 1997). The FRC is run jointly by the PRO & ONS. Underground: Angel (Northern line). Farringdon (Hammersmith & City, Metropolitan & Circle lines).

Guildhall Library, Manuscripts Section, Aldermanbury, LONDON EC2P 2EJ Tel: 0171 3321863 **Fax:** 0171 6003384 **E-mail:** manuscripts.guildhall@ms.corpof london.gov.uk
Internet: http://ihr.sas.ac.uk/ihr/ghmnu.html
Opening Hours: M.-Sat 9.30-4.45 Closure: Public hols.
Parking: None.
Disabled: Disabled friendly.
Children: At staff's discretion.
Appointments: Prior booking for viewers. Entry-register+ID for certain archives. 24 seats+1 film+2 fiche-1 reader/printer.
Ordering System: Prior ordering by letter/tel-1 day. Catalogue nos required. Three ordered & produced. Delivery 15 mins max. Some business records, chiefly 19-20thC's, require 1 day prior notice. No production Sat 12-2. Last order: 4.30. P/copying restricted, by staff-post. Typing/taping/laptops (power supply)/ cameras (subject to copyright) at archivist's discretion.
Records: the City of London local RO. Diocesan RO for Diocese of London/Archdeaconry of London/City of London parish records. Dean & Chapter of St. Paul's Cathedral. PRs-film/Ts (a

few in Printed Books Section of Library)/originals if not filmed or film illegible-on 24 hr call. BTs (poor survival)-on 24 hr call. City Wards. City Livery Companies. Christ's Hospital School. Corporation of Trinity House. Extensive business records incl. Lloyds Marine collection/London Stock Exchange, etc. Families. Probate. Nonconformist.
Research Service: Limited specific enquiry only (no printouts).
Facilities: Toilet. No public tel-nearby. Room for own food. Café/pub/shops nearby.
Publications: Free: leaflets on specific records. For sale: *Guide to Genealogical Sources in Guildhall Library. Handlist of PRs at Guildhall Library-Part 1 & Part 2. Handlist of Nonconformists/Roman Catholic/Jewish Burial Grounds at Guildhall Library. The British Overseas: A Guide to Records of their Births/Marriages/Deaths & Burials. City Livery Companies & Related Organisations: A Guide to their Archives in Guildhall Library.* Maps. Bookshop in Library. **Note:** A Guide to Archives & MSS at Guildhall Library is now available on Internet as are some free leaflets.
O.R: Guildhall Library (address as above) holds extensive collection of books & directories for London & rest of the country. Maps/prints/drawings for London.
Remarks: Bags allowed-lockable coat racks only. Postal donations appreciated-cheques payable to Chamberlain of London. Underground: Moorgate: Bank.

House of Lords Record Office, House of Lords, LONDON SW1A OPW Tel: 0171 2193074 **Fax:** 0171 2192570 **E-mail:** hlro@parliament.uk
Internet: www.parliament.uk
Opening Hours: M.-F. 9.30-5. Closure: Public hols+last 2 wks in Nov.
Parking: None.
Disabled: Lift. Toilet.
Children: At archivist's discretion.
Appointments: Prior booking for seats/viewers-1 wk. Entry-register+ID. 8 seats+2 film+1 fiche-2 reader/printers.
Ordering System: Prior ordering by letter/tel. Catalogue nos helpful. Six ordered & produced. Printed Parliamentary Papers require 48 hrs prior ordering. No production 1-2.15; 4-5. Delivery 30 mins. P/copying by staff-same day/post/collection depending on size of order. Typing not permitted. Taping/cameras/laptops (power supply) at discretion of supervisor.
Records: Archives of both Houses of Parliament. Sources for local & family history-plans/associated documents/mins of evidence for canals/railways/road/docks etc from 1794 on. Estate & Enclosure Acts 16thC on. Protestation Returns 1641/2. Certain Papist returns. 1698 Petitions re: Woollen Trade. Acts of Parliament 1497 on. Witnesses to private Bills now on database.
Research Service: Limited specific enquiry-post only.
Facilities: Toilet. No public tel/refreshment facilities. Café/pub/shops nearby.
Publications: Free: Info. leaflet incls. map. List of publications.
Remarks: Bags allowed-cupboard storage. There is a comprehensive description of the records by M.E. Bond, *Guide to the Records of Parliament* (HMSO 1971)-subsequent accessions are listed in the RO Annual Reports.
Note: Access to the office is by the public entrance nearest to the Victoria Tower in the west front of the Houses of Parliament. The adjacent Pass Office will issue a day pass for admission to the RO on proof of identity & on confirmation of appointment. Underground: Westminster (District line & from 1998 Jubilee line). Mainline Stations: Victoria/Waterloo/Charing Cross.

Imperial War Museum, Department of Documents, Lambeth Road, LONDON SE1 6HZ Tel: 0171 4165221/4165222/4165226 **Fax:** 0171 4165374
Opening Hours: M.-Sat 10-5 Sat-limited service. Closure: Public hols+preceding Sat+stocktaking-usually 2 wks Nov.
Parking: None.
Disabled: Lift to Reading Rooms. Ramp to Museum. Limited special parking by prior arrangement.
Children: Accompanied: 12 yrs+ Unaccompanied: 16 yrs+
Appointments: Prior booking-1 day. Entry-form+check against appointments list. 40 seats+5 film+1 fiche-1 reader/printer.
Ordering System: Prior ordering by letter/tel. Catalogue nos sometimes required. Number order & produced at archivist's discretion. Delivery 45 mins max. Last order: 4 p.m. P/copying by staff-same day/post/DIY-reader printer only. Typing/taping/laptops (power supply) permitted. Cameras not allowed.
Records: for Britain & Commonwealth at War 1914 to present. Allied & 'enemy' war experience. Military & Civil events. Mainly British Private papers. Private papers of senior British Armed Services Commanders & other personalities associated with 20thC warfare. M/f-copies of broad selection of administrative files from German occupation of Channel Islands.
Research Service: None.
Facilities: Toilets/public tel/restaurant. Café/pub/shops nearby.
Publications: Free: Info. leaflet-map. (SAE).
Remarks: Bags not allowed-museum entrance cloakroom. Donations appreciated. See *Sources in British Political History 1900-1951*, by Chris Cook (2nd & 6th vols.). *The*

Two World Wars: a Guide to Manuscript Collections in the United Kingdom by S.L. Mayer & W.K. Koenig. *List of Accessions to Repositories* (pub. annually HMSO). Station: Waterloo. Underground: Lambeth North. Elephant & Castle-also mainline station. Also see *The Imperial War Museum* by Sarah Paterson (FFHS 'News and Digest' April 1998)

The Jewish Museum, London's Museum of Jewish Life, 80 East End Road, Finchley, LONDON N3 2SY Tel: 0181 3491143 **Fax:** 0181 3432162
Internet: http://www.ort.org/jewmusm/
Opening Hours: M.-Th. 10.30-5; Sun 10.30-4.30 Closure: Fri/Sat+Public hols+Jewish festivals+Sun in Aug+ Dec 24-Jan 4.
Parking: None.
Disabled: Tel. for info.
Children: Tel. for info.
Appointments: Prior booking necessary-3 days. Entry-register (in case of sensitive material, letter of reference may be required). 2 seats.
Ordering System: Prior ordering by letter/tel. Catalogue nos sometimes required. P/copying-DIY at curator's discretion. Typing/taping/cameras not permitted. Laptops allowed.
Records: the archives relate mainly to Jewish social history & Jewish East End in London. Personal papers & records incl. trades. Theatre. Synagogues. Refugees from Nazi persecution. Jewish Friendly Society. Oral & photographic collections. Reference library.
Research Service: None.
Facilities: Toilet/public tel/refreshment facilities. Café/pub nearby.
Publications: List available. *Educational Resources. Audio-visual Resources. Research Papers. 1901 Map of Jewish East End. Yiddish Theatre in London (1880-1987). East End Synagogues. 150 Years of Progressive Judaism in Britain 1840-1990. London's Jewish Cemeteries* (addresses, contact nos etc.). *A Bibliography of Jewish Life in East London. The Jewish East End of London 1840-1940. Sources for Jewish Family History Research.*
Remarks: Donations appreciated. **Note:** The Museum does not hold records of a genealogical nature but holds Family History workshops six times a year in tracing Jewish Family History. The Museum produces a quarterly newsletter available to Friends of the Museum.

Lambeth Palace Library, LONDON SE1 7JU (entrance in Lambeth Palace Road). **Tel:** 0171 9286222
Opening Hours: M.-F. 10-5 Closure: Public hols+10 days beg Christmas Eve+Good Friday.
Parking: None.
Disabled: Limited facilities-library on ground floor.
Children: Not allowed.
Appointments: Prior booking for viewers. Entry-register+letter of introduction from person of recognised standing. 17 seats+1 film+1 fiche.
Ordering System: Prior ordering by letter only. Five ordered, one loose item/five vols produced. Delivery 30 mins. No production 1-2. Last order: 4.30. P/copying restricted, by staff-same day depending on how busy Reading Room is. Typing/taping/cameras not permitted. Laptops (power supply) allowed.
Records: Archives of Province of Canterbury incl. Vicar General/Court of Arches/ Temporalities. Archives of the Archbishop of Canterbury, e.g. Archbishops Papers/registers. Collection of the Bishop of London relating to Colonial America & West Indies (Fulham Papers). Faculty Office & Vicar General marriage allegations. Archbishops Peculiars of Arches/Croydon/Shoreham. Ecclesiastical records of Commonwealth 1643-1660. Doctors Commons. Some foreign churches, e.g. Basra/Khartoum/Shanghai/ Shangtung. Various Anglican societies, e.g. Church of England Mens Society/Church of England Temperance Society/Clergy Orphan Corporation, etc. Printed books c200,000+ some dating before 1700. M/f-Carew Papers-Elizabethan Ireland & Settlement of Ulster/The Shrewsbury Papers/Papers of Anthony Bacon. Catalogues of MSS & archives available+unpublished lists & indexes.
Research Service: Limited specific enquiry.
Facilities: Toilets. No public tel. Room for own food+tea/coffee facilities.
Publications: Free leaflet: *Lambeth Palace Library*-with map (SAE). For sale: Handlist of published catalogues. Slides & cards.
Remarks: Bags not allowed-limited storage. Donations appreciated. Underground: Waterloo /Lambeth North/Vauxhall/Westminster.

London Metropolitan Archives (formerly Greater London Record Office), **40 Northampton Road, LONDON EC1R OHB Tel:** 0171 3323820 **Fax:** 0171 8339136
Opening Hours: M.W.F. 9.30-4.45; T.Th. 9.30-7.30 Closure: Public hols+1st 2 wks in Nov+Christmas-New Year. **Parking:** None.
Disabled: Disabled friendly. Parking for Orange Badge holders. Minicom 0171 8339135
Children: At archivist's discretion.
Appointments: Prior booking unnecessary. Entry-register. 30 seats (Reading room)+viewers-2 reader/printers.
Ordering System: Prior ordering by letter/tel. Catalogue nos required. Five ordered, one produced. Ordering times: every 30 mins from 9.45-4.15 M.W.F; & 9.45-5.45 T.Th. Delivery 15 mins after collection times. P/copying restricted, by staff-post/collection within 2

working days. Typing/taping/laptops (power supply) at archivist's discretion. Cameras not allowed.
Records: for former counties of London & Middlesex for deposited records. Greater London area for inherited records. Diocesan RO for London & Southwark. PRs-film/Ts/originals if not copied. BTs-Ts. Parish Chest. Poor Law. Middlesex Registry of Deeds. Significant holdings of local govt, from 16thC incl. Middlesex Sessions. London County Council (LCC) & its predecessors. Greater London Council (GLC). Inner London Education Authority (ILEA). Important series of electoral registers. Photograph collection. Large topographical library for London. Large map/print collection. Large deposits of hospital records/local & national charities. Nonconformist. Manorial. Family & estate. Business. Cemeteries. M/f-IGI.
Research Service: Charge made-2 hrs max. Tel: 0171 3323820 Minicom 0171 8339136.
Facilities: Toilets/public tel/room for own food/drink vending machine. Café/pub nearby.
Publications: Free info leaflets: *London Metropolitan Archive-Discover, Your Quick Guide*-with map. *Tracking down PRs in the London Metropolitan Archives*. 1. *Family History in London*. 2. *IGI*. 3. *Licensed Victuallers Records*. 5 *The City of London & Tower Hamlets Cemetery*. 7. *The Middlesex Deeds Registry 1709-1938*. 8. *London School Attendance Medals*. 9. *History of Nursing-major sources in the L.M.A.* 10. *The evacuation of children from the county of London during the Second World War*. 11. *Records of gardening and horticulture among the L.M.A. holdings*. 13. *Hospital Records*. 14. *An Outline of Sources for the History of Education in the L.M.A.* 15. *Records of Patients in London Hospitals*. 17.*The German Community in London*. (A4 SAE). For sale: various publications.
Remarks: Bags not allowed-lockers £1 coin.
Note: The L.M.A. is very near to the Family Records Centre & the Society of Genealogists. Underground: Farringdon/Angel.

London Transport Museum, 39 Wellington Street, Covent Garden, LONDON WC2E 7BB Tel: 0171 3796344 Appt. London Transport archives c1810 on. Poster archive c1908 on.

Museum In Docklands Library & Archive, Unit C 14, Poplar Business Park, 10 Prestons Road, LONDON E14 9RL Tel: 0171 5151162 This repository is currently closed to researchers as it is expected there will be a move to **Warehouse No 1 North Quay, West India Docks, London E14**, towards the end of 1999, re-opening January 2000. Probable opening hours T-10-5. Full disabled access. Facilities in the new Museum Library & Archive will be in a purpose built Research Room & accessible via Canary Wharf Station, DLR & Jubilee Line-5 mins walk. Records: The staff records relate only to the permanent establishments of private dock companies in the Port of London 1800-1909 & of the Port of London Authority 1909 on. Registers of vessels licensed to operate on the tidal R. Thames 1890-1950. Thames Navigation Authorities 1770 on. Newspapers. Photographs. The minute books of the private dock companies are unique & tell the story of one of the world's greatest ports.
Note: This archive contains no records relating to the millions of casual dock labourers who worked in the docks & wharves of the Port of London as such records are virtually non-existent. From January 2000 write for further info. **O. R: Island History Trust**, Docklands Settlement, Westferry Road, LONDON E14.

Museum of London, 150 London Wall, LONDON EC27 5HN Appt. Varied collections incl. Port of London Authority records from 1911. Business. Deeds. Maps & plans. Photographs. Library.

National Army Museum, Royal Hospital Road, LONDON SW3 4HT Tel: 0171 7300717 **Fax:** 0171 823 6573 **E-mail:** nam@enterprise.net
Internet: http://www.failte.com/nam/
Opening Hours: T.-Sat 10-4.30 Closure: Public hols+preceding Sat+Dec 24- Jan 1+last 2 wks in Oct.
Parking: None.
Disabled: Lift & ramp to galleries & reading room. Toilet. Access to shop/cafe.
Children: Not allowed.
Appointments: Prior booking for viewers-2 days. Entry-register+National Army Museum reader's ticket obtained in advance of visit. 18 seats+2 film+3 fiche-1 reader/printer.
Ordering System: Prior ordering by letter/tel. Catalogue nos required. Eight ordered & produced. Delivery 10-20 mins. No production 12-2. Last order: 4.15. P/copying by staff-post/collection (next day not guaranteed). Typing/cameras not permitted. Taping/laptops (power supply) allowed.
Records: Private papers/diaries/letters/memoirs/poems etc. of officers & men of British Army incl. former Indian Army regiments/former Irish regiments prior to 1922/various other regiments 17thC on. Regimental books. Photographs/prints/drawings. Maps. Oral histories. Films. Military music. United Services Club 1815-1970. Collection of papers of major officers 18thC on. Regimental records of 9th/12th Royal Lancers/Middlesex Regiment/Womens Royal Army Corps (& predecessors)/ Westminster

Dragoons/Surrey Yeomanry 4th Battn/London Regiment/various Indian Army units. Business archives of Gaunt & other military tailors. Tidworth Tattoo records 1920-1939.
Research Service: None.
Facilities: Toilets/public tel/refreshment facilities. Café/pub/shops nearby.
Publications: Free: computer print-outs or p/copies of lists of some collections can be produced in response to specific enquiries. (SAE).
Remarks: No bags allowed-storage at main entrance cloakroom. Donations appreciated. Underground: Sloane Square.

National Maritime Museum, Library & Archive, GREENWICH, London SE10 9NF
Tel: 0181 3126691 **Fax:** 0181 3126722
Internet: http://www.nmm.ac.uk
Opening Hours: M.-F. 10-4.45 Closure: Public hols+last 2 wks in Feb.
Parking: None.
Disabled: Library on ground floor-room for w/chair users. Large magnifying stand available.
Children: Not generally allowed.
Appointments: Prior booking unnecessary. Entry-register+ reader's ticket+ID. 22 seats+ 2 film+2 fiche-3 reader/printers.
Ordering System: Prior ordering by letter/tel. Catalogue nos sometimes required. Six ordered, three produced. Delivery, at present:10.30; 11.45; 2.30 due to building works-normally 30 mins. Most ship plans & older charts all require 1 wks notice. P/copying restricted, by staff-post. Typing/cameras not permitted. Taping/laptops (power supply) allowed.
Records: Numerous collections of personal papers incl. Nelson's. Admiralty Records (National collection). Navy Board. Dockyards. Books. Photographs. Charts. Portulan Charts. Letter & order books. Masters certificates/crew lists/ships logs. Lloyds Surveys. Business records except P&O.
Research Service: Charge made.
Facilities: Toilets/public tel/restaurant facilities. Café/pub/shops nearby.
Publications: For sale: *National Maritime Museum Guide to the Manuscripts* (2 Vols).
Remarks: Bags not allowed-lockers. Donations appreciated. Station: BR. Maze Hill.

Post Office Archives, Freeling House, Mount Pleasant Complex, LONDON EC1A 1BB. (Entrance-Phoenix Place). **Tel:** 0171 2392570 **Fax:** 0171 2392576 **E-mail:** catherine.orton@postoffice.co.uk
Opening Hours: M.-F. 9-4.15 Closure: Public hols+Maundy Thurs pm.
Parking: None.
Disabled: Access. Toilet.
Children: Not allowed.
Appointments: Prior booking unnecessary. Entry-register+ID. 14 seats+1 film+1 fiche-1 reader/printer.
Ordering System: Prior ordering by letter/tel. Catalogue nos required. Six ordered & produced. Delivery 5 mins. Last order: 3.45. P/copying-DIY. Typing/laptops (power supply) permitted. Taping/cameras not allowed.
Records: The history of the British Post Office reflecting the great variety of operations & services provided since its creation over 350 years ago. Numerous subjects incl. pillar boxes/postage stamps/post office products/ service/transport & distribution of mail. Family historians will find records of appointments/ pensions/gratuities which can provide name/rank/job/years of service/wages/ appointments held. Local historians can find information about the growth of the Post Office in their area. Mails/transport/ telecommunications in G.B. & overseas. Internal operation of early colonial service. Local postal services. Reports to the Post Master General 1790-1836/1847-1859. Reports from post masters. Sketches of local post & petitions. Volumes containing proof impressions of date & cancellation stamps since 1825. Packet Service from 1680s. Mail Coach Service from 1780s. Mail by rail from 1830. Air Mail from 1920s. Post Office Savings. Broadcasting. Reproduction maps of Cary's Survey of the High Road from London 1790. Photographs.
Research Service: None.
Facilities: Toilet. No public tel. Room for own food/drink vending machine. Café/pub nearby.
Publications: Free: Brochures. Info. sheets (A4 SAE). For sale: Books. Videos. Maps. Posters. Postcards. Prints. Engravings. Historical miniatures.
O.R: National Postal Museum, King Edward Street, LONDON EC1A 1LP Tel: 0171 2395420. Official collection of British Stamps.
Remarks: Bags not allowed-storage facilities. Underground: Chancery Lane/Farringdon. Station: King's Cross.

Principal Probate of the Family Division, First Avenue House, 42-49 High Holborn, LONDON WCN 6NP Tel: 0171 9367000 (Probate): 0171 9366940 (Divorce). Voice-mail: 0171 9367189/0171 9367574 for concise instructions on how to search for and order copies of grants of probate - for England and Wales only.
Opening Hours: M.-F. 10-4.30 Closure: Public hols.
Parking: None.
Disabled: No facilities-steps to entrance.
Children: Accompanied: At staff's discretion. Unaccompanied: 16 yrs+
Appointments: No prior booking.
Ordering System: No prior ordering. Unlimited number taken from the Probate

Indexes at a time. Small fee for viewing wills. Copies of requests sent by post.
Records: Wills & Administrations for England & Wales from 1858 to present. Divorce petitions 1858 on. Index to all decrees absolute issued by England & Wales 1858 on. Divorce Index inspected by staff only. Postal applications: apply to the Chief Clerk, Probate Sub Registry, Duncombe Place, York YO1 2EA who will send requisite request form.
Facilities: Toilets/public tel. No refreshment facilities. Café/pub nearby.
Remarks: This entry has been compiled from the previous entry in the 3rd Ed. & updated where possible. **Note:** Divorce petitions through private Acts of Parliament 1668-1857 have been indexed & are available at the House of Lords RO (see entry). **Note:** The search room only houses indexes to wills and administrations already proved and granted.

Public Record Office, KEW, Richmond, Surrey TW9 4DU Tel: 0181 8763444
Fax: 0181 8788905 **E-mail:** enquiry.pro.rsd.kew@gtnet.gov.uk
Internet: http://www.open.gov.uk/pro/prohome.htm Website address will soon become http://www.pro.gov.uk
Opening Hours: M.W.F.Sat 9.30-5; T. 10-7; Th. 9.30-7 Closure: Public hols+1st 2 wks in Dec.
Parking: Yes-free.
Disabled: Disabled friendly+sign language.
Children: At staff's discretion.
Appointments: Prior booking unnecessary. Entry-PRO reader's ticket+ID. 400 seats+60 film+30 fiche-6 reader/printers.
Ordering System: Prior ordering by letter/tel-with reader's ticket name & number. Catalogue nos required-Tel: 0181 3925261. Three ordered, one produced-bulk orders by prior arrangement. Last order: M.W.F. 4.00; T.Th. 4.30; Sat 2.30. Delivery 35 mins. P/copying restricted, by staff-same day/post/collection. DIY-M/f only. Typing/taping/laptops (power supply) permitted. Cameras not allowed.
Records: of Central Government. Central Courts of Law 11thC to present. Army. Navy. Royal Marines. Royal Air Force. Poor Law Union Correspondence. Maps & plans. Photographic collection.
Research Service: Limited specific enquiry. List of professional researchers available. (SAE).
Facilities: Toilets/public tel/restaurant/room for own food/drink vending machine.
Publications: The PRO has a bookshop with a wide range of family, military & general history books. **Tracing Your Ancestors in the PRO*. **New to Kew?* a first time guide for family historians. Series of guides on various categories of records held in the PRO. Numerous free info leaflets on a wide variety of topics-available on a self-help basis only (not by post).
Remarks: Bags not allowed-lockers/cloakroom. Donations appreciated. **Note:** It is recommended that prior to a first visit to the PRO guides to the PRO and the *books should be consulted-these should be available in most major reference libraries. Most records over 30 yrs old are available to the public with some exceptions. Car access off Mortlake Road (A205). From Kew Bridge, first left turn after Ruskin Avenue. Underground & rail: Kew Gardens. Station: Kew Bridge. To contact Friends of the PRO-tel: 0181 8763444 Ext. 2226. Also see entry for Family Records Centre, London.

Railtrack PLC Records Centres for civil engineering and architectural records relating to the past and present appearance of currently operational main-line railway infrastructure in Great Britain, i.e. not closed or preserved railways and railways in Ireland. Railtrack also holds property records (e.g. title deeds & land plans) relating to the railway estate – all of these records were transferred to Railtrack from British Railways on 1st April 1994. Enquiries in writing (SAE) only to the appropriate Records Manager as shown below.
Scotland (whole of) civil engineering & architectural records – **Railtrack Scotland Records Manager**, Buchanan House, 58 Port Dundas Road, GLASGOW G4 0HG
London North Eastern (N.E. England, Yorkshire & N. Lincs East Coast Main Line from Scottish Border to London Kings Cross) – **Railtrack London North Eastern Zone Records Manager**, D007 Hudson House, YORK YO1 1HP
Midlands (N.W. England, East & West Midlands, North & Central Wales, West Coast Main Line from Scottish Border to London Euston, main lines to boundary of London St. Pancras [Note: London St. Pancras is not owned by Railtrack] and London Marylebone) – **Railtrack Midlands Zone Records Manager**, 4th Floor East Stanier House, 10 Holliday Street, BIRMINGHAM B1 1TG.
Great Western (South Central & South Wales, Welsh Borders, the West Country, Gloucestershire, Herefordshire, Worcestershire, Wiltshire, Oxfordshire, Berkshire & mainline into Paddington) – **Railtrack Great Western Zone Records Manager**, WH 157 125 House, (Milford Wing), 1 Gloucester Street, SWINDON SN1 1GW.
Southern (Southern England south of the Thames & the GWR Main Line west to Exeter, all lines radiating from London Liverpool Street & London Fenchurch Street into East Anglia, North London Line from Richmond to North Woolwich) – **Railtrack Southern**

Zone Records Manager, Plan Arch 236D Waterloo Street, LONDON SE1 8SW.
Property Records (England, Wales & Scotland) - **Drawing Office and Land Records Manager**, Railtrack Property, 7th Floor, Tournament House, Paddington Station, LONDON W2 1FT.
In case of difficulty contact - Head of Records Management, Railtrack PLC, DP 13 Legal & Secretariat, Railtrack House, Euston Square, LONDON NW1 2EE.
Remarks: Historians who wish to access records of parliamentary authorisations or private acts of Parliament relating to railways should apply to the House of Lords Record Office, London (see entry). It should be noted that no business records prior to 1st April 1994 are held by Railtrack and no other post 1st April 1994 business records are open to the public. For reasons of security and commercial confidentiality decisions on granting access to records will have to be made on a case by case basis and are entirely at the discretion of the records manager. Record Centres exist primarily to provide a service to Railtrack and its suppliers and this work will always take priority. A charge will be levied in accordance with local policy. It should be noted that no historical personnel records are held by Railtrack and that many of these are at the Public Record Office, Kew. Also see *Railway Ancestors: A guide to the Staff Records of the Railway Companies of England & Wales 1822-1947* by David T. Hawkings (Alan Sutton Publishing 1995).

Library of the Religious Society of Friends (Quakers), Friends House, Euston Road, LONDON, NW1 2BJ Tel. 0171 6631000/6631135 **Fax:** 0171 6631001
Opening Hours: M.T.Th.F. 1-5; W. 10-5; Sats in the year 10-3 these vary-phone for info. Closure: Public hols+2 wks in Spring & Autumn.
Parking: None.
Disabled: Disabled friendly.
Children: At librarian's discretion.
Appointments: Prior booking for viewers-1 wk. Entry-register+ID+library reader's ticket+letter of introduction. 12 seats+2 film.
Ordering System: Prior ordering by letter/tel. Catalogue nos sometimes required. Three ordered, one produced. P/copying restricted, by staff-post/collection. Typing/taping/cameras at staff's discretion. Laptops (power supply) permitted.
Records: for the Religious Society of Friends in Great Britain. Quaker registers/papers/books/ diaries/MSS collection/letters. Early Quaker writings. Meetings. Great Book of Sufferings 1659-1800. Periodicals-*The Friend* 1843 on/*The Friends Quarterly* 1867/The British Friend 1843-1913.
Research Service: None.
Facilities: Toilets/public tel/refreshment facilities/drink vending machine. Café/pub/ shops nearby.
Publications: Quaker Bookshop in same building.
Remarks: Bags not allowed-lockers (limited). Donations appreciated. Quaker registers have been deposited with the PRO & are available on film at the Family Records Centre (see entry). Other Quaker registers & minutes of Quarterly Meetings may be found in CROs & archive repositories. Underground: Euston Square.

Department of Research & Information Services, R.A.F. Museum, Grahame Park Way, HENDON, London NW9 5LL Tel: 0181 2052266 **Fax:** 0181 2001751
Opening Hours: Th. 10-5 Closure: Mon/Tues/Wed/Fri+Public hols+Christmas period.
Parking: Yes.
Disabled: Lift.
Children: Accompanied: 12 yrs+ Unaccompanied: 16 yrs+
Appointments: Prior booking for seats/viewers-2 wks min. Entry-register. 7 seats+2 film/fiche-dual.
Ordering System: Prior ordering by letter/tel. Three ordered & produced. Delivery 5 mins. No production 12-2. P/copying restricted, by staff-same day(small amounts)/post. Typing/taping/laptops (power supply) permitted. Cameras not allowed.
Records: for all theatres in which the RAF & its antecedents have operated. Large collections of private papers from personnel of all ranks. Aircrew logbooks. WW1 casualty records. Records for RAF aircraft/vehicles/marine craft. Photographs & films.
Research Service: None.
Facilities: Toilets/public tel/restaurant. Room for own food-in preparation.
Publications: Info leaflet on research topics (A5 SAE).
Remarks: Bags not allowed-cloakroom. Donations appreciated. **Note:** The PRO, Kew also holds RAF records. Station: Underground: Colindale. B.R. Thameslink: Mill Hill Broadway.

Society of Genealogists, 14 Charterhouse Buildings, Goswell Road, LONDON EC1M 7BA Tel: 0171 2500291/0171 2518799 **Fax:** available on application. **E-mail:** Computers in Genealogy=http:www.gold.ac.uk/~cig/ For articles & correspondence to the editor of Computers in Genealogy: cig@gold.ac.uk
Internet:http://www.cs.ncl.ac.uk/genuki/SoG
Opening Hours: T.F.Sat 10-6; W.Th. 10-8 Closure: Mon+Public hols+preceding Fri pm+1st full wk in Feb.
Parking: None.
Disabled: Ground floor contains most of the major sources-w/chair access. An able-bodied

friend can be admitted free to fetch & carry-by prior arrangement with librarian.
Children: Accompanied: under 12 yrs by permission of librarian. Unaccompanied: 13 yrs+
Appointments: Prior booking for CD-Rom computer-2 wks. Entry-register+member's ticket (fee for non-members). c75 seats+9 film+26 fiche-4 reader/printers.
Ordering System: No prior ordering. Three ordered & produced (closed access material only). Possible delay Sat 12.30-2.30. Delivery 5 mins. Last order: 15 mins before closure. **Note:** Large roll pedigrees cannot be produced if lecture theatre is in use. P/copying by staff for pedigrees-those larger than A3 can be copied at nearby printshop. Taping not permitted. Typing allowed. Cameras/laptops (power supply+small donation) by prior arrangement.
Records: Worldwide with emphasis on areas receiving British immigrants+ British Isles. Largest genealogical library in G.B. PRs/BTs-film/fiche/Ts. Boyd's Marriage Index/Inhabitants of London/London burials. Bernau Index-Chancery & other court proceedings. Great Card Index. MIs. Directories. Poll books. Schools/Universities. Calendars of wills/marriage licences. Apprentices/Masters Index. Local histories. Pedigrees/family histories. Australian/New Zealand state registration indexes. M/f-census/GRO Indexes/ Scottish GRO Indexes/Scottish OPR Indexes/ IGI for world.
Research Service: Charge made for limited searches in indexed sources+p/copies/film or fiche printouts.
Facilities: Toilet/public tel/room for own food+facilties for tea/coffee. Café/pub/shops nearby.
Publications: Free: Info. leaflets. Bookshop stock list. SoG Publications catalogue. Microfiche stock list (A5 SAE). For sale: Numerous SoG & other publications-genealogy/local history/social history covering G.B. & overseas+surnames/trades/ professions /railwaymen etc. Record Guides to various sources.
Remarks: Bags not allowed-lockers. Donations appreciated. Underground: Islington/Barbican.

United Reformed Church History Society, 86 Tavistock Place, LONDON WC1H 9RT. Tel: 0171 9162020 Appt. Open F. 11.30-3.30. Denominational records of Presbyterian Church of England. Congregational Church-England/ Wales. Some baptism registers. Biographical information of former ministers. Unique collection of 17thC religious pamphlets. Over 6,000 books. **Note:** This collection will be moving to Westminster College, Cambridge in 1998.

Westminster Abbey Muniment Room & Library, East Cloister, LONDON SW1P 3PA
Tel: 0171 2225152 Ext. 228 **Fax:** 0171 2226391
Opening Hours: M.-F. 10-1; 2-4.45 Closure: Occasional closures owing to special services+Public hols.
Parking: None.
Disabled: No facilities-spiral staircase to Search room.
Children: 16 yrs+
Appointments: Prior booking for seats. Entry-register. 4 seats.
Ordering System: Prior ordering by letter/ tel. Catalogue nos sometimes required. Five ordered & produced-according to size. Delivery-10 mins. P/copying by staff-same day. Typing/taping/cameras not permitted. Laptops (power supply strictly subject to a 'portable appliance certificate' produced) allowed.
Records: Administrative archives of the medieval monastery of Westminster & of post-reformation Collegiate Church. Extensive estates held until mid 19thC. PRs-film/Ts of the Abbey. M/f of St. Margaret's Westminster-PRs available ONLY at Westminster City Archives (see entry). Various other records of St. Margaret's Westminster. Personal papers. City of Westminster coroners inquests 1760-1880. Photographs & plans. 14,000 printed books.
Research Service: Limited specific enquiry-fee.
Facilities: Toilet. No public tel. Coffee stall in cloisters. Café/pub nearby.
Publications: Various for sale.
Remarks: Donations appreciated. Underground: Westminster/St. James Park.

Westminster Diocesan Archives, 16A Abingdon Road, Kensington, LONDON W8 6AF Tel: 0171 9383580. This is the private archive of the Roman Catholic Archbishop of Westminster & is not open to the public, nor is access allowed at anytime to the material stored here. There are a few church registers which are being transcribed by the Catholic Family History Society & copies of all these are deposited with the Society of Genealogists as they become available. These are mainly registers of baptisms with some marriages & deaths which, in some cases, date back to the 18th century (nothing earlier). Occasional access is allowed to those registers not yet transcribed from 10-4 by appt. only. Address requests to the Catholic Family History Society, c/o Mrs B. Murray, General Secretary, 2 Winscombe Crescent, Ealing, London W5 1AZ.

Dr. Williams's Library, 14 Gordon Square, LONDON WC1H OAG Tel: 0171 3873727. Appt. Opening Hours: M.W.F. 10-5; T.Th. 10-6.30 Closure: Tues/Thurs+1st 2 wks in Aug+Easter+Dec 24-Jan 2. Publications:

LONDON (Useful Addresses)

Various guides to collections. This library holds a large collection of material in MSS & print, relating to the history of English Protestant dissent, particularly in its Presbyterian/Unitarian/Congregational forms. The librarian is able to sometimes assist with enqs. about ministers in these denominations. The Congregational Library formerly at the Memorial Hall, Farringdon Street, is contained within this building & comes under the librarian. Nonconformist registers may also be found at the Family Records Centre, PRO, Kew and CRO's. **Note:** Records of Dr. Williams's Library & Wesleyan Metropolitan Registry have been filmed & are available at the PRO & Family Records Centre (RG 5).

LONDON-USEFUL ADDRESSES:

British Transport Police Headquarters, 15 Tavistock Place, LONDON WC1H OSJ-GWR Transport Police records.

Business Archives Council, The Clove Building, 4 Maquire Street, LONDON SE1 2NQ

Charity Commission for England & Wales, St. Albans House, 57/60 Haymarket, LONDON SW1Y 4QX

Church of England Record Centre, 15 Galleywall Road, South Bermondsey, LONDON SE16 3PB

Grand Lodge of England, Freemasons Hall, Great Queen Street, LONDON WC2B 5AZ

Huguenot Society of Great Britain and Ireland, Huguenot Library, University College London, Gower Street, LONDON WC1E 6BT

National Monuments Record Centre (London Office), 55 Blandford Street, LONDON W1H 3AF-connection with Swindon Office by Monarch.

National Portrait Gallery Archive, Heinz Archive & Library, St. Martin's Place, LONDON WC2H OHE Access-Orange Street.

Tate Gallery Archive, Millbank, LONDON SW1P 4RG

The College of Arms, Queen Victoria Street, LONDON EC4V 4BT

The Royal Commission on Historical Manuscripts, Quality House, Quality Court, Chancery Lane, LONDON WC2A 1HP

The Theatre Museum, 1E Tavistock Street, LONDON WC2E 7PA (Postal address). Library & Archive Public entrance-Russell Street, Covent Garden

LORD COUTANCHE LIBRARY, see St. Helier.

Lowestoft Record Office, Central Library, Clapham Road, LOWESTOFT, Suffolk NR32 1DR Tel: 01502 405357 **Fax:** 01502 405350 **E-mail:** gwyn.thomas@libber.suffolkcc .gov.uk
Internet:http://www.suffolkcc.gov.uk/libraries_and_heritage/
Opening Hours: M.W.-F. 9.15-5.30; T. 9.15-6; Sat 9.15-5 Closure: Public hols.
Parking: Public nearby.
Disabled: Ramp. Lift. Toilet.
Children: At archivist's discretion.
Appointments: Prior booking for viewers-2/3 days. Entry-register+CARN. 18 seats+4 film+6 fiche-1 reader/printer.
Ordering System: Prior ordering by letter/tel. Catalogue nos helpful. Number ordered at archivist's discretion, four produced. Delivery 10-15 mins. Sometimes no production 12-2. Last order: 4.45 except for Tues when 5.45. P/copying restricted, by staff-same day/post. Typing not permitted. Taping/cameras by arrangement. Laptops (power supply by arrangement) allowed.
Records: for North East Suffolk, but countywide coverage of census & PRs. Diocesan RO for St. Edmundsbury & Ipswich. PRs-fiche/Ts/originals if not copied. BTs available. Manorial. Business. Local authority. Education. Shipping. Enclosure. Probate. Poll books. Electoral registers. Books. Directories. Pamphlets. Maps. Photographs. M/f-newspapers/census/IGI.
Research Service: Charge made.
Facilities: Toilets/public tel/restaurant. Café/pub/shops nearby.
Publications: Free: Info leaflets: *Notes for Searchers. PRs/Census on M/F.* (SAE) For sale: Leaflets: *Newspapers on M/f. IGI. Local History catalogue. Manorial records.* New edition of *The Guide to Genealogical Sources in the Suffolk RO* is due to be printed in sections, which will be available as a whole or separately.
Tourist Office: Tel: 01502 523000 Fax: 01502 539023
Remarks: Bags not allowed-lockers. Donations appreciated.

Ludlow Museum, Castle Street, LUDLOW, Shropshire SY8 1AS Tel: 01584 875384 Appt. Local History collection. Photographs. Costumes.

LUTON, see Bedford.

Luton Central Library, St. George's Square, LUTON, Beds LU1 2NG Tel: 01582 30161 Usually open. Local Studies collection for Luton & Bedfordshire.

Luton Museum & Art Gallery, Wardown Park, Old Bedford Road, LUTON, Beds LU2 7HA Tel: 01582 546723 Appt. Disabled: Access. Lift. Toilet. Prior booking for seats-1/2 wks. Entry-register. The hat & lace industry in Beds & further afield. Archive collection & library relating to it.

Lydd Town Council, Town Clerk's Office, Guildhall, LYDD, Romney Marsh, Kent TN29 9AF Tel: 01797 320999 Appt-1/2 wks. Entry-register+ID+letter of recommendation. P/copying. Area covered by the old Borough of Lydd-most prior to 1850+the history of the Cinque Ports, of which Lydd was a chartered member+the history of small chartered towns. Legal docs-Court & Plea Books. Militia. Oath Rolls. Burgess Rolls. Freemen. Some parish & charity. Records are catalogued & a list is available on site or at the Centre for Kentish Studies, Maidstone (see entry).

MAIDENHEAD-USEFUL ADDRESS:

Commonwealth War Graves Commission, 2 Marlow Road, MAIDENHEAD, Berks SL6 7DX. Maintains computerised records of burials & commemorations of Commonwealth war dead from the two World Wars in 140 countries & names of citizens of Commonwealth & Empire killed in UK 1939-45 (60,000+).

Centre for Kentish Studies, County Hall, MAIDSTONE, Kent. ME4 1XQ (opposite railway station) **Tel:** 01622 694363 **Fax:** 01622 694379
Opening Hours: T.W.F. 9-5; Th. 10-5; 2nd & 4th Sat 9-1 Closure: Mon+Public hols+2 wks in June. Report in first instance to security staff at County Hall entrance & then to Centre receptionist in bookshop.
Parking: Public nearby-paying. All day parking at Station or multi-storey parks.
Disabled: W/chair & disabled access. Deaf loops. Easy Reader. Special parking by prior arrangement.
Children: Accompanied: At archivist's discretion. Unaccompanied: 10 yrs+
Appointments: Prior booking for viewers-1 wk. Entry-CARN (2 passport-sized photos+ID). 14 seats+15 film+ 2 fiche-1 reader/printer.
Ordering System: Prior ordering by letter/tel. Catalogue nos sometimes required. Number ordered at archivist's discretion, three produced. Delivery 10 mins. Last order: 4 pm. **Note:** Microfilm room closes 15 mins before main searchroom. P/copying restricted, by staff-same day/post/collection. Typing/taping/cameras not permitted. Laptops allowed.
Records: for historic county of Kent. Diocesan RO for Rochester & Canterbury. PRs for Archdeaconries of Maidstone/Malling/Shoreham/Sevenoaks/Tonbridge/Tunbridge Wells-film/fiche/Ts/originals if not copied. BTs & Marriage licences for diocese of Rochester. Wills & inventories. Manorial. Schools & education. Apprenticeship. Taxation. PLU. Royal West Kent Regiment 18-20thC's. Royal East Kent Yeomanry 18-20thC's. Hearth Tax returns. Public house licenses. Nonconformist. Local Government. Rural District Council for E. & W. Ashford/Cranbrook/Faversham/Hollingbourne/Maidstone/Malling/ Sheppey/Swale/Tenterden/Thanet. Urban District Council for Ashford/Sheerness/ Sittingbourne & Milton/Swanscombe/ Tonbridge/Walmer. Borough records for Dartford/Deal/Dover/Faversham/Gillingham/Gravesend/Maidstone /New Romney/ Queenborough/Romney Marsh/Sandwich/ Tenterden. Charities & societies. Hospitals. Business, Trade & industry. Family & estate. Shipping register incl. fishing crew lists. Quarter/General Sessions. Electoral registers & Poll books. Directories. Maps & plans. Tithe Maps & Awards. Illustrations. Photographs. Ephemera. Periodicals. M/f-census/IGI. **Note:** The Centre has an extensive collection of printed books on history & topography of Kent+related subjects. Also see entry for Lydd Town Council.
Research Service: Charge made.
Facilities: Toilet/public tel/restaurant. Café/pub/shops nearby.
Publications: Guidance leaflet on collections. Copies of catalogues & lists. Maps. (Bookshop).
O.R: Maidstone Library, St. Faith's Street, MAIDSTONE. ME14 1LH. Tel: 01622 752344
Tourist Office: Tel: 1622 673581 Fax: 01622 673581
Remarks: Bags not allowed-lockers. Donations appreciated. **Note:** From 1st April 1998 a new Unitary Authority-Medway Authority will be responsible for the Rochester upon Medway & Gillingham areas. This office comprises the collections of the West Kent Archives Office & the County Local Studies Library. See Publications: *West Kent Sources: Guide to Genealogical Research in Diocese of Rochester* (N.W. Kent FHS). *New Maidstone Gaol Order Book 1805-23* (Kent Archives Society). See entry for E. Kent Archive Centre, Whitfield, Dover. Station: Maidstone East (from London-Victoria/Charing Cross)

MAN, ISLE OF, see Douglas.

Chetham's Library, Long Millgate, MANCHESTER, Greater Manchester M3 1SB Tel: 0161 8347961 **Fax:** 0161 8395797 **E-mail:** chetlib@dial.pipex.com

MANCHESTER

Opening Hours: M.-F. 9-12.30; 1.30-4.30 Closure: Public hols+Christmas.
Parking: 2 spaces.
Disabled: Limited access to building but full access to the collections.
Children: Accompanied: 16 yrs+ Unaccompanied: 18 yrs.
Appointments: Prior booking for seats-few days. Entry-register+ID+references. 25 seats.
Ordering System: Prior ordering by letter/tel. Number ordered & produced at librarian's discretion. P/copying restricted, by staff. Typing/taping/cameras/laptops (power supply) permitted.
Records: for Manchester & surrounding area. Manchester Sunday School. Societies. Hospital minute books. Hulme Trust deeds. Business-Belle Vue/Jennison collections. Family & estate. Societies. Sutton nr. Macclesfield & Over Knutford poor house & constable's accounts. Newspapers. Scrapbooks. Tracts & broadsides. Photographic collection of slides.
Research Service: None.
Facilities: Toilet/public tel. No refreshment facilities. Café/pub/shops nearby.
Remarks: Donations appreciated. Station: Manchester Central.

Documentary Photography Archive, c/o Room GO11, Tylecote Building, Cavendish Street, MANCHESTER, Greater Manchester M15 6BG. Tel: 0161 247 1765 Appt. Contemporary & historical photographic collection relating to N. West.

Greater Manchester County Record Office, 56 Marshall Street, New Cross, MANCHESTER, Greater Manchester M4 5FU Tel: 0161 8325284 **Fax:** 0161 8393808
E-mail: archives@gmcro.u-net.com
Internet:http://www/u-net.com/~gmcro/home.htm
Opening Hours: M. 1-5; T.-F. 9-5; 2nd & 4th Sat 9-12; 1-4 Closure: Public hols+preceding Sat+1 wk stocktaking.
Parking: None
Disabled: Steps to lift. Toilet. Induction loop in conference room.
Children: At archivist's discretion.
Appointments: Prior booking for viewers-2/3 wks. Entry-register+CARN. Entrance fee for residents of Stockport MBC only. 10 seats+10 film+5 fiche.
Ordering System: Prior ordering by letter/tel. Catalogue nos required. Number ordered & produced at archivist's discretion. Delivery 5-10 mins. Possible restriction lunchtime. Last order: 4.30 pm. P/copying by staff-same day. Typing/taping/laptops (power supply-subject to electrical equipment being certified) at archivist's discretion. Cameras not allowed.
Records: for Greater Manchester county. Local authority records for Bury & Trafford Districts (also see Trafford Central Library, Sale). Coroners-Bolton/Bury/Manchester/Oldham/Rochdale. Hospitals-Altrincham/Bury. Valuation books (see Manchester City Archives). Family. Business incl. Manchester Ship Canal (see Manchester Local Studies Archives), Rochdale Canal (see Rochdale Central Library). Trade Unions. Solicitors. Motor vehicle licensing-Bury/Oldham/Rochdale/Stockport. Societies. Maps. Documentary Photographic Archive. National collection-The Paul Graney Memorial Folk Trust (Introductory guide available). M/f-GRO Indexes 1837-1950 (appt. nec.)/Probate Index 1858-1945/IGI.
Research Service: Charge made.
Facilities: Toilet/public tel/room for own food/drink vending machine. Café/pub nearby. Shops 10 mins.
Publications: Free: Information for Visitors. *G.M. Archives: A Guide to local repositories* (A5 SAE).For sale: *GMCRO Guide.* Leaflet pack. Courier-newsletter of GMCRO (also by subscription). *Caring for your Family Photographs. Manchester Fire Brigade Book. Kingswater-Story of Debdale. Rochdale Canal* booklet. *Dark Days-Memories of Lancashire & Cheshire Coal Mining.* Publications of the Record Society of Lancashire & Cheshire.
O.R: The Registrar, Agecroft Cemetery, Langley Road, SWINTON, Manchester M27 2SS Tel: 0161 7362512 for burial records of Weaste Cemetery & Agecroft Cemetery. Please supply as many details as possible; **The Registrar**, 716 Liverpool Road, ECCLES, Manchester, Greater Manchester M30 7LW Tel: 0161 7891901 for burial records of Peel Green Cemetery. Please supply as many details as possible. **Manchester District Probate Registry**, 9th Floor, Astley House, 23 Quay Street, MANCHESTER, Greater Manchester, M3 4AT Tel: 0161 8344319
Tourist Office: Tel: 0161 2343157/8 Fax: 0161 2369900
Remarks: Bags not allowed-lockers. Donations appreciated. **Note:** Negotiations are proceeding for re-location of office but is not likely in less than 2 yrs. Station: Manchester Piccadilly: Manchester Victoria.

Greater Manchester Police Museum, Newton Street, MANCHESTER, Greater Manchester M1 1ES. Tel: 0161 8563287 (Voice mail facility) Fax: 0161 856 3286. Open M.-F. for research purposes by staff, Tues for research interviews. Police Museum staff are able to provide more detailed information, due to their training and experience, being able to interpret 'police phraseology' or 'annotations' etc. Family history & similar enquiries are normally answered in 3-4 wks but can take longer if more extensive research is required. Appts. can be made for enquiriers to visit & speak with a researcher to discuss any particular case or problem (letter/fax). **Note:** That some archive material will be subject to 30 or 75 yr. closure. Records relate to the history of the police & their records in the Greater Manchester area-Manchester/Oldham/Salford/Rochdale/Stockport. Personal records of police officers & aliens registers for Salford. Manchester Court Leet. Constables accounts. Watch Committee papers for Oldham/Salford/Manchester. Oldham Beadles Book 1827. Personnel appointment ledgers for Manchester City/Oldham Borough/Rochdale Borough/ Salford City/Stockport Borough Police Forces. Personnel files for Bolton Borough/Manchester City/Manchester & Salford/Greater Manchester Police Forces. Documentation for WW2. Court records-Calenders of Prisoners/Manchester Assize/Quarter Sessions. Manchester Summons Books. Oldham Felony. J.Ps. Journal 1852-1935. Museum also holds a small ref. section of secondary sources relating to the development of policing, individual force histories, biography, crime & forensic science. Research is free of charge but donations towards this service are appreciated. Publications: Free: *Greater Manchester Police Museum*. Information for Visitors (guided tours, research etc). Police F.H. Enquiry Form. *Policing Crime in Victorian Times. Summary of Archive Collection* (A5 SAE). **Note:** Enquiries must relate to deceased police officers of the Greater Manchester area only.

Jewish Museum, 190 Cheetham Hill Road, MANCHESTER, Greater Manchester M8 8LW. Tel: 0161 8349879. Appt. Deposited records of the Jewish communities in the Greater Manchester region. For records of official Jewish organisations see entry for Manchester Local Studies Archives.

John Rylands University Library of Manchester (Special Collections Division), 150 Deansgate, MANCHESTER, Greater Manchester M3 3EH Tel: 0161 8345343/6765 **Fax:** 0161 8345574 **E-mail:** (Head of Special Collections) pmcniven@fs1.li.man.ac.uk
Internet: http://rylibweb.man.ac.uk
Opening Hours: M.-F. 10-5.30; Sat 10-1 Closure: Public hols+Christmas Eve-New Year's Day.
Parking: None.
Disabled: Very difficult-no w/chair access. Lift for more able-bodied. Situation under review.
Children: Accompanied: At librarian's discretion. Unaccompanied: Normally 18 yrs+
Appointments: Prior booking unnecessary. Entry-Manchester University card or letter of recommendation+ID. c40 seats+3 fiche. No m/film readers-under review.
Ordering System: Prior ordering by letter/tel. Catalogue nos required. Number ordered & produced at librarian's discretion. Delivery 5-30 mins. Last order: 30 mins before closure. P/copying restricted, by staff-same day/post. Typing/taping at librarian's discretion. Laptops (power supply) permitted. Cameras not allowed.
Records: for Cheshire & Lancashire. Rare books & MSS (Division of University Library). Nonconformist. Private genealogical & family papers. Manchester Medical Society. English textile companies. Business. Deeds. Newspapers.
Research Service: None.
Facilities: Toilets. No public tel/refreshment facilities. Café/pub/shops nearby.
Publications: Free: *Guide to the building & research resources.* (SAE). For sale: Prospectuses relating to the Library. Exhibition catalogues. Offprints from the Library's Bulletin incl. Handlists of Holdings, postcards.
O.R: Methodist Archives & Research Centre situated at above address Tel: 0161 8345343. Methodist records excluding Circuit, Chapel & genealogical records. Periodicals. Local histories. Portraits. Photographs.
Remarks: Bags not allowed-manned cloakroom. Donations appreciated. Station: Salford Central; Manchester Victoria.

Manchester Local Studies Archives, Central Library, St. Peter's Square, MANCHESTER, Greater Manchester M2 5PD. Tel: 0161 2341980 **Fax:** 0161 2341927
E-mail: archives@mcrl.poptel.org.uk
Opening Hours: M.-Th. 10-4.30 Closure: Fri/Sat+Public hols.
Parking: None.
Disabled: Disabled friendly. 10 disabled parking spaces. Visually impaired unit on 2nd floor.
Children: Accompanied: At archivist's discretion. Unaccompanied: 10yrs+
Appointments: Prior booking necessary-1 wk. Entry-ID (CARN accepted as ID). 10 seats+c20 film (2 in searchroom+others in separate unit)-3 reader/printers.
Ordering System: Prior ordering by letter/tel. Approx eight ordered per day, one produced. Order times: 10.30; 11.30; 1.00; 2.00; 3.00. All originals to be returned by 4.10. Delivery 20 mins after ordering time. P/copying restricted, by staff-same day/post/collection. Typing/taping/cameras not permitted (flexible in certain circumstances). Laptops (power supply if electrical certificate produced) allowed.
Records: for City of Manchester-early deposits cover wider area-Cheshire/Lancs, etc. Diocesan RO for Manchester. PRs- film/fiche /Ts

MANCHESTER

(Lancashire Parish Register Society)/originals if not copied. Nonconformist incl. Roman Catholic/Jewish synagogues & organisations. Manchester Overseers of Poor. Local authority incl. Turnpike Trusts. PLUs for Manchester/Chorlton/Prestwich (see Lancs RO entry for other area PLUs). Schools & School Board. Salford Hundred Court of Record. Manchester City/Petty Sessions. Burial Authorities. Hospitals. Valuation maps. Territorial Army. Crew agreements. Solicitors. Family. Business-Manchester Ship Canal/Quarry Bank Mill/Calico Printers Association (M75/)/English Sewing Cotton Co. Political & Trade Unions. Charities & societies. Womens Suffrage collection (M50/) Boys & Girls Welfare Society (M 189/-restricted issue). Electoral registers. Maps. Newspaper cuttings files. National Index of wills 1858-1935. Local History collection. M/f-GRO Indexes/ newspapers/MIs & Cemetery/Rate Book/Trade Directories/census/IGI.
Research Service: None.
Facilities: Toilets/public tel/restaurant/drink vending machine. Café/pub/shops nearby.
Publications: Free leaflets: *Access to Archives*+map. *Sources for Family History in the L.S. Unit. Family History Catalogue in the L.S. Unit. Census Returns on Microfilm in the L.S. Unit. St. Catherine's House Indexes & Local Registration Districts. Local Newspapers on Microfilm in the L.S. Unit. A Guide to the L.S. Unit. Manchester Mapped Out in the L.S. Unit.* (A4 SAE). For sale: *Registers in the L.S. Unit of Manchester Central Library* (Manchester & Lancs. FHS.)
O.R: Greater Manchester Museum of Science & Industry. Liverpool Road, CASTLEFIELD, Manchester M3 4JP Tel: 0161 8322244. Appt. Business incl. Engineering/electrical engineering/locomotive & motor car manufacture etc; **Superintendent Registrar**, Cumberland House, Spinningfield, off Deangate, MANCHESTER M60 3RG Tel: 0161 2347878
Remarks: The L.S. Unit contains an alphabetical list of family names being researched by visitors. If you wish to add your interests to the file, make enqs. at the L.S. Unit.
Note: see *Guide to Greater Manchester Record Office* by V.McKeman & J. Hodkinson (1992). *Handbook, a guide to genealogical sources.* 4th ed. (1996). Station: Manchester, Oxford Road.

National Museum of Labour History, 103 Princess Street, MANCHESTER, Greater Manchester M1 6DD Tel: 0161 2287212. Appt.-letter of introduction. Labour history. Photographs. Posters etc.

North West Film Archive, Manchester Metropolitan University, Minshull House, 47-49 Chorlton Street, MANCHESTER, Greater Manchester M1 3EU. Tel: 0161 2473097. Appt. 21,000 items showing life in Greater Manchester/Lancashire/Cheshire/ Merseyside 1896 to present.

MANCHESTER, GREATER, see Irlam; Middleton; Oldham; Salford; Rochdale; Stockport.

Mansfield Library, Local Studies Dept., Four Seasons Centre, Westgate, MANSFIELD, Notts NG18 1NH Tel: 01623 27591 Usually open. Newspapers. Wills of the Peculiar of Manor of Mansfield. Census name indexes. M/f-PRs/census for Mansfield & surrounding district.

MANX NATIONAL HERITAGE LIBRARY, see Douglas.

Local Studies Collection, Margate Library, Cecil Square, MARGATE, Kent. CT9 1RE
Tel: 01843 223626 **Fax:** 01843 293015
Opening Hours: T. 2-5; F. 2-6; Every 1st Sat 9.30-1; 2-5 **Note:** Opening hours are liable to change by unexpected closures. Closure: Public hols.
Parking: None.
Disabled: No facilities.
Children: Accompanied: 7 yrs+ Unaccompanied: 11 yrs+
Appointments: Prior booking as opening hours are liable to change by unexpected closures. Entry-register. 12 seats+4 film+3 fiche-1 reader/printer.
Ordering System: Prior ordering by letter. Catalogue nos sometimes required. Number ordered & produced at librarian's discretion. P/copying by staff. Typing/cameras not permitted. Laptops allowed.
Records: for Isle of Thanet. Heritage collection for Margate area. PRs-film/Ts indexed of St. John the Baptist. Rowe collection (part) local families/buildings/streets. White MSS, Parker Collection, Theatre Bills & posters. Political posters. Scrapbooks. Illustrations. Maps. Photographs. Books. Pamphlets. Ephemera. Kent & Isle of Thanet Directories. M/f-St. Lawrence/Minster St. Peter/census/ newspapers. See *Handlist of PRs in Thanet Libraries*-available at Library.
Research Service: None.
Facilities: No toilet/public tel/refreshment facilities. Café/pub/shops nearby.
Publications: Free leaflet: *Heritage Services in Thanet* (SAE).
O.R: Margate Museum, Old Town Hall, Market Square, MARGATE.
Tourist Office: Tel: 01843 220241 Fax: 01841 230099

MARYLEBONE, see London, Westminster, City of.

Derbyshire Record Office, New Street, MATLOCK, Derbyshire. Postal address: County Hall, Matlock DE4 3AG **Tel:** 01629 585347 (searchroom). 01629 580000 Ext. 35207 (duty archivist). **Fax:** 01629 57611
Opening Hours: M.-F. 9.30-4.45 Closure: Public hols.
Parking: Limited-free.
Disabled: Disabled friendly. Large print guidance notes etc..
Children: Accompanied: At archivist's discretion. Unaccompanied: 12 yrs+
Appointments: Prior booking for viewers-1 wk. Entry-register+register as user of DRO+ID (CARN). 22 seats+12 film+4 fiche-3 reader/printers.
Ordering System: Prior ordering by letter. Catalogue nos required for archives other than PRs & tithe maps etc. Three ordered, one produced. Ordering at set times: 9.45; 10.30; 11.15; 12; 12.30; 2.15; 3.00; 3.45. Delivery 10 mins after order time. P/copying restricted, by staff-same day/post/collection. Typing/taping permitted but not in searchroom. Laptops allowed. Cameras not permitted.
Records: for Derbyshire & City of Derby. Diocesan RO for Derby. PRs-film/fiche/Ts/originals if not copied. BTs-some Ts. Official. Ecclesiastical. Business. Family. Estate. Societies. Schools. Hospital. Industrial. Quarter Sessions. Probate. Police. Nonconformist. Poor Law. PLUs. M/f-some nonconformists & Roman Catholic series.
Research Service: Charge made (see DRO Info. leaflet).
Facilities: Toilet. No public tel. Room for own food by arrangement. Café/pub/shops nearby.
Publications: Monthly News Update-free to visitors+free info. leaflets (A5 SAE). For sale: Archives First-Beginners guides-user friendly introductions to archives & archive techniques (series). Outline county maps for Derbyshire. *Derbyshire ecclesiastical parishes. Derbyshire Poor Law Unions in 1857. Methodist church archives in Derbyshire RO.* Facsimile broad sheets (e.g. Crimes & Spectacles). *Derbyshire RO Guide* (2nd ed.). *Derbyshire RO Parish Register list* (revised ed). *Nonconformist Register Guide.* Publication & price list available.
Tourist Office: Tel: 01629 55082 Fax: 01629 56304
Remarks: Bags not allowed-lockers. Donations appreciated.

Local Studies Library, County Hall, MATLOCK, Derbyshire DE4 3AG Tel: 01629 585579 **Video Conference-Tel:** 01629 760050 **Fax:** 01629 585049
Opening Hours: M.-F. 9-5; Some Sat by appt. (six Sat per yr) 9.30-1 Closure: Public hols+Tues following Spring/Easter/Autumn+3 days at Christmas.
Parking: Yes but can fill quickly.
Disabled: Disabled friendly. 2 disabled car spaces. Special assistance as needed.
Children: At staff's discretion.
Appointments: Prior booking for viewers-2 wks. Entry-register. 12 seats+6 film+4 fiche-1 reader/printer.
Ordering System: Prior ordering by letter/tel. Number ordered & produced at librarian's discretion. Delivery 5 mins. P/copying by staff/DIY. Typing/taping/laptops permitted. Cameras not allowed.
Records: for Derbyshire+national & international genealogical research tools, e.g. GRO Indexes incl. Misc. GRO Indexes, Filby Passenger & Immigrations lists (also see Derbyshire RO entry). Mapping 1880 for Derbyshire to date. Comprehensive collection of printed material on Derbyshire past & present. Photographs. Will Indexes & copies. M/f-Derbyshire census 1841-1891/1881 Census Index for England & Wales/Directories-trade & tel/Electoral registers & poll books/Lambeth Palace marr. licences Indexes 1543-1850/MIs/Mining deaths 1850-1914/"Strays"/newspapers/Nonconformist/Roman Catholic registers/IGI.
Research Service: Charge made.
Facilities: Toilet/public tel/restaurant/drink vending machine. Café/pub/shops nearby.
Publications: Free leaflet: *Local Studies Library, Matlock*+publications list (SAE). For sale: *Microfilms in Derbyshire Libraries. Local Newspapers in Derbyshire Libraries. Happy Hunting Ground*-a checklist of different kinds of material useful to family historians in the L.S. Library, Matlock. *How to Start Tracing your Family Tree in Derbyshire. Family History in Derbyshire: A Guide to Library Resources. Derbyshire Directories. Local Studies in Derbyshire.*
Remarks: Also see entry for Derby Local Studies Library 25B Irongate, Derby which is now the library of the new Derby City Unitary Authority.

MERSEYSIDE POLICE HEADQUARTERS, see Liverpool.

MERSEYSIDE, see Huyton; Liverpool; Port Sunlight; Southport; St. Helen's; Waterloo.

MERSEYSIDE-USEFUL ADDRESS:

Port Sunlight Heritage Centre & Information Services, 95 Greendale Road, PORT SUNLIGHT, Wirral, Merseyside L62 4XE. Publication: *Sunlighters-Story of a Village, First Hundred Years.*

MERTHYR TYDFIL

Merthyr Tydfil Central Library, High Street, MERTHYR TYDFIL, S. Wales CF47 8AF Tel: 01685 723057 **Fax:** 01685 722146
Opening Hours: M.-F. 9-6.30; Sat 9-12 Closure: Public hols.
Parking: None.
Disabled: Facilities available.
Children: At staff's discretion.
Appointments: Prior booking for viewers-1 day. 25 seats+5 film+3 fiche-2 reader/printers.
Ordering System: Prior ordering by letter/tel. P/copying DIY. Typing/taping/cameras/ laptops (power supply) permitted.
Records: for parish of Merthyr Tydfil. PRs-film. BTs-Ts. Original rate books. Original chapel records. Electoral registers. Maps. Pamphlets. Photographs. Oral history. Genealogical material. M/f-church records/chapel records/census 1841-1891 (arranged by computer in surname order)/newspapers.
Research Service: None.
Facilities: No toilet/public tel/refreshment facilities. Café/pub/shops nearby.
Publications: Various free & for sale.
O.R: Cyfarthfa Castle Museum, Brecon Road, MERTHYR TYDFIL.
Remarks: Note: Merthyr Tydfil Local Authority has no record office but contributes towards the upkeep of the Glamorgan Record Office, Cardiff (see entry).

MERTON, see London Borough of.

METHODIST ARCHIVES, see Manchester.

Teeside Archives (formerly Cleveland County Archives), **Exchange House, 6 Marton Road, MIDDLESBROUGH, Teeside TS1 1DB Tel:** 01642 248321
Opening Hours: M.W.Th. 9-5; T. 9-9; F. 9-4.30 Closure: Public hols.
Parking: None.
Disabled: Toilets. Lift.
Children: At archivist's discretion.
Appointments: Prior booking for seats/ viewers-as long as possible. Entry-register+ CARN. 35 seats+7 film+1 fiche-2 reader/ printers.
Ordering System: Prior ordering by letter/tel. Catalogue nos required. Number ordered & produced at archivist's discretion. Delivery 5 mins. P/copying by staff-post. Typing not permitted. Taping/cameras/laptops (power supply) by special arrangement.
Records: for the former county of Cleveland, now unitary authorities of Middlesbrough/ Stockton/Hartlepool/Redcar/Cleveland. Diocesan RO for York-former county of Cleveland parishes. PRs-film/fiche/Ts. BTs-film. Local authority. Local collections.
Research Service: None.
Facilities: Toilets. No public tel/refreshment facilities. Café/pub/shops nearby.
O. R: Middlesbrough Central Library, Victoria Square, MIDDLESBROUGH, Teeside TS1 2AY Tel: 01642 248155. Usually open. Local History of Cleveland county/N. Yorks/South Durham. Captain Cook collection.
Tourist Office: Tel: 01642 243425 Fax: 01642 264326
Remarks: Bags not allowed-lockers.

MIDDLESEX, see Hounslow, London Borough of.

MIDDLESEX, UXBRIDGE, see London Borough of Hillingdon.

Middleton Library, Long Street, MIDDLETON, Greater Manchester M24 6DY Tel: 0161 6435228 **Fax:** 0161 6540745
Opening Hours: M. 10-7.30; T.Th.F. 10-5.30; W. 10-12.30; Sat 9.20-1; 2-4 Closure: Public hols.
Parking: 1-2 spaces.
Disabled: No facilities (Local Studies on 1st Floor).
Children: At librarian's discretion.
Appointments: Prior booking for viewers-1 day. 14 seats+2 film+2 fiche-1 reader/printer.
Ordering System: No prior ordering. Number ordered & produced at librarian's discretion. P/copying restricted-DIY. Typing/taping not permitted. Laptops/cameras allowed.
Records: for Middleton & limited surrounding area. PRs-film/Ts. Local authority. Highway rates. Poor Law. Administration. Middleton Poor Book 1838. Sheffield rental 18thC. Church records-rates/tithe/plans/deeds. Pamphlets. Theatre posters. Political handbills. Newspaper Index. Edgar Wood, architect,-cuttings files/photographs.
Research Service: Charge made for copies of records & M/f.
Facilities: No toilet/public tel/refreshment facilities. Cafe/pub/shops nearby.
Remarks: Note: This library comes under Rochdale Metropolitan Council. Station: Manchester Central.

MIDLANDS WEST, see Coseley; Coventry; Smethwick; Solihull; Stourbridge; Sutton Coldfield.

MIDLOTHIAN, see Loanhead.

MILITARY ARCHIVES, see Dublin.

MILITARY MUSEUM OF DEVON & DORSET, THE KEEP, see Dorchester.

MODERN RECORDS CENTRE, see Coventry.

Clogher Diocesan Archives, Bishop's House, MONAGHAN, co. Tyrone, N. Ireland Tel: 047 81019 Hours: M.-F. 10-1 Closure: Public hols+Church Holy Days. Appt. by letter-1 mth in advance. P/copying. 20 parking spaces. Disabled-no facilities. Records: PRs-originals but can be seen on film/fiche at the PRO of Northern Ireland, Belfast. Baptism/marriage records from c1825 to present.

The Nelson Museum & Local History Centre, Priory Street, MONMOUTH, Newport NP5 3XA Tel: 01600 713519
Opening Hours: M.-Sat 10-1; 2-5; Sun 2-5
Parking: None.
Disabled: Access.
Appointments: Prior booking for seats-2 days. Entry-register+fee if not a local resident. 4 seats+fiche.
Ordering System: No prior ordering. P/copying by staff-same day.
Typing/taping/laptops/cameras not permitted.
Records: Museum collection of Monmouth Borough archive. Collection relating to Horatio Nelson incl. large MSS letter collection/ships logs etc. Newspapers. Photographs. Prints. Paintings. Ephemera.
Research Service: Limited specific enquiry.
Facilities: No toilet/public tel/refreshment facilities. Café/pub/shops nearby.
Publications: Local history based on the Museum archive of Borough documents.
Tourist Office: Tel: 01600 713899
Remarks: Bags not allowed-storage. Donations appreciated.

MONMOUTHSHIRE, see Monmouth; Newport.

Angus Archives, Montrose Library, 214 High Street, MONTROSE, Angus, Scotland DD10 8HE Tel: 01674 671415 **Fax:** 01674 671810
Opening Hours: M.-F. 9.30-5 Closure: Public hols.
Parking: None.
Disabled: No facilities.
Children: 14 yrs+
Appointments: Prior booking for viewers-1 wk. Entry-register. 2 seats+1 fiche (library shares the building & has 4 film readers).
Ordering System: Prior ordering by letter/tel. Catalogue nos where possible. Four ordered, one produced. Delivery depending where records stored. P/copying restricted, by staff-same day. Typing/cameras not permitted. Taping/laptops (power supply) allowed.
Records: for all of county Angus, formerly Forfarshire. Burgh records for Arbroath/Brechin/Carnoustie/Forfar/Kirriemuir/Monifieth/Montrose. Angus County Council/ District Council. Trade Incorporation records-Arbroath (Glovers/Hammermen/ Shoemakers /Guildry)/Brechin (Guildry/Bakers /Tailors/ Hammermen/Weavers)/Forfar (Tailors/ Shoemakers/Weavers)/Montrose (Hammermen). Montrose Lunatic Asylum & Dispensary. Burgesses. Criminals. Landowners. Schools. Industry. Jacobites. Valuation Rolls. Poor. Business & Societies incl. Forfar Militia/Brechin Soup Kitchen/Montrose & Arbroath harbours etc. Indexes to militia/burgesses/weavers/shoemakers/tailors /burials/MIs/witches, etc. Building plans 1890 to present. Research files. Slide collection. Local History collection. **Note:** The William Coull Anderson Library of Genealogy was est. at Arbroath in 1970 to help people trace their family trees. In 1997 this collection was amalgamated with Angus Archives to provide a service for family historians.
Records: OPRs-film/p/copies/Ts. Valuation rolls. Kirk session. Sasines/Deeds indexes. Fasti Ecclesiae Scoticanae. Scots Peerage pre 1855. MIs. Families of Burns/Coull etc. Indexes to pre-1855 burial records for parishes of Arbroath & St. Vigean. Photographs. M/f-census/post 1855 BMD certs/IGI. Family trees researched are now on database.
Research Service: Charge made incls. Family Trees, Local History & House history-apply for details. No charge for specific archival & local history enqs.
Facilities: No toilets/public tel/refreshment facilities. Café/pub/shops nearby.
Publications: Free: Info. leaflets (SAE). Lists of resources for Angus burghs. All Angus libraries archival lists/indexes & Ts. available. Local History publications. Heritage trails.
Tourist Office: Tel: 01674 672000
Remarks: Bags not allowed-lockers.

MORAY, see Elgin; Forres.

MORDEN, SURREY, see London Borough of Merton.

MORPETH RECORDS CENTRE, see Loansdean.

Motherwell District Library, Local Studies Centre, Hamilton Road, MOTHERWELL, Borders, Scotland ML1 3BZ Tel: 01698 51311 Appt. Some original newspapers. M/f-OPRs/census/newspapers.

Much Wenlock Town Council, The Corn Exchange, MUCH WENLOCK, Shropshire TF13 6AE Tel: 01952 727509 Appt. Much Wenlock Borough records-minutes/manor court/parish/rates/voters lists.

MUSEUM OF DARTMOOR LIFE, see Okehampton.

N. IRELAND, see Armagh; Belfast; Ballymena; Ballynahinch; Monaghan; Omagh.

N. YORKSHIRE, see Malton; Pickering; Richmond; Scarborough; Whitby; York.

NATIONAL ARCHIVES, see Dublin.

NATIONAL LIBRARY OF IRELAND, see Dublin.

NATIONAL LIBRARY OF SCOTLAND, see Edinburgh.

NATIONAL LIBRARY OF WALES, see Aberystwyth.

NATIONAL MONUMENTS RECORDS CENTRE, see London; Swindon

NATIONAL MONUMENTS RECORD OF SCOTLAND, see Edinburgh.

NATIONAL MUSEUM OF LABOUR HISTORY, see Manchester.

NELSON MUSEUM & LOCAL HISTORY CENTRE, see Monmouth.

Royal Army Chaplains Dept., Netheravon House, Salisbury Road, NETHERAVON, Wilts SP4 9SY (temporary accommodation). Tel: 01980 604911 **Note:** all archives, museum, library, etc. are in store for a year pending a move to The Armed Forces Chaplaincy Centre, Amport House, Amport, Andover, Hants SP11 8BG. World-wide records. Church services registers. Protestant marriages/baptisms/deaths. Registers of overseas military cemeteries. P.O.W. material of various chaplains over the years. **Note:** Other related records are in the PRO, Kew. A book on the history & records of army chaplains is in active preparation by Dr. Garth Thomas of the PRO.

Newark Museum, Appletongate, NEWARK, Notts NG24 1JY Tel: 01636 702358 Appt. Local History. Militaria of Sherwood Foresters.

Newcastle Upon Tyne Heritage Information Centre, City Library, Local Studies Section, Princess Square, NEWCASTLE UPON TYNE NE99 1DX Tel: 0191 2610691 **Fax:** 0191 2326885 **E-mail:** Heritage@dial.pipex.com
Opening Hours: M.Th. 9.30-8; T.W.F. 9.30-5; Sat 9-5 Closure: Public hols.
Parking: None.
Disabled: Lift. Toilet.
Children: At staff's discretion.
Appointments: Prior booking unnecessary. Entry-register. 40 seats+5 viewers+5 fiche-5 reader/printers.
Ordering System: No prior ordering. Six ordered & produced. Delivery on request. P/copying restricted-DIY. Taping not permitted. Typing/cameras/laptops (power supply) allowed.
Records: Mostly on open shelves in Genealogy Room. PRs-Ts incl some nonconformists. Various Marriage Indexes 1813-1837. Boyd's Marriage Index for Northumberland & Durham to 1812. Durham Marriage Bonds (incls. Northumberland) 1594-1815. Family histories & pedigrees. Durham Wills 1576-1735 (6 Vols. indexed). 122 Northumberland wills late 18th/early 19thC's. Newspapers. Directories. Entertainment programmes. Electoral registers 1832 on. Poll books 1705-1871. Maps & plans. Photographs. Audio material. MIs-Ts. Local heraldry. M/f-GRO Indexes 1837-1992/census/newspapers/IGI.
Research Service: Charge made incls. p/copies to max. 5 A4. (see Research Info. leaflet).
Facilities: Toilet/public tel/restaurant. Café/pub/shops nearby.
Publications: Free & for sale. (A4 SAE). Genealogy guides-1) *Tracing Your Ancestors: A Brief Guide for the Beginner.* 2) *Tracing Your Ancestors in North East England.* 3) *Genealogical Sources*-PRs/Pedigrees/Family Notices/Epitaphs/Census Returns etc. 4. *Census Records on Microfilm.* 5. *PR Transcripts & Indexes.* 6) *MIs.* 7) *Electoral Registers & Poll Books.* 8) *Genealogical Researchers*+a number of others.
O.R: Northumberland & Durham FHS Library & Research Centre, 2nd Floor, Bolbec Hall, Westgate Road, NEWCASTLE UPON TYNE NE1 1SE Tel: 0191 2612159 Appt. Tel. for opening hours. The Society operates a limited research service.
Tourist Office: At this library. Tel: 0191 2610610 Fax: 0191 2210115
Remarks: Note: Wills & Inventories for Diocese of Durham 1540-1858 are in Durham University Library, Archives & Special Collections (see entry). Wills for the Peculiar of Hexham & Hexhamshire are at the Borthwick Institute, York (see entry). Copies of wills 1858-1940 are at Northumberland RO (see entry), & also in Durham University Library, Archives & Special Collections. Metro: Monument.

Tyne and Wear Archives Service, Blandford House, Blandford Square, NEWCASTLE UPON TYNE, Tyne & Wear NE1 4JA Tel: 0191 2326789 **Fax:** 0191 2302614
Internet:
http://www.swinhope.demon.co.uk/genuki/nbl/tynewearas/
Opening Hours: M.W.F. 9-5.15; T. 9-8.30 Closure: Thurs+Public hols.
Parking: Limited nearby-paying.
Disabled: Disabled friendly.
Children: At archivist's discretion.

Appointments: Prior booking for viewers-3 days. Entry-register. 14 seats+11 film+3 fiche-1 reader/printer.
Ordering System: Prior ordering by letter/tel. Catalogue nos required. Number ordered unlimited, three produced. Delivery 5-10 mins. Last order: 4.45. P/copying restricted, by staff-post/collection. Typing not permitted. Taping/cameras/laptops (power supply) allowed.
Records: for Tyne & Wear. PRs-film/Ts. Local authority. Methodist Circuit registers. Nonconformist incl. Jewish/Quakers. Shipbuilding-port registers/business. Shipping guilds-apprenticeships/freemen. Hospitals. Building plans. Quarter/Petty Sessions. Magistrates/County Courts. Coroners. Police. Schools. Manorial. Trade Unions. Transport. Business. Fenwick-circus material. Electoral registers. Maps & plans. Photographs. Printed sources. M/f-census.
Research Service: Charge made.
Facilities: Toilets/public tel/restaurant/room for own food/drink vending machine. Café/pub/shops nearby.
Publications: Free leaflets: User Guides to particular sources (A5 SAE). For sale: *How to Use the Archives Service. Sources for Family History at Tyne & Wear Archives Service*+other publications/videos.
Remarks: Bags not allowed-lockers.

NEWCASTLE, see North Gosforth

NEWHAM, see London Borough of.

Newport Libraries, Reference Library, John Frost Square, NEWPORT, Glamorgan, S. Wales NP9 1PA Tel: 01633 211376 Opening Hours: M.T.W. 9.30-6; Th. Sat 9.30-5; F. 9-6. Disabled friendly. Appt. for viewers-3 wks. Covers Monmouthshire/Gwent. Electoral registers & poll books. Tithe maps. Maps. Directories. Chartist riots, trial reports re: Newport & district (in vols.). PRs-Ts. M/f-census. All records listed on Internet. http://www.earl.uk/earl/members/newport. Research details available on request. Publications-all family history material available on Internet through 'Familia' address: www.earl.org.uk/familia (200 local authorities holdings listed).

Isle of Wight Record Office, 26 Hillside, NEWPORT, Isle of Wight PO30 2EB Tel: 01983 823820/1 **Fax:** 01983 823820
Opening Hours: M. 9.30-5; T.-F. 9-5; 1st Wed of month 9-7.30 Closure: Public hols+Christmas to New Year.
Parking: 5 spaces.
Disabled: No facilities.
Children: Accompanied: At archivist's discretion. Unaccompanied: 14 yrs+
Appointments: Prior booking for viewers-1 wk, essential for late night Wed 5-7.30. Entry-register+CARN. 16 seats+1 film+4 fiche-2 reader/printers.
Ordering System: Prior ordering by letter/tel. Catalogue nos required. Four ordered & produced. Delivery 10 mins max. Last order: 30 mins before closure. P/copying restricted, by staff-same day(small orders)/post/ collection (large orders). Typing/taping/cameras not permitted. Laptops (power supply) allowed.
Records: for Isle of Wight. PRs-original post 1900 only. PRs-film/bound photocopies (1837-1900 marriage registers)/Ts pre-1900 fully indexed (card index). Diocesan RO for Portsmouth (Isle of Wight) parish records. BTs are at Hampshire RO Winchester (see entry). Local authority. Local collections. Papers of the Oglander family of Nunwell. Barrington/Simeon families of Swainston.
Research Service: Charge made.
Facilities: Toilets. No public tel/refreshment facilities. Café/pub/shops nearby.
Publications: Free leaflets (A5 SAE).
O. R: Isle of Wight County Library, Lord Louis Library, Orchard Street, NEWPORT, Isle of Wight PO30 1LL Tel: 01963 823800.Usually open. Local History. Maritime History collection. Directories. Some 19thC newspapers.
Tourist Office: Tel: 01983 867979-info 01983 525450-accommodation. Fax: 01983 822929.
Remarks: Donations appreciated. No station for Isle of Wight-ferry/hovercraft only from Portsmouth/Southsea.

Railway Studies Library, Newton Abbot Library, Bank Street, NEWTON ABBOT, Devon TQ12 2RP Tel: 01626 336128. Appt. Railway history in U.K. G.W.Railway. L&S.W. Railway. Southern Railway. Free Intro leaflet. Reader's Guide (SAE).

NORFOLK, see Aylsham; Great Yarmouth; Norwich.

NORRIS LIBRARY, see St. Ives.

NORTH AYRSHIRE LIBRARIES, see Ardrossan

NORTH DEVON MARITIME MUSEUM, see Appledore.

NORTH DEVON RECORD OFFICE, see Barnstaple.

NORTH EASTERN EDUCATION & LIBRARY BOARD, see Ballymena, co. Antrim.

NORTH EAST LINCOLNSHIRE ARCHIVES, see Grimsby.

NORTH EAST OF SCOTLAND LIBRARY SERVICE, see Old Meldrum.

NORTH EAST OF SCOTLAND MUSEUMS SERVICE, see Peterhead.

NORTH EAST SOMERSET, see Bath.

Northumberland Record Office, Melton Park, NORTH GOSFORTH, Newcastle, Northumberland NE3 5QX Tel: 0191 2362680 **Fax:** 0191 2170905
Internet: http://www.swinhope.demon.co.uk/genuki/NBL/NorthumberlandRO/ (Info re records).
Opening Hours: M. 9.30-1; 2-8; T.F. 9.30-1; 2-5 Closure: Wed/Thurs+Public hols.
Parking: 12 spaces
Disabled: Tel. in advance for required assistance.
Children: Accompanied: At archivist's discretion. Unaccompanied: School age.
Appointments: Prior booking unnecessary. Entry-register. 16 seats+2 film+1 fiche.
Ordering System: No prior ordering. Three ordered & produced. Delivery 15 mins. Last order: 30 mins before closure-am & pm. P/copying by staff-same day/post/collection. Typing/cameras not permitted. Taping/laptops (power supply) allowed.
Records: for the present county of Northumberland. Diocesan RO for Diocese of Newcastle (extends south to Newcastle & all of Tyneside north of R. Tyne). PRs & BTs now held at Morpeth Records Centre, Loansdean (see entry). Manorial. Family. Estate. Business. Coal mining. Miscellaneous accessions. N. of England Institute of Mining & Mechanical Engineers. Society of Antiquaries of Newcastle upon Tyne. Maps-tithe/enclosure/O.S/plans. Estate-widest range of maps available for Northumberland. Photographic collection.
Research Service: Charge made.
Facilities: Toilets. No public tel/refreshment facilities. Drink vending machine. No café/pub/shops nearby.
Publications: Free leaflets: General Info with area map. *Introduction to the RO.* Northumberland Archives publication list. (A5 SAE).
Tourist Office: Central Library: Tel: 0191 2610610 Fax: 0191 2210115; Central Station: 0191 2300030 Fax: 0191 2210115
Remarks: Bags not allowed-lockers. Donations appreciated. **Note:** See entry for Berwick-upon-Tweed RO & Morpeth Records Centre. Metro: Regent Centre then bus service-Northern buses Nos 41-45.

NORTH HIGHLAND ARCHIVE, see Wick.

Local Studies, Central Library, Northumberland Square, NORTH SHIELDS NE30 1QU Usually open. Local History collection. PRs-Ts/M/f.

NORTH OF ENGLAND OPEN AIR MUSEUM, see Beamish.

NORTH SOMERSET LOCAL STUDIES LIBRARY, see Weston-super-Mare.

NORTH WEST FILM ARCHIVE, see Manchester.

NORTH WEST SOUND ARCHIVE, see Clitheroe.

NORTH YORKSHIRE, see Leyburn; Northallerton.

North Yorkshire County Record Office, Malpas Road, NORTHALLERTON, N. Yorks Postal address: County Record Office, County Hall, Northallerton, N. Yorks DL7 8AF **Tel:** 01609 777585 **Fax:** 01609 777078
Opening Hours: M.T.Th. 9-4.45; W. 9-8.45; F. 9-4.15 Closure: Public hols+extra day May & Aug.
Parking: Yes+additional parking at back of building.
Disabled: Disabled friendly.
Children: At archivist's discretion.
Appointments: Prior booking for seats/viewers. Initial entry by signing an enquirer's card+entry in register with subject & purpose of enquiry.
Ordering System: Prior ordering by letter/tel. Catalogue nos required or exact description. Number ordered & produced at librarian's discretion. Usually open lunchtime but may be subject to closure 1-2. P/copying by staff (see Leaflet SR3).
Records: for North Yorkshire. Diocesan RO for Bradford/Ripon/York. Most records including PRs available on M/f, facsimiles, transcripts & typed abstracts. (see Leaflet SR9). PRs in progress of being transcribed & indexed by computer. Parish chest. Nonconformists. Quarter Sessions/House of Correction. Family & estate. Business. Maps. M/f-census.
Research Service: Charge made. (see Leaflet SR4).
Facilities: Toilet/public tel/room for own food.
Publications: Free: Info. leaflets (A5 SAE). For sale: large number of publications incl. *Calendars/Ts/M/f in the RO* (Guide 1). *PRs/census/land tax assessments/tithe apportionments/enclosure awards in the RO* (Guide 2). *Maps & plans in the RO-N. Yorkshire & N. Riding* (Guide 3). *Enclosure awards in the RO*-detailed list (Guide 4). *N. Yorkshire PRs incl. dates & whereabouts/Ts/M/f* (Guide 5). *N. Yorkshire gazetteer of townships & parishes* (Guide 6). Publications & price list available.

O.R: North Yorkshire County Library, 21 Grammar School Lane, NORTHALLERTON DL6 1DF Tel: 01609 776271 Census. Photographic collection; **Northallerton Library**, 1 Thirsk Road, NORTHALLERTON DL6 1PT. GRO Indexes 1837-1947
Tourist Office: Tel: 01609 776864
Remarks: Note: The Borthwick Institute, York has a quantity of N. Yorks PRs (see entry).

Northampton Central Museum, Boot & Shoe Section, Guildhall Road, NORTHAMPTON, Northants NN1 1DP. Tel: 01604 233500 Ext. 5105. Postal service only as Boot & Shoe Index is not open to the public. FOC on receipt of SAE. Records: Shoemakers Index-mostly British/Europe/USA. Mostly 19-20thC's with a few from 17thC & earlier. At present records are kept on 5"x3" filing cards with the name clearly written on top followed with as much info. as possible which includes dates/precise occupations/addresses/relevant family details/apprenticeship. Contributions are welcomed from those with shoemaker (cordwainer) ancestry+any ancestors in the footwear industry. Index is currently being computerised. This facility is provided by Northampton Borough Council.

Northamptonshire Record Office, Wootton Hall Park, NORTHAMPTON, Northants. NN4 8BQ Tel: 01604 762129 **Fax:** 01604 767562 **E-mail:** archivist@nro .northamptonshire.gov.uk
Internet: http://www.nro.northamptoshire.gov .uk
Opening Hours: M.-W. 9-4.50; Th. 9-7.45; F. 9-4.30; 1st & 3rd Sat in mth 9-12.15 Closure: Public hols.
Parking: Yes.
Disabled: Disabled friendly.
Children: Accompanied: 10 yrs+ Unaccompanied: At archivist's discretion.
Appointments: Prior booking essential for lunchtimes/late eve/Sat. Entry-register. 70 seats+8 film+15 fiche-3 reader/printers.
Ordering System: Prior ordering by letter/tel. Catalogue nos sometimes required. Number ordered at archivist's discretion, four produced. Ordering on the half hour only. P/copying restricted, by staff-same day/post/collection. Typing/taping not permitted. Laptops (power supply) allowed. Cameras by prior arrangement.
Records: for Northamptonshire/ Peterborough+other places throughout the U.K./Ireland/World integral to local collections. Diocesan RO for Peterborough. PRs-fiche/p/copies/Ts/originals only for illegible entries. BTs-p/copies of all to 1812. Parish chest. PLU. Nonconformist. Probate. Quarter Sessions. Manorial. Borough. Local authority-Urban/Rural District Councils. Hospital. Family & estate. Borough collection. Militia. Canals. Diaries. Directories. Newspapers. Maps & photographs. M/f-census.
Note: Diocesan records for Northampton are housed at Shropshire RO, Shrewsbury (see entry).
Research Service: None.
Facilities: Toilet/public tel/room for own food/drink vending machine. Café/pub nearby.
Publications: For sale: *Tracing Your Ancestors in Northamptonshire* by Colin Chapman.
O.R: Northampton Central Library, Local Studies Collection, Abington Street, NORTHAMPTON NN1 2BA.
Tourist Office: Tel: 01604 22677 Fax: 01604 604180
Remarks: Bags not allowed-lockers. Donations appreciated.

NORTHAMPTONSHIRE, see Northampton.

NORTHUMBERLAND RO, see North Gosforth.

NORTHUMBERLAND, THE FUSILIERS OF NORTHUMBERLAND MUSEUM, see Alnwick.

NORTHUMBERLAND, see Alnwick; Berwick-upon-Tweed; Blyth; Hexham; Loansdean; Newcastle; North Gosforth.

Northwich Library, Wilton Street, NORTHWICH, Cheshire CW9 5DR Tel: 01606 44221 Appt. Local History collection. Maps. Photographs. M/f-PRs/census/ newspapers.

Norfolk Record Office, Gildengate House, Anglia Square, Upper Green Lane, NORWICH, Norfolk NR3 1AX Tel: 01603 761349 **Fax:** 01603 761885 **E-mail:** norfrec.nro@norfolk.gov.uk
Internet: http://www.ecn,co.uk/norfolkcc/ htm/council/departments/no/nr oindex.html
Opening Hours: M.-F. 9-5; Sat 9-12 Closure: Public hols+preceding Sat+following Mon+additional day at Christmas.
Parking: Public nearby-paying.
Disabled: Disabled friendly+car parking outside by prior arrangement.
Children: At archivist's discretion.
Appointments: Prior booking for original MSS & maps-few days (longer for maps). Entry-register+CARN (for use of MSS only). 16 seats+11 film+13 fiche.
Ordering System: Prior ordering by letter/tel. Catalogue nos or sufficient description to identify. Records stored elsewhere require 1 wk prior ordering. Requests collected 9.10 & 9.30 then at half hourly intervals to 4.30 Mon-Fri; 11.30 Sat. No production 12.30-2. Delivery 5-30

mins. P/copying restricted, by staff-post/collection (within 2 wks). Typing/laptops (power supply available but certificate of electrical safety+proof of purchase within last 12 mths) permitted. Taping not allowed. Cameras restricted.
Records: for county of Norfolk & Diocese of Norwich which included most of Suffolk to 1914. Present Diocese incls. parishes in the Lothingland Deanery in N.E. Suffolk. Also Diocesan RO for Ely-Deaneries of Feltwell & Fincham. PRs-film/fiche/p/copies/Ts/originals if not copied-if not legible/not too fragile. BTs-original/some Ts. Earliest Quarter Sessions in England/Wales. Medieval records incl. Norwich Cathedral for late 11thC. Family & estate. Business. Literary MSS. King's Lynn Borough archives stored elsewhere require prior ordering. M/f-some parish records/nonconformist/pre-1858 probate/marr. licence bonds/Quarter Sessions/PLUs/manorial/land tax/rate lists/pre 1915 electoral registers/registers of freemen & apprentices (at Norwich/King's Lynn/Gt. Yarmouth)/cemetery records (Norwich/Yarmouth). Finding aids available in searchroom.
Research Service: Limited specific enquiry-charge made. List of Record Agents available.
Facilities: Toilets/public tel. No refreshment facilities. Café/pub/shops nearby.
Publications: Free: Info. leaflet (with map). Series of free guides to sources. Publications list. (A5 SAE). For sale: *Parish Registers & Transcripts in the Norfolk RO. Free Church Registers & Related Records in the NRO. Guide to Genealogical Sources* (3rd ed. 1993). Norfolk parish map. *A Guide to sources for Tracing the History of a House or Property in Norfolk.*
O.R: Norfolk Studies Library, address as above (2nd floor). Usually open. M/f-GRO Indexes/census/newspapers/IGI.
Tourist Office: Tel: 01603 666071 Fax: 01603 765389
Remarks: Bags not allowed-lockers (20p coin). Donations appreciated. **Note:** Some of the ROs holdings were damaged by water following a fire in the strongroom in 1994 & cannot be produced until they have been restored. A new Norfolk RO & East Anglia Studies Centre will open at the University of East Anglia, Norwich in 2001 if Heritage Lottery funding is received. Station: Norwich (Thorpe). Bus stop: Magdalen Street, outside Anglia Square. Depart: Castle Meadow.

Nottinghamshire Archives, County House, Castle Meadow, NOTTINGHAM, Notts NG2 1AG Tel: 0115 9581634/9504524 **Fax:** 0115 9413997
Opening Hours: M.W.F. 9-4.45; T. 9-7.15 Closure: Thurs+Public hols+following Tues.
Parking: 9 spaces.
Disabled: Disabled friendly.
Children: At archivist's discretion.
Appointments: Prior booking unnecessary. Entry-register+CARN. 12 seats+1 film+27 fiche-1 reader/printer.
Ordering System: Prior ordering if order slips are presented up to 1 wk. in advance. Catalogue nos required. Three items or groups ordered, ten pieces produced. Ordering times-quarter past the hour. Delivery 10-30 mins depending on number of requests. P/copying restricted, by staff-post/collection.
Typing/taping/cameras/laptops (power supply if disclaimer signed) by prior arrangement.
Records: for Nottingham County & City. Diocesan RO for the Peculiar of Southwell. PRs/film/fiche/Ts/originals if not copied. BTs-film. County/City Council. Boroughs of Mansfield & Retford. District Council. Nonconformist. Probate. Poor Law. Court. Family & estate. Business. Societies. Correspondence. Diaries. Electoral registers. Trade Directories. Cemeteries. Maps & plans. Extensive genealogical library. Cuckney apprentice registers (Toplis & Co.). M/f-census/IGI. **Note:** BTs for the Peculiar of Southwell are at Southwell Minster Library, Southwell.
Research Service: None-list of Record Agents on request.
Facilities: Toilets/public tel/room for own food/drink vending machine. Café/pub/shops nearby.
Publications: Free Info. leaflets: *Nottinghamshire Archives*-with map. *Discovering Your Family History in Nottinghamshire.* (SAE). For sale: Resource packs.
O.R: Nottingham Central Library, includes Local Studies & Arts Library, Angel Row, NOTTINGHAM NG1 6HO Tel: 0115 9412121; **Nottingham Diocese Roman Catholic Archives**, Willson House, Derby Street, NOTTINGHAM NG1 5AW Tel: 0115 9241968; **Galleries of Justice**, Shire Hall, High Pavement, Lace Market, NOTTINGHAM NG1 1HN Tel: 0115 9520555 Appt. Law archives. Ross Sims Police collection; **Nottingham District Land Registry**, Chalfont Drive, NOTTINGHAM NG8 3RN Tel: 0115 9291166 Land registration for counties of S & W. Yorkshire/Derbyshire/Nolttinghamshire/Leicestershire before 1990; **Nottingham Probate Sub Registry**, Butt Dyke House, 33 Park Row, NOTTINGHAM Tel: 0115 9414288.
Tourist Office: Tel: 0115 9470661 Fax: 0115 9350883
Remarks: Bags not allowed-lockers.

University of Nottingham, Department of Manuscripts & Special Collections, Hallward Library, University Park, NOTTINGHAM, Notts NG7 2RD Tel: 0115 951 4565 **Fax:** 0115 951 4558 **E-mail:** mss-library@nottingham.ac.uk
Internet: mss.library.nottingham.ac.uk
Opening Hours: M.-F. 9-5 Closure: Public hols+additional University hols.
Parking: Yes-paying.
Disabled: Lift. Toilet.
Children: Accompanied: 10 yrs+ Unaccompanied: Not allowed.
Appointments: Prior booking unnecessary for viewers but university members have priority. Entry-register+register for University ticket. 12 seats+1 film+1 fiche.
Ordering System: Prior ordering by letter/tel. Catalogue nos required. Number ordered & produced at archivist's discretion. Delivery 15-30 mins. Occasional closure lunch times. Last order: 3.45. P/copying restricted, by staff-post. Typing/taping/laptops/cameras not permitted.
Records: Archdeaconry of Nottingham. Family & estate collections of East Midlands. Manorial. Business & Trade Unions. Marr licence bonds. Nonconformist. Hospital. University. Maps & plans. Photographs. Posters. Political papers of 18/19thC's. Literary papers.
Research Service: None.
Facilities: Toilets/public tel/room for own food/drink vending machine.
Publications: Free: *A Guide to the Department, Its Holdings & Services. Guide to East Midlands Collection.* (SAE). For sale: *Nottinghamshire Marriage Bonds 1791-1800. Abstract of the Bonds for Marriage Licences of the Archdeaconry Court of Nottingham.*

NOTTINGHAMSHIRE, see Mansfield; Newark; Southwell.

OFFICE OF THE CHIEF HERALD, see Dublin.

The Museum of Dartmoor Life, 3 West Street, OKEHAMPTON, Devon EX20 1HQ Tel: 01837 52295 Appt. Local Studies material. Photographic & oral history archives. M/f-PRs for area/tithe maps & apportionments/registers of some Methodist, URC churches & Society of Friends. This is a Devon RO Service point-staff attend once a mth in the afternoon, for info tel: 01392 384252.

Oldham Local Studies Library and Archives Service, 84 Union Street, OLDHAM, Greater Manchester OL1 1DN Tel: 0161 9114654 **Fax:** 0161 9114669 **E-mail:** localstudies@oldham.gov.uk or archives@oldham.gov.uk
Opening Hours: M.Th. 10-7; T. 10-2; W.F.Sat 10-5 Closure: Public hols.
Parking: Public nearby (Ashworth's behind library)-paying.
Disabled: Disabled friendly-ramp access at Greaves St. entrance.
Children: At staff's discretion.
Appointments: Prior booking unnecessary. Entry for archives only-register+CARN/other reader's ticket+ID. 17 seats+6 film+3 fiche+1 film/fiche-1 reader/printer.
Ordering System: Prior ordering by letter/tel. Catalogue nos required. Number ordered & produced at staff's discretion. Delivery 10 mins. P/copying restricted, by staff (archives)-same day where possible. Typing/taping not permitted. Laptops (power supply) allowed. Cameras by prior arrangement.
Records: for Oldham Metropolitan Borough Council & predecessor authorities-Oldham/Chadderton/Crompton/Failsworth/Lees/Royton/Saddleworth/Springhead/Uppermill. PRs-film/p/copies/Ts. Business-Highams Textile 1874-1979. Textile Trade Unions. Co-operative Society. Family papers. Rowbottom Diaries (daily events in Oldham 1787-1829). Newspapers. Oral history. Local Studies collection: Photographs/plans/books/pamphlets on history of Oldham. M/f-nonconformist registers/census.
Research Service: None.
Facilities: Toilets. No public tel. Room for own food. Café/pub/shops nearby
Publications: Free booklet: *Greater Manchester Archives: A Guide to local repositories.* (A5 SAE).
Tourist Office: Tel: 0161 6271024 Fax: 0161 9114077
Remarks: Note: There may be a possible move of this repository by 2000/2001. Station: Oldham Mumps.

Saddleworth Museum, Archives Room, High Street, Uppermill, OLDHAM, Greater Manchester OL3 6HS Tel: 01457 874093
Opening Hours: Every day: Apl-Oct 10-5; Nov-Mch 12-4
Parking: Limited-free.
Disabled: Chairlift.
Children: At curator's discretion.
Appointments: Entry-payment for Museum+name & address for archive enquiry. 5 seats+1 film+2 fiche.
Ordering System: Prior ordering by letter/tel. Number ordered & produced at curator's discretion. Delivery few mins. P/copying by staff-same day. Typing/taping/cameras/laptops (power supply) permitted.
Records: for Saddleworth villages-Delph/Dobcross/Uppermill/Diggle/Greenfield & hamlets. Saddleworth Museum & Historical Society collection. PRs-film/fiche/p/copies. Deeds. Wills. Enclosures. Canal/turnpikes/

railways with Acts & maps. Extensive records of closed local woollen mills. Religious & social collections-Methodist/education/friendly societies/co-operative movement. Poor Law relief book. Genealogy. Works of local authors. Bound local newspapers & cuttings. Oral history. M/f-St. Chad's parish/nonconformist chapels/census.
Research Service: None.
Facilities: No toilets/public tel/refreshment facilities. Café/pub/shops nearby.
Publications: For sale: Leaflets on source documents-Architecture/Education/Leisure pursuits/Religion/Social history/Transport/Urban growth/Village histories. *Saddleworth Archives-Archives for Research & Education.* (SAE for info).
Remarks: Donations appreciated. Station: Greenfield.

Salford : Roman Catholic Diocesan Archives, Sacred Heart Presbytery, Whetstone Hill Road, OLDHAM, Greater Manchester OL1 4NA The archive deals with diocesan records & associated material only. Parish registers are either in the parish of origin or have been deposited with the Lancashire RO, Preston (see entry). M/f of such registers c1870 on are also at Lancashire RO. See Catholic Family History series by M. Gandy (1996):- *Catholic missions & registers 1700-1880* by M. Gandy (1993). Vol. 4. *North east England.* Vol. 5. *North west England. Catholic parishes in England, Wales & Scotland, an index.* ed. M. Gandy (1993).

The North East of Scotland Library Service, Meldrum Megway, The Meadows Industrial Estate, OLDMELDRUM, Aberdeen, Scotland AB51 OGN. Tel: 01651 872707. Appt. Family & local history relating to former districts of Banff & Buchan/Gordon/Kincardine/Deeside. Estate papers. Maps. Photographs.

Ulster-American Folk Park, 2 Mellon Road, Castletown, OMAGH, co. Tyrone, N. Ireland BT78 5QY. Tel: 01662 243292 Appt. Emigration history & database.

Western Education & Library Board, Irish & Local Studies Dept., Library Headquarters, 1 Spillars Place, OMAGH, co. Tyrone, N. Ireland BT78 1HL Tel: 01662 244821 Ext. 133/134 **Fax:** 01662 246716 **E-mail:** omalib.demon.co.uk
Opening Hours: M.W.F. 9.15-5.30; T.Th. 9.15-8; Sat 9.15-1; 2-5 Closure: 17 Mch+Easter Mon & Tues+12 Jly+Christmas Eve-Boxing Day+New Year's day.
Parking: Limited.
Disabled: Disabled friendly.
Children: At staff's discretion.
Appointments: Prior booking for viewers-1 day. 12 seats+2 film+2 fiche-1 reader/printer.
Ordering System: No prior ordering as immediate delivery. P/copying by staff-same day/DIY. Typing/laptops/cameras permitted. Taping not allowed.
Records: for co. Tyrone. M/f-1901 census. 1860 Griffiths Valuation+Griffiths Valuation updates for 1920s/1934-1935/1957. Earlier lists of people available in Hearth Money roll 1666. Militia officers 1761. Muster Roll 1630-31. Access to Emigration Database 1750-1900-this project based at the Ulster-American Folk Park, Omagh (see entry). Family History periodicals-various. Church/school registers are held at Public Record Office of N. Ireland (PRONI), Belfast-librarian is able to give information as to which are held for Omagh.
Research Service: Limited specific enquiry.
Facilities: Toilets/public tel/refreshment facilities. Café/pub/shops nearby.
Publications: Free: Info leaflets incl. *Tracing Your Family Tree* (SAE). For sale: Books of Irish Interest (covers recent additions to stock). Irish Periodicals published before 1901.
O.R: The Irish Genealogical Project has four centres in N. Ireland: **Armagh Ancestry**, 42 English Street, ARMAGH, co. Armagh BT61 7AB Tel: 01861 527808 Fax: 01861 528329-City & co. Armagh; **Heritage World**, The Heritage Centre, DONAGHMORE, co. Tyrone BT70 3HG Tel: 018687 67039 Fax: 018687 67663-Fermanagh & Tyrone; **Genealogy Centre**, Inner City Trust, 14 Bishop Street, LONDONDERRY, co. Londonderry BT48 6PW Tel: 01504 269792 Fax: 01504 360921; **Ulster Historical Foundation,** Balmoral Buildings, 12 College Square East, BELFAST BT1 6DD Tel: 01232 332288 Fax: 01232 239885-City of Belfast & co's Antrim & Down.
Remarks: Note: Access to the Emigration Database is also available through the Londonderry & Enniskillen libraries. Also see *Tracing the past* by W. Nolan (1982) for background reading. Station: Ulsterbus Station, Drumragh Avenue Omagh.

ORKNEY, see Kirkwall.

Oswestry Town Council, Powis Hall, OSWESTRY, Shropshire, SY11 1PZ Tel: 01691 652776 **Fax:** 01691 671080
Opening Hours: M.T.Th.F. 9.30-12.45; 2.15-4.30 Closure: Public hols.
Parking: Public-paying.
Disabled: Powis Hall: no facilities. Guildhall: Disabled friendly.
Children: At staff's discretion.
Appointments: Prior booking for seats-2 days. Entry first visit-registration form+proof of identity+register. 3 seats.

Ordering System: Prior ordering by letter/tel. Catalogue nos if possible. Number ordered & produced at staff's discretion. Delivery 15 mins (Powis Hall). 5-10 mins (Guildhall). P/copying restricted, by staff-same day/post/collection. Typing/taping/laptops-under review. Cameras at Town Clerk's discretion.
Records: of Oswestry Town Council & its predecessors. A few items relate to surrounding areas. Burgess books. Court records of civil actions 17-19thC's. Deeds. Quarter Sessions 18-20thC's. Petty Sessions 19thC. Correspondence. Charities. A catalogue of the archives will be available for consultation at the Guildhall. Copies also available at Oswestry Library/Shropshire Records & Research Centre, Shrewsbury (see entry).
Research Service: None.
Facilities: Toilets. No public tel/refreshment facilities. Café/pub/shops nearby.
O.R: Oswestry Library, Arthur Street, OSWESTRY.
Tourist Office: At Mile End Services Tel: 01691 662488 (Info.)/01691 657876 (accommodation). Fax: 01691 662883
Remarks: Bags/briefcases/lockers/donations -under review. **Note:** The Town Council's offices & archives will be moving to the Guildhall, Oswestry SY11 1PZ sometime in 1998.

Centre for Oxfordshire Studies, Central Library, Westgate, OXFORD, Oxon OX1 1DJ Tel: 01865 815749 Photographic Archive: 01865 815432 **Fax:** 01865 810187 **E-mail:** cos.occdla@dial.pipex.com
Internet: Under development: http://www.oxfordshire.gov.uk/
Opening Hours: T.Th.F. 9.15-7; W.Sat 9.15-5 Closure: Mon+Public hols+2 wks stocktaking Jan/Feb.
Parking: None. Park & Ride Service.
Disabled: Lift from ground floor.
Appointments: Prior booking for viewers-2 days+fee. Entry-register. 60 seats+4 film+13 fiche-1 reader/printer.
Ordering System: Prior ordering by letter/tel. Catalogue nos sometimes required. Four ordered & produced. Delivery 10-15 mins. Last order: 15 mins before closure. P/copying by staff-post/collection after 3/4 working days, or DIY. Taping/cameras not permitted. Typing/laptops (power supply-at owner's risk) allowed.
Records: for post 1974 Oxfordshire. PRs-Ts. MIs. Printed books. Pamphlets & maps. Oxfordshire Local History. Oral History Archive. Photographic Archive. Oxfordshire Sites & Monuments Record. Newspapers from 1640s. Family History/Heraldry books. Local Obituaries Index 1820 on. Surname Index (Eng/Wales). Oxford & Berkshire Marr. Indexes 1538-1837. M/f-GRO Indexes 1837-1992/Oxon census/1881 Census Index/Probate 1858-1957/IGI.
Research Service: Limited specific enquiry-charge made max. 2 hrs. List of professional researchers available.
Facilities: Toilets/public tel. No refreshment facilities. Café/pub/shops nearby.
Publications: Free leaflets: *User's Guide-Centre for Oxfordshire Studies & Oxfordshire Archives. Finding out about Oxfordshire Centre for Oxfordshire Studies & Oxfordshire Archives. Studying Your Family History using Oxfordshire Newspapers. Your House-How to trace its history. Using Oxfordshire Maps. Using Oxfordshire Photographic Archive. Oral History.* (A5 SAE).
Remarks: Bags allowed at owner's risk-10 small/6 large lockers. Donations appreciated.
Note: This centre holds a wide range of Local Studies & Family History resources. Permanent displays of oral history, photographic archive, Family History, maps, archaeology.

Oxfordshire Archives, County Hall, New Road, OXFORD, Oxon OX1 1ND Tel: 01865 815203/810801 E-Mail & Internet-in process of being set up-contact for details
Opening Hours: M.-Th. 9-5 Closure: Fri.+Public hols+last wk in Jan & 1st wk in Feb.
Parking: None. Park & Ride Service.
Disabled: Lift. Toilet.
Children: 8 yrs+
Appointments: Prior booking for viewers-1 wk. Entry-register+CARN+2 photos. 16 seats+2 film+2 fiche.
Ordering System: No prior ordering. Number ordered & produced at archivist's discretion. Delivery 5 mins unless records held at outstore. Last order: 4.30. P/copying restricted, by staff-same day/post/collection. Typing/cameras/laptops (power supply) permitted. Taping not allowed.
Records: for pre 1974 Oxfordshire+records deposited from the Vale of White Horse (formerly Berkshire) since 1974-pre this date see Berkshire RO, Shinfield Park, Reading entry. Diocesan RO for Oxford-Archdeaconry of Oxford. Oxford Archdeaconry archives & parishes in Archdeaconry. PRs-Ts/originals. BTs. Local authorities-Banbury/Chipping Norton/Henley-on-Thames incl. Boroughs/courts. Quarter Sessions since 1687. Coroners-c20thC. PLUs. Nonconformist. Estate. Manorial. Business. Private deposits. Enclosure. Electoral registers. Deeds. Access to Oxford/Woodstock borough records. University College-estates/records of staff & students. St. Edward's School.
Research Service: Charge made.
Facilities: Toilets/public tel/restaurant/room for own food/drink vending machine. Café/pub/shops nearby.

OXFORD

Publications: Free: Info. sheets series-A4 guides to various types of records held. (A4 SAE). For sale: Publications by Oxfordshire FHS. *Calendars of Oxford Diocesan Court Records* (4 vols). Books pub. by members of staff using Oxfordshire sources. Brief Guides to Family/House History sources.
O.R: Bodleian Library, Dept. of Western MSS, Broad St, OXFORD, Oxon OX1 3BG reader's ticket by personal application only+letter of introduction by a responsible person. The Bodleian is a copyright library; **Oxfordshire Health Archive**, The Warneford Hospital, Warneford Lane, Headington, OXFORD, Oxon OX3 7JX. Appt. only. Administrative records (local health) subject to 30 yr. closure & medical records to 100 yrs.
Remarks: Bags not allowed-lockers. Donations appreciated. **Note:** As the archive storage is now over full, visitors should check in advance that the particular collections they need are available. Most colleges hold their own archives. **Note:** There is a possibility of relocation in 1999 to new premises at St. Luke's Church, Cowley (2 mls from City Centre, just off the Ring road).

Regent's Park College, Angus Library, Pusey Street, OXFORD OX1 2LB Appt. Written application & letter of reference. Fee payable for Family History research. Baptist Union of Great Britain & Ireland archives. Baptist Missionary Society. Some Baptist churches.

OXFORDSHIRE-USEFUL ADDRESSES:

Local Studies Centre, Abingdon Library, ABINGDON, Oxon. Local census returns.
Centre for Banburyshire Studies, Banbury Library, BANBURY, Oxon Tel: 01295 262282 Appt. PRs-Ts.+ Oxfordshire FHS's Marriage Index 1538-1837. Directories. Newspapers. Maps. Photographs. Ephemera. The Centre has lists of all Banbury related material deposited in Oxfordshire Archives. M/f-census/school log books/IGI. Info. leaflet (SAE). **Note: Banbury Museum**, 8 Horsefair, BANBURY, Oxon OX16 0AA. Tel: 01295 259855 has a bookshop with a good selection of local history publications.
Local Studies Centre, HENLEY-ON-THAMES, Oxon. Local census returns.

Local Studies Library, Central Library & Museum Complex, High Street, PAISLEY, Renfrewshire PA1 2BB Tel: 0141 8892360 **Fax:** 0141 8876468
Opening Hours: M.-F. 10-8; Sat 10-5 Closure: Public hols.
Parking: None.
Disabled: By prior arrangement.
Children: At staff's discretion.
Appointments: Prior booking for viewers-1 day. 24 seats (shared with Ref. Library)+3 fiche-2 reader/printers.
Ordering System: Prior ordering by letter/tel. Catalogue nos sometimes required. Number ordered & produced at librarian's discretion. Records stored elsewhere require prior ordering. Last order: before 5 pm. P/copying restricted, by staff-post/DIY. Typing/taping/ cameras/ laptops (power supply under some circumstances) permitted.
Records: Burgh records for Renfrew/Paisley/ Johnstone/Barrhead. Indexes to local newspapers from 1824. Paisley Burgess Rolls 1682-1872. Society of Hammermen of Paisley 1761-1955. Poll Tax rolls of Renfrew parishes 1695. Voters rolls 1832-1879; 1872-1913. Crawfurd & Metcalfe's History of the Shire of Renfrew. The Cairn of Lochwinnoch. Lochwinnoch & its families BMDs 1827-1845 (45 vols+index). Paisley & surrounding areas. Poor Law 1839-1948 (some closed)-some indexed. Renfrewshire MIs pre 1855. Minute Books for Paisley Society of Tailors 1666-1783. Sasines for Renfrewshire 1781-1947 (later ones indexed). Confirmations & Inventories 1876-1936. Directories. M/f-OPRs for Renfrewshire from 1670/census. IGI on CD-Rom.
Research Service: None.
Facilities: No toilet/public tel/refreshment facilities. Café/pub/shops nearby.
Publications: Free leaflet: *Records for Family Historians* (SAE). Guide for family history records in the collections of the Library & the Museum.
O. R: Paisley Museum & Art Galleries (same building) Tel: 0141 8893151 Some records are held jointly by the two repositories, some exclusively by this museum.
Tourist Office: Tel: 0141 8890711
Remarks: Station: Paisley Gilmour Street.

PALMERS GREEN, see London Borough of Enfield.

Peebles Area Library, Chambers Institution, High Street, PEEBLES EH45 8AG Tel: 01721 720123 Appt. Peebleshire Local History. Freedom collection-city/town/ burgh-relates to the Governor General of Canada.

PEMBROKESHIRE, see Haverfordwest.

PENZANCE, see Cornwall

Local Studies Dept., A. K. Bell Library, 2-8 York Place, PERTH, Perth & Kinross PH2 8EP Tel: 01738 444949. Appt. for viewers-3 film+2 fiche-2 reader/printers (fee charged). Vols of MIs-pre 1855. Newspaper Index. Brief details of wills 1876-1936. Parish histories. Maps. Photographs. 1891 census index. M/f-OPRs for Perth & Kinross district+Perthshire OPRs within Stirling area/census/IGI. See leaflet: *A Guide to family history resources in the Local Studies Dept. of the A. K. Bell Library* (SAE). For sale: Local History publications.

Perth & Kinross Council Archive, A. K. Bell Library, 2-8 York Place, PERTH, Perth & Kinross, PH2 8EP Tel: 01738 477012 **Fax:** 01738 477010
Opening Hours: M.-F. 9.30-5; Th. 5-8 (appt. only). Closure: Public hols.
Parking: Yes 2 hrs free-paying afterwards.
Disabled: Lift. Parking.
Children: At archivist's discretion.
Appointments: Prior booking for viewers (L.S. Dept)-1 day. Entry-register. 10 seats+3 film+2 fiche-2 reader/printers in L.S. Dept.
Ordering System: Prior ordering by letter/tel. Number ordered & produced at archivist's discretion. Delivery 5 mins. P/copying by staff-same day. Typing not permitted. Taping/laptops (power supply) allowed. Cameras at archivist's discretion.
Records: for Perth & Kinross Council. M/f-OPRs in L.S. Dept (see entry). Perth/Perth & Kinross/Kinross County Councils. Burghs of Aberfeldy/Abernethy/Alyth/Auchterarder/Rattray/Blairgowrie/Blairgowrie & Rattray/Coupar Angus/Crieff/Kinross/Pitlochry. Perth & Kinross District Council+retransmitted records of City & Royal Burgh of Perth. County of Perth/Kinross JPs. Perth Outport District/Blairgowrie Customs & Excise. Perth County Constabulary/Burgh Police. Nonconformist. Poor Law. Criminals. Hospitals. Schools. Lieutenancy. Valuation rolls & cess books from 1650. Industry. Family. Business. Trade Union. Solicitors. Voters lists. Cemetery. Maps & plans. Photographs.
Research Service: Charge made.
Facilities: Toilets/public tel/restaurant. Café/pub/shops nearby.
Publications: Free: General Info. leaflet: *Archives & L.S.* (SAE). For sale: *Summary List of Holdings*. Various other publications.
O.R: Perth Museum & Art Gallery, George Street, PERTH PH1 5LB. Tel: 01738 632488. Appt. Local History. Trade. Plans. Photographic (negatives) collection; **The Regimental Archives of The Black Watch,** Balhousie Castle, Hay Street, PERTH, Perth & Kinross PH1 5HR Tel: 0131 3108530 Appt. Regimental service records/diaries/casualty rolls/order books etc.(42nd & 73rd Highland Regiments).
Tourist Office: Tel: 01738 638353.
Remarks: Note: On 1st April 1996 this facility became The Libraries & Archives Division, Leisure & Cultural Services Dept. Perth & Kinross Council.

Peterborough Central Library, Broadway, PETERBOROUGH, Cambs PE1 1RX Tel: 01733 348343 Appt. Local History collection for Peterborough & surrounding area. Photographic collection. Maps & plans. **Note:** Peterborough became a Unitary Authority in April 1998.

North East of Scotland Museums Service, Arbuthnot Museum, St. Peter's Street, PETERHEAD, Aberdeenshire AB42 6QD. Tel: 01779 477778. Appt. North East Scottish Local History. Fishing. Shipping. Port books. Photographs. M/f-fishing boat records.

West Devon & Plymouth Record Office, Unit 3, Clare Place, Coxside, PLYMOUTH, Devon PL4 OJW Tel: 01752 223939 **E-mail:** pbrough@devon-cc.gov.uk
Opening Hours: T.-Th. 9.30-5; F. 9.30-4 Closure: Mon+Public hols+Dec 25-Jan 1.
Parking: Limited.
Disabled: Rear access-by appointment.
Children: Accompanied: At archivist's discretion. Unaccompanied: 12 yrs+
Appointments: Prior booking for seats/viewers-1 day. Entry-CARN+ID+fee. 7 seats+2 film+9 fiche-1 reader/printer.
Ordering System: Prior ordering by letter/tel. Catalogue nos required. Three ordered, one produced. Delivery 5 mins. No production 12-2 (but self service fiche available) Last order: T.-Th. 4.30; F. 3.30. P/copying restricted, by staff-collection next day. Typing/taping not permitted. Cameras/laptops (power supply) allowed.
Records: for the City of Plymouth & West Devon. Diocesan RO for West Devon parishes & parts of the South Hams. PRs-film/fiche/originals if not copied. BTs-originals. Local authority. Families. Estates.
Research Service: None.
Facilities: Toilets. No public tel/refreshment facilities. Café/pub nearby.
Publications: Various. Those which include this area are obtainable from Devon RO, Exeter (see entry).
O.R: Plymouth Central Library, Local Studies Reference Library, Drake Circus, PLYMOUTH PL4 8AL Tel: 01752 385907/8 Appt. Local History. Naval & Maritime History.
Tourist Office: Discovery Centre: 01752 266030/1 Fax: 01752 266033 Island House: 01752 264849 Fax: 01752 257955
Remarks: Bags not allowed-lockers. **Note:** Plymouth became a Unitary Authority (Plymouth City) from 1st April 1998 & now has its own separate archives service, but no major change is anticipated.

Poole Reference Library, Local Studies Collection, Dolphin Centre, POOLE, Dorset BH15 1QE Tel: 01202 671496 **Fax:** 01202 670253

PORTSMOUTH

Opening Hours: M. 10-7; T.-F. 9.30-7; Sat 9-1 Closure: Public hols.
Parking: None.
Disabled: Access-stairs or stairlift.
Children: At staff's discretion-may be provided with project files instead of original material (level & type of material depends on child).
Appointments: Prior booking for viewers-3 days or more. 6 seats+70 in adjacent Ref. library+ 4 film+3 fiche-1 reader/printer.
Ordering System: Prior ordering by letter/ tel. Class nos sometimes required. Number ordered & produced at librarian's discretion. P/copying restricted, sometimes by staff-same day/DIY. Typing not permitted. Taping/cameras/laptops (power supply) by prior arrangement.
Records: for Poole, East Dorset & Dorset in general incl. Parkstone/Canford/Longfleet/ Lytchett Minster. PRs -film. P/copies of various local govt. elections & electors/Newfoundland connections (Gosse Collection)/Council mins/Health reports. Newspapers. Press cuttings. Maps. Directories. Photographs. M/f-census/newspapers/IGI-incl Newfoundland.
Research Service: Charge made.
Facilities: No toilets/public tel/refreshment facilities. Café/pub/shops nearby.
Publications: For sale: Leaflets: *Poole Local Studies Collection-an Introduction*. Index of PRs on M/f. Directories. Electoral Lists. Local Newspapers. Local History publications, e.g. *Genealogical Sources* (Libraries in Dorset). Photographs.
O.R: Poole Museum Service, Waterfront Museum, 4 High Street, POOLE, Dorset.
Tourist Office: Tel: 01202 673322/668855 (accommodation). Fax: 01208 684531
Remarks: Note: Poole is now a Unitary Auhority. The extensive Poole Borough Archive collection has been transferred to Dorset RO Dorchester (see entry). The L.S. Library has a Poole Newspaper Indexing Project to mark the 150th Anniversary of the Poole & Dorset Herald (see Info. leaflet). See *Dorset parishes & neighbouring parishes* by B. Percival & V. Davies.

Portsmouth City Council Central Library, Historical Collections (2nd Floor), Guildhall Square, PORTSMOUTH, Hants PO1 2DX Tel: 01705 819311 Ext. 234 **Fax:** 01705 839855
Opening Hours: M.-F. 9.30-7; Sat 9.30-4 Closure: Public hols.
Parking: Public nearby-paying (very expensive).
Disabled: W/chair access from Guildhall Square (opposite end). Lifts. Magnifying glasses available. Toilet-see Facilities.
Children: Accompanied: At staff's discretion. Unaccompanied: 8 yrs+must have ID.
Appointments: Prior booking for viewers-3 wks phone Ext. 232. Entry-register+ CARN/other reader's ticket (Hampshire or Portsmouth)+ID. 20 seats+4 film+8 fiche-1 reader/printer.
Ordering System: Prior ordering unnecessary-most items on open access. Number ordered & produced at librarian's discretion. Prior ordering for a few items held in store. P/copying restricted, by staff-same day/post/collection. DIY-after permission from staff. Typing allowed (separate room). Taping/laptops (power supply-by prior arrangement) permitted. Cameras by prior arrangement.
Records: for Hampshire, West Sussex & Isle of Wight-especially Portsmouth/S.E. Hants. PRs-fiche (Portsea Island only)/p/copies/Ts. Important Naval collection of printed books. Charles Dickens collection. Theatre playbills. Local newspapers 1799-1976. Books-Clergy lists/Crockford's Directories. Missing persons. School/College/University registers. Directories. Genealogical manuals. Heraldry. Commonwealth War Graves Commission lists+other war records. Maps. M/f-GRO Indexes 1837-1983/census/National Probate calendars 1858-1943/IGI.
Research Service: Limited specific enquiry-free at librarian's discretion.
Facilities: Toilets-until 5 p.m/3.30 Sat. Public tel/cafe. Café/pub/shops nearby.
Publications: Free: *Trace your family history in the library. The Genealogical Collection at Portsmouth Central Library. The IGI. Indexes to births, marriages, deaths on M/f. Brief Notes on the Dickens Collection*. Local Publications for sale incl Portsmouth/ Hampshire Papers Series (A4 SAE).
O.R: Local Studies Collections in libraries at GOSPORT, FAREHAM and WATERLOOVILLE (Havant), also Museums at GOSPORT, FAREHAM and HAVANT.
Remarks: Station: Portsmouth & Southsea-2 mins.

Portsmouth City Museums & Records Service, Museum Road, PORTSMOUTH, Hants PO1 2LJ Tel: 01705 827261 **Fax:** 01705 875276 **E-mail:** Portmus@compuserve.com
Internet: http://ourworld.compuserve.com/homepages/portmus
Opening Hours: M.-F. 10-5 Closure: Public hols+Dec 24.
Parking: Nearby-in Museum Road.
Disabled: Disabled friendly.
Children: Accompanied: At archivist's discretion. Unaccompanied: 12 yrs+
Appointments: Prior booking for viewers. Entry-register+CARN. 11 seats+2 film+7 fiche.
Ordering System: Prior ordering by letter/tel. Number ordered & produced at archivist's

discretion. No production 12.45-1.30. Last order: 4.45. P/copying restricted, by staff-same day/post/collection.
Typing/taping/cameras/laptops (power supply) permitted.
Records: of Portsea Island & surrounding area. Diocesan RO for Portsmouth-three deaneries of Portsmouth (Anglican) covering Havant/ Alverstoke/Portsea Island. PRs-film/fiche/p/ copies/originals if not copied. Portsmouth City Council & predecessor authorities from 14thC. Anglican records from 16thC. Quarter Sessions. Nonconformists/ Roman Catholic churches. Deeds. Correspondence. Poor Law. Schools. Cemetery. Local business. Groups. Families & individuals. Electoral registers. Index of Consistory Court of Winchester wills 1571-1858 (originals in Hampshire RO, Winchester). Maps. Photographs & postcards. Census indexes 1841-1891. M/f-census/IGI.
Research Service: Charge made.
Facilities: Toilet. No public tel. Cafe-drinks & snacks. Café/pub nearby.
Publications: Free leaflets: Searchroom guide-plan of search room+map. *Dead men don't tell tales. Portsmouth Museum & Records Service.* (A5 SAE). The Museum shop sells a selection of local books.
O.R: Superintendent Registrar for Portsmouth, Milldam House, Burnaby Road, PORTSMOUTH, Hants PO1 3AF Tel: 01705 829041; **Superintendent Registrar for South East Hampshire**, 4-8 Osborne Road, FAREHAM, Hants PO16 7DG Tel: 01329 280493
Tourist Office: The Hard: Tel: 01705 826722 Fax: 01705 822693 Commercial Road: Tel: 01705 838382
Remarks: Bags not allowed-lockers. Donations appreciated. **Note:** No official naval or army service records kept here-see entry for PRO, Kew. Station: Portsmouth/Southsea

Portsmouth Roman Catholic Diocesan Archives, St. Edmund House, Edinburgh Road, PORTSMOUTH, Hants PO1 3QA Tel: 01705 822166. These are private archives & there are no set opening hours. Prior arrangement must be made with the archivist. No parking. Disabled-no facilities. Records cover the former counties of Hampshire, Berkshire, Isle of Wight & the Channel Islands. **Note:** This is a small part of the General Offices of the Roman Catholic Diocese of Portsmouth. It does not usually hold parish registers but has a list of their whereabouts & has details of any printed copies. The archive contains histories of each parish. See series by Michael Gandy-*Catholic Family History. Catholic Missions & Registers.*

Royal Naval Museum Archive, H.M. Naval Base, PORTSMOUTH, Hants PO1 3NU Tel: 01705 733060 Appt. Midshipmans journals. WRNS Historic collection. Oral history. Photographic collection.

POWYS, see Brecon; Llandrindod Wells.

PRESBYTERIAN HISTORICAL SOCIETY OF IRELAND, see Belfast.

Lancashire Record Office, Bow Lane, PRESTON, Lancs PR1 2RE Tel: 01772 263026 **Fax:** 01772 263050 **E-mail:** lancsrecords@treas.lancscc.gov.uk
Internet: http://www.lancashire.com/lcc/ro/index.htm
Opening Hours: M.W.Th. 9-5; T. 9-8.30; F. 9-4 Closure: 1st full wk of each mth+Public hols+Tues following Easter & Spring.
Parking: 10 spaces.
Disabled: Access. Toilet.
Children: At archivist's discretion.
Appointments: Prior booking unnecessary. Entry-register+CARN. 46 seats+15 film+13 fiche-1 reader/printer.
Ordering System: No prior ordering. Three ordered & produced. Delivery 10-15 mins. P/copying restricted, by staff-post/collection. Typing/taping/laptops (power supply) permitted. Cameras by prior arrangement.
Records: for historic county (pre 1974) of Lancashire+others to post 1974 boundaries. Diocesan RO for Blackburn/Bradford (part of)/Liverpool (part of)/Manchester (part of). PRs-fiche/Ts/originals if not copied. BTs-film. Some records relate to Furness/parts of Merseyside/Greater Manchester. Local authority. Nonconformist & Roman Catholic. Quarter Sessions. Coroners. Probate. Family. Business. Swinton Industrial School of Manchester Union. PLUs. Records from 12thC on. See *Guide to the Lancashire Record Office* for archive collection.
Research Service: None.
Facilities: Toilet/public tel/room for own food/drink vending machine. Café/pub nearby. Shops-10 mins.
Publications: Free: small handouts re: Regulations/Reprographic/Policy (SAE). For sale: *Finding Folk: Handlist of Genealogical Sources in Lancashire RO. Guide to the Lancashire RO* (3rd ed.) & Supplement (1977-89)-2 vols.
O.R: Preston District Library & Local Studies, Harris Library, Market Square, PRESTON PR1 2PP Tel: 01772 404000 Family History. Local History. Maps; **Lancashire County & Regimental Museum**, Stanley Street, PRESTON PR1 4YP Tel: 01772 264075 Appt. Duke of Lancaster's Own Yeomanry/14th/20th Hussars. Photographs.
Tourist Office: Tel: 01772 253731
Remarks: Bags not allowed-racks at security desk. **Note:** Blackburn & Blackpool became

Unitary Authorities from 1st April 1998 but have indicated their intention to operate a joint service with Lancashire from these premises. (See entries for Blackburn & Blackpool). See *Basic facts... about family history research in Lancashire* by R. Hirst. (FFHS1997).

Regimental Museum, Queen's Lancashire Regiment, Fulwood Barracks, PRESTON, Lancs PR2 4AA Tel: 01772 260362 Appt. Officers/soldiers of the Queen's Lancashire Regt.-E. Lancs. Regiment-20th & 59th Regts of Foot/Lancashire Regt-40th & 62nd Regts of Foot/the Loyal Regt-North Lancashire, 47th & 81st Regts of Foot.

PRIAULX LIBRARY, see St. Peter Port.

PRINCESS OF WALES & QUEEN'S REGIMENT MUSEUM, see Dover.

PUBLIC RECORD OFFICE OF NORTHERN IRELAND, see Belfast.

QUEEN ALEXANDRA'S ROYAL ARMY NURSING CORPS MUSEUM, see Aldershot.

QUEEN'S LANCASHIRE REGIMENTAL MUSEUM, see Preston.

QUEEN'S OWN HIGHLANDERS REGIMENT MUSEUM, see Inverness.

RAILWAY STUDIES LIBRARY, see Newton Abbot.

Thanet Branch Archive, Ramsgate Library, Guildford Lawn, RAMSGATE, Kent CT11 9AY Tel: 01843 593532 **Fax:** 01843 852692
Opening Hours: Th. & every 3rd Sat 9.30-1; 2-5
Parking: Yes.
Disabled: W/chair access-no special facilities in archive room.
Children: At archivist's discretion.
Appointments: Prior booking for viewers-1 wk. Entry-register. 6 seats+2 film+2 fiche-1 reader/printer.
Ordering System: Prior ordering by letter/tel. Catalogue nos sometimes required. Number ordered & produced at archivist's discretion. Delivery 5-10 mins. P/copying by staff-same day/post/collection. Typing/taping/cameras not permitted. Laptops (silent) allowed.
Records: for Isle of Thanet-former boroughs of Margate/Ramsgate. Former Urban District Councils of Broadstairs/St. Peter's+Rural District Council. Ancient parishes of Minster/Monkton/St. Nicholas at Wade/St. Lawrence/St. John/St. Peter/All Saints/Birchington. Ramsgate Borough-Garrett MSS. Conynyham MSS. Congregational (Ebenezer), Ramsgate. Theatre bills & programmes. 19/20thC's political posters & scrapbooks. Maps. Periodicals & journals. Directories. M/f-census/newspapers.
Research Service: Charge made.
Facilities: No toilet/public tel/refreshment facilities. Café/pub/shops nearby.
Publications: Various free & for sale.
O.R: Ramsgate Museum (same premises); **Maritime Museum**, Harbour Yard, Royal Harbour, RAMSGATE, Kent.
Tourist Office: Tel: 01843 583333 Fax: 01843 591086 Dover: 01304 205108 Fax: 01304 225498
Remarks: Note: In 1998 a new small repository, the East Kent Archive, will open at Whitfield, Dover which will house the archival records now held at Ramsgate & Folkestone (S.E. Kent Archive Office). This centre will be open for a limited number of days a week-see Folkestone entry. The Ramsgate & Folkestone libraries will still retain their own Local Studies collections.

Rawtenstall Central Library, Rossendale Collection, Queen's Square, Haslingden Road, RAWTENSTALL, Lancs BB4 6QU
Tel: 01706 227911/2 Fax: 01706 217014
E-mail: lancs-co-lib-hq@mcr1.poptel.org.uk
Internet: http://www.earl.org.uk/earl/members/lancashire **Note:** E-mail & Internet are for county headquarters-E-mail will be forwarded to the Library.
Opening Hours: M.T. 10-7.30; W. 10-1; Th.F. 10-5; Sat 10-4 Closure: Public hols.
Parking: Nearby-on street.
Disabled: No facilities-stairs.
Children: At staff's discretion.
Appointments: Prior booking for viewers. 22 seats+4 film+2 fiche-1 reader/printer.
Ordering System: Prior ordering by letter/tel. Number ordered & produced at librarian's discretion. Delivery usually immediate. P/copying by staff-post/collection/DIY. Typing/taping not permitted. Laptops/cameras allowed.
Records: for Rossendale District of Lancashire-Bacup/Haslingden/Rawtenstall/Whitworth. PRs-film/fiche. Rawtenstall & Rossendale Council mins/electoral registers. Rawtenstall burial board. Housing Scheme 20thC. Cooperative Societies. Sunday School. Haslingden Gospel Mission. Copies of music scores written & used by Deighn Layrocks-18thC musicians (originals in Lancashire RO, Preston). Newscuttings. Photographs. M/f-Rossendale Free Press.
Research Service: None.
Facilities: No toilet/public tel/refreshment facilities. Café/pub/shops nearby.
O.R: Rossendale Museum, Whitaker Park, Haslingden Road, RAWTENSTALL, Lancs BB4 6RE
Tourist Office: Tel: 01706 226590 Fax: 01706 226590

Remarks: Donations appreciated. Booklet detailing archive material in stock-parish records/newspapers etc. **Note:** Blackburn & Blackpool became Unitary Authorities outside Lancashire but should not affect this collection..

County Studies Library, 1st Floor, Reading Central Library, Abbey Square, READING, Berks RG1 3BQ Tel: 0118 9509243. Appt. Local History. Mins of Berks County Council from 1892. Reading Borough Council mins from 1911. Ts-PRs/MIs. Electoral rolls. Directories. Ephemera/Scrapbooks. Maps. M/f-census/ newspapers/IGI. **Note:** Reading became a Unitary Authority on 1st April 1998.

Rural History Centre, The University, Whiteknights, P.O. Box 229, READING, Berks RG6 6AG Tel: 0118 9318660 **Fax:** 0118 9751264 **E-mail:** jhbrown@reading.ac.uk; jscreasey@reading.ac.uk (Note. J.H. Brown, Archivist & J.S. Creasey, Librarian).
Internet: http://www.reading.ac.uk/instits/im/home.html
Opening Hours: M.-F. 9.30-5 Appt.
Parking: 10 spaces.
Disabled: On ground floor-appt. for access.
Records: Agricultural engineering records-national collection. Farm records-national collection (via Reading University Library at present). Agricultural Trade Unions. Societies/Cooperatives/Council for the Protection of Rural England (CPRE). Photograph library.
Publications: Free Info. leaflets: *The Researchers' Guide to the Rural History Centre*. Publications List. (SAE). Publications for sale from Museum bookstall.
Remarks: Note: Planned re-location to another site on University Campus within the next four years.

READING, see Shinfield Park.

REDBRIDGE, see London Borough of.

Redcar Reference Library, Central Library, Coatham Road, REDCAR TS10 1RP Tel: 01642 489292. Usually open. Local History collection incls. photographic collection. Redcar is now a Unitary Authority.

Cornish Studies Library, 2-4 Clinton Road, REDRUTH, Cornwall TR15 2QE Tel: 01209 216760 **Fax:** 01209 314763
Opening Hours: T.W.Th. 9.30-12.30; 1.30-5; F. 9.30-12.30; 1.30-7; Sat 9.30-12.30 Closure: Mon+Public hols+Easter Sat+Christmas.
Parking: Public-paying.
Disabled: No facilities-library on 1st floor. Contact library staff for info.
Children: At staff's discretion.
Appointments: Prior booking for viewers-10 days min. 10 seats+9 film+2 fiche-1 reader/printer.
Ordering System: Prior ordering-no restrictions usually. Delivery few mins. P/copying restricted, by staff-same day/post/DIY depending on items. Typing/ taping not permitted. Laptops allowed. Cameras permitted subject to copyright restrictions.
Records: Cornwall's principal collection of printed & published material. PRs-Ts (incl. Phillimore's Marriages for Cornwall). BTs-film. Indexes to Archdeaconry of Cornwall probate records 1600-1857. Printed family histories. Plans-railway/sea charts. Newspapers. Directories. Local tel. directories from 1968. Maps. Photographs. Pamphlets. Video recordings. M/f-GRO indexes 1837-1939/ census/1881 census index/newspapers/IGI.
Research Service: None.
Facilities: Toilets. No public tel (one outside building). No refreshment facilities. Café/pub/shops nearby.
Publications: For sale: *List of the Transcripts of PRs Available at the Cornish Studies Library*. Leaflets: *The Cornish Studies Library: an introduction*-with map. *Cornish Directories at the Cornish Studies Library. Family History in Cornwall.*
O.R: Cornish American Connection, Murdoch House, Cross Street, REDRUTH, Cornwall TR15 2BU
Remarks: Bags not allowed-at staff desk. **Note:** There will be a re-location to the new Heritage Centre, Alma Place, Redruth c1999/2000.

REGENTS PARK COLLEGE, ANGUS LIBRARY, see Oxford.

RELIGIOUS SOCIETY OF FRIENDS IN IRELAND, see Dublin.

RENFREWSHIRE, see Giffnock; Paisley.

REPRESENTATIVE CHURCH BODY LIBRARY, see Dublin.

The Green Howards Regimental Museum, Trinity Church Square, RICHMOND, N.Yorks DL10 4QN Tel: 01748 822133. Regimental history of the Green Howards from 1688.

RICHMOND UPON THAMES, SURREY, see London Borough of Richmond; Kew.

Rochdale Local Studies Library, The Arts and Heritage Centre, The Esplanade, ROCHDALE OL16 1AQ Tel: 01706 647474 Ext. 4915 Enquiries: 01706 864915

ROCHDALE

Opening Hours: T.W.F. 10-1; 2-5.30; Th. 10-1; 2-7.30; Sat 9.30-1; 2-4 Closure: Mon+Public hols.
Parking: Nearby.
Disabled: Disabled friendly. Parking.
Children: Unaccompanied: 7yrs+
Appointments: Prior booking for viewers-few days. 23 seats+4 film+3 fiche-2 reader/printers.
Ordering System: Prior ordering by letter/tel. Number ordered & produced at librarian's discretion. Records stored elsewhere need 1 wk prior notice. P/copying restricted. Typing/taping/cameras not permitted. Laptops allowed.
Records: for the area covered by Rochdale (Middleton & Heywood are in separate units)-Littleborough/Wardle/Milnrow/some Whitworth records. PRs/BTs-M/f. Wills 1553-1810. Municipal & other administrative records. Trade Unions/Political. Rochdale Pioneers mins. Methodist archives+other nonconformist registers-Baptist/Presbyterian in hard copy & M/f. MIs. C. of E. Industrial. Commercial. Manorial. Family. Burgess rolls. Poor Law. Landowners. Almanacks. Newspapers-original & M/f. Theatre posters. Maps & plans. Photographs. M/f-census/IGI.
Research Service: None.
Facilities: Toilets. No public tel/refreshment facilities. Café/pub nearby. Shops-10 mins.
Publications: Free: *Genealogical Sources in Rochdale Local Studies Library* (SAE). For sale: various.
Tourist Office: Tel: 01706 356592
Remarks: Donations appreciated.
Note: There will be a move to temporary accommodation (location not yet known) some time in 1998 for renovations & restoration of present premises. MSS material currently difficult to access-contact librarian for details. Change to Unitary Authority. Manchester RO also has other Rochdale records (see entry).

ROCHDALE, see also Heywood, Middleton

Rochester-upon-Medway Studies Centre, Civic Centre, Strood, ROCHESTER, Kent ME2 4AW Tel: 01634 732714 **Fax:** 01634 297060 **E-mail:** s-dixon@gateway.rochester.gov.uk
Internet: As yet Main City Council Home page only: rochester.gov.uk
Opening Hours: M.Th.F. 9-5; T. 9-6 Closure: Wed+Public hols+two full wks in Nov.
Parking: Yes-free.
Disabled: Lift. Toilet. Loop system.
Children: Accompanied: At archivist's discretion. Unaccompanied: 14 yrs+
Appointments: Prior booking for viewers-1 wk. Entry-register+CARN+ID. 6 seats+9 film+2 fiche-2 reader/printers.
Ordering System: No prior ordering. Three ordered, one produced. Delivery 2 mins. No production 1-2. Last order: M.Th.F 4.30; T. 5.30. P/copying restricted, by staff-collection by arrangement. Typing/taping/laptops (power supply) by prior arrangement. Cameras not allowed.
Records: for Rochester-upon-Medway local authority area+adjacent areas of historical local authority overlaps. Diocesan RO for Rochester Archdeaconry area. PRs-film/Ts. BTs-film (originals at Maidstone, see entry). Rochester City archives-Quarter/Petty Sessions/Courts of-Admiralty/Portmate/Leet. Oyster Fishery. Council mins/rates/rentals. Freemens registers. Strood Extra Parish Meeting records. Borough of Chatham. Board of Health. PLU. Municipal burial records. Building plans. Council mins. Medway District/Borough Councils. Rochester-upon-Medway Borough/ City Councils. Strood Rural District Council-mins/building plans. Rochester Highway Board. Hoo Rural District Council-mins/plans. Hospital of Sir John Hawkins, Kt. in Chatham 16thC on. E.H. Couchman collection of ephemera 18thC on. Charities. Naval collection. Poor Law relief. Hospitals. Trades. Industry. Education. Family & estate. Dean & Chapter of Rochester c1080-1983. Nonconformists. Cemeteries. Maps & plans. Photographs & prints. M/f-census for Rochester-upon-Medway area & Wouldham/newspapers/IGI.
Research Service: None.
Facilities: Toilets. Public tel. in Civic Centre main building. No refreshment facilities. Café/pub/shops nearby.
Publications: Free: Info. leaflets (SAE). For sale: *Subject guide. Family History. Armed Forces guide.*
O.R: Local Studies Section (same building); **Guildhall Museum**, High Street, ROCHESTER.
Tourist Office: Tel: 01634 84366.
Remarks: Bags not allowed-rack near main door. Donations appreciated. **Note:** From 1st April 1998, with the creation of a new Unitary Authority, there will be a change of name, as yet unknown, but no change of location & the collections will remain unchanged. As yet, no comment can be offered regarding arrangements for Gillingham Borough Archives. Station: Strood.

ROMAN CATHOLIC RECORD OFFICE, see Aldershot.

ROMFORD, ESSEX, see London Borough of Havering.

Archives & Local Studies Section, Central Library, Walker Place, ROTHERHAM, Yorks S65 1JH Tel: 01709 823616 **Fax:** 01709 823650 **E-mail:** archives@rotherham.gov.uk
Opening Hours: T.W.F. 10-5; Th. 1-7; Sat 9-1. Closure: Mon+Public hols+1st wk in

Dec+Christmas to New Year. **Parking:** Public-at rear of library.
Disabled: Lift.
Children: At staff's discretion.
Appointments: Prior booking for viewers-1 wk. Entry-register. 16 seats+4 film+2 fiche-1 reader/printer.
Ordering System: Prior ordering by letter/tel. Number ordered & produced at archivist's discretion. Delivery 5-10 mins. P/copying by staff. Typing/taping/laptops (power supply) permitted. Cameras by prior arrangement.
Records: for Metropolitan Borough of Rotherham-former authorities of Rotherham county borough/Kiveton Park/Rotherham Rural & Urban District Councils-Maltby/Swinton Rawmarshe/Wath-upon-Dearne. PRs film/ fiche/p/copies/Ts. Quarter Sessions/Courts. Nonconformist. Hospital. PLU. Business. Cemeteries. Police. Newspapers. Photographs.
Research Service: Charge made.
Facilities: Toilets/public tel/restaurant. Café/pub/shops nearby.
Publications: Free: brief leaflets on family history sources. For sale: range of Local History publications.
O.R: York & Lancaster Regiment Museum, Regimental Library & Archives, ROTHERHAM Tel: 01709 382121 Ext. 3625 Appt. only.
Tourist Office: Tel: 01709 823611 Fax: 01709 823650
Remarks: Donations appreciated. Station: Rotherham Central.

Bute Museum, Stuart Street, ROTHESAY, Isle of Bute Argyll & Bute PA20 OBL Tel: 01700 502540. Appt. Winter: T.-Sat 2.30-4.30 Summer from 1st April 7 days10.30-4.30 P/copying. Rothesay Town Council /Parish Session. Rothesay Examination rolls/bapt/marr 1775-1835 (incomplete). Kingarth deeds & papers+Ascog Estate 16th-18thC's. Kingarth Parish Session. Photographs. Station: Wymss Bay with ferry connection to Bute. **Note:** This small museum is mainly run by volunteers. Donations appreciated.

ROYAL ARMOURED CORPS & ROYAL TANK MUSEUM, see Bovington Camp.

ROYAL ARMY CHAPLAINS' DEPT., see Netheravon.

ROYAL ARMY MEDICAL CORPS, see Aldershot.

ROYAL COLLEGE OF NURSING ARCHIVES, see Edinburgh.

ROYAL COLLEGE OF SURGEONS OF EDINBURGH, see Edinburgh.

ROYAL CORPS OF SIGNALS MUSEUM, see Blandford Forum.

ROYAL ELECTRICAL & MECHANICAL ENGINEERS (REME) MUSEUM, see Arborfield.

ROYAL ENGINEERS LIBRARY, see Chatham.

ROYAL HIGHLAND FUSILIERS REGIMENTAL HEADQUARTERS MUSEUM, see Glasgow.

ROYAL INNISKILLING FUSILIERS REGIMENTAL MUSEUM, see Enniskillen.

ROYAL LOGISTICS CORPS MUSEUM, see Deepcut, Surrey.

ROYAL MARINES MUSEUM, see Southsea.

ROYAL NAVAL MUSEUM ARCHIVE, see Portsmouth.

ROYAL NAVY SUBMARINE MUSEUM, see Gosport.

ROYAL SCOTS REGIMENTAL MUSEUM, see Edinburgh.

ROYAL ULSTER RIFLES REGIMENT MUSEUM, see Belfast.

RURAL HISTORY CENTRE, see Reading.

Denbighshire Record Office, 46 Clwyd Street, RUTHIN LL15 1HP Tel: 01824 703077 **Fax:** 01824 705180
Internet: http://www.llge.org.uk/cac/cac0011 .html
Opening Hours: M.-Th. 9-4.45; F. 9-4.15 Closure: Public hols+1 wk late Jan/early Feb.
Parking: 5 spaces-free
Disabled: Access by prior arrangement. Toilet.
Children: At archivist's discretion.
Appointments: Prior booking for viewers-3 days. Entry-register+CARN. 18 seats+5 film+2 fiche-reader/printer.
Ordering System: Prior ordering by letter/telephone. Catalogue nos preferred. Number ordered & produced at archivist's discretion. Delivery 10-15 mins. No production 12-1.30. Last order: M-Th. 4.30; F. 4.00. P/copying restricted, by staff-same day/post. Typing/taping/laptops (power supply) by arrangement. Cameras not allowed.
Records: for Denbighshire & former county of Clwyd. PRs-film/p/copies/Ts. Parish. Nonconformists. Quarter Sessions. Local Government. Business. Industries. Families. Estates. School log books. Newspapers. Maps. Photographs. M/f-GRO Indexes/census/Index

to Probate registers for England/Wales 1858-1928.
Research Service: Charge made-see Denbighshire RO Research Service leaflet.
Facilities: Toilets. No public tel. Room for own food/drink vending machine. Café/pub/shops nearby.
Publications: Free leaflets: *Denbighshire RO. Denbighshire RO Services to Schools.* (SAE). List of Publications. For sale: *Guide to the Parish Records of Clwyd. Handlist of Denbighshire Quarter Sessions Records* 2 vols. *Handlist of the Grosvenor/Halkyn MSS*-lead/coal mining/quarrying in north east Wales. *Handlist of Chapel Registers.* Parish Map. *Handlist of the Topographical Prints of Clwyd.* Llangollen Directory-1886 facsimile. Facsimiles of maps/prints/posters. *Ruthin Gaol. The Mold Riots. The Tithe War.* Leaflets-List of PRs/Sources for the Genealogist.
O. R: Clwyd FHS Genealogical Centre, Mwrog Street, RUTHIN. Limited opening.
Tourist Office: Tel: 01824 7903992
Remarks: Bags not allowed. Donations appreciated. **Note:**This RO came under a Unitary Authority on 1st April 1996-formerly Clwyd RO (Ruthin Branch). The RO Indexes-computer database arranged under subject & place. The Local Studies are scheduled to be on this site by Summer 1998. Nearest Station: Rhyl.

RUTLAND, see Leicestershire RO, Leicester

JOHN RYLANDS UNIVERSITY, see Manchester.

S. YORKSHIRE, see Sheffield.

SADDLEWORTH MUSEUM, see Uppermill.

Saffron Walden Library & Arts Centre, Victorian Studies, 2 King Street, Market Square, SAFFRON WALDEN, Essex CB10 1ES Tel: 01799 523178. Local History collection. M/f-census/newspapers.

Saffron Walden Town Council, 18 High Street, SAFFRON WALDEN, Essex CB10 1AX Tel: 01799 527661 Appt. by letter to Town Clerk. Borough council & court records 14thC-1974

St. Albans Central Library, The Maltings, Victoria Street, ST. ALBANS, Herts AL1 3JQ. Tel: 01727 860000 (Library). 01727 866100 (City Council). Usually open but prior appt. for archives. St. Albans Council-docs/ letters/municipal/manorial 16thC on. Charity mins.

Hay Fleming Reference Library, St. Andrews Branch Library, Church Square, ST. ANDREWS, Fife KY16 9NN Tel: 01334 412685
Opening Hours: M.T.W.F. 10-7; Th.Sat 10-5 Closure: Public hols+Christmas Day & New Year.
Parking: None.
Disabled: No facilities.
Children: At librarian's discretion.
Appointments: Prior booking-1 day. 20 seats+1 film+1fiche.
Ordering System: Prior ordering by letter/tel. Number ordered & produced at librarian's discretion. P/copying by staff-same day/post. Typing not permitted. Taping/laptops/cameras allowed.
Records: OPRs-Ts. David Hay Fleming Collection-archives relating to St. Andrews. Deeds. Nonconformists. Ecclesiastical. Business. Local trades. Maps. Pamphlets. Photographs.
Research Service: None
Facilities: No toilet/public tel/ refreshment facilities. Café/pub/shops nearby.
Tourist Office: Tel: 01334 472021
Remarks: Station: Leuchars.

St. Andrews University Library, Manuscripts Dept., North Street, ST. ANDREWS, Fife KY16 9TR Tel: 01334 462324 **Fax:** 01334 462282 **E-mail:** nhr1@st-and.ac.uk
Internet: http://www.st-and.ac.uk University Home Page-through menus to Library.
Opening Hours: M.-F. 9-5; Sat 9-12.15 (Academic term only). Closure: Christmas-New Year (open other public hols.)
Parking: None.
Disabled: Disabled friendly-by appt.
Children: At staff's discretion.
Appointments: Prior booking unnecessary. Entry-register. 24 seats+2 film+2 fiche-1 film/1 fiche reader.
Ordering System: No prior ordering. Number ordered & produced at staff's discretion. Delivery 3 mins. P/copying restricted, by staff-same day/post/collection-depending on volume/pressure of work. Typing/cameras not permitted. Taping (if quiet)/laptops (power supply) allowed.
Records: primarily for North East Fife. Muniments: former burghs of N.E. Fife area-Anstruther/Auchtermuchty/Crail/Cupar /Elie & Earlsferry/Falkland/Kilrenny/Ladybank /Newburgh/Newport/Pittenweem/St. Andrews /St. Monance/Tayport+parishes in former presbyteries of St. Andrews & Cupar. Local estates. Dundee Royal Infirmary mins. Various indices/guides etc. available for consultation-see WEB page. Library MSS Dept: Photographic Collection.
Research Service: None.
Facilities: Toilet/public tel. No refreshment facilities. Café/pub/shops nearby.

ST. AUSTELL, see Cornwall

Museum of Welsh Life, ST.FAGANS, Cardiff CF5 6XB Tel: 01222 573437 Appt.+letter of introduction. Local History/folklore collections. Dialect. Farming. Heraldry. Trades. Books. Periodicals. Photographs. Sound & film archives.

ST. GERMANS, see Cornwall

St. Helens Local History & Archives Library, Central Library, Gamble Institute, Victoria Square, ST. HELENS, Merseyside WA10 1DY Tel: 01744 456952 **Fax:** 01744 20836
Opening Hours: M.W. 9.30-8; T.Th.F. 9.30-5; Sat 9.30-4 Closure: Public hols.
Parking: Public nearby-Birchley Street (5 mins).
Disabled: Lift. Parking outside library-disabled badge.
Children: Accompanied: 10 yrs+ Unaccompanied: At staff's discretion.
Appointments: Prior booking for viewers. Entry-register+ID depending on docs. required. 25 seats+7 film+5 fiche-1 reader/printer.
Ordering System: Prior ordering by letter/tel essential-1 day. Catalogue nos required. Number ordered & produced at staff's discretion. P/copying restricted, by staff-same day depending on quantity. Typing not permitted. Taping/laptops allowed. Cameras by permission.
Records: for St. Helen's Borough & adjacent villages. PRs-film/fiche/p/copies/Ts. Newspapers+Index. Borough/Council. Poor Law for Township of Parr 17thC-1828. Estate. Business. Parr papers. SmithKline Beecham Archives (closed-require permission to consult from SmithKline Beecham). Maps. Pamphlets. Photographs. M/f-GRO Indexes/census.
Research Service: None.
Facilities: No toilet. Public tel. No refreshment facilities. Café/pub/shops nearby.
Publications: Free: *Tracing Your Family Tree* (SAE).
Remarks: Station: St. Helens Central.

Jersey Archives Service, Jersey Museum, The Weighbridge, ST. HELIER, Jersey, Channel Islands JE2 3NF Tel: 01534 633303 **Fax:** 01534 633301
Internet: http://www.jersey/gov.uk/StatesofJerseyHeritageIcon
Opening Hours: M.-F. 9-5 Closure: Public hols+May 9.
Parking: None.
Disabled: Disabled friendly.
Children: School age.
Appointments: Appointment essential. Entry-register+registration form.
Ordering System: Prior ordering by letter/tel. Catalogue nos sometimes required. Number ordered at archivist's discretion, four produced. P/copying restricted, by staff-same day/post/collection. Typing/cameras/laptops (power supply) permitted. Taping not allowed.
Records: for the States of Jersey. The Anglican church in the Channel Islands is in the Diocese of Winchester but their records are not protected by the Parochial Registers & Records Measure of 1978 & therefore may be classed as 'at risk'. (see Remarks). States Committees & depts, the Royal Court. H.E. Lt. Governor. Parishes. Churches. Business. Societies. Social Security Dept. Individuals relating to the Island. Occupation Registration cards. Bailiffs & States Greffe files. Schools. Motor registration. M/f-Jersey census. Computerised indexes & catalogues to the collections.
Research Service: None.
Facilities: Toilets/public tel/restaurant. Café/pub/shops nearby.
Publications: Free: Info. leaflet.
Remarks: Bags not allowed. **Note:** A new Archives Centre is in process of being built at Clarence Road, St. Helier, which will open to the public in 2000. Once the Archives Service has its own premises it is hoped that many parishes will consider deposit of their vital records & allow easier public access to them-see Jersey Archives Service Annual Report 1996.

Judicial Greffe, Westaway Chambers, Don Street, ST. HELIER, Jersey, Channel Islands JE2 4TR Tel: 01534 502300 **Probate Registry**: Wills of personalty+combined wills of personalty & realty. The Registry is not open to the general public but searches can be carried out (time permitting) & in most cases copies can be issued. Some earlier documents are not in a suitable condition to be copied. Search fee £10 per half hour+25p per photocopied sheet. Please supply as much information as possible, i.e. full names of deceased person, incl. maiden name where applicable and date of death. Failing this a reasonable time span in which to search. **Public Registry**: The "Loi sur les Testaments d'Immeubles" passed in 1851 gave persons the right to dispose of their real estate by will, subject to certain conditions. There are few such wills of an earlier date. The index is integrated with the index of Deeds of Sale & Hypothecation of real estate. If a request is made to the Department for copies it is also essential to provide as much information as possible. Search fee is £5 per half hour+50p per photocopied sheet.

Lord Coutanche Library, Societe Jersiaise, 7 Pier Road, ST. HELIER, Jersey, Channel Islands JE2 4XW Tel: 01534 30538 **Fax:** 01534 888262

Opening Hours: M.T.W.F. 9.30-4.30; Th. 9.30-7; Sat 9.30-12.30 Closure: Public hols.
Parking: None.
Disabled: Lift. Toilet.
Children: Accompanied: At staff's discretion. Unaccompanied: 10 yrs+
Appointments: Prior booking unnecessary. Entry-register. 15 seats+1 film+1 fiche-1 reader/printer.
Ordering System: Prior ordering by letter/tel. Five ordered & produced. Delivery 15 mins (next day for photographs). P/copying restricted, by staff-same day/post/collection. Typing/taping/cameras not permitted. Laptops (power supply) allowed.
Records: for Jersey & other Channel Islands. PRs-p/copies/Ts Indexes to parish records/civil registers. Nonconformist & Roman Catholic churches. Military census 1809;1815. Rate lists 1858 to date. Local & Family History for Jersey. German Occupation-maps/newspapers/ almanacs/prints/photographs. Ephemera. Jersey Merchant Seamens Benefit Society registers 1835-1900-names of seamen & ships registered in Jersey (incomplete-some on M/f)). Business. Family papers & correspondence. MIs. Index to wills in Judicial Greffe. Photographs. Scrapbooks of newspaper cuttings. Societe Jersiaise & States of Jersey publications. M/f-census+indexes 1841-1891.
Research Service: Charge made+cost of copies of certs. from Superintendent Registrar.
Facilities: Toilet/public tel/room for own food by arrangement. Café/pubs/shops nearby.
Publications: Free leaflets: *Introduction to Family History Research. Guide to the Library & Photographic Archive.* Publications List. For sale: Various+some children's books. Back issues of Societe Bulletin.
O.R: Superintendent of Cemeteries (parish of St. Helier only), Mont a l'Abbe Cemeteries Office, St. John's Road, ST. HELIER, Jersey JE2 3LE. Tel: 01534 30788 Fax: 01534 888047; **Superintendent Registrar** (BMDs), 10 Royal Square, ST. HELIER, Jersey JE2 4WA Tel: 01534 502335; **Jersey Public Library**, Halkett Place, ST. HELIER, Jersey JE2 4WH Tel: 01534 59991; **Channel Islands FHS**, P.O. Box 507, ST. HELIER, Jersey JE4 5TN-Research Room open Tues & Thurs am only & is staffed by volunteers. On 1st floor of Bo-Kay (florist), 22 Hilgrove Street, St. Helier. The Research Room will eventually be accommodated in the Archives Centre, Clarence Road, St. Helier.
Remarks: Bags not allowed. Donations appreciated. **Note:** Most of the family archives are in French. See *Family History in Jersey* by M. L. Backhurst (1991).

Norris Library, The Broadway, ST. IVES, Huntingdon, Cambs PE17 4BX Tel: 01480 465101
Opening Hours: T.-F. 10-1; 2-4; (5 May to Sept) Sat 10-12 Closure: Public hols.
Parking: None.
Disabled: W/chair access.
Children: Accompanied: 12 yrs+ Unaccompanied: 18 yrs.
Appointments: Prior booking for seats-1 wk. Entry-register. 4 seats.
Ordering System: Prior ordering by letter/tel. Number ordered & produced at librarian's discretion. Delivery 5 mins. P/copying by staff-post. Typing/taping/cameras/laptops (power supply) permitted.
Records: for historic county of Huntingdon. 16th-19thC's wills & legal documents. Local Government minute books. Local charities. Newspaper collection. Civil War pamphlets. Maps. Photographs. Notes by local historians. Book collection on history of Huntingdonshire.
Research Service: None.
Facilities: No toilet/public tel/refreshment facilities. Café/pub/shops nearby.
Remarks: Donations appreciated. Nearest Station: Huntingdon.

Isles of Scilly Museum, Church Street, ST. MARY'S, Isles of Scilly TR21 OJT Tel: 01720 422337
Opening Hours: Daily in Summer season: 10-12; 1.30-4.30 Librarian attends Tues/Fri; Oct-March W. 2-4
Parking: None.
Disabled: Chairlifts.
Children: Not allowed.
Appointments: Prior booking for seats-1 wk. Entry-register+ID+entrance fee. 2 seats.
Ordering System: Prior ordering by letter/tel. Three ordered & produced-Tues/Fri only. P/copying restricted, by staff-post. Typing/cameras not permitted. Taping/laptops allowed.
Records: for the Isles of Scilly. PRs-Ts. Custom house books. Court record books. Ships logs. Lifeboat records. Wills. Scrapbooks. Local History collection. Photographs. Oral history.
Research Service: None
Facilities: Toilet. No public tel/refreshment facilities. Cafe/pub/shops nearby.
Publications: For sale: various.
O. R: Superintendent Registrar, Town Hall, ST. MARY'S, Scilly Tel: 01720 22537
Tourist Office: Tel: 01720 422536 Fax: 01720 422049
Remarks: Bags not allowed-storage facilities. Nearest Station on mainland: Penzance.

Island Archives Service, 29 Victoria Road, ST PETER PORT, Guernsey, Channel Islands GY1 1HU. Tel: 01481 724512 Appt. only. No disabled facilities. St. Peter Port Hospital-trade & occupation records/lunatic asylum/children's home/outdoor relief/ stranger poor etc. States committee &

departmental records. **Note:** Family historians are requested to make their first enquiries from the Priaulx Library (see entry) who will then contact the Island Archives Services if necessary.

Priaulx Library, Candie Road, ST. PETER PORT, Guernsey, Channel Islands GY1 1UG Tel: 01481 721998 **Fax:** 01481 713804
Opening Hours: M.-Sat 9.30-5 Closure: Public hols+9 May (Liberation Day).
Parking: 8 spaces.
Disabled: W/chair ramp.
Children: Accompanied: At librarian's discretion. Unaccompanied: 15 yrs+
Appointments: Prior booking for viewers-1 day. Entry-register. 20 seats+7 film+3 fiche-1 reader/printer.
Ordering System: No prior ordering. One ordered & produced. P/copying by staff-same day. Typing/taping/ laptops not permitted. Cameras allowed.
Records: for Bailiwick of Guernsey. PRs-film/fiche. Roman Catholic. Some Methodist. Cemetery. Army Lists. Regimental histories. Royal Guernsey Militia. Constables. Newspaper collection 1791 to present for Guernsey & Jersey. Family files. Photographs & postcards. Genealogy/Heraldry books. M/f-GRO Indexes/census 1841-1891 for Guernsey/Jersey.
Research Service: Charge made.
Facilities: Toilets. No public tel/refreshment facilities. Café/pub/shops nearby.
Publications: Free: leaflets.
O.R: St. Peter Port Societe, F.H. Section, P.O. Box 314, Candie, ST.PETER PORT, Guernsey GY1 3TG
Tourist Office: Tel: 01481 723552 (enqs)/723555 (accommodation). Fax: 01481 714951
Remarks: Donations appreciated.

The Greffe, Royal Court House, ST. PETER PORT, Guernsey, Channel Islands GY1 2PB Tel: 01481 725277 **Fax:** 01481 715097
Opening Hours: M.-F. 9-1; 2-4 Searchers should initially attend in the afternoon when staff can introduce them to the records.
Parking: None.
Disabled: Lift. Toilet.
Children: At staff's discretion.
Appointments: By written application to Her Majesty's Greffier+letter of introduction for researchers outside Guernsey+ID.
Ordering System: Prior ordering by letter only. Number ordered & produced at staff's discretion. P/copying by staff. Typing/taping/laptops permitted. Cameras not allowed.
Records: of Deanery Court of Guernsey from 1662. Judicial Records of the Royal Court of Guernsey 1526 on. Legislative records 1553 on. Royal Court letter books 1737 on. Land conveyances etc 1576 on. The Assembly of the States of Guernsey 1605 on. PRs-p/copies/Ts. Registers of BMDs 1840 on. Wills of Real Property from 1841 (Wills of Personalty are held by the Ecclesiastical Court. Tel: 01481 721732). Company registry 1882 on. Docs. issued by the Royal Court c1350 on. Feudal Court registers especially Cour St. Michel from 1532. Private collections of local families. Ts of docs held elsewhere i.e. Mont St. Michel Collection+minute books of Calvinist regime in Guernsey c1558-1660. Identity card files 1940-1945 (c20,000 personal forms & photographs). Maps & plans. M/f-major classes of records such as registers of conveyances/criminal trials/BMDs on reader/printer. Finding aids-Summary of Family History sources at the Greffe & detailed application forms for BMD certs-copies on request.
Research Service: None.
Facilities: Toilet/public tel. No refreshment facilities. Café/pub/shops nearby.
Publications: Free: General Info on records held. Research facilities, etc.
Remarks: Bags not allowed-lockers. **Note:** All genealogical enquiries should first be addressed to the Priaulx Library (see entry). For a general introduction to records see *The Records of the Royal Court* by J.C. Davies (La Societe Guernesiase Report & Transactions, xvi (1956-60), 404.

Trafford Local Studies Centre, Sale Library, Tatton Road, SALE, Cheshire M33 1YH Tel: 0161 9123013 **Fax:** 0161 9123019
Opening Hours: M.Th. 10-7.30; T.F. 10-5; Sat 10-4 Closure: Wed+Public hols.
Parking: None.
Disabled: Lift.
Children: At staff's discretion.
Appointments: Prior booking for viewers-few days/24 hrs for archives. Entry-register. 30 seats+4 film+3 fiche-1 reader/printer.
Ordering System: Prior ordering by letter/tel. Six ordered, three produced. P/copying by staff-same day. Typing not permitted. Taping/laptops (power supply) allowed. Cameras by prior arrangement.
Records: for Trafford Metropolitan Borough Council+archives of preceding councils-Sale/ Ashton under Mersey/Bowdon/Hale/Dunham/ Carrington/Warburton/Partington/Flixton/ Urmston/Davyhulme Stretford/Old Trafford. PRs-film/Ts. MIs. Trade directories. Will Indexes. Electoral registers. Local Societies. Newspapers/ newspaper cuttings. Maps. Photographs. M/f-census/newspapers/IGI/ BigR.
Research Service: Limited specific enquiry-free. Up to 1 hr-charge made.

Facilities: Toilet. No public tel/refreshment facilities. Café/pub/shops nearby.
Publications: Free leaflets: *Sources for Family History at Trafford L.S. Centre. Short Guide to sources for Family History. Trafford L.S. Centre. Local Newspapers. Photographic Services.* Publications list. (A5 SAE). For sale: Local history books for Altrincham/Sale/Stretford/Trafford/Urmston areas.
O.R: Register Office, Town Hall, Sale, TRAFFORD, Cheshire Tel: 0161 912 3026; **Altrincham Crematorium**, Whitehouse Lane, DUNHAM MASSEY, Cheshire WA14 5RH Tel: 0161 928 7771-holds the five cemeteries' records for Trafford.
Remarks: Station. Metrolink Sale.

Salford Local History Library, Peel Park, SALFORD, Greater Manchester M5 4WU Tel: 0161 7362649 **Fax:** 0161 7459490
Opening Hours: T.Th.F. 10-5; W. 10-8; Closure: Mon+Public hols.
Parking: Yes.
Disabled: Disabled friendly.
Children: At staff's discretion.
Appointments: Prior booking for viewers-1 day. Entry-register. 15 seats+ 5 film+ 3 fiche-1 reader/printer.
Ordering System: Prior ordering by letter/tel. Number ordered & produced at staff's discretion. Delivery few mins. P/copying by staff-same day. Typing/taping/cameras/laptops (power supply) permitted.
Records: for the City of Salford. R.C. Registers for St. John's Cathedral & other parishes. Electoral registers for S.E. Division of Lancs 1836-1869/Borough of Salford 1857 on/Salford area 1842-43. Burgess Rolls 1851-1915. Schedules of buildings. O/S & Tithe maps for Barton-upon-Irwell & Broughton. MIs-Ts. Newspapers. Local histories. Directories. Photographs. M/f-census/nonconformist registers/IGI.
Research Service: None.
Facilities: Toilets. No public tel. Restaurant/drink vending machine. Café/pub/shops nearby.
Publications: Free & for sale.
O.R: Working Clan Movement Library, Jubilee House Crescent, SALFORD M5 4WX; **Lancashire Mining Museum,** Buile Hill, Eccles Old Road, SALFORD, Greater Manchester M6 8GL Tel: 0161 7361832. Appt. Large Mining Library-coal mining/metalliferous mining/quarrying; **Salford University Library,** Academic Information Services, Clifford Whitworth Building, University of Salford, SALFORD, Greater Manchester M5 4WT Tel: 0161 7365843 Appt. Bridgwater Estates. Correspondence. Canal & railway engineers. Free: Info.leaflets (A5 SAE).
Remarks: Donations appreciated. Station: Salford Crescent.

SALFORD, see Irlam; Oldham.

Royal Gloucestershire, Berkshire & Wiltshire Regiment, Museum of the Duke Of Edinburgh's Royal Regiment, The Wardrobe, 58 The Close, SALISBURY, Wilts SP1 2EX Tel: 01722 414536 Appt. Archives of the 49th/62nd/66th/99th Regts of Foot, Volunteers & Militia incls. the Penruddocke Papers & Militia Rolls. **Note:** Other Wiltshire Militia records are at Wiltshire & Swindon R.O, Trowbridge (see entry).

SALISBURY, see Trowbridge.

SALTASH, see Cornwall

SANDWELL COMMUNITY HISTORY & ARCHIVE SERVICE, see Smethwick.

Scarborough Central Library, Vernon Road, SCARBOROUGH, N. Yorks YO11 2NN Tel: 01723 364285 **Fax:** 01723 353893
Opening Hours: M.T.F. 9.30-5; W. 9.30-1; Th. 9.30-7; Sat 9.30-4 Closure: Public hols.
Parking: None.
Disabled: Ramp.
Children: At librarians's discretion.
Appointments: Prior booking for viewers. Entry-ID for Local History Room. 35 seats (shared with Ref. Library)+3 film+2 fiche-1 reader/printer.
Ordering System: Prior ordering by letter/tel. Number ordered & produced at librarians's discretion. Delivery on demand. P/copying by staff/DIY. Typing not permitted. Taping/laptops/cameras allowed.
Records: for Scarborough+30 mile radius. PRs-p/copies/Ts+published Ts. Scarborough & district school log books & minute books for area. Town rate books. Scarborough Harbour Commissioners mins & accounts. Societies. Family papers. Indentures. Ships logs. Deeds. Directories. Burgess lists. Maps & plans. Prints. Photographs.
M/f-PRs/MIs/census/newspapers/Ts for St. Mary (unindexed)+Ts (9 vols unindexed)..
Research Service: None.
Facilities: Toilets. No public tel/refreshment facilities. Café/pub/shops nearby.
Publications: For sale: *Family History in Scarborough Library.*
O.R: Rotunda Museum, Vernon Road, SCARBOROUGH, N. Yorks; **Superintendent of Cemeteries**, Woodlands Crematorium, SCARBOROUGH, N. Yorks YO12 7SN Tel: 01723 372652-records for Dean Rd/Manor Rd/Woodlands Cemeteries; **Superintendent Registrar**, 14 Dean Road, SCARBOROUGH, N. Yorks Tel: 01723 360309
Tourist Office: Tel: 01723 373333 Fax: 01723 363785

Remarks: See under 'Yorkshire addresses' for other Superintendent Registrars' addresses.

SCILLY, ISLES OF, see St. Mary's.

SCOTTISH BORDERS ARCHIVE & LOCAL HISTORY CENTRE, see Selkirk.

SCOTTISH FISHERIES MUSEUM, see Anstruther.

SCOTTISH GENEALOGICAL SOCIETY LIBRARY & FAMILY HISTORY CENTRE, see Edinburgh.

SCOTTISH RECORD OFFICE, see Edinburgh.

SCOTTISH UNITED SERVICES MUSEUM, see Edinburgh.

SCUNTHORPE, see Grimsby.

SEFTON METROPOLITAN BOROUGH COUNCIL LIBRARIES, see Liverpool; Southport; Waterloo.

Scottish Borders Archive & Local History Centre, Library Headquarters, St .Mary's Mill, SELKIRK, Scottish Borders TD7 5EW Tel: 01750 20842 **Fax:** 01750 22875 **E-mail:** library1@netcomuk.co.uk
Opening Hours: M.-Th. 9-1; 2-5; F. 9-1; 2-3.30; Closure: Public hols+2nd Jan.
Parking: Yes nearby-free.
Disabled: Parking. Ramp-ground floor premises.
Children: At archivist's discretion.
Appointments: Prior booking for viewers-2 wks. Entry-register. 5 seats+1 film+ 4 fiche-2 reader/printers.
Ordering System: Prior ordering by letter/tel. Catalogue nos sometimes required. Records stored elsewhere need prior ordering-1 wk. Four ordered & produced. Delivery 5-10 mins. P/copying by staff-same day. Typing/taping/laptops (power supply) permitted. Cameras by prior arrangement.
Records: for Scottish borders-pre 1975 counties of Berwickshire/Peebleshire/Roxburghshire/Selkirkshire. PRs-film. Commissioners of Supply (valuation rolls). Highway Authorities (turnpike trusts). County council mins. School log books. Parish records. Business. Societies. Individuals. Maps & plans. Newspapers. M/f-OPRs+index/census/newspapers/IGI.
Research Service: None.
Facilities: Toilets. No public tel/refreshment facilities on site or nearby.
Publications: Free leaflet: *Scottish Borders Archive & Local History Centre: An Introduction*-with map (SAE).
O. R: Scottish Borders Museum Service, Municipal Buildings, SELKIRK Tel: 01750 20096
Tourist Office: Tel: 01750 20054
Remarks: Donations appreciated. **Note:** This archive is situated on the North Riverside Industrial Area. Nearest station: Edinburgh-40 miles.

Sevenoaks Archives, Sevenoaks Library, Buckhurst Lane, SEVENOAKS, Kent, TN13 1LQ Tel: 01732 453118/452384 **Fax:** 01732 742682
Opening Hours: M.T.F. 9.30-5; Th. 9.30-7; Sat 9-5 Closure: Wed+Public hols.
Parking: Public nearby-paying.
Disabled: Ramp. Lift.
Children: At staff's discretion.
Appointments: Prior booking for seats/viewers-1 day. Entry-form for archives. c30 seats+2 film+1 fiche-1 reader/printer.
Ordering System: Prior ordering unnecessary. Three ordered & produced. P/copying restricted, by staff-same day/post. Taping by prior arrangement. Laptops permitted. Typing/cameras not allowed.
Records: for Sevenoaks district. PRs-film/fiche/Ts. Local authority. Local collections.
Research Service: None.
Facilities: No toilets/public tel/refreshment facilities. Café/pub/shops nearby.
Remarks: Note: Sevenoaks collection will remain here for the foreseeable future.

SHAKESPEARE BIRTHPLACE TRUST RO, see Stratford upon Avon.

West Yorkshire Archive Service (Leeds), Leeds District Archives, Chapeltown Road, SHEEPSCAR, Leeds, West Yorks LS7 3AP Tel: 0113 2628339 **Fax:** 0113 2624707
E-mail: leeds@wyashq.demon.co.uk
Internet: http://www.wyashq.demon.co.uk
Opening Hours: T.-F. 9.30-5 Closure: Mon+Public hols+day following+1 wk in Feb.
Parking: None.
Disabled: No facilities.
Children: Accompanied: At archivist's discretion. Unaccompanied: 12 yrs+
Appointments: Prior booking for seats/viewers-2 days. Entry-register. 15 seats+1 film+6 fiche-1 reader/printer.
Ordering System: Prior ordering by letter/tel. Catalogue nos required. Some documents in outstore require 3 days notice. Four ordered & produced. Delivery 10 mins. No production 12.15-2. P/copying by staff-post. Typing/taping/laptops (power supply) permitted. Cameras allowed but no flash.
Records: for the historical West Riding & Diocese of Ripon which includes parts of North Riding. Diocesan RO for Ripon & Bradford.

PRs-fiche/Ts/originals if not copied. BTs available. Local authority. Family & estate-including Fountains Abbey/Earls of Harewood/Lord Canning/Ripley Castle. Business. Industry. Voluntary bodies.
Research Service: Charge made.
Facilities: Toilets. No public tel. Room for own food. Café/pub nearby.
Publications: Free: Info leaflets: *Guide to RO. Probate records. Parish records. BTs.* (SAE) For sale: *Guide: Leeds Archives.*
Tourist Office: Tel: 0113 2425242
Remarks: Bags not allowed-lockers. Donations appreciated. Station: Leeds City.

Sheffield Archives, 52 Shoreham Street, SHEFFIELD, S. Yorks S1 4SP Tel: 0114 2734756 **Fax:** 0114 2735066 **E-mail:** sheffield.archives@dial.pipex.com
Internet: http://www.earl.org.uk/earl/members/sheffield/arch.htm
Opening Hours: M.-Th. 9.30-5.30; Sat 9-1; 2-4.30; Closure: Fri+Public hols+Tues following+2 wks in Feb.
Parking: Public nearby-paying. Park & Ride service.
Disabled: Disabled friendly.
Children: Accompanied: At archivist's discretion. Unaccompanied: Registration+ID.
Appointments: Prior booking for seats/viewers-2 wks. Entry-Reader's ticket+ID-2 official proofs+registration form. 24 seats+6 film-reader/printer+10 fiche-1 reader/printer.
Ordering System: Prior ordering by letter/tel-essential for Sat by 5pm previous Thurs. Catalogue nos required. Number ordered & produced at archivist's discretion. Original docs. collected from strongroom at regular intervals between 10-11.45; 1 small issue 1 p.m; 2-4. Delivery time varies. P/copying restricted, by staff-same day/post/collection. Typing/taping/laptops (power supply) permitted. Cameras not allowed.
Records: for Sheffield/South Yorkshire/parts of North Derbyshire. Diocesan RO for Archdeaconry of Sheffield. Roman Catholic Diocese of Hallam. PRs-film/fiche/p/copies/Ts/originals if not copied. BTs-film. Nonconformist. Quarter Sessions. Magistrates Courts. Coroners. Hospitals. Printed probate calendars. Local Government. Police 1831-1975. Charities. Schools. Business. Family & estate. Maps. Photographs incl. aerial photographs. Audio recordings. National Coal Board for S. Yorks 19/20thC's. Yorkshire Water Authority. Personal papers of Earl of Stafford (Thomas Wentworth), 2nd Marquess of Lockingham & Edmund Burke's Arundel Castle MSS (Duke of Norfolk). M/f-census.
Research Service: Charge made (see Sheffield Archives Postal Research Service & List of Professional Genealogists & Record Searchers).
Facilities: Toilets. No public tel/refreshment facilities. Café/pub nearby. Shops-10 mins.
Publications: Free leaflets: *Sheffield Archives*-with map. *Family Search*-Mormon files & indexes on CD-Rom with instructions. (SAE). For sale: Family History Guides-1) *Census Returns* 2) *MIs.* 3) *BTs.* 4) *PRs.* 5) *Copies of PRs held by other ROs.* 6) *Nonconformist Registers.* 7) *Registers of burials in churchyards, chapel yards & cemeteries.*
O.R: Sheffield Cemeteries & Crematoria, Head Office, City Road Cemetery, City Road, SHEFFIELD S2 1GD Tel: 0114 2396068; **The Cutlers' Company Archive**, The Cutlers' Hall, Church Street, SHEFFIELD S1 1HG. Tel: 0114 2728456. Appt. only. The Cutlers' Company 1624 to present; **Sheffield Probate Sub Registry**, PO Box 832, 50 West Bar, SHEFFIELD S3 8YR Tel: 0114 2812596; **Sheffield Register Office**, Surrey Place, SHEFFIELD S1 1YA Tel: 0114 2735321/2; **Local Studies Library**, Sheffield Central Library, Surrey Street, SHEFFIELD S1 1XZ Tel: 0114 2734753 Usually open. Printed sources. Pamphlets. Newspapers. Maps. Electoral rolls. Photographs. Films. Videos/audio tapes.
Tourist Office: Tel: 0114 2734671/2 Fax: 0114 2724225
Remarks: Bags not allowed-storage. Donations appreciated. Station: Sheffield Midland-5 mins.

SHETLAND, see Lerwick.

Berkshire Record Office, SHINFIELD PARK, Reading, Berks. RG2 9XD Tel: 0118 9015132 **Fax:** 0118 9015131)
Opening Hours: T.W. 9-5; Th. 9-9; F. 9-4.30; Mon-appt. only 2-4.30 Closure: Public hols+2 wks in Nov.
Parking: Yes-free.
Disabled: Access-by appt.
Children: Accompanied: 6 yrs+ Unaccompanied: 12 yrs+
Appointments: Prior booking for seats/viewers-few days (longer for GRO Indexes)-several wks in advance for Thurs evenings. Entry-register+CARN. 20 seats+13 film+7 fiche-1 fiche reader/printer.
Ordering System: Prior ordering by letter/tel. Catalogue nos required (can be checked over phone). Six ordered, one vol/ten pieces produced. Ordering & delivery at set times (see Leaflet No. 5. Getting Started-ordering documents) P/copying restricted, by staff-post/collection. Typing/taping/cameras not permitted. Laptops (power supply) allowed.
Records: for historic county of Berkshire which incls. Vale of White Horse-transferred to Oxfordshire in 1974 (some records at Oxfordshire RO-see entry). Very limited coverage for Slough & surrounding area-transferred from Buckinghamshire in 1974

(main source for Slough is still Buckinghamshire RO Aylesbury - see entry). Diocesan RO for Archdeaconry of Berkshire (see Remarks). PRs-film/fiche/Ts/originals if not copied. BTs-not generally but some BTs of missing PRs have been transcribed. Parish Chest. Estate. Family. Quarter/Petty Sessions. Police. Borough. Education. PLUs. Nonconformist. Marr. Licences & Bonds. Probate 1508-1857+wills for Faringdon 1547-1853 (Indexes). Tithe. Inclosure. Cemeteries. Poll books & Electoral registers. Maps. M/f-GRO Indexes/census/IGI. Probate Indexes 1858-1935.
Research Service: Charge made-min ½ hr, max 1 hr.
Facilities: Toilets/public tel. Access to canteen/small shop now restricted-bring own food. Room for own food. No café/pub/shops nearby.
Publications: Free leaflets: Nos 1-8. Getting Started series incl. Family History, Houses, Transport. Research, Fees, Essential Information, Talks & Visits etc. Publications leaflet (A5 SAE). For sale: *Finding Your Family: a Genealogist's Guide to Berkshire RO. Handlist of PRs. Handlist of non-parochial registers incl. workhouse & cemetery registers. Handlist of Poor Law records 1835-1948.* Maps.
O.R: Berkshire FHS Research Centre, Prospect School, Honey End Lane, TILEHURST, Reading Tel: 0118 9413223 (Cliff Debney)/0118 9503072 (Robert Houseman). Information leaflet (SAE); **Bracknell Library** (for Bracknell Forest Borough Council) Tel: 01344 423149; **Newbury Library** (for West Berkshire Council) Tel: 01635 40972; **Slough Library** (for Slough Borough Council) Tel: 01753 535166; **Maidenhead Library** Tel: 01628 625657 or **Windsor Library** Tel: 01753 860543 (for Royal Borough of Windsor & Maidenhead); **Wokingham Library** (for Wokingham District Council) Tel: 0118 9781368.
Tourist Office: Reading Tel: 0118 9566226 Fax: 0118 9566719
Remarks: Bags not allowed-lockers. Donations appreciated. **Note:** From 1st April 1998 the RO will be run by Reading Borough Council on behalf of all the Unitary Authorities in Berkshire. The location of the RO will stay the same until a new record office is built for Spring 2000. Access will not change but tel/fax nos will-see above. Many Berkshire parishes came under the jurisdiction of the Diocese of Sarum (Salisbury) & various diocesan records-BTs/probate are in the Wiltshire & Swindon RO, Trowbridge-see entry. There is no mainline station at Shinfield.

Shropshire Records & Research Centre, Castle Gates, SHREWSBURY, Shropshire SY1 2AQ Tel: 01743 255350 **Fax:** 01743 255355
Opening Hours: T. 10-9; W.Th.F. 10-5; Sat 10-4. Closure: Mon+Public hols.
Parking: None-nearest Raven Meadows & rear of Station. Park & Ride Service between town centre & Harlescott/Meole Brace/Shelton.
Disabled: Disabled friendly. Induction loop system. 2 parking spaces at Castle Gates entrance-by prior arrangement.
Children: Accompanied: At archivist's discretion. Unaccompanied: Students under 17 yrs need signature of parent/tutor/teacher.
Appointments: Prior booking for viewers-4 days. Entrance-register+RO reader's ticket+ID+2 passport photos. 60 seats+5 film+16 fiche-2 reader/printers.
Ordering System: Prior ordering by letter/tel. Catalogue nos required. Number ordered at archivist's discretion, two produced. Delivery 10 mins. P/copying restricted, by staff-same day. Typing/taping/cameras/laptops (power supply) permitted.
Records: for Shropshire. Diocesan RO for Hereford-Archdeaconry of Ludlow/Lichfield-Archdeaconry of Salop. PRs-film/fiche/Ts/originals if not copied. Parish chest. Nonconformist. PLU. Schools. Quarter Sessions. Borough Corporations. County/District Councils. Manorial. Business. Solicitors. Deeds. Plans. Landed estates & families incl. pedigrees. Clubs & societies. Shewsbury newspapers 1772 on-indexed with biographical information from 1892 on. Prints. Drawings. Water colours. Photographs from 1842. Directories. Books. Pamphlets & periodicals. King's Shropshire Light Infantry collection. M/f-Shropshire census 1841-1891/some newspapers/IGI/maps-incl. O.S/tithe/apportionments. **Note:** Diocesan records for Northampton now housed with this R.O.
Research Service: Charge made.
Facilities: Toilets/public tel/room for own food/drink vending machine. Café/pub/shops nearby.
Publications: Free: Info leaflets (SAE). For sale: *Shropshire Family History: a guide to sources in the Shropshire Records & Research Centre.*
Tourist Office: Tel: 01743 350761 Fax: 01743 358780
Remarks: Bags not allowed-lockers. Donations appreciated. **Note:** The Shropshire Records & Research Centre comprise the former Shropshire RO & the L.S. Library. Prior notice for lengthy specialist research is advised. Catalogue of Oswestry Town Council archives available (see Oswestry). Friends of Shropshire Records & Research memberships available-c/o address above.

SHROPSHIRE

SHROPSHIRE, see Ironbridge; Ludlow; Much Wenlock; Oswestry; Shrewsbury.

SIGNALS ROYAL CORPS OF, MUSEUM, see Blandford Forum.

Sandwell Community History & Archives Service, Smethwick Library, High Street, SMETHWICK, Warley B66 1AB Tel: 0121 558 2561 **Fax:** 0121 555 6064
Opening Hours: M.F. 9.20-7; T.W. 9.30-6; Th. 9.30-1; Sat 9-1 Closure: Public hols.
Parking: Public nearby.
Disabled: W/chair access.
Children: At archivist's discretion.
Appointments: Prior booking for viewers-few days/1 wk for Sat. Entry-register. 14 seats+2 film+4 fiche-1 reader/printer. **Ordering System:** Prior ordering by letter/tel. Number ordered & produced at archivist's discretion. Delivery depends on staffing levels. P/copying by staff-same day. Typing/taping not permitted. Laptops (power supply-permission required) allowed.
Records: for Sandwell Metropolitan Borough. Diocesan RO for Birmingham-Warley Deanery only. PRs-film/fiche/p/copies/Ts. Nonconformist. Deeds. Local authority. Business. Large collection of mining maps.
Research Service: None.
Facilities: No toilet. Public tel/room for own food. Café/pub/shops nearby.
Publications: Free: Info leaflet. For sale: Lists of Parish & Nonconformist Church Registers.
Remarks: Station: Smethwick Rolfe Street.

Local Studies Collection, Solihull Library, Homer Road, SOLIHULL, West Midlands BG1 3RG Tel: 0121 7046977 Usually open except Tues. following Bank hols+extra day at Christmas. Disabled facilities. Toilets/public tel/refreshment facilities. 60 seats+2 film+9 fiche+reader/printer. P/copying. Numerous Local History publications for sale. PRs-film/Ts. MIs. Business. Local Studies collection-newspapers/maps/photographs. M/f-census/IGI. **Note:** Building works during 1998 on car park adjacent to Library-nearest car park 10 mins walk.

SOMERSET ARCHIVE & RECORD SERVICE, see Taunton.

SOMERSET, see Bath; Bridgwater; Taunton; Wells; Weston-super-Mare; Yeovilton.

SOUTH EASTERN EDUCATION & LIBRARY INFO. SERVICE, see Ballynahinch, Co. Down.

Local History Department, South Tyneside Central Library, Prince Georg Square, SOUTH SHIELDS, Tyne & Wear NE33 2PE Tel: 0191 4271818 Ext. 2135 **Fax:** 0191 4558085 **E-mail:** stlib.ref@dial.pipex.com
Internet: South Tyneside Libraries http://www.zebra.co.uk/heritage-north/st1/index.htm
Opening Hours: M.-Th. 9.30-7; F. 9.30-5; Sat 9.30-1. Closure: Public hols+Tues following.
Parking: Public-paying.
Disabled: Lift to basement where department is situated.
Children: At librarian's discretion.
Appointments: Prior booking for viewers-1 wk. 20 seats+4 film+5 fiche-2 reader/printers.
Ordering System: Prior ordering by letter/tel. Number ordered & produced at librarian's discretion. P/copying by staff/DIY. Typing/taping/cameras not permitted. Laptops allowed.
Records: for South Tyneside-South Shields/Jarrow/Hebburn/Boldons/Cleadon/Whitburn/Westoe & Harton. PRs-film/Ts. Kelly collection-posters (business/industry/entertainment in South Shields). Local photographers-various collections incl. Jarrow March/slums of South Shields in 1930s-most catalogued & indexed.
Research Service: None.
Facilities: Toilets/public tel/restaurant. Café/pub/shops nearby.
Publications: Free: Publications list (SAE). For sale: Various local history publications. Postcards.
Tourist Office: Museum & Art Gallery. Tel: 0191 454 6612

SOUTH TYNESIDE LIBRARY, see South Shields.

SOUTH WALES BORDERERS & MONMOUTHSHIRE REGIMENT MUSEUM OF ROYAL REGIMENT OF WALES, see Brecon.

SOUTH YORKSHIRE, see Doncaster; Sheffild.

Southampton Archives Service, Civic Centre, SOUTHAMPTON, Hants. SO14 7LY Tel: 01703 832251/223855 Ext 2251 **Fax:** 01703 336305
Opening Hours: T.-F. 9.30-4.30 One late eve a mth by appt. only-contact office for details. Closure: Mon+Public hols.
Parking: None.
Disabled: Access.
Children: At archivist's discretion.
Appointments: No prior booking. Entry-register. 9 seats+1 film+2 fiche.
Ordering System: Prior ordering by letter/tel. Three ordered & produced. No production 12.30-1.30. Delivery under 15 mins. P/copying restricted, by staff-same day.

Typing/taping/laptops (power supply) by prior arrangement. Cameras permitted.
Records: for geographic area of Southampton. Diocesan RO for Winchester-Southampton City parishes. PRs-fiche/Ts/originals. BTs-Ts. City/borough from 1199. Parish chest. Nonconformist-Methodist/Congregational/Baptist/Presbyterian/ Evangelical/Unitarian/ French Church. Quarter Sessions. Court Leet. Poor Relief. PLU. Military incl. muster books/militia. Town administration incl. electoral rolls/burgesses. Property records. Finance & trade accounts incl. debts/port books/brokage books. Board of Health. Water Works. Pavement & Improvement Commissioners. School Boards. Hospitals. Charities & societies. Solicitors. Family & estate. Merchant ships crew lists. Ships drawings. Photographs. Printed sources. Directories. Maps.
Research Service: Limited specific enquiry-free. Charge for more detailed work.
Facilities: Toilets/public tel. No refreshment facilities. Café/pub/shops nearby.
Publications: Free: Info leaflet. Publications leaflet (SAE). For sale: Southampton Papers (series). Southampton maps. *Guides to Records incl. Southampton Crew Lists 1863-1913. Sources for Family History in Southampton City RO. Hampshire Archivist's Group Joint Guides to Records.* The Southampton RO leaflet+others.
Tourist Office: Tel: 01793 221106 Fax: 01703 631437
Remarks: Donations appreciated.

Southampton City Heritage Services, Collection & Management Centre, 18 Melbourne Street, SOUTHAMPTON, Hants SO14 5FB Tel: 01703 237584 Opening Hours: M.-F. 8-5. Appt.-2 wks. Royal Mail Steamship Co. Officers lists from 1850. Photographic collection of associated British ports. British Power Boat Co. archives. Research Service. Free info. leaflets & photograph lists. (A5 SAE). Various for sale. Donations appreciated. **Note:** Maritime photographs will be available on Internet (see Southampton Pages).

Southampton Maritime Museum, Wool House, Bugle Street, SOUTHAMPTON SO1 0AA Tel: 01703 223941 Appt. Southampton Maritime history-liners/ship & port employees.

SOUTHAMPTON USEFUL ADDRESS:

Ancient Order of Foresters, Friendly Society, Forester's Heritage Trust, College Place, SOUTHAMPTON, Hants SO15 2FE See *My forebears were members of the Ancient Order of Foresters Friendly Society* (1993).

Essex Record Office, Southend Branch, Central Library, Victoria Avenue, SOUTHEND-ON-SEA, Essex SS2 6EX Tel: 01702 464278 **Fax:** 01702 464253
Opening Hours: M. 10-5.15; T.W.Th. 9.15-5.15; F. 9.15-4.15 Closure: Public hols.
Parking: Yes-paying.
Disabled: Lift to 1st Floor.
Children: Accompanied: At archivist's discretion. Unaccompanied: 11 yrs+
Appointments: Prior booking for viewers-3 days. Entry-register+CARN (for original docs.). 4 seats+4 film+5 fiche.
Ordering System: Prior ordering by letter/tel. Catalogue nos required. Five ordered, one bundle/up to five vols produced. Delivery 15 mins. Limited production 12-2. Last order: M.-Th. 4.30; Fri 3.30. P/copying restricted, by staff-same day. Typing/taping/cameras not permitted. Laptops (power supply) allowed.
Records: for Southend-on-sea/Castle Point Borough Councils/Rochford District Council/S. E. Essex. Diocese RO for Chelmsford-Deaneries of Hadleigh/Rochford/Southend-on-Sea. PRs-fiche/Ts-(PRs for all Essex on M/f). Local authority. Poor Law. Nonconformist. Schools. Quarter Session rolls (calendars to 1714). Maps & plans. Deeds & Sale catalogues. Estate. Building plans. MIs. Photographs & engravings. Directories. Catalogues to all Essex RO collections/Marriage licences/Settlements etc. M/f-Index to Essex 1881 census+30 other counties (approx.)/Index to Essex Wills 1400-1858/IGI.
Research Service: Charge made.
Facilities: Toilets/public tel. No refreshment facilities at present. Café/pub/shops nearby.
Publications: Free Info leaflets: *Surname Indexes. Out-County Sources. Sources for House History. Sources for Family History.* (A5 SAE). For sale: Various publications incl. *Essex Family History: A Genealogist's Guide to the Essex RO* (5th Ed).
O.R: Local Studies Library, Central Library, Victoria Avenue, SOUTHEND-ON-SEA, Essex SS2 6EX (adjacent to RO). holds M/f-census 1841-1891.
Tourist Office: Tel: 01702 215120 Fax: 01702 431449
Remarks: Bags not allowed-lockers. Donations appreciated. **Note:** Southend-on-Sea became a Unitary Authority on 1st April 1998. This service will probably continue unchanged but no decision has yet been made. Station: Southend Victoria from London Liverpool Street.

SOUTHERN EDUCATION & LIBRARY BOARD, see Armagh.

Sefton Metropolitan Borough Council Libraries, Southport Library, Local History Unit, Lord Street, SOUTHPORT, Merseyside PR8 1DJ. Tel: 0151 934 2119

Opening Hours: M.T.F. 10-5; W. 10-8; Sat 10-1. Appt. Disabled: Automatic doors+lift. Research charges. Local Government records pre-1974. Local History collection.

The Royal Marines Museum, (Archives & Library), Eastney, SOUTHSEA, Hants PO4 9PX Tel: 01705 891385 Appt. Archives of the Royal Marines/diaries/letters. Photographic collection. **Note:** Other Royal Marine records are with the Public Record Office, Kew. See *Records Of The Royal Marines* by Garth Thomas (PRO Readers' Guide No. 10.1994)

SOUTHWARK, see London Borough of.

Southwell Minster Library, c/o Minster Office, Trebeck Hall, Bishop's Drive, SOUTHWELL, Notts NG25 OJP Tel: 01636 812649 Appt.-1 wk min. No disabled facilities. Children: Accompanied 16 yrs+. Diocese of Southwell (BTs). Southwell Minster archive MSS from 1600. Marriage licences for Nottinghamshire. Local photographs. Local History material referring to Southwell Minster & Diocese. Holdings on computer database. **Note:** Nottingham CRO is the Diocesan RO. Southwell is a Peculiar.

Essex Police Museum, Police Headquarters, P.O. Box 2, SPRINGFIELD, Essex CM2 6DA. Tel: 01245 491491 Ext. 50770 Curator-Fredk. Feather. Appt. P/copying. Original police personnel records for Essex Police District which includes former police force records for Southend-on-Sea/ Saffron Waldon/Harwich/ Maldon/Colchester. Disciplinary registers. Registers of service. Some records for special constables & local railway police. Bound vols. of *The Truncheon* (incls. deaths & obituaries of local police personnel) 1926-1980s. An Index is available to police personnel. A charge may be made & donations are appreciated. See article in *Family Tree Magazine* Nov 1995 by Avril Cross about the Essex Police Museum, its records & bibliography. **Note:** Police records are usually subject to 100 & 75 yr closure ruling.

Staffordshire Record Office, Eastgate Street, STAFFORD, Staffs ST16 2LZ Tel: 01785 278380/01785 278372 (Bookings only)/278379 (Archives enqs.) **Fax:** 01785 278384
Opening Hours: M.T.W.Th. 9-1; 1.30-5; F. 9-1; 1.30-4.30; Sat (appt. only) 9-12.30. Closure: Public hols+preceding Sat+following Tues.
Parking: None.
Disabled: Ramp access. Toilet.
Children: 11 yrs+
Appointments: Prior booking for viewers-as long as possible. Entry-register+reader's ticket. 16 seats+7 film.
Ordering System: No prior ordering. Three ordered, number produced at archivist's discretion. Delivery 20 mins max. No production 12.45-2. Last order: M.-Th. 4.30; Fri-4. P/copying restricted, by staff-same day/post. Typing/taping not permitted. Laptops (power supply)/cameras (hand-held) allowed.
Records: for Staffordshire. Diocesan RO for Archdeaconry of Stafford (Lichfield is the main Diocesan RO-see entry). PRs-film/fiche/ originals if not copied. Local authority. Public. Anglican parish. Nonconformist. Family. Estate. Business. Professional. Societies. Personal. Institutions & Organisations. Dartmouth Papers (Govt. & Colonies). Birmingham Rail, Carriage & Wagon Works (Worldwide connections)-19thC.
Research Service: Charge made.
Facilities: Toilet. No public tel/refreshment facilities. Café/pub/shops nearby.
Publications: Free leaflets: *Staffordshire R.O: an introduction. Lichfield R.O: an introduction. Burton-upon-Trent Archives: an introduction. Dwelling in the Past* (House history). Publications List. (A5 SAE). For sale: Summary list of PRs incls. outline maps of ancient Staffordshire parishes, etc. List of registers of Staffordshire Nonconformist Churches. Parish/County maps. Family History packs. Transport-Canal/Railway records. Guides to Maps. Enclosure Acts, Awards & Maps. Tithe Maps & Awards. Estate Maps before 1840. Business Records, etc.
Tourist Office: Tel: 1785 240204 Fax: 01785 240204
Remarks: Bags not allowed-lockers. Donations appreciated. See *Staffordshire family collections, a handlist of family papers in Staffordshire RO.* (1992).

William Salt Library, Eastgate Street, STAFFORD, Staffs ST16 2LZ Tel: 01785 278372 **Fax:** 01785 278384
Opening Hours: T.-Th. 9-1; 2-5; F. 9-1; 2-4.30; 2nd/4th Sat in mth only 9.30-1 Closure: Mon+Public hols.
Parking: None.
Disabled: Limited facilities-contact in advance.
Children: 11 yrs+
Appointments: Prior booking unnecessary. Entry-register+reader's ticket. 15 seats+1film+1 fiche.
Ordering System: No prior ordering. Three ordered & produced. Delivery 5 mins-depending how busy. P/copying restricted, by staff-post/collection. Typing/ taping not permitted. Cameras/laptops (power supply) allowed.
Records: PRs-Ts. Books. Drawings. Pamphlets. Prints. William Salt MSS Collection 9th-20thC's. Copy of 1676 Compton Census. Misc. pedigrees & family notes. Newspapers.

Research Service: None.
Facilities: Toilets. No public tel/refreshment facilities. Café/pub/shops nearby.
Publications: Leaflets on holdings, maps & cards. Details of opening hours etc. (SAE).
Remarks: Donations appreciated.

STAFFORDSHIRE, see Burton on Trent; Lichfield; Stafford; Stoke on Trent; Walsall; Wolverhampton.

Tameside Local Studies Library, Stalybridge Library, Trinity Street, STALYBRIDGE, Cheshire SK15 2BN Tel: 0161 3382708/3383831 or 0161 3037937 **Fax:** 0161 3038289 **E-mail:** tamelocal@chal.pipex .com
Opening Hours: M.-F. 9-7.30; Sat 9-4 Closure: Public hols.
Parking: Public nearby-paying.
Disabled: None-steps. Tel. about possible arrangement.
Children: At staff's discretion.
Appointments: Prior booking for viewers-3 days. Entry-register. 10 seats+2 film+1 fiche-1 reader/printer.
Ordering System: Prior ordering by letter/tel. Catalogue nos sometimes required. Prior ordering for records held elsewhere. Three ordered & produced. Delivery 2-5 mins. Last order: 30 mins. before closure. P/copying restricted, by staff-same day. DIY for some printed material. Typing/taping/laptops (power supply) permitted. Cameras at archivist's discretion.
Records: for Tameside & Authorities which previously made up the Borough-Ashton-under-Lyne/Audenshaw/Denton/Droylsden/ Dukinfield/Hyde/Longdendale/Mossley/ Stalybridge. PRs-film/fiche/Ts-vols. pub. by Lancashire Parish Register Society. Local authority. Nonconformists. Schools. Hospital. Business. Family. Trade Unions. Manchester Regt. collection. Manchester Studies tape collection (oral history). MIs. Directories. Photographs. Printed Index to wills held at Lancashire/Cheshire ROs. M/f-census/census returns street index/ newspapers/Index to some newspapers/ Surname Index (incomplete).
Note: Further Regimental research concerning the Manchester Regiment-**RHQ(I) The King's Regiment**, Ardwick Green, MANCHESTER M12 6HD. More material may be found in the PRO, Kew.
Research Service: Limited specific enquiry-free+charge for p/copies.
Facilities: No toilet/public tel. (some close by). No refreshment facilities. Café/pub/shops nearby.
Publications: Free: Info. leaflets: *Family History at Tameside L.S. Library. Manchester Regt. Archive Collection. House History at Tameside L.S. Library: Getting into Print.* (A4 SAE). For sale: *Guide to Tameside Archive Service* (1994). Local publications for sale in library.
O. R: Tameside District Register Office, Dukinfield Town Hall, King Street, DUKINFIELD, Cheshire SK16 4LA Tel: 0161 3301177/1454
Remarks: Donations appreciated. **Note:** There is a possibility this library may be relocated some time after 1999/2000. Station: Stalybridge (5 mins. walk).

Stockport Archive Service, Central Library, Wellington Road South, STOCKPORT SK1 3RS Tel: 0161 4744530 **Fax:** 0161 4747750 **E-mail:** stockport.cenlibrary@dial.pipex.com
Opening Hours: M.T.Th.F. 10-8; W. 10-5; Sat 9-4 Appt. necessary after 5pm+Sat. Closure: Public hols.
Parking: None.
Disabled: Stairlift.
Appointments: Prior booking for viewers-several days. Entry-register for archives only. 30 seats+2 film+4 fiche-1 reader/printer.
Ordering System: Prior ordering by letter/tel. Catalogue nos sometimes required. Three ordered & produced. Records stored elsewhere need several days prior ordering. Delivery 5-10 mins. P/copying by staff-same day. Typing/taping/cameras at archivist's discretion. Laptops permitted.
Records: for the new Metropolitan Borough-Bredbury & Romiley/Cheadle & Gatley/Hazel Grove & Bramhall/Marple. PRs-film/p/copies/Ts. Local authority. Borough Magistrates Court. Nonconformist-Methodist. Stockport Sunday school. Family. Business incl. Christy Hat manufacturers. Societies.
Research Service: None.
Facilities: Toilet. No public tel/refreshment facilities. Café/pub/shops nearby.
Publications: *Genealogy in Stockport. Guide to archive calendars* 1-14.
Tourist Office: Tel: 0161 4743320/1

Stockton Reference Library, Church Road, STOCKTON ON TEES, Teeside TS18 1TU Tel: 01642 672680 Appt. Local History collection. Maps. Photographs. M/f-census/ newspapers. See leaflet *Sources for Family Historians in Stockton Reference Library.* **Note:** Stockton on Tees is now a Unitary Authority.

Hanley Library, Bethesda Street, Hanley, STOKE ON TRENT, Staffs ST1 3RS Tel: 01782 281242/215108 Appt. Local Studies collection. School board mins & log books. Title deeds for Staffs. Methodist records.

Western Isles Libraries, 2 Keith Street, STORNAWAY, Isle of Lewis PA87 2QG Tel:

01851 703064. Appt. Local History of the Western Isles. School. Minute books of area, parochial boards & parish councils. Housing registers/rent accounts. Newspapers-some on m/f. Photographs.

Western Isles Islands Council, Sandwich Road, STORNAWAY, Isle of Lewis PA87 2SW Tel: 01851 703773 Appt. Town/Western Isles Islands Council. Parochial boards/parish councils of Ross & Cromarty/Invernesshire. Education. Valuation rolls. Housing.

Stourbridge Library, Crown Centre, STOURBRIDGE, W. Midlands DY8 1YE Tel: 01384 394004. Usually open. Local History. Maps. Photographs. M/f-census/newspapers.

STOW ON THE WOLD, see Gloucester.

Stranraer Museum, 55 George Street, STRANRAER, Dumfries & Galloway DG9 7JP Tel: 01776 705088 **Fax:** 01776 704420
Opening Hours: Museum: M.-Sat 10-5 Archives: M.-F. 10-5
Parking: None.
Disabled: Toilets.
Children: At staff's discretion.
Appointments: Archives: Prior booking for seats-2 wks. Entry-register. 2 seats.
Ordering System: Prior ordering by letter/tel. Two ordered & produced. P/copying restricted, by staff-same day. Typing/taping/laptops (power supply) permitted. Cameras not allowed.
Records: Burgh records for Stranraer/ Whithorn/Wigtown/Newton Stewart. Minute books. Accounts. Police. Wigtownshire County Council. Machais & Rhins Council administrative records. Stranraer Court book. Photographs.
Research Service: Under review.
Facilities: Toilet. No public tel/refreshment facilities. Café/pub/shops nearby.
Publications: Various.
Tourist Office: Tel: 01776 702595

STRATFORD, see London Borough of Newham.

Shakespeare Birthplace Trust Record Office, Henley Street, STRATFORD-UPON-AVON, Warwicks CV37 6QW (Postal Address) Access for visitors-Guild Street. **Tel:** 01789 201816/204016 **Fax:** 01789 296083 **E-mail:** records@shakespearetrust.demon.co.uk
Opening Hours: M.-F. 9.30-1; 2-5; Sat 9.30-12.30 Closure: Public hols+preceding Sat.
Parking: None
Disabled: Lift
Children: Accompanied: At archivist's discrection. Unaccompanied: 9yrs+
Appointments: Prior booking unnecessary. Entry-registration card+register. 14 seats+1 film+2 fiche+2 dual.
Ordering System: Prior ordering by letter/tel. Catalogue nos preferred. Number ordered at archivist's discretion, five produced. Delivery 5-15 mins. P/copying restricted, by staff-same day depending on size of order/post/collection. Typing/taping/laptops (power supply) permitted. Cameras allowed+fee charged+ copyright notice to be included in frame.
Records: for Warwickshire & neighbouring parts of Gloucestershire & Worcestershire. Diocesan RO for Stratford-upon-Avon/ Shottery. PRs-film/photocopies/Ts/ originals if not copied. Stratford-upon-Avon Borough-incls vestry/settlement/bastardy/poor law apprenticeships. Borough Police. Nonconformists. Stratford Probate. Manorial. Canals. Railways. Business. Family. Newspapers. Prints. Drawings. Photographs. Trade Directories M/f-census/MIs/Obituaries. Lists & Indexes to collections.
Research Service: None.
Facilities: Toilet/public tel. No refreshment facilities. Café/pub/shops nearby.
Publications: Free leaflets: *The Shakespeare Birthplace Trust RO*+13 other info. leaflets on collection incl. *History of a House. Sources for Genealogists. O/S Maps.* (A5 SAE)
Tourist Office: Tel: 01789 293127 Fax: 01789 295262
Remarks: Bags not allowed-lockers. Donations appreciated. A reference and reading room is available. This office will be on Web site soon.

SUFFOLK, see Bury St. Edmunds; Ipswich; Lowestoft.

Thames Valley Police Museum, Sulhamstead House, SULHAMSTEAD, Berks RG7 4DU Tel: 0118 932 5748 Appt. Donations appreciated. Thames Valley Police-Berks/Bucks/Oxon. Oxford City/ Reading Borough Police archives. Charge made. Curator-Susan Healy.

Sunderland City Library & Arts Centre, Fawcett Street, SUNDERLAND, co. Durham SR1 1RE Tel: 0191 5141235 Usually open. Large Local History collection for Sunderland.

SURREY HISTORY CENTRE, see Woking.

SURREY RO KINGSTON UPON THAMES, see Woking.

SURREY, CROYDON, see London Borough of Croydon.

SURREY, KINGSTON UPON THAMES, see London Borough of Kingston upon Thames.

SURREY, MORDEN, see London Borough of Merton.

SURREY, RICHMOND, see Kew; London Borough of Richmond upon Thames.

SURREY, see Chertsey; Deepcut; Egham; Kew; Kingston upon Thames; Sutton; Woking.

SURREY, SUTTON, see London Borough of.

SURREY, TWICKENHAM, see London Borough of Richmond upon Thames.

SUSSEX, see Brighton; Chichester; Lewes.

Sutton Coldfield Local Studies Dept., Sutton Coldfield Library, 43 Lower Parade, SUTTON COLDFIELD, West Midlands B72 1XX Tel: 0121 3542274 **Fax:** 0121 3544504
Opening Hours: M.W.F. 9-6; T.Th. 9-8; Sat 9-5 Closure: Public hols.
Parking: Public-paying.
Disabled: Lift to 2nd floor-if working.
Children: At staff's discretion.
Appointments: Prior booking unnecessary. 16 seats+3 film+2 fiche.
Ordering System: Prior ordering by letter/tel. Catalogue nos sometimes required. Records stored elsewhere need 2 days prior ordering. Number ordered & produced at librarians's discretion. No production 12-2. Last order: 30 mins before closure. P/copying restricted, by staff-post/collection/DIY. Typing not permitted. Taping/laptops allowed. Cameras under review.
Records: PRs-film/fiche/Ts-Sutton Coldfield parish church/St. Chad's, Tachbrook. P/copies of coroners inquests. Sutton Coldfield rate books. Will Index 1630-1710 (in progress). Directories. Electoral registers. Corn rent schedules. Borough rental books 1742-1890. Periodicals (genealogical & local). Photographs. Genealogical research guides etc. M/f-GRO Indexes 1837-1912 (fee for use)/census for Sutton Coldfield & surrounding area (fee for use of 1891 census)/ newspapers/vestry mins/IGI.
Research Service: None.
Facilities: Toilet/public tel. No refreshment facilities. Café/pub/shops nearby.
Publications: Various info leaflets+*Discover Your Family Tree at Sutton Coldfield Library* (A5 SAE).

SUTTON, SURREY, see London Borough of Sutton

West Glamorgan Archive Service, County Hall, Oystermouth Road, SWANSEA, South Wales SA1 3SN Tel: 01792 636589 **Fax:** 01792 636340
Internet: Welsh Archives Network
Opening Hours: Swansea searchroom: M. 9-5 Need appt. for 5.30-7.30; T.-Th. 9-5 Closure: Fri+Public hols. Neath Library: M.-W.F. 9.30-12.30; 1.30-5.30; Th. 9.30-12.30; 1.30-5 (see Remarks).
Parking: Yes-free.
Disabled: Disabled friendly.
Children: At archivist's discretion.
Appointments: Prior booking for viewers-1 wk. Entry-register. 20 seats+2 film+12 fiche-1 reader/printer.
Ordering System: Prior ordering by letter/ tel. Catalogue nos required. Three ordered & produced. Delivery 5 mins. P/copying restricted, by staff-same day/post. Typing/cameras not permitted. Taping/laptops (power supply) allowed.
Records: for former county of West Glamorgan & City of Swansea. PRs-p/copies/originals if not copied. Local authority. Ecclesiastical parish records. Civil parish/Community Council. Nonconformist. Poor Law/Workhouse. Manorial. Estate & family. Maritime. Business. Societies. Maps & plans. Official records of Swansea City Council & its predecessor authorities 18th-20thC's. Prints. Photographs. Cine films/video tapes/sound archive tapes. Pamphlets.
Research Service: Charge made.
Facilities: Toilets/public tel/restaurant/room for own food/drink vending machine. Café/pub/shops nearby.
Publications: Free leaflets: Info leaflet with maps. Publications list. (SAE). For sale: *Tracing Your Family History*. Annual Reports of the West Glamorgan County Archivist. *Nonconformist Registers of Wales. On the Parish, the Poor Law before 1834 Source Book. Welsh Family History*. Maps. Posters etc.
O.R: Swansea Museum, Victoria Road, Maritime Quarter, SWANSEA, SA1 1SN Tel: 01792 653763 Local History library-Swansea & South Wales area. Photographs; **University of Wales-Swansea**, Singleton Park, SWANSEA, SA2 8PP Tel: 01792 205678 Ext. 4048. Appt. S.Wales Coal Archive. Trade Unions. Family. Estate. Industry. Railway. St. David's Priory parochial registers & records. Swansea & Gower Methodist records (not registers). M/f-census (Swansea & Gower); **South Wales Miners' Library**, Hendrefoelan House, Sketty, SWANSEA, SA2 7NB Tel: 01792 201231 Ext. 2003 Appt.; **West Glamorgan County Library**, West Glamorgan House, 12 Orchard Street, SWANSEA, SA1 5AZ Tel: 01792 642044 Appt. Local History collection. Welsh collection. Index to 19thC Cambrian newspapers.
Tourist Office: Tel. 01792 468321
Remarks: Bags not allowed-lockers. Donations appreciated. **Note:** This archive service now comes under the City & County of Swansea/Neath/Port Talbot County Borough. Neath Library, Victoria Gardens, Neath (see

Opening Hours) now has a Service Point-Tel: 01639 620139. Documents available on Tues/Thurs by prior appointment. **Note:** County Hall has a separate room dedicated to Family History research which contains on M/f-GRO Indexes 1837-1992/Glamorgan census returns 1841-1891/IGI-a small charge is made for use of M/f reader.

National Monuments Record Centre, Kemble Drive, SWINDON, Wilts SN2 2GZ Tel: 01793 414600.
Opening hours: T-F 9:30-5, 3rd Sat in month 10-4 but need to confirm. Closed Mon. Car park nearby. Public archive of the Royal Commission on the Historical Monuments of England. Photographs-buildings. Air photographs-over 3 million. Drawings/plans/reports of buildings. Books. Pamphlets. **Note:** This office is in connection with the London office via 'Monarch'.

SWINDON RAILTRACK, see London Other Repositories-Railtrack.

Wiltshire & Swindon Record Office, Regent Circus, SWINDON, Wilts SN1 1QG Tel: 01793 463240 Opening Hours: M.-Th. 9-8; F. 9-5; Sat 9-4. Appt. M/f-PRs for Borough of Swindon parishes-Bishopstone, Blunsdon St. Andrew, Chiseldon, Eaton Castle, Hannington, Highworth, Inglesham, Liddington, Marston South, Rodbourne Cheney, Stanton Fitzwarren, Stratton St. Margaret, Swindon (Christ Church/St. Barnabas/St. John/St. Mark/St. Paul/St. Saviour), Wanborough, Wroughton/ BTs/electoral registers/census/ newspapers (incl.The Times)/directories. **Note:** Once a month a member of the RO at Trowbridge is available at Swindon to give advice. Swindon Local Studies library holds books & pamplets/Wiltshire Record Society publications/Wiltshire Notes & Queries/ Wiltshire Archaeological & Natural History Magazine from 1854/maps/plans/ illustrations /magazines/pamphlets/ephemera/collection of books on the Great Western Railway-particularly Swindon Railway Works. See also entry for Wiltshire & Swindon RO, Trowbridge.
O. R: District Registrar, Aspen House, Temple Street, SWINDON SN1 1SQ Tel: 01793 522140.

SWINTON, see Irlam.

SYDNEY JAMES LIBRARY, see Liverpool.

TAMESIDE LOCAL STUDIES LIBRARY, see Stalybridge.

Somerset Archive & Record Service, Somerset Record Office, Obridge Road, TAUNTON, Som TA2 7PU Tel: 01823 337600 (appts.)/ 01823 278805 (other enqs.) **Fax:** 01823 325402 **E-mail:** somerset-archives@compuserve.com
Internet: www.somerset.gov.uk
Opening Hours: M. 2-4.50; T.W.Th. 9-4.50; F. 9-4.20; 1st & 3rd Sat in mth 9.15-12.15 Closure: Public hols+2 wks beg last Mon in Jan.
Parking: Limited.
Disabled: W/chair access. Toilet.
Children: 8 yrs+
Appointments: Prior booking for seats/viewers-2 wks. Entry-register+CARN or ID. 20 seats+4 film+18 fiche-2 reader/printers.
Ordering System: Prior ordering by letter/tel. Catalogue nos sometimes required. Prior ordering for Modern District & Council records-3 days. Four ordered, four vols/one bundle produced. Delivery 15 mins. No production 12.45-2. Last order: 4 p.m. P/copying restricted, by staff-same day. DIY-M/f. Typing not permitted. Taping at archivist's discretion. Cameras/laptops (power supply-state when booking) allowed.
Records: for historic county of Somerset. Diocesan RO for Bath & Wells. PRs-fiche/Ts/originals if not copied. BTs-fiche. Local authority. Quarter Sessions. Parish chest. Manorial. Marriage licences. Apprenticeships. Family & estate. Trade-overseas. Dr. Campbell's Index (1million Somerset names from PRs). Subject Indexes-in progress:-1851 census/marriages 1754-1827/marriage licences 1765 on/ Apprenticeships/ Settlements/Bastardy.
Research Service: Charge made.
Facilities: Toilet. No public tel. Room for own food/drink vending machine. Café pub nearby.
Publications: For sale: *Your Somerset Family. Your Somerset House.* Summary List of PRs.
O.R: Somerset Studies Library, Central Library, Paul Street, TAUNTON, Som TA1 3PF Tel: 01823 340300. Usually open. Local history of historic Somerset.
Tourist Office: Tel: 01823 336344 Fax: 01823 340308
Remarks: Bags not allowed-lockers. Donations appreciated.

Tavistock Public Library, Market Road, TAVISTOCK, Devon Opening Hours: M.T.Th.F. 9.30-7; W. 9.30-1; Sat 9.30-4. M/f-area PRs/tithe maps & apportionments/registers of some nonconformist churches in area. **Note:** This is a Devon RO Service point & a member of DRO staff attends once a month in the afternoon. Tel: 01752 385940 for info.

TAYSIDE, see Dundee; Forfar.

TEESIDE ARCHIVES, see Middlesbrough.

TEESIDE, see Middlesbrough; Stockton on Tees.

TELFORD, see Ironbridge.

THAMES VALLEY POLICE MUSEUM, see Sulhamstead.

THANET BRANCH ARCHIVE, see Ramsgate.

TIPPERARY S.R.CO.MUSEUM, see Clonmel.

Tiverton Museum,The Old School, St. Andrew Street, TIVERTON, Devon EX16 6PH Tel: 01884 256295
Opening Hours: Search Room: M. 2-4.30; W. 10.30-4.30 Closure: Wed. before Christmas to 1st Mon in Feb.
Parking: Public nearby-paying.
Disabled: By arrangement-some facilities can be provided on ground level.
Children: Accompanied: 10 yrs+ Unaccompanied: 11 yrs+
Appointments: Prior booking for seats/viewers-1 wk. Entry-register+entrance fee. 5 seats+1 film+4 fiche.
Ordering System: Prior ordering by letter/tel. Number ordered & produced at curator's discretion. Delivery 5 mins. Last order: 4p.m. P/copying restricted, by staff-same day. Typing/cameras not permitted. Taping/laptops (power supply) by prior arrangement.
Records: for mid-Devon-11 mile radius of Tiverton. PRs-film/fiche parishes of the area. John Heathcoat & Co, lace manufacturers of Tiverton 1816-1947-logbooks/pension registers/staff magazines. Ephemera. Books. Documents. Directories. Maps. Family histories & Info files on local families. M/f-census/tithe maps apportionments/nonconformist/ newspapers/IGI.
Research Service: None.
Facilities: Toilet. No public tel/refreshment facilities. Café/pub/shops nearby.
Publications: Free: Info leaflet on material held. Publications list. (SAE).
Tourist Office: Tel: 01884 255827 Fax: 01884 257594
Remarks: Donations appreciated. **Note:** The Museum acts as a Service point with the Devon RO, Exeter. An archivist visits 2nd Mon afternoon of each month Apl-Oct to give advice & bring M/f of material not held at Museum-such items to be ordered by Wed preceding archivist's visit. Station: Tiverton Parkway-5 mls (bus service to Tiverton)/Exeter St. David-15 mls-bus to Taunton/Cullompton for Tiverton.

Tonbridge Central Library, Avebury Ave, TONBRIDGE, Kent TN9 1TG Tel: 01732 352754 Appt. Local History collection. Family records incl. wills. M/f-census for Tonbridge/Malling districts.

Torpoint Archives, Council Offices, Buller Road, TORPOINT, Cornwall PL11 2LD Tel: 01752 812203 Opening Hours: T.& F. Appt. No disabled facilities. Parking. Torpoint town+very limited records for villages of Antony/Wilcove. PRs-Ts. School. Photographic archive-10,000 photographs/slides+other Torpoint records. M/f-census. **Note:** Torpoint Town was est. 1750 to house Royal Dockyard workers & naval personnel. Because of WW2 bombing & 1974 Local Govt. re-organisation many of the town's day to day records were lost, but this is now in process of being rectified. The archivists have a considerable knowledge of family history & events & will search their records for a donation. **Note:** This archive is a registered charity with volunteer workers therefore donations are appreciated. See entries for Cornwall RO, Truro & West Devon RO, Plymouth.

Torquay Central Library, Lymington Road, TORQUAY, Devon TQ1 2DT Tel: 01803 386505 Appt. Torbay District council archives of former authorities of Torbay-Brixham/ Churston Ferrers/Cockington/Paignton/St. Marychurch/Tormonhun. Local History collection. Maps. Newspapers. Some local nonconformist churches. M/f-PRs/census/tithe maps & apportionments. **Note:**This is a Devon RO Service point & DRO staff attend once a month in the afternoon. Tel: 01392 384252 for info. **Note:** Torbay became a Unitary Authority on 1st April 1998 but will have an archive service provided by Devon.

Totnes Museum Trust, 70 Fore Street, TOTNES, Devon TQ9 5RU Tel: 01803 863821 Nonconformists. Documents. Photographs. M/f-PRs/census/tithe maps & apportionments for Totnes area. **Note:** This is a Devon RO Service point & DRO staff attend once a month in the afternoon. Tel: 01392 384255 for info.

TOWER HAMLETS, see London Borough of.

TRAFFORD LOCAL STUDIES CENTRE, see Sale.

Treorchy Library, Local Studies Dept., Station Road, TREORCHY, Rhondda, S. Wales CF42 6NN Tel: 01443 773204 **Fax:** 01443 777047
Opening Hours: M.-Th. 9.30-5.15; F.1-8; Sat 9-12 Closure: Public hols.
Parking: None.
Disabled: Access to library-Reference & Local Studies on ground floor.
Appointments: Prior booking for viewers. 14 seats+2 film+2 fiche-2 reader/printers.
Ordering System: Prior ordering by letter/tel-mostly for census on viewers.

P/copying by staff-same day. Typing/taping not permitted. Laptops/cameras allowed.
Records: for Rhondda Valleys & some areas bordering-whole of Ystradyfodwg/parts of Llanwonno/Llantrisant parishes (Pontypridd Registration District). PRs-film. Local History archives. Welsh Congregational Church. Cemetery 1877 on (Rhondda). Maps. Photographs. M/f-census/newspapers.
Research Service: Limited specific enquiry answered by letter+charge for p/copies.
Facilities: No toilets/public tel/refreshment facilities. Café/pub/shops nearby.
Remarks: Note: Treorchy became a Unitary Authority on 1st April.1996-Rhondda, Cynon Taff county.

Wiltshire County Council Reference & Local Studies Library, Bythesea Road, TROWBRIDGE, Wilts BA14 8BS Tel: 01225 713732. Usually open. Appt. for viewers. Magazines. Illustrations. Collection of structure & local plans. Ephemera. Local History collection. Large photographic collection. M/f-census 1841-1891/1881 Census Index for England & Wales/GRO Indexes 1837-1901/Prerogative Court of Canterbury Wills/Directories-Kelly's 1848-1939/Swindon & N.Wilts 1852-1952/Devizes area 1858-1958/W. Wilts 1908-1953/Surveyor's drawing for first O/S survey of southern England/IGI-U.K. Commonwealth & USA/Wilts newspapers+ 18thC *Bath & Sherborne Mercury* 1737-1867. Church of Jesus Christ of Latter-day-Saints. CD-Rom-Family Search/ Ancestral File/F.H. Catalogue-appt. for 30 min sessions £2.50 per session. The Wiltshire Buildings Record (Tues. only) is at above address. Tel: 01225 713740. **Note:** The Library is situated at County Hall East, opposite County Hall & in the same building as the RO. **O. R: Salisbury Local Studies Library**, Market Place, SALISBURY, Wilts SP1 1BL Tel: 01720 410073; **Salisbury & S. Wilts Museum**, The King's House, 65 The Close, SALISBURY, Wilts SP1 2EN Tel: 01720 332151

Wiltshire & Swindon Record Office, County Hall, Bythesea Road, TROWBRIDGE, Wilts BA14 8JG Tel: 01225 713139 **Fax:** 01225 713715
Opening Hours: M.T.TH.F. 9.15-5; W. 9.15-7.45 Closure: Public hols+last 2 wks in Jan.
Parking: 7 spaces+others in Visitors' car park-County Hall West.
Disabled: Disabled friendly. 2 disabled car spaces.
Children: At archivist's discretion.
Appointments: Prior booking for viewers-few days. Prior booking for some records on Wed eve. Entry-register+CARN. 53 seats+3 film+17 fiche-1 reader/printer.
Ordering System: Prior ordering by letter/tel. Catalogue nos required. Six ordered & produced. No production 12.20-1.30. Last order: M.T.Th.F. 4.30; Wed 7.30. P/copying restricted, by staff-same day/post/collection. Typing/taping/laptops (power supply) permitted. Cameras by prior arrangement.
Records: for historic county of Wiltshire. Diocesan RO for Sarum incls. some parishes of Berkshire/Dorset/one in Devon. Bristol parish records Swindon Archdeaconry. PRs-film/ fiche/p/copies/Ts. BTs-film/some originals. Parish Chest. PLU. Official county records. Quarter/Petty Sessions. Clerk of the Peace. Probate incls. some for Berks & Dorset. Marr. Licence Bonds & Allegations. Coroners. Parish Councils. Urban/Rural District Councils. Borough. Hospitals. Police. Schools. Nonconformist. Charities & societies. Business. Deeds. Family & estate. Solicitors. Maps & plans.
Research Service: Limited specific enquiry (SAE).
Facilities: Unisex/disabled toilet. Public tel. Room for own food/drink vending machines (under review). Restaurant (Byway), County Hall West (12-2)-able-bodied only. Café/pub/shops 15 mins.
Publications: Free: Info. leaflet: *Wiltshire Records: An Introduction to the CRO*-with map. *House History* (SAE). For sale: *Sources for Wiltshire Family History*. List of PRs. Parish map.
O.R: District Register Office, Chestnut House, Bythesea Road, TROWBRIDGE, Wilts
Tourist Office: Tel: 01225 77054
Remarks: Bags not allowed-lockers. Donations appreciated. **Note:** The RO is situated at County Hall East, opposite County Hall. Wiltshire Family History Society, 10 Castle Lane, DEVIZES, Wilts SN10 1HU have transcriptions of many Wiltshire records incl. baptism/burial registers by Wiltshire FHS members for sale (SAE for list).

Cornwall Record Office, County Hall, TRURO, Cornwall TR1 3AY Tel: 01872 323127/273698 **Fax:** 01872 270340
Opening Hours: T.W.Th. 9.30-1; 2-5; F. 9-4.30; Sat 9-12 Closure: Public hols+usually 1st 2 wks in Dec.
Parking: Free-spaces on main County Hall sites.
Disabled: W/chair access. Large print info. leaflets. Disabled parking immediately outside office.
Children: At archivist's discretion, but space limitations may restrict.
Appointments: Prior booking necessary, particularly for map table. Entry-register+ CARN+ID. 12 seats+2 film+14 fiche.
Ordering System: Prior ordering by letter/tel. Catalogue nos required where possible.

Number ordered at archivist's discretion, two items/five wills produced. Delivery 4-6 mins. Last order: 15 mins before closure. P/copying restricted, by staff on 2 levels of service: Express-same day service limited to documents already in use in searchroom. By quantity-post/collection. Typing not permitted. Taping only if note taking physically impossible. Laptops (quiet) permitted. Cameras in accordance with copyright restrictions.
Records: for the County of Cornwall. Diocesan RO for Truro. PRs-fiche/Ts/originals if not copied. BTs-shared with Exeter (Cornwall's mother diocese until 1877). Parish Chest. Poor Law. Nonconformists. Quarter Sessions. Plans. County Council Mins. Borough/district/parish council mins/accounts/ratebooks. Schools. Hospitals. Turnpikes. Tithe. Estate deeds/leases/rentals/plans. Mine settlements & cost books. Engineering. Shops. Solicitors. Societies & clubs. Families. Abandonment plans of mines. Arundell archive-national & local significance especially for medieval period. Maritime records-crew lists/log books from 1860-1913. Ports & fisheries. Probate records 1600-1858. **Note:** Wills & other probate records of the Archdeaconry of Cornwall 1600-1857 available at this office but probate records for the 28 parishes which were peculiars of the Bishop/Dean & Chapter of Exeter were destroyed in Exeter during the bombing of WW2. M/f-census
Research Service: Charge made (see Info. Leaflet No. 2)
Facilities: Toilets. No public tel/refreshment facilities. Café-supermarket next door. Pub/shops 10 mins.
Publications: Free: Info leaflet with map. Other leaflets: 1) *An Introduction to Cornwall RO.* 3). List of Publications. 4). *Cornish Probate Records.* 5). *Cornish Family History.* 6). *Sources for the History of a House.* 7). *Maritime History.* (A5 SAE). For sale: Booklets & Handlists-*Sources for Cornish Family History. Guide to Sources at the Cornwall RO: Guide to Cornish Probate Records. Index to Cornish Estate Duty & Deanery of St. Buryan Wills. Pedigrees & Heraldic Documents. Parish Poor Law Papers. A List of Cornish Manors. Introduction to the Arundell Archives: Index to Accessions 1979-1993.* Review & Accession List pub. each June 1994-95: 1995-1996. *Records of School* (reprint pending).
O.R: Cornwall Family History Society, 5 Victoria Square, TRURO, Cornwall TR1 2RS. Open part time only (no phone). Research aids. GRO Indexes. Census returns. IGI etc; **The West County Studies Library**, Castle Lane, EXETER, holds the collection of PRs & Nonconformist transcriptions of the Devon & Cornwall Record Society (fee payable for research). (see entry).
Remarks: Bags not allowed-lockers. Donations appreciated. **Note:** Other Maritime records for Cornwall, i.e. crew lists/agreements/logbooks of voyages may be found at the National Maritime Museum (see entry); the Maritime History Group, Memorial University of Newfoundland, St. John's, NEWFOUNDLAND, Canada; the PRO, Kew (see entry). Also see entries for the Courtney Library, Royal Institution of Cornwall, Truro, & the Cornish Studies Library, Redruth.

The Courtney Library, The Royal Institution of Cornwall, River Street, TRURO, Cornwall TR1 2SJ Tel: 01872 272205 **Fax:** 01872 240514 E-mail connection imminent
Internet:http://www.cornwall-on-line.co.uk/ric 'home page'.
Opening Hours: M.-Sat 10-1; 2-5 Closure: Public hols.
Parking: Public nearby.
Disabled: Disabled friendly.
Children: Accompanied: At librarian's discretion. Unaccompanied: 12 yrs+
Appointments: Prior booking for viewers. Entry-register. 14 seats+2 film+3 fiche-2 reader/printers.
Ordering System: Prior ordering by letter/tel. Catalogue nos sometimes required. Ten ordered & produced depending on items. Delivery 5 mins. P/copying restricted, by staff-same day/post/collection. Typing/taping permitted. Cameras (sign copyright form)/laptops (power supply) by prior arrangement.
Records: for geographical county of Cornwall. PRs-film/Ts-incls. Phillimore Marrs. for Cornwall with card index to surnames. Methodist Church History collection. Cornish Estates. Photographs. Henderson MSS collection-archives of Cornish families 12th-19thC's. Printed books-Rex Hall collection of 300 maritime vols. incl. histories of mercantile shipping companies/foreign vessels/war losses/periodicals. Lloyd's Registers. Newspapers. Indexes in progress-emigration from newspapers. Extensive collection on Cornish shipwrecks. Post Office Packet Service. M/f-Ross Index of Cornish marr/IGI.
Research Service: Charge made.
Facilities: Toilets/restaurant. Café/pubs/ shops nearby.
Publications: For sale: Info leaflets. Access & Scale of Charges. *Copyright & Copying from Books & MSS in the Courtney Library. PRs on Microfilm. PR Transcripts. Sources for Maritime Research.*
Remarks: Bags not allowed-left with librarian. Donations appreciated towards the library's Book Fund. This is the oldest established Cornish History research centre in the county

(Journal pub. since 1864). Annual Membership available.

TULLIE HOUSE MUSEUM & ART GALLERY, see Carlisle.

TWICKENHAM, SURREY, see London Borough of Richmond upon Thames.

TYNE & WEAR, see Gateshead; Newcastle upon Tyne; South Shields.

TYRONE, COUNTY, see Monaghan; Omagh.

ULSTER FOLK & TRANSPORT MUSEUM, see Holywood.

ULSTER-AMERICAN FOLK PARK, see Omagh.

ULVERSTON, see Barrow-in-Furness.

UXBRIDGE, MIDDX, see London Borough of Hillingdon.

W. MIDLANDS, see Stourbridge.

W. YORKSHIRE, see Barnsley; Bradford; Calderdale; Halifax; Huddersfield; Keighley; Kirklees; Leeds; Sheepscar; Wakefield.

Wakefield Libraries & Information Services, Local Studies Dept., Library Headquarters, Balne Lane, WAKEFIELD, W. Yorks WF2 ODQ Tel: 01924 302224 **Fax:** 01924 302245
Opening Hours: M. 9.30-7; T.W.Th.F. 9.30-5; 2nd Sat of each mth 9.30-1 Closure: Public hols.
Parking: Yes-collect permit on arrival.
Disabled: Disabled friendly.
Children: At staff's discretion.
Appointments: Prior booking for viewers-3 days. 8 seats+5 film+1 fiche-reader/printer.
Ordering System: Prior ordering by letter/tel. Number ordered & produced at librarian's discretion. P/copying restricted, DIY. Typing not permitted. Taping/laptops (power supply possible) allowed. Cameras by prior arrangement.
Records: for West Riding-Wakefield Metropolitan District in particular. The collection covers all aspects of life in Wakefield Metropolitan District past & present in all formats. PRs-film/Ts. Family papers. Wakefield Street Commissioners. Wakefield Corporation mins. Maps. Illustrations.
Research Service: None.
Facilities: Toilets/public tel. No refreshment facilities. Café/pub nearby.
Publications: Free & for sale depending on availability. Guides to Collections/leaflets presently under revision.

O.R: John Goodchild Collection, Local Studies Centre, The Basement, Drury Lane, WAKEFIELD, W. Yorks WF1 2TE Tel: 01924 891871 Appt. Industry/transport/government/ social/political/religious life in central W. Riding from 12thC on. MSS. Books. Pamplets. Maps & illustrations.
Tourist Office: Tel: 01924 305000/1 Fax: 01924 305293
Remarks: Station: Wakefield Westgate.

West Yorkshire Archive Service-Wakefield Headquarters, Registry of Deeds, Newstead Road, WAKEFIELD, West Yorks WF1 2DE Tel: 01924 305980 **Fax:** 01924 305993 **E-mail:** hq@wyashq.co.uk all enquiries must be sent by post not E-mail.
Internet: www.http=//www.wyashq.demon.co .uk
Opening Hours: M. 9.30-1; 2-8; T.W. 9.30-11; 2-5 Closure: Thurs/Fri+Public/Council hols+ stocktaking wks.
Parking: 10 spaces.
Disabled: No facilities.
Children: At archivist's discretion.
Appointments: Prior booking for seats-1 wk at least. Entry-register. 5-6 seats for original docs/6 for Registry of Deeds+2 film+9 fiche.
Ordering System: Prior ordering by letter/tel. Catalogue nos required. Four ordered, one produced. Delivery 5-10 mins. Last order: 15 mins before closure. P/copying restricted, by staff-same day/post/collection. Typing/ taping /cameras +fee/laptops (power supply) permitted.
Records: for West Riding. West Riding official records. W. Yorkshire official & public records. Wakefield Metropolitan District Council-official & District based private deposits. Diocesan RO for Wakefield. PRs-fiche/p/copies/Ts/originals if not copied. West Riding Registry of Deeds 1704-1970. British Waterways Board (Northern Region). West Riding Quarter Sessions/Magistrates. Coroners. West Riding House of Correction (later Wakefield Prison). W. Yorks Metropolitan Police & predecessors. Vehicle Registration authority. Industries. Hospitals. Schools. Copy wills of Wakefield Probate Registry 1858-1941+printed calendars of Somerset House wills. Maps. Nonconformist-Methodist/Baptist/URC. Business. Charities. Trade Unions. Families. Solicitors.
Research Service: Charge made-limited to 30 mins.
Facilities: Toilets. No public tel. Area for own food. Café/pub/shops nearby.
Publications: Free: Info leaflets on individual offices. Visitors' Procedures leaflet. (SAE) For sale: various publications.
Remarks: Bags not allowed-lockers. Donations appreciated. See entries for West Yorkshire Archive Services at Bradford/

Calderdale/Kirklees/Leeds. See *Basic facts...about Family History Research in Yorkshire* by Pauline Litton (FFHS).

Walsall Local History Centre, Essex Street, WALSALL, Staffs WS2 7AS Tel: 01922 721305 **Fax:** 01922 634954
Internet: http://www.earl.org.uk/earl/members/walsall/
Opening Hours: T.Th. 9.30-5.30; W. 9.30-7; F. 9.30-5; Sat 9.30-1 Closure: Mon+Public hols.
Parking: Limited.
Disabled: Ramp. Toilet.
Children: At staff's discretion.
Appointments: Prior booking for viewers-2 days. Entry-register. 12 seats+3 film+8 fiche-2 reader/printers.
Ordering System: No prior ordering. Four ordered & produced. P/copying by staff. Typing/taping/laptops/cameras permitted.
Records: for Walsall Metropolitan Borough. PRs-film/fiche/Ts. Nonconformist registers+ film of local pre-1837 ones at PRO. Quarter Sessions/Magistrates. Coroners. Local Government of Walsall Metropolitan incls. Urban Districts of Aldridge/Brownhills/Darlaston/Willenhall/Walsall Corporation. Business. Organisations. Societies. Hospital. Electoral registers. Posters. Pamphlets. Trade & sale catalogues. Directories. Photographs. Tape records (oral histories). M/f-census/newspapers/cemetery records.
Research Service: None.
Facilities: Toilets. No public tel. Room for own food. Café/pub/shops nearby.
Publications: Free: List of publications (SAE). For sale: *Something Very Special: A History of the Reedswood Open Air School. Fairs & Circuses in the Black Country. Black Country Graveyards, Cemeteries, Epitaphs. Trace Your Family Tree in Walsall Metropolitan Borough.* Maps. *Popular Education in Walsall*+many others on local & social history, incl. the magazine of the Black Country Society-*The Black Countryman.*
Remarks: Donations appreciated.

WALTHAM FOREST, see London Borough of.

WALTHAMSTOW, see London Borough of Waltham Forest.

WANDSWORTH, see London Borough of

WARLEY, see Smethwick.

Warrington Library, Museum Street, WARRINGTON WA1 1JB Tel: 01925 571232 Appt. Town council mins & rate books. Early poor law rate/account books. Manorial. Newspapers. Nonconformists. Police. Photographs. M/f-PRs/census/sources held at Chester archives.

Warwickshire County Record Office, Priory Park, Cape Road, WARWICK, Warks CV34 4JS Tel: 01926 412735 **Fax:** 01926 412509
Opening Hours: T.W.Th. 9-1; 2-5.30; Sat 9-12.30 Closure: Mon+Public hols.
Parking: Yes.
Disabled: Ramp (intercom from driveway to Reception).
Children: At staff's discretion.
Appointments: Prior booking unnecessary. Entry-register+Warwick RO reader's ticket+ID. 18 seats+13 film+6 fiche-1 reader/printer.
Ordering System: Prior ordering only for Sat-by letter/tel. Catalogue refs. required. Three ordered & produced. Delivery 10 mins. P/copying by staff-same day. Typing/taping not permitted. Cameras (without flash)/laptops (power supply) allowed.
Records: for Warwickshire. Diocesan RO for Coventry & part of Birmingham. PRs-film/Ts/originals if not copied. BTs-some Ts (originals/marriage bonds & allegations held at Worcester RO & Lichfield Joint RO-see entries). Nonconformist/Roman Catholic registers. Some wills-most copies & original wills (indexed) for five small parishes around Temple Balsall. Hearth tax. Electoral registers. Rate books. Index of parish poor law docs 1660-1835 with over 80,000 names, administered by the Birmingham & Midland Society for Genealogy & Heraldry. County/district/parish councils. Quarter/Petty Sessions. PLU. MIs. Hospitals. Charities. Schools. Urban/Rural District councils. Canals. Railways. Turnpike. Industries. Business. Deeds. Maps. Family & estate. Solicitors. Lists & Indexes available in RO. Photographs & prints. M/f-census/IGI. **Note:** An index to Warwickshire burials 1813-1837 is complete/one up to 1813 is in progress-administered by the Birmingham & Midland Society for Genealogy & Heraldry (details from RO).
Research Service: Charge made.
Facilities: Toilets/public tel. No refreshment facilities. Café/pub/shops nearby.
Publications: Free: Leaflets-*Tracing Warwickshire Ancestors*-with map. General Information. (SAE). For sale: *PRs, Nonconformist registers & Census returns in the Warwickshire CRO. Family History & Local Studies Sources in the County Library.* Map. *Tracing Your Ancestors in Warwickshire (excluding Birmingham)* by June Watkins & Pauline Saul (Birmingham & Midland Society for Genealogy & Heraldry. 4th ed 1997)-essential reading.
Tourist Office: Tel: 01926 492212 Fax: 01926 494837
Remarks: Bags not allowed-limited space available-locked cupboard for valuables. Donations appreciated. For information re. Roman Catholic registers & whereabouts see

WARWICKSHIRE

Catholic Missions & registers 1700-1880 Vol 2. The Midlands & East Anglia by Michael Gandy available from *Family Tree Magazine.* **Note:** Other Warwickshire records are held at Stratford-upon-Avon/Coventry/Birmingham City/Worcester/Lichfield (see entries). Local history material is held in Warwickshire libraries.

WARWICKSHIRE, see Coventry; Stratford-upon-Avon; Warwick.

Sefton Metropolitan Borough Council Libraries, Crosby Library, Local History Unit, Crosby Road North, WATERLOO, Merseyside L22 OLQ Tel: 0151 928 6487 Appt. Disabled: Ramps+automatic doors. Research charges. Local History collection.

British Waterways, Willow Grange, Church Road, WATFORD, Herts WD1 3QA Tel: 01923 226422 Waterways archive.

Watford Museum, 194 High Street, WATFORD, Herts WD1 2HG Tel: 01923 232297. Local History collection. Printing. Brewing. Maps. Photographs.

WATT LIBRARY, see Greenock.

WELCH REGIMENT MUSEUM, see Cardiff.

Wells City Record Office, Town Hall, WELLS, Som BA5 2RB Tel: 01749 673091 Appt.-1 wk. Opening Hours: Th.F. 10-4. City council records incl. title deeds & plans. Rate books. Surveys. Tithe. Petty Sessions. Electoral registers/burgess rolls. Building records. Railway papers incl. subscription lists. Public Health. Education. Business. Societies. Photographs.

WESLEY JOHN, CHAPEL, see Bristol.

WEST COUNTRY STUDIES LIBRARY, see Exeter.

WEST DEVON RO, see Plymouth.

WEST LOTHIAN, see Bathgate; Blackburn.

WEST MIDLANDS, see Coseley; Coventry; Smethwick; Solihull; Sutton Coldfield.

WEST YORKSHIRE, see Barnsley; Bradford; Calderdale; Halifax; Huddersfield; Keighley; Kirklees; Leeds; Sheepscar; Wakefield.

WESTERN ISLES LIBRARIES: WESTERN ISLANDS COUNCIL, see Stornaway.

WESTERN EDUCATION & LIBRARY BOARD, see Omagh

North Somerset Local Studies Library, Central Library, The Boulevard, WESTON-SUPER-MARE, Som BS23 1PL Tel: 01934 636638 Usually open. Local History collection.

Cumbria Record Office & Local Studies Library, Scotch Street, WHITEHAVEN, Cumbria CA28 7BJ Tel: 01946 852920 **Fax:** 01946 852919
Opening Hours: M.T.Th.F. 9.30-5; W. 9.30-7; Sat 9.30-1 Closure: Public hols+Tues following Easter & Spring.
Parking: Limited.
Disabled: Disabled friendly.
Children: At archivist's discretion.
Appointments: Prior booking unnecessary. Entry-register+CARN. 28 seats+6 film+4 fiche-2 reader/printers.
Ordering System: Prior ordering only for Wed eve/Sat. Two ordered & produced. Delivery 15 mins max. P/copying restricted, by staff-same day/post/collection. Typing/taping/cameras/ laptops (power supply) by prior arrangement.
Records: for West Cumbria-south of R. Derwent to Millom. Diocese RO for Carlisle. PRs-film/Ts/originals if not copied. BTs-held at CRO Carlisle. Ecclesiastical. Probate. Electoral registers. Poor Law. Maps & plans. Deeds. Family-Curwen of Workington/Pennington of Muncaster. Business. Local authority. Schools. Coal mining. British Steel. Directories. Photographs. M/f-census.
Research Service: Charge made.
Facilities: Toilets. No public tel. Room for own food. Café/pub/shops nearby.
Publications: Free: Info. leaflets-Archives. Rules. Reader's Ticket System. Exhibition of Archives (Archives in the Community). Services to Secondary Schools-Teachers' Leaflet. Publications List. (A5 SAE). For sale: *Cumbrian Ancestors. Notes for Genealogical Searchers* (2nd ed 1993). *Vital Statistics-The Westmorland Census of 1787* (1992). Information Packs. Maps. Posters etc.
O.R: Beacon Centre, West Strand, WHITEHAVEN, Cumbria CA28 7LY
Tourist Office: Tel: 01946 695678
Remarks: Bags not allowed-lockers. Donations appreciated. See entries for other Cumbrian ROs-Barrow in Furness/Carlisle/Kendal. See *Cumbrian Ancestors* (Cumbria Archive Service).

East Kent Archives Centre, Enterprise Business Park, Honeywood Road, WHITFIELD, Dover CT16 3EH The Centre will open in Summer 1998 & records will be transferred from Folkestone & Ramsgate Libraries (see entries).

North Highland Archive, Wick Library, Sinclair Terrace, WICK, Caithness KW1 5AB Tel: 01955 606432 **Fax:** 01955 603000
Opening Hours: M.T.Th.F. 10-1; 2-5.30; W. 10-1 Closure: Sat+Public hols.
Parking: Limited-on street.
Disabled: None-1st floor location.
Children: 12 yrs+
Appointments: Prior booking for viewers-3 days. Entry-register. 8 seats+3 film+3 fiche-reader/printer.
Ordering System: No prior ordering. Two/three ordered & produced. Delivery 2 mins. P/copying restricted, by staff-same day. Typing/taping not allowed. Laptops (power supply) permitted. Cameras by prior arrangement.
Records: for Caithness county. OPRs-film/originals. Wick & Thurso Burgh. Thurso Police Commissioners. Thurso River Harbour Trust. Wick Harbour Trust. Caithness County Council. Schools. Parochial Board. Hospital. Private. Solicitors. Architectural collection. Maps & plans. Printed resources-Abridgements of Sasine, Caithness 17-20thC's. Calendars of Confirmations 19/20thC's. Minute Books of Inhibitions & Adjudications 19/20thC's. Index to the Services of Heirs in Scotland 19/20thC's. M/f-census/Ordnance Survey Original Object Name Book 1871-1873/IGI.
Research Service: Charge made.
Facilities: Toilets. No public tel/refreshment facilities. Café/pub/shops nearby.
Publications: Free: Info. leaflet with area map. (SAE).
O.R: Wick Heritage Centre, WICK, Caithness.
Tourist Office: Tel: 01955 602596

Wigan History Shop, Rodney Street, WIGAN, Lancs. WN1 1DG Tel: 01942 828128 Opening Hours: M. 10-7; T.-F. 10-5; Sat 10-1. By appt. for the Research Centre. Maps. Photographs. Incorporates the Wigan Local History Collection & a genealogical centre. M/f-PRs/census for Metropolitan Wigan area 1841-1891. Original archives are at Wigan RO, Leigh (see entry). **O. R: Leigh Local History Services**, Turnpike Centre, Leigh Library, LEIGH. See Info. leaflet with map (SAE).

WIGAN, see also Leigh.

WIGHT, ISLE OF, see Cowes, Newport.

Leicestershire Record Office, Long Street, WIGSTON MAGNA, Leicester, Leics LE18 2AH Tel: 0116 2571080 **Fax:** 0116 2571120
Opening Hours: M.T.Th. 9.15-5; W. 9.15-7.30; F. 9.15-4.45; Sat 9.15-12.15 Closure: Public hols+preceding Sat+following Tues+1st wk in Oct.
Parking: 10 spaces. Public nearby-free.
Disabled: Disabled friendly. Induction loops.
Children: At archivist's discretion.
Appointments: Prior booking for viewers-1 wk. Entry-register+CARN+ID. 44 seats+8 film+18 fiche-1 film+1 fiche reader/printer.
Ordering System: Prior ordering by letter/tel. Catalogue nos required. Three ordered & produced. Delivery 15 mins. Production may be suspended due to heavy demand. Last order: 30 mins before closure. P/copying restricted, by staff-same day/post/collection. Typing/taping/ cameras at archivist's discretion. Laptops (power supply) permitted.
Records: for Leicestershire, Rutland & City of Leicester. Diocesan RO for Leicester, Peterborough (Archdeaconry of Rutland). PRs-fiche/Ts/originals if not copied. BTs-film. Leicestershire/Rutland County Councils. Borough of Leicester from 1103. Quarter/Petty Sessions. PLU. Probate Registry wills from 1858. Nonconformist. Archdeaconry of Leicester-incls. wills & inventories from 1496. Landed estates & families. Solicitors. Commercial firms & manufacturers. Clubs/Societies/other organisations. Electoral registers. Files of local newspapers. Illustrations of people & places. Books/ magazines/ pamphlets. Directories. Maps. Photographic collections. Archive films. Oral history & sound recordings. M/f-census (Leicestershire & Rutland).
Research Service: Charge made (see Leaflet Leicestershire Genealogical Service)
Facilities: Toilet/public tel/room for own food/drink vending machine. Café/pub/shops nearby.
Publications: Free: Info leaflet with map (SAE). For sale: Books of local interest. Maps. Posters. Postcards. Handlists of records.
O.R: Leicestershire & Rutland FHS Research Centre & Library, Free School Lane, LEICESTER, Leics. Access through an entrance door inside gateway to right of the Library windows. Their Bookshop is situated 'in-store' at Typewriter Centres, 87 High Street, LEICESTER LE1 4JB Open: M.-Sat 9-5.
Tourist Office: Leicester Tel: 0116 2650555 Fax: 0116 2555726
Remarks: Bags not allowed-lockers. Donations appreciated. **Note:** The City of Leicester & Rutland are now Unitary Authorities. No relocation of Leicester RO but agreement on continuation of the present joint service for Leicestershire, Leicester & Rutland is not yet achieved. Rutland has agreed but no discussion with Leicester yet. Present service continuing pro tem. See *Tracing Your Ancestors in Rutland* by C.R. Chapman (1997). *Family forebears: a guide to tracing your family tree in the Leicestershire RO* by J. Farrell. (1987). Station: Leicester (No. 48. bus from outside station to Wigston Magna). South Wigson Station (bus available).

WILLIAM SALT LIBRARY, see Stafford.

WILTSHIRE & SWINDON RO, see Swindon, Trowbridge.

WILTSHIRE ARCHAEOLOGICAL & NATURAL HISTORY SOCIETY, see Devizes.

WILTSHIRE COUNTY COUNCIL REFERENCE & LOCAL STUDIES LIBRARY, see Trowbridge.

WILTSHIRE, see Cricklade; Devizes; Netheravon; Salisbury; Swindon; Trowbridge.

WIMBLEDON, see London Borough of Merton

Hampshire Record Office, Sussex Street, WINCHESTER, Hants SO23 8TH Tel: 01962 846154 **Fax:** 01962 878681 **E-mail:** sadeax@hants.gov.uk
Internet: http://www.hants.gov.uk:80/record-office/index.html
Opening Hours: M.-F. 9-7; Sat 9-4 Closure: Public hols.
Parking: 11 spaces. Parking is often easier after 5 p.m. Public nearby-paying.
Disabled: Disabled friendly.
Children: At archivist's discretion.
Appointments: Prior booking for viewers. Entry-register+CARN+ID. 30 seats+12 film+28 fiche-2 reader/printers.
Ordering System: Prior ordering by letter/tel. Catalogue nos preferred. Six ordered & three vols/ten numbered pieces produced (all docs counted in & out). Delivery 20 mins max. Last order: 30 mins before closure. No production 12.45-1.30 on Sat. P/copying by staff-same day. Typing/taping/laptops (power supply) permitted. Cameras not allowed.
Records: for Hampshire except where records relate primarily to Southampton or Portsmouth. Diocesan RO for Winchester-also original parish records from Bishops Waltham+Petersfield deaneries in Portsmouth diocese. PRs-film/fiche/p/copies/Ts/originals if not copied. Fiche copies of all Hampshire PRs incl. those in Portsmouth/Southampton/Guildford ROs. BTs-film/Ts. Winchester City archives. Local authority. Quarter Sessions. PLU. Winchester Bishopric Estate. Parish chest. Nonconformists. Probate. Education. Militia. Political papers. Families. Business. Societies. Diaries. Deeds. Maps/prints/photographs. Trade Directories. M/f-census. **Note:** Wessex Film & Sound Archive is on the 2nd Floor-see Info leaflet.
Research Service: Charge made.
Facilities: Toilets/public tel/room for own food/drink vending machine/chilled water dispenser-2nd Floor. Café/pub/shops nearby.
Publications: Free leaflets: *Find Your Way Around Hampshire R.O: Hampshire R.O:* Hampshire RO Education Service. History Curriculum Resource Packs & Videos. (A5 SAE). For sale: Hampshire Record Series Publications-List of Guides to Sources-e.g. *Maps & Plans. Tracing the History of your Hampshire House. History of Winchester Buildings. Quarter Sessions Records. Records of the Diocese of Winchester. Sources for Family History. PRs of Hampshire & Isle of Wight. A Guide to Winchester City Archives. Hampshire Papers*. Portsmouth Record Series.
O.R: Winchester Library, Local Studies Library, Jewry Street, WINCHESTER, Hampshire SO23 8RX Tel: 01962 862748; **Reference Library**, North Walls, WINCHESTER. **District Probate Registry**, Cromwell House, 15-23 Andover Road, WINCHESTER. SO23 7EW Indexes.
Tourist Office: Tel: 01962 840500 Fax: 01962 841365
Remarks: Bags not allowed-lockers/coat hangers. Donations appreciated. Station: Winchester-2 mins.

WIRRAL ARCHIVES SERVICE, see Birkenhead.

Wisbech & Fenland Museum, Museum Square, WISBECH, Cambs PE13 1ES Tel: 01945 583817
Opening Hours: T.-Sat 10-5 (Apl-Oct); 10-4 (Oct-Apl) Closure: 25/26 Dec+1 Jan.
Parking: Nearby-free.
Disabled: No facilities.
Children: Accompanied: 10 yrs+ Unaccompanied: Not allowed.
Appointments: Prior booking for viewers-1 wk. Entry-register+CARN. 2 seats+2 film+1 fiche.
Ordering System: Prior ordering by letter/tel. Catalogue nos sometimes required. Five ordered, one produced. Delivery 10 mins. P/copying by staff-same day/post/collection. Typing/taping/laptops/cameras permitted.
Records: within 5 mile radius of Wisbech (Norfolk & Cambridgeshire). PRs-fiche/film/p/copies/Ts/originals in exceptional circumstances. Terriers. Churchwardens Accounts. Overseers accounts. Cemetery. MIs. Some wills. Diaries. Wisbech Town Council & predecessors. Manorial. Family. Maps. Newspapers. Playbills & posters. Photographs. Ephemera. Library.
Research Service: Limited specific enquiry-only when staff available.
Facilities: No toilets/public tel/refreshment facilities. Café/pub/shops nearby.
Publications: Free: leaflet on List of holdings (SAE). For sale: A5 booklets on local history & local personages.
O.R: Wisbech Library, Ely Place, WISBECH, Cambs.

Tourist Office: Tel: 10945 583263 Fax: 01945 582784
Remarks: Donations appreciated. Station: nearest-Peterborough/March (limited service).

Surrey History Centre, 130 Goldsworth Road, WOKING, Surrey GU21 1ND (see Remarks) **Tel:**: 01483 594594 **Fax:** 01483 594595 in operation from Oct 1998. **E-mail:** shs@dial.pipex.com
Internet:
www.surreycc.gov.uk/librariesleisure/shs/shs index.html
Opening Hours: to be announced.
Parking: Limited.
Disabled: Entrance ramps. Toilet.
Children: At archivist's discretion.
Appointments: Prior booking unnecessary. Entry-register+CARN+ID. 30 seats+ 30 M/f viewers-2 reader/printers.
Ordering System: Prior ordering by letter/tel. Catalogue nos required. Ten ordered, one produced. Delivery 15 mins. P/copying restricted, by staff-same day/post/collection. Typing not permitted. Cameras/laptops (power supply) allowed.
Records: PRs-fiche/Ts/originals if not copied. Usual CRO archives+Broadwood (piano manufacturers). Dennis Vehicles (Guildford). It will be necessary to make enquiries about collections after this office has opened.
Research Service: Charge made.
Facilities: Toilet/public tel/room for own food/drink vending machine. Café/pub/shops nearby.
Publications: List will be available later.
Remarks: Bags not allowed-lockers. Donations appreciated. **Note:** This new Surrey History Centre includes the former Surrey RO at Kingston upon Thames & the Guildford RO. The move from these offices will take place mid 1998. Until this time, phone 0181 5419065 (Kingston upon Thames) for info. Only minumum info is able to be supplied in this guide. Various guides to Surrey research as follows: *Guide to parish registers.* Surrey Record Office guide No 2 (1993). *A guide to Surrey genealogy & records.* (1991). *A guide to Surrey manorial records.* (1993). *London, Middlesex & Surrey workhouse Records: a guide to their nature & location.* (1992). The Surrey Local Studies Library situated at Guildford will also be moving to Woking in 1998 (M/f-PRs/census/newspapers. Maps. Photographs.)

Wolverhampton Archives & Local Studies, 42-50 Snow Hill, WOLVERHAMPTON, Staffs WV2 4AG (1st Floor above 'Netto') **Tel:** 01902 717703 **Fax:** 01902 311073
Opening Hours: M.T.F.Sat 10-5; W. 10-7 Closure: Thurs+Public hols+one wk in Nov.
Parking: Public nearby.
Disabled: Disabled friendly.
Children: At staff's discretion.
Appointments: Prior booking for viewers-3 days. Entry-register+CARN+ID-day ticket available. 22 seats+3 film-1 reader/printer+11 fiche-2 reader/printers. Reader/printers bookable.
Ordering System: Prior ordering by letter/tel-essential for Sat. Catalogue nos preferred. Number ordered at archivist's discretion, four produced. Delivery 5 mins. Some restrictions 12-2. P/copying restricted-DIY. Typing/taping/laptops permitted. Cameras allowed+fee.
Records: for Wolverhampton Metropolitan Borough including former Urban District Councils of Bilston/Heath Town/Tettenhall/ Wednesfield/Penn/some items for South Staffs-census. PRs-film/fiche/Ts. Nonconformist. Education incl. The Chantry (Bluecoat School)/The Royal Wolverhampton School. Quarter/Petty Sessions. Magistrates. Coroners. Local organisations. Business. Private individuals papers. Electoral Registers. Maps. Photographs. Library of books about Wolverhampton. M/f-census/newspapers. Indexes to Archives & Local Studies collections.
Research Service: Charge made-max 1 hr. List of researchers available.
Facilities: Toilets/public tel nearby. No refreshment facilities. Café/pub/shops nearby.
Publications: Leaflets: *Wolverhampton Archives & Studies*-with map. 1). *Education.* 12). *Wolverhampton at War 1939-1945*+others (SAE for listing). For sale: *Tracing Your Family Tree: a brief guide for beginners. Using Wolverhampton Archives & Local Studies: a Guide for Students.*
O. R: Wolverhampton Register Office, Civic Centre, St. Peter's Square, WOLVERHAMPTON WV1 1RU Tel: 01902 314989
Remarks: Bags not allowed-lockers. Donations appreciated.

WOOL, DORSET, see Bovington Camp.

(Hereford &) Worcester Record Office, County Hall, Spetchley Road, WORCESTER, Worcs WR5 2NP Tel: 01905 766351 **Fax:** 01905 766363
Opening Hours: M. 10-4.45; T.W.Th. 9.15-4.45; F. 9.15-4 Closure: Public hols+2 wks mid Nov.
Parking: Yes.
Disabled: Parking.
Children: At staff's discretion.
Appointments: Prior booking for viewers-2 wks. Entry-register+CARN+ID. 10 seats+ 20 film+10 fiche-1 reader/printer.
Ordering System: Prior ordering by letter/tel. Catalogue nos essential. Three ordered, one produced. Delivery 10-15 mins. No production 12-30-1.30. Last order: M.-Th. 4.15; F. 3.30.

P/copying restricted-DIY. Typing not permitted. Taping/laptops allowed. Cameras+fee permitted.
Records: for historic administrative area of Worcester county. Diocesan RO for Worcester. PRs-film/photocopies/Ts/originals if not copied. BTs-film. Nonconformists. Quarter/Petty Sessions. Coroners. Hospitals. PLU. Probate. Marriage bonds & allegations incl. William Shakespeare's marriage bond. Schools. Land tax. Directories. Central Govt.-vehicle licensing records. Church Commissioners-mainly deeds/valuations/manorial/property. West Mercia Police. Worcester/Evesham/ Droitwich Boroughs. District/Parish councils. Extensive Worcester Photographic Survey. M/f-census/cemetery records/newspapers/ nonconformist. IGI on computer as part of the Family Search system incl. Ancestral File/Family History Catalogue of holdings in Salt Lake City, Utah.
Research Service: Charge made (see Info. leaflet No. 15)
Facilities: Toilets. No public tel. Room for own food. Café/pub nearby.
Publications: Free: Brief Guides to location of records. General Info. *Hereford & Worcester RO-Which branch do I need? Using the RO for Family History Research. House Hunting at the Worcester RO.* (A5 SAE). For sale: various.
O. R: Museum of the Worcestershire Yeomanry Cavalry, City Museum & Art Gallery, Foregate Street, WORCESTER, Worcs WR1 1DT Tel: 01905 35371 Appt. Documents & photographs of the Worcestershire Volunteers & Territorial Cavalry Regiment 18-20thC's.
Tourist Office: Tel: 01905 726311
Remarks: Bags not allowed-lockers. Donations appreciated. **Note:** On 1st April 1998 the new Worcestershire County Council was formed separating from Hereford. RO facilities should remain the same, in the short term at least. Station: Worcester. Foregate Street.

Worcester Record Office, St. Helen's, Fish Street, WORCESTER, Worcs WR1 2HN Tel: 01905 765922 **Fax:** 01905 765925
Opening Hours: M. 10-4.45; T.W.Th. 9.15-4.45; F. 9.15-4 Closure: Public hols+2 wks mid Nov.
Parking: None.
Disabled: No facilities.
Children: Accompanied: At archivist's discretion. Unaccompanied: 9 yrs+
Appointments: Prior booking unnecessary. Entry-register+CARN. 14 seats+1 film+1 fiche.
Ordering System: Prior ordering by letter/tel. Catalogue nos required. Three ordered, one produced. Orders every half hour & on the hour 9.30; 10; 10.30 etc. No production 1.00. Last order: 30 mins before closure. P/copying-DIY. Typing not permitted. Taping/laptops allowed. Cameras permitted+fee.
Records: for County of Worcester. Diocesan RO for Worcester. PRs/BTs are at County Hall, Spetchley Road. Parish poor rate books. Rates & Rents. Manorial. Church Schools. Parish records. Glebe terriers. Churchwardens presentments. Nonconformist. Large estates. Charity. Solicitors. Worcester City Corporation archives. Register of Papists estates 1715-1740/1762. Maps & plans. Tithe Sale particulars. Inclosures. Elgar Papers. M/f-hearth tax returns.
Research Service: Charge made+costs of travelling & p/copies (see Info. leaflet).
Facilities: No toilet/public tel/refreshment facilities. Café/pub/shops nearby.
Publications: Free leaflets: *Using the RO for Family History Research.* General Info. *House Hunting at Worcester RO. Which Branch Do I Need?*-a brief guide to location of records. (A5 SAE).
O. R: The Worcester & Sherwood Foresters' Regiment, Regiment Archives RHQ WFR, Norton Barracks, WORCESTER, Worcs WR5 2PA Tel: 01905 354359 Appt. Regimental records of officers & soldiers. Regimental history. Photographs.
Remarks: Bags not allowed-lockers. Donations appreciated. County Hall (see entry-Remarks).
Note: Records are not transferable between the ROs.

WORKINGTON, see Barrow in Furness..

The Fleet Air Arm Museum, Box D6, Royal Naval Air Station (RNAS), YEOVILTON, Nr. Ilchester, Som BA22 8HT Tel: 01935 840565 Appt. History of the Fleet Air Arm/Royal Naval Air Service. Photographs.

Borthwick Institute of Historical Research, The University of York, St. Anthony's Hall, Peasholme Green, YORK, N. Yorks YO1 2PW Tel: 01904 642315 **Fax:** 01904 633284
Internet: http:/www.york.ac.uk/inst/bihr
Opening Hours: M.-F. 9.30-12.50; 2-4.50 Closure: Wk at Easter+extended Christmas period.
Parking: None.
Disabled: By special arrangement.
Children: Sixth formers only.
Appointments: Prior booking necessary-2/3 wks. 16 seats+6 film+1 fiche
Ordering System: Prior ordering by letter/tel. Catalogue nos required. Six ordered & produced. Ordering times: As soon as possible after arrival; 11.00; 12 noon; 2.15; 3.00; 3. 45. Delivery as soon as possible after ordering. P/copying by staff-post. Typing/taping/laptops (power supply) permitted. Cameras not allowed.

Records: Diocese of York+Province in some cases. Archdeaconry of York. Diocesan. Parochial. Archbishopric of York from 13thC. Probate records of Exchequer/Prerogative Courts of York 14-19thC's. PRs-film/ photocopies/Ts. BTs-film. Marriage Bonds & Allegations. Quaker. Archives of mental asylum 'The Retreat'. York families. Political papers.
Research Service: Charge made (see Info. leaflets: Searching Service. Professional Record Searchers & Genealogists).
Facilities: Toilets. No public tel/refreshment facilities. Cafe/pub/shops nearby.
Publications: Free: Brief Guides-*Genealogical Sources. Document Reproduction. Yorkshire ROs. Records of Civil Registration from 1837. Services at the Branch Genealogical Libraries of the Mormon Church. Sources for the History of Houses. Archive Conservation. Regulations. Catalogue of Publications.* (A5 SAE) For sale: Borthwick Papers. Borthwick Wallets. Borthwick Studies in History-Occasional Papers incl. *A Guide to Genealogical Sources in the Borthwick Institute of Historical Research* 3rd ed (1996). Lists & Indexes.
Remarks: Bags not allowed-lockers. Donations appreciated. More details about the Institute's facilities can be found on the Institute Web site.

York City Library, Reference Library, Local Studies Collection, Museum Street, YORK, N. Yorks YO1 2DS Tel: 01904 552824/655631/654144 Usually open. Appt. for viewers. ID required for archives. Local collection. Family papers. Films of local interest. Illustrations/slides. PRs-publications/copyTs. Local Newspaper Index. Calendars of York Assizes. M/f-GRO Indexes 1837-1947/ census/IGI.

York City Archives, Art Gallery Buildings, Exhibition Square, YORK, N. Yorks YO1 2EW Tel: 01904 551878/9 **Fax:** 01904 551877
Opening Hours: M.-F. 9.30-1: 2-5 Closure: Public hols.
Parking: None.
Disabled: Ramp up internal steps-advance notice necessary.
Children: At staff's discretion.
Appointments: Prior booking for seats/viewers-few days. Entry-register. 12 seats+ 2 film+ 2 fiche-1 reader/printer.
Ordering System: Prior ordering by letter/tel. Catalogue nos sometimes required. Number ordered & produced at archivist's discretion. Delivery 1-15 mins. P/copying by staff-same day. DIY-printed sources. Typing not permitted. Taping/laptops (power supply with permission) allowed. Cameras by arrangement.
Records: for City of York & area. No PRs. City records inc. Ainsty area. City of York-Freemen's Rolls. Quarter Sessions/Magistrates/early Wardmote Courts. Local collections. Nonconformists. Enclosures. Manorial. York cemetery registers. Photographs/negative collection of properties demolished during 1920s slum clearance. Maps & plans. Poor Law. York PLU incl. outdoor relief books/weekly lists/creed registers/admission & discharge registers/childrens records. Police. School board. Acomb/Dringhouses parish councils 18-20thC's. Foss Navigation 17thC on. Vaccination records in the poor law collection (unindexed)-copy of birth cert with vacc. date & signatory to vacc. for City District 1872-89; 1899-1907. Rural District 1872-85; 1887-89; 1889-1907. Rural District divided into sub-districts of villages-Bishopthorpe from 1904. Dunnington incl. Osbaldwick from 1901. Escrick incl. Heslington from 1901. Skelton incl. Clifton w'out 1904. Earswick & Huntington from 1904. Flaxton. Education Dept.-returns of births 1946-72. Indexes to birth registers 1945-86. Apprenticeship Registers 1573-1688; 1721-1945. Registry of boys/girls in Farm Service 1910-1914. Estates. Families. Charities. Solicitors. Entertainments. Maps & plans. Photographs/illustrations.
Research Service: Charge made (Info leaflet available).
Facilities: Toilets. No public tel. Room for own food. Café/pub/shops nearby.
Publications: Free leaflets: *Tracing Your Ancestors in Yorkshire. York City Archives-Main Sources for Genealogists.* (A5 SAE). For sale: *Brief Guide to Records. Richard III & York Wallet. Lords of the City* (Lord Mayors of York). *York City Archives.* Local history publications.
O. R: York Health Archives, c/o The Wheelchair Centre, Shipton Road, YORK YO3 6SF Tel: 01904 628183 for details. **Note:** Staff details closed for 75 yrs/patient records for 100 yrs.
Tourist Office: The De Grey Rooms & York Railway Station Tel: 01904 621756 Fax: 01904 625618.
Remarks: York is noe a Unitary Authority. **Note:** There may be a possible move to the Library, Museum Street, YORK sometime during the next 5 yrs. There will be no storage for records - these will have to be ordered in advance.

York Minster Archives, Dean's Park, YORK, N. Yorks YO1 2JD Tel: 01904 611118 **Fax:** 01904 611119
Opening Hours: M.T.W.Th. 9-1; 2-5 Closure: Fri.+Public hols+Christmas-New Year.
Parking: None at present but maybe 2-3 spaces by Sept 1998.
Disabled: None at present but new extension will have lift & disabled toilet.
Children: Accompanied: At archivist's discretion. Unaccompanied: 14 yrs+

YORK

Appointments: Prior booking for viewers-1 wk. Entry-register. 3 seats (10 in future)+1 film+1 fiche-1 reader/printer.
Ordering System: Prior ordering by letter/tel. Catalogue nos sometimes required. Six ordered, up to three produced. Delivery 5-10 mins. P/copying restricted, by staff-same day/post. Typing/taping not permitted. Laptops (power supply) allowed. Cameras with written permission.
Records: for York Minster/Dean & Chapter. PRs-film/originals. York Gospels-various illuminated MSS. Vicars Choral deeds. Lease Registers of the Dean & Chapter. Local History. Hailstone Collection-deeds/docs mainly relating to West Riding 12th-19thC's. 19thC York Wesleyan Methodist. Database of 250,000 names of Yorkshire people before 1550.
Research Service: 1st half hour free-charge made for further research.
Facilities: Toilet. No public tel/refreshment facilities. Café/pub/shops nearby.
Publications: Various for sale.
Remarks: Bags not allowed-storage cloakroom. Donations appreciated. **Note:** The new extension will allow longer opening hours with more reader places & facilities.

YORK & LANCASTER REGIMENT MUSEUM, see Rotherham.

YORK RAILTRACK, see London Other Repositories-Railtrack

YORKSHIRE EAST, see Beverley; Kingston-upon-Hull.

YORKSHIRE NORTH, see Leyburn; Northallerton; Richmond; Scarborough; York.

YORKSHIRE SOUTH, see Doncaster; Sheffield.

YORKSHIRE, see Malton; Pickering; Rotherham; Whitby; York.

YORKSHIRE WEST, see Barnsley; Bradford; Calderdale; Halifax; Huddersfield; Keighley; Kirklees; Leeds; Sheepscar; Wakefield.

YORKSHIRE-USEFUL ADDRESSES:

Superintendent Registrar, Rydedale House, MALTON, Yorks YO17 OHH Tel: 01653 692285

Superintendent Registrar, 38 The Mount, PICKERING, Yorks YO18 8AD Tel: 01751 476708

Superintendent Registrar, Eskholme, Upgang Lane, WHITBY, Yorks YO21 3DR Tel: 01947 602731

York Probate Sub-Registry, Duncombe Place, YORK YO1 2EA Tel: 01904 624210 Wills & administrations 1858 to date.

National Railway Museum, Leeman Road, YORK YO2 4XJ
Reference book: *Basic facts...about family history research in Yorkshire* by P.M. Litton (FFHS 1995)

NOTES